THE WOLF KING

A volume in the series

Medieval Societies, Religions, and Cultures
Edited by M. Cecilia Gaposchkin and Anne E. Lester

A list of titles in this series is available at cornellpress.cornell.edu.

THE WOLF KING

IBN MARDANĪSH AND THE CONSTRUCTION OF POWER IN AL-ANDALUS

ABIGAIL KRASNER BALBALE

CORNELL UNIVERSITY PRESS
Ithaca and London

First published 2022 by Cornell University Press

Library of Congress Cataloging-in-Publication Data

Names: Balbale, Abigail Krasner, author.
Title: The Wolf King : Ibn Mardanish and the construction of power in al-Andalus / Abigail Krasner Balbale.
Description: Ithaca [New York] : Cornell University Press, 2022. | Series: Medieval societies, religions, and cultures | Includes bibliographical references and index.
Identifiers: LCCN 2022006096 (print) | LCCN 2022006097 (ebook) | ISBN 9781501765872 (hardcover) | ISBN 9781501765889 (epub) | ISBN 9781501765896 (pdf)
Subjects: LCSH: Ibn Mardanīsh, Muhammad ibn Sa'd, approximately 1124-1172. | Muslims—Spain—Andalusia—History—To 1500. | Islam—Spain—Andalusia—History—To 1500. | Power (Social sciences)—Spain—Andalusia—History—To 1500. | Islam and politics—Spain—History—To 1500. | Andalusia (Spain)—Kings and rulers—Religious aspects. | Andalusia (Spain)—Civilization—Islamic influences. | Andalusia (Spain)—History—To 1500. | Spain—History—711-1516.
Classification: LCC DP302.A5 B35 2022 (print) | LCC DP302.A5 (ebook) | DDC 946.8088/297—dc23/eng/20220712
LC record available at https://lccn.loc.gov/2022006096
LC ebook record available at https://lccn.loc.gov/2022006097

For Zayd, my travel companion and fellow history lover

Man is a classifying animal, and he has the incurable propensity to regard the network he has himself imposed on the variety of experience as belonging to the objective world of things.

—Ernst Gombrich, *Norm and Form*

Contents

Acknowledgments

In the decade since I began the research that would eventually become this book, the world and my life have transformed. I write these acknowledgements at what we all hope is the tail end of a global pandemic, after nearly two years of intermittent lockdown and teaching, researching and parenting from home. I could not have gotten from research to the conclusion of this work without the help and support of far more people than I will be able to name here. From the teachers, mentors, and colleagues who have encouraged, critiqued, and improved my work, to the extended family who have fed, housed, and cared for my family, to the women who have helped me raise my children, this book required a village.

I am grateful to the scholars of Ibn Mardanīsh in Spain who have so generously shared their time and research with me. Julio Navarro Palazón has been an unfailingly generous interlocutor, sending me images, pdfs of his articles, inviting me to conferences, and even accompanying me on visits to his archaeological sites and museum exhibitions. He and Pedro Jiménez Castillo, who conducted most of the first modern excavations of Ibn Mardanīsh's buildings, have also generously shared their drawings and plans with me and have allowed me to include some in this book. The Universidad de Murcia's eminent Arabist, Alfonso Carmona, was similarly generous with his time and his research, even though he admitted to me that he had always wanted to write a book about Ibn Mardanīsh. Jorge Eiroa at the Universidad de Murcia also gave me personal tours of his new archaeological sites in Murcia and the exhibit he co-curated with Mariángeles Gómez Ródenas at the Museo Arqueológico de Murcia. Many thanks to Mariángeles for facilitating the process of gaining permission to reproduce images from the museum's collection in this book. Thanks are due to Tawfiq Ibrahim of the impressive Tonegawa collection in Madrid, for allowing me to handle and photograph Ibn Mardanīsh's coinage. Ángel Velasco opened the Museo Almodí for me in Xàtiva so I could see the Jativa basin and the remnants of Pinohermoso, even though the museum was closed for renovations.

In the broader sphere of North African and Andalusī studies, many colleagues and friends have helped me refine my ideas and gain access to important materials. Maribel Fierro has, over the course of a decade, welcomed me at CSIC in Madrid, recommended readings, and generously offered corrections and suggestions. J. Santiago Palacios and Carlos Ayala invited me to a fruitful conference in Portugal on the concept of "Reconquista"; an earlier version of part of chapter 7 appears in Spanish in the conference volume they edited. Concha Herrero Carretero and Javier Rodrigo del Blanco at the Patrimonio Nacional de España facilitated access to images from the Museo de Telas Medievales at Las Huelgas in Burgos. Antonio Almagro and the Real Academia de Bellas Artes de San Fernando have made his extraordinary architectural drawings and plans widely accessible. In Tunisia, Sihem Lamine at the CMES Harvard Tunis office made my trip both more productive and more enjoyable. Director Raja Ben Slama, Rachida Smine, and Hayat Abdelli at the Bibliothèque Nationale de Tunisie facilitated access to the Ibn Ghaṭṭūs Quran and allowed me to publish images of it.

Brian Catlos and Sharon Kinoshita organized the transformative NEH Summer Institute in Barcelona in 2010 that led me to start thinking in a "Mediterranean" frame. Brian also introduced me to the Archivo de la Corona de Aragón. Thank you to the rest of the participants in this summer institute, especially Yuen-Gen Liang, Camilo Gómez-Rivas, and Andrew Devereux, my co-conspirators in the Spain-North Africa Project, for an intellectual community that has lasted long past that brief summer. D. F. Ruggles and Nikolas Bakirtzis's Getty Connecting Art Histories program on Mediterranean Palimpsests has also made me think much more comparatively about the layered cities I study, and about the effects of nationalism on understandings of the medieval past. Participants in the University of Minnesota Mediterranean studies conference on Mediterranean violence offered helpful feedback on earlier version of chapter 2. Gülru Necipoğlu and the Aga Khan Program in Islamic Architecture at Harvard gave important feedback on an earlier version of chapter 3, and Gülru informed me of the existence of the newly discovered Quran of Ibn Ghaṭṭūs attributed to the patronage of Ibn Mardanīsh in Tunis. Students and colleagues at Princeton's Near Eastern Studies and Religion departments offered helpful suggestions on two different early versions of chapter 4.

Thanks for germinating the seed that would become this book are due firstly to María Rosa Menocal, whose charismatic lecture on Don Quixote first inspired me to study the Iberian Peninsula. Her generosity—as a teacher, coauthor, and friend—over the course of the next fourteen years until her untimely death was unparalleled. Jerrilynn Dodds has been an extraordinary mentor and friend for nearly twenty years. At Harvard, my advisor Roy Mottahedeh urged me to stick with al-Andalus when I was tempted to focus on the east but made sure that I was well versed in the history and literature of the broader Islamic world. Susan Gilson Miller introduced me to the study of Morocco and insisted I engage seriously with North Africa. Bill Granara helped me read the texts of the western Mediterranean and think about the literature of jihad. Dan Smail introduced me to thing theory, the material turn, and transregional approaches to medieval history. He remains a generous and astute reader and advisor.

My time at Bard Graduate Center taught me how to engage seriously with material culture, and the support of the Trehan fund for Islamic Art allowed me to bring together groups of scholars I admire. Colleagues including Peter Miller, Jeffrey Collins, Andrew Morrall, and Ittai Weinryb offered feedback on various parts of this book. At New York University, conversations with several colleagues have helped me develop my ideas relating to this project: Ismail Alatas, Marion Katz, Finbarr Barry Flood, Sarah Pearce, Justin Stearns, Ayşe Baltacioglu-Brammer, and Zvi Ben-Dor Benite. Beyond NYU, I'm grateful to a broader community of Iberianists who have inspired me and offered feedback at various stages: Mohamad Ballan, Maria Judith Feliciano, Simon Doubleday, Cynthia Robinson, Pamela Patton. My pandemic zoom writing group with Intisar Rabb, Najam Haider, and Adnan Zulfiqar has made this time of isolation far more enjoyable and productive.

Thank you to NYU's Center for the Humanities for a book subvention grant and also for funding my first book colloquium, as well as Carolyn Dinshaw and NYU's Office of the Dean of the Humanities for assistance in defraying publication costs. An NYU Global Research Initiative grant allowed me to spend a crucial summer in Madrid toward the end of this project. Support from the National Endowment for the Humanities allowed me to spend a year finishing the book manuscript. The Medieval Academy of America's Olivia Remie Constable Award supported research in Spain. The Barakat Trust awarded a subvention that helped to cover costs associated with images.

Antonio Musto helped me to use digitized Arabic sources and Mathilde Monpetit assembled the bibliography. Rosa Klein-Baer helped me track down digital versions of texts to double-check citations while the pandemic had shut down our libraries. Mike Bechtold created the beautiful maps. Hanna Siurua meticulously copyedited the draft and saved me from many embarrassing mistakes. I am grateful to the series editors Cecilia Gaposchkin and Anne Lester for their careful readings, insightful suggestions, and support throughout the process. Mahinder Kingra and Bethany Wasik at Cornell University Press kept the process on track through difficult pandemic years. Thank you to the two anonymous reviewers of the manuscript, whose comments were enormously valuable as I revised the book.

In a time of upheaval and uncertainty, my students have been an inspiration. They participate our classes with enthusiasm and verve, in spite of financial challenges, health issues, childcare problems, and ill family members. My ability to continue teaching and writing during these difficult years would have been impossible without the support of my family. Special thanks are due to my parents, Deborah and Michael Krasner, and my sister, Lizzie Krasner, for stepping in at several crucial points to help care for children and put food on the table so I could focus on writing. Thank you to all the caregivers who have allowed me to write this book during the infancy and preschool years of my children: Cynthia, Jihan, Josselly, Rania and Yeye. Thank you also to the Weston Balbales for housing us during the first months of the pandemic. The biggest thanks of all go to my husband, Musab, for supporting my work.

Abbreviations

ACA Archives of the Crown of Aragon
BNF Bibliothèque Nationale de France
BNT Bibliothèque Nationale de Tunisie
EI^2 *Encyclopaedia of Islam*, 2nd ed., edited by P. J. Bearman, Th. Bianquis, C. E. Bosworth, E. van Donzel, and W. P. Heinrichs. Leiden: E. J. Brill, 1960–2005.

Note on Transliteration

All transliteration from the Arabic follows the *International Journal of Middle Eastern Studies* guidelines. Dates are generally listed in Hijri with Gregorian equivalents following. All translations are my own, unless otherwise noted. Citations from the Quran follow A. J. Arberry, *The Koran Interpreted* (New York: Macmillan, 1955).

THE WOLF KING

Introduction

Ibn Mardanīsh as Historical Figure and Historiographic Subject

Muḥammad ibn Sa'd ibn Aḥmad ibn Mardanīsh became ruler of eastern al-Andalus in 542/1147, as Almoravid power waned. Andalusī by birth, he was the son of a commander of the Marrakech-based Almoravid armies who had, according to legend, given King Alfonso I of Aragon a deadly blow at the Battle of Fraga (528/1134). During his quarter-century in power, Ibn Mardanīsh was the single most formidable enemy of the Almohad Empire, which by the mid-twelfth century stretched across most of North Africa and conquered the rest of al-Andalus in the decades that followed. He continued to fight off Almohad armies until his death in 567/1172. This fascinating figure does not fit neatly into the typical paradigms for the histories of the eleventh and twelfth centuries in al-Andalus. Those histories often portray the North African–based Berber dynasties of the Almoravids and Almohads locked in conflict with Andalusīs. Neither does he fit into the teleological narrative of Christian-Muslim enmity often called the Reconquista, a construct that imagines Christians united to fight Muslim invaders for a period of some seven hundred years.

Ibn Mardanīsh, known in Christian sources as *el rey lobo* or *rex lupus*—the Wolf King—broke every mold. He allied with the kings of Castile, Aragon, and Barcelona, formed trade agreements with the Italian merchant cities of Genoa and Pisa, and garnered posthumous praise from a pope as "Wolf King of Glorious Memory." He even appeared in Castilian documents as a vassal to Alfonso VIII, the child-king, whose regency caused strife among the noble families of Castile and Aragon. At the same time, Ibn Mardanīsh was at pains to present himself as a standard-bearer for the Abbasid caliphate in the east, and to make his court a major cultural center in the Islamic west. He minted gold coins in the name of the Abbasid caliph in Baghdad for the first time on the Iberian Peninsula since 138/755, when the Umayyad ʿAbd al-Raḥmān al-Dākhil invaded al-Andalus and sent the Abbasid governor packing. As an Andalusī emir for the Abbasids, vassal to a Castilian king, rival to the nascent Almohad caliphate, who managed to gain and maintain power over nearly half of al-Andalus for twenty-five years, "the Wolf King" deserves our attention.[1]

This book unfurls the story of Ibn Mardanīsh, both in his lifetime and in the eight and a half centuries that have followed. I situate him in the Islamic world of the Middle Period (1000–1500), when vast numbers of non-Arabs converted to Islam and began to integrate themselves into Islamic political systems, and in the particular context of the twelfth century, when the rivalry between the Abbasid and Fatimid caliphates accelerated the rise of new kinds of religious and military leaders. He also operated in the polyglot setting of the western Mediterranean, and drew on traditions near and far to legitimate his authority. Finally, I trace how ideas about Ibn Mardanīsh have transformed over time, as his territory was lost first to the Almohads and then split between Castile and Aragon, as the last kingdoms of al-Andalus fell, and as scholars in Spain and beyond attempted to make sense of the Iberian Peninsula's Islamic past. Ibn Mardanīsh's story illuminates not only the dynamism of politics and culture in the medieval western Mediterranean, but also how its complexity has been flattened to serve more modern ideologies. Historians writing after Ibn Mardanīsh's death have often sought to fit him into categories—geographic, genealogical, temporal—the twelfth-century figure would not have recognized.

---

1 The best brief overview of Ibn Mardanīsh's time in power is Emilio Molina López, "Apuntes en torno al perfil biográfico de un dirigente local andalusí, Muḥammad b. Saʿd b. Mardanīš (siglo XII)," in *Regnum Murciae: Génesis y configuración del Reino de Murcia*, ed. A. Robles Fernández and I. Pozo Martínez (Murcia: Comunidad Autónoma de la Región de Murcia, 2008), 87–101. In addition, two books in Arabic have focused on Ibn Mardanīsh and his family. They provide a valuable survey of the Arabic sources that discuss this figure: Jābir Khalīfa Jābir, *Banū Mardanīsh wa-dawrahum al-siyāsī wa-l-ʿaskarī fī al-Andalus* (Damascus: Dār Amal al-Jadīda, 2017); Sīmūn Ḥāyik, *Ibn Mardanīsh aw al-Muwaḥḥidūn* (Jūnīya, Lebanon: al-Maṭbaʿa al-Būlīya), 1993.

In the 1840s, the eminent Dutch Arabist Reinhart Pieter Anne Dozy sat down to write about a curious incident in the history of Granada, for his book on the political and literary history of medieval Spain. After the fall of the Marrakech-based dynasty of the Almoravids in 1147, he wrote, the struggle for power in al-Andalus came down to two parties: the Berber loyalists, who supported the rival Moroccan Almohad dynasty, and the "Andalusian or national party, who tried yet to maintain the independence of the country."[2] The chief of this latter party, he wrote, was a man known as Abū Abd Allāh Muḥammad ibn Saʿd ibn Aḥmad ibn Mardanīsh (518–67 AH/1124–72 CE), king of Murcia, Valencia, and all of southeastern Spain, a man difficult to classify, characteristic of contexts in which "many nationalities and different religions" have contact.[3] But, Dozy wondered, to which nation did Ibn Mardanīsh belong?[4] Over the next several pages, Dozy weighed the ruler's own claims to be Arab against the distinctive, non-Arabic, name of his great-great grandfather (Mardanīsh), determining that he must have been of "Spanish" Christian origin. Dozy noted that Ibn Mardanīsh did not seem to want to hide his Christian roots, as later Arabic authors reported he liked to employ Christians and dress like them. His foreign policy consisted of alliances with Christians against the Almohads, and Arabic chronicles say he was known for his feasting, drinking, bedding of slave girls, bravery in battle, and cruelty to his enemies.[5] After several pages, Dozy paused. "If, even in the eyes of impartial history, such men cannot be taken for

---

2 "Le parti andalous ou national, qui tâchait encore de maintenir l'indépendance du pays"; Reinhart Dozy, "Sur ce qui se passa á Grenade en 1162," in *Recherches sur l'histoire politique et littéraire de l'Espagne pendant le moyen âge*, 3rd ed. (Leiden: Brill, 1881), 365. Originally published 1849, republished as *Recherches sur l'histoire et la littérature de l'Espagne pendant le moyen âge* in 1860. My citations throughout are to the 1881 edition. The later nineteenth-century Spanish Orientalist Francisco Codera y Zaidín translated Dozy and copied him verbatim in his *Decadencia y desaparición de los almoravides de España* (originally published 1899). This work was republished as Codera, *Decadencia y desaparición de los almorávides en España,* ed. María Jesús Viguera Molins (Pamplona: Urgoiti Editores, 2004). In Codera's version, he interestingly replaced "andalous ou national" with just "nacional"; see 112–13.

3 Dozy, *Recherches*, 365: "C'était une de ces figures caractéristiques et difficiles à classer, que le contact de plusieurs nationalités et de différentes religions produisait parfois dans la Péninsule." Codera, *Decadencia y desaparición*, 113.

4 Though this ruler referred to himself as Muḥammad ibn Saʿd, and was called the same by most of his peers, the near universal use of his ancestor's name, Mardanīsh, to refer to him in the time since has led me to call him Ibn Mardanīsh throughout this book, except when directly quoting a source that refers to him as Muḥammad ibn Saʿd.

5 Dozy, *Recherches*, 365–70; Codera, *Decadencia y desaparición*, 113–16.

good Muslims, what aversion and horror must they have inspired in the Almohads, ignorant Berbers, animated by the most ardent fanaticism?"[6]

For Dozy, the complex events in al-Andalus and North Africa during the twelfth century could be explained through race, religion, and nation–the terms and concepts that defined the nineteenth century. Ibn Mardanīsh had Christian roots, therefore his behavior and politics were philo-Christian, whereas the "ignorant Berber" Almohads fought him because they were fanatical Muslims opposed to Christians as a matter of faith. Dozy believed his narration was "impartial history," and his assessment of this period has remained largely unchallenged for more than a century and a half. But, as I will show in this book, modern understandings of Ibn Mardanīsh, and of al-Andalus more generally, are anything but impartial. They have been formed in the political context of Western European ascendancy over North Africa and much of the Islamic world, and serve to reinforce racial and religious hierarchies that privilege the European, the Christian, or the secular over others. The historical processes that have yielded these visions are complex, for it was not Dozy who invented the idea that Ibn Mardanīsh dressed like a Christian or drank. The failure of Ibn Mardanīsh's dynasty and the eventual fall of al-Andalus led to explanations emphasizing his decadence (and that of al-Andalus as a whole) as a reason for the loss of territory. But medieval ideas have been filtered through modern preconceptions in ways that distort them even further.

Dozy's assessment of Ibn Mardanīsh and his Almohad rivals echoes pejorative sources stretching back to the twelfth century. The Almohads, whose caliphate lasted from 515–668 AH/1121–1269 CE, worked hard in their chronicles and chancery documents to present their dynasty (*dawla*) as pious, God-guided, and focused on the hereafter and their rivals, such as Ibn Mardanīsh, as impious, sensual, dangerously close to Christians, and tangled in the snares of the material world.[7] But for Dozy, as for most of the nineteenth- and twentieth-century scholars who

6 Dozy, *Recherches*, 369–70: "Que si, même aux yeux de l'histoire impartiale, de tels hommes ne pouvaient pas être comptés parmi bons musulmans, quelle aversion, quelle horreur ne devaient-ils pas inspirer aux Almohades, a ces Berberes ignorants et animés du plus ardent fanatisme?"

7 The Almohad movement began in 515/1121 when Ibn Tūmart, their charismatic founder, is said to have declared himself the mahdī, a messianic figure who rules during the end times. ʿAbd al-Muʾmin became Ibn Tūmart's successor (*khalīfa*) after his death, beginning what would become the Muʾminid caliphate. The Almohad dynasty defeated the Almoravids and took their capital, Marrakech, in 541/1147.

read these Arabic sources, the chronicles that aimed to legitimate the Almohads and their divine mission by denigrating Ibn Mardanīsh became, in the new framework of modernity, evidence of protomodernity in the past. That is, the very same tools used by the Almohads to discredit Ibn Mardanīsh's quest for power later gained legitimacy as hallmarks of Western secular modernity. The result of this strange confluence is that the Almohads' evaluation of Ibn Mardanīsh as a "bad Muslim" has turned him, in more recent years, into an exemplar of a "good Muslim," according to Mahmood Mamdani's categorization: one who is secular, flexible, and Western.[8] At the same time, the Almohads are classified as "fanatical," and their perceived piety becomes a mark of their danger.

I discuss this nineteenth-century historiography not to denigrate Dozy, a great scholar who worked almost exclusively with manuscripts and who valorized Arabic sources as integral to the history of Spain and of Europe—approaches still rare today. Nor do I mean to imply that scholarship on Ibn Mardanīsh and on al-Andalus began and ended in the nineteenth century. Rather, I begin here because so many of the questions historians work with today are echoes of nineteenth-century preoccupations. To what nation did Ibn Mardanīsh belong? Was his Islam sincere or simply pragmatic? How did his fight against the Almohads reflect a nascent Spanish identity that could transcend religious difference? What is the relationship between his race, his religion, and his politics? Were the Almohads fierce fanatics as opposed to flexible, protosecular Andalusīs?

Behind all of these questions, omnipresent in the scholarship about Ibn Mardanīsh, is another set of broader questions about the history of al-Andalus and of Spain, about geography, ethnicity, national identity, and religion. These questions, in turn, encode even bigger concerns—about how humans construct their identities through classifying and categorizing, labeling people, ideas, places, and periods as like or unlike themselves and their own experiences. Many of the ideas that frame contemporary understandings of the western Mediterranean in the Middle Ages are born of the nineteenth-century construction of academic knowledge: the creation of the medieval to separate the ancient and the modern, the invention of Islam as the singular, monolithic Other

8 This juxtaposition of the "good," secular, modern Muslim, who is allied with Christians, with the "bad," religious, premodern, fundamentalist Muslim persists in contemporary discourse about twenty-first century events. See Mahmood Mamdani, *Good Muslim, Bad Muslim: America, The Cold War, and the Roots of Terror* (New York: Penguin Random House, 2005).

for Europe's Christianity, and the assertion of secularism, science, and progress as the modern, against religion, tradition, and culture as the past. The nineteenth century is when the written record was enshrined as the primary source of the historian, and objects and artifacts were relinquished to the "antiquarian." It was the century that championed history as a science, a positivist undertaking that could reveal how things really were, and simultaneously, endorsed a vision of history as the scaffolding for human progress, enabling humanity to move inexorably toward a more perfect future.

Even as, in the twentieth century, scholars of medieval France and postcolonial India advocated history from below, even as new generations of scholars from wider swaths of the world and of increasingly diverse backgrounds began to question the power structures inherent in traditional modes of research, the architecture of knowledge has remained mostly intact. In spite of a push toward interdisciplinarity, historians, art historians, archaeologists, and literary scholars frequently do not read each other's work, and they engage even less frequently with each other's sources. Notwithstanding a growing interest in transregionalism and global approaches, most scholars still focus on regions defined according to national boundaries created in the nineteenth century. The hegemony of the discipline, and of the nation-bounded region, operate so forcefully that it is easy to miss the interstices and those slippery subjects that refuse to rest peacefully in one discipline or nation.

Ibn Mardanīsh is one such slippery subject. He minted dinars in the name of the distant Abbasid caliph and constructed a palace, Dār al-Ṣughrā, that incorporated new architectural forms from the Islamic East. He also served as vassal to King Alfonso VII of Castile-Leon and King Alfonso VIII of Castile, paid tribute to the count-kings of Barcelona, and executed trade agreements with the Italian city-states of Genoa and Pisa. Written sources, from the twelfth-century Almohad chronicler Ibn Ṣāḥib al-Ṣalā to the seventeenth-century historian al-Maqqarī, focused on his alliances with his Christian neighbors and suggested that he was an infidel. Yet records from his court, especially its material culture, suggest that Ibn Mardanīsh sought to connect himself to the caliphate in the east much more closely than any earlier Andalusī ruler had. In this book, I untangle the complex threads of Ibn Mardanīsh's identity, politics, and legacy. By bringing together evidence from chronicles, chancery documents, poetry, architecture, coins, and portable objects, I trace Ibn Mardanīsh's transformation from warrior to the founder of a dynasty. I also show how he adapted language and forms from around the Islamic world to articulate a vision that was powerful enough to allow him to gain and maintain power. Using methodologies from history, religious studies, and art history, I examine processes of political legitimation and identity formation and then explore how narratives about the dynasty—and al-Andalus more generally—shifted after its dissolution.

Considering Ibn Mardanīsh's ruling culture through written and material sources allows me to situate him (and his rivals and successors) in complex networks of affiliation and resistance. I investigate how rulers aspiring to great power legitimated their authority; what they said, wrote, and did to present themselves as righteous. I look at how they constructed their palaces and houses of worship, and the motifs and language they imprinted on their coins. Every choice a would-be ruler made situated him amongst the caliphs, sultans, and kings of his day and his predecessors. The specific forms and legends minted on a ruler's coins reflected not just what would be deemed acceptable in the marketplace but also whom he sought to emulate and whom he sought to challenge. These relationships were in some cases hyperlocal—building a palace could demonstrate resistance to a dangerously ambitious brother, for example—but they could also span the Mediterranean or the Pyrenees or reach back across centuries to honorable predecessors.

Reconstituting this web of connections helps to challenge the paradigm of al-Andalus as a peripheral or exceptional place. Like in the Islamic East, in al-Andalus the twelfth century was a time when newly Muslim populations began to integrate themselves more fully into systems of government and to assert their power. In the East, such populations were mostly Turkic peoples; in the west, they were Berbers and former Christians.[9] Ibn Mardanīsh was likely descended from Iberian

9 I use the word *Berber* here following the vast majority of sources dealing with the Almoravids and Almohads, in both medieval Arabic works and contemporary scholarship, but I am cognizant of recent challenges to the term on the grounds that its roots in the Greek word for foreigner (*barbaros*) can be seen as pejorative. Even more problematically, as Ramzi Roughi has recently shown, the category Berber effaces the enormous heterogeneity of peoples, languages, and cultures that are now lumped together as Berber. Roughi shows that the idea of the inhabitants of North Africa as a cohesive group called Berbers was elaborated by historians writing in Arabic in al-Andalus, beginning with Ibn Ḥazm (d. 456/1064) and culminating in Ibn Khaldūn (d. 808/1406). Rouighi describes the colonial roots of the now-preferred term for contemporary indigenous peoples of North Africa, Amazigh/Imazighen, and emphasizes that it functions as a calque for Berber rather than offering more specificity or historicity. Ramzi Rouighi, *Inventing the Berbers: History and Ideology in the Maghrib* (Philadelphia: University of Pennsylvania Press, 2019). For a more traditional overview of the peoples known as Berbers, see Michael Brett and Elizabeth Fentress, *The Berbers* (Oxford and Cambridge, MA: Blackwell, 1996).

Christian stock (though, as I discuss later, this is a fraught question), and he fought the Berber Almohads. Throughout the Islamic world, Jews and Christians lived under Muslim rule or negotiated alliances and enmities along the Islamic empire's borders. Al-Andalus was no more peripheral than any other border region, and the regular circulation of people and goods between the Maghrib and the Mashriq guaranteed that its people had considerable familiarity with the Islamic East. Nor was the attitude toward non-Muslim subjects and rivals substantially different in the two regions. Like Ibn Mardanīsh in al-Andalus, his contemporary Saladin in the Levant was occasionally chastised by companions for spending too much time fighting fellow Muslims and making alliances with neighboring Christians.

Instead of suggesting that al-Andalus was a special site of tolerance, I show that later teleological interpretations of al-Andalus's eventual collapse imbued its earlier history with a fablelike simplicity: al-Andalus was perpetually doomed, either because its glories, like those of the Garden of Eden, were too wonderful for fallible humans to maintain or because its cosmopolitan population cared too little about its religious duty to fight the infidels. Both of these narratives have made Ibn Mardanīsh into an embodiment of tolerance (whether conceived as a virtue or an evil) and envisioned his enemies, the Almohads, as pious and violent. This book traces how this historical memory crystallized as Ibn Mardanīsh's story transformed over time from that of a rebel against the Almohads to a proximate cause for the fall of al-Andalus, and further to an emblem of modern nationalist and secularist visions of the past. In the nineteenth century, ideas about the superiority of al-Andalus (and Europe) were sometimes used to justify European colonial ventures in North Africa and the Middle East. In the twentieth century, Ibn Mardanīsh became a proto-Spanish nationalist or a hero of a tolerant "European Islam," vaunted and celebrated by European historians, Arab nationalists, and regional governments alike. Today, debates about tolerance and violence and essentialist declarations about the nature of Islam and "the West" dominate headlines, and Ibn Mardanīsh appears in Spanish newspapers as evidence of a cosmopolitan, flexible, Iberian Islam. Ibn Mardanīsh's historiographic treatment therefore parallels the broader othering of al-Andalus, which went from being seen as an important component of a diverse collection of Islamic territories to being cast as a unique, particularly advanced corner of the empire by virtue of its location in what would come to be known as Europe. His uses in the legitimating processes of new, modern forms of domination has obscured much of the complexity of his story and, by highlighting him as an exception, has reinforced distorted conceptions of a normative Islamic culture that would never be flexible, complex, or generous to Christian inhabitants.

Ibn Mardanīsh's quest for power demonstrates how deeply imbricated rulers in the western Mediterranean were in overlapping spheres of culture and authority. Ibn Mardanīsh; his Almohad rivals; and the kings of Castile, Barcelona, and Sicily, among others, traded gifts, exchanged women, borrowed architectural forms, and sent scholars and poets to each other's courts. The motifs and people they exchanged hailed, in many cases, from points further east. Rather than a world defined by conflict between Muslims and Christians or between the forces of cosmopolitanism and those of strict religiosity, we find constantly shifting, kaleidoscopic arrangements of alliance and violence, in which the Almohad caliph and the king of Navarre might ally against Castile, and Barcelona and Murcia might unite against the Almohads and Navarre, only to shift alliances again. Ibn Mardanīsh was intensely eastward-looking in his ruling culture, and the visual forms and language he imported from Baghdad and Cairo made their way to his allies in Castile. He sent gifts of silk, gold, and camels to King Henry II of England, indicating his position as a member of a brotherhood of kings. He also joined the Castilian armies in fights against Navarre and received their help in his fights against the Almohads. After his death, Ibn Mardanīsh's children were incorporated into the highest echelons of the Almohad elite, with his daughters marrying the current caliph and the future caliph, and his descendants included later Almohad caliphs. Ibn Mardanīsh's relationships transcend the binaries by which the study of the Iberian Peninsula has often been defined (Islamic/Christian, Arabic/Latin, Berber/Andalusī) as well as the broader binaries that have formed the architecture of academic knowledge (Europe/not-Europe, secularism/religiosity, medieval/modern, text/art).

By illuminating Ibn Mardanīsh's world before the dominance of such binaries distorted the picture, this book offers a portrait of an al-Andalus that was more closely integrated with its Christian neighbors and with the Islamic East than is typically understood. And by tracing Ibn Mardanīsh's story over time, it reveals how the history of medieval Iberia was demolished in order to construct a European identity for a Spain built in opposition to Islamic and African others. Ibn Mardanīsh's story demonstrates the dangers of academic disciplinary divisions in reifying regions, periods, and religions as separate categories. Finally, it counteracts the idea of a pure, white European Middle Ages that is now being weaponized by racist extremists, while simultaneously indicating the inadequacy of visions of medieval coexistence that ignore religious motivations.

As the title of this book indicates, I focus on the construction of power. By power, I mean not simply the Weberian imposition of control over bodies and territories but also the assertion of a connection to the divine. As I discuss in the first two chapters, the conflict between Ibn Mardanīsh and the Almohads was, at root, about who had the right to proclaim divine guidance, to act as the deputy of God on earth, and to unify the global Muslim community. Their fundamentally different perspectives on the caliphate led to the development of different religious and governmental systems, rituals, spaces, and objects. At the same time, they expressed their differences through violence—on the battlefield, against the bodies of rebels, and in the destruction or transformation of objects and spaces. The administrative systems they created, their alliances and treaties, and their cultural programs constituted a mode of constructing their power, often explicitly in relation to their rivals. So, too, did their battles and acts of violence, which served to perform their righteousness by painting their rivals as enemies of God and their acts of destruction as signs of divine justice. Power, in the hands of these new dynasties, was expansive and flexible. Divine favor could be proven through success on the battlefield, through the splendor of a new monument, or through the relationships of loyalty demonstrated in alliances, tribute, or marriage.

Throughout the book, I also use the frame of genealogy as a mode of thinking about the practice of power, from the familial and cultural genealogies that Ibn Mardanīsh and the Almohads presented in texts and material culture to the *salāsil* (sing. *silsila*) or chains of transmission scholars used to authenticate their knowledge. At the same time, I think about genealogy as Foucault did, following Nietzsche, as *Herkunft*, the descent of an idea, in order to excavate how and why people thought about the history of Ibn Mardanīsh in a particular way.[10] I think about genealogies on three levels: familial lineage, cultural and intellectual expressions of filiation, and the genealogy of ideas (al-Andalus, Europe, secularism). On each level, those expressing their genealogy have the

10 Michel Foucault, "Nietzsche, Genealogy, History," in *Language, Counter-Memory, Practice: Selected Essays and Interviews*, ed. D. F. Bouchard (Ithaca, NY: Cornell University Press, 1977).

chance to formulate their identity, to understand their relationships to one another, and to articulate their legitimacy. Tracing back these lines of descent does not yield a narrative of origins or promise linearity. Instead, like Foucault, I aim to discover "the accidents, the minute deviations—or conversely, the complete reversals—the errors, the false appraisals and the faulty calculations that gave birth to those things that continue to exist and have value for us."[11] The narratives about Ibn Mardanīsh crafted by historians after his death, made in different contexts and to legitimate new powers, also constructed distinct visions of religion, identity, and geography that continue to exist today. The varied ways in which the histories of this period were constructed across centuries led to the accretion of new layers of meaning that express new forms of domination. Teleological narratives, which impose linearity on complexity, relegate failed dynasties and subjects that do not fit neatly into the narratives' categories to the periphery. In the case of Ibn Mardanīsh and the Almohads, and al-Andalus more generally, the construction of geographical, racial, and temporal hierarchies has fundamentally distorted how the period is understood. As I will discuss in the last chapter of the book and in the postscript, the ideas constructed around this period, born from "minute deviations" and "false appraisals" of early sources, have become dangerously potent ideologies in recent years.

In seeking to understand how historical narratives produce systems of power, I follow historians of women and other marginalized groups who, in the last fifty years, have worked to expand the range of sources historians use to interpret the past in order to illuminate the stories of figures often left out of written narratives.[12] What Joan Wallach Scott has called "the invisibility of women" in historical narratives not only reflects but helps construct a world organized by hierarchies that silence those who are deemed Other.[13] Most of this book focuses on how historical knowledge was constructed to naturalize the ascendance of later powers, from the Almohads to the modern nation of Spain, transforming

11 Foucault, "Nietzsche, Genealogy, History," 146.

12 Gayatri Chakravorty Spivak, "Can the Subaltern Speak?" in *Marxism and the Interpretation of Culture*, eds. Cary Nelson and Lawrence Grossberg (Basingstoke: Macmillan, 1988), 271–313. For an overview of the field of women's history in the late 1980s, and its approach to sources in particular, see the essays collected in S. Jay Kleinberg, ed., *Retrieving Women's History: Changing Perceptions of the Role of Women in Politics and Society* (Oxford: Berg Publishers, 1988), especially the introduction by the editor, ix–xii.

13 Joan Wallach Scott, "The Problem of Invisibility," in *Retrieving Women's History*, ed. Kleinberg, 5–29; Joan Wallach Scott, *Gender and the Politics of History*, Thirtieth Anniversary ed. (New York: Columbia University Press, 2018).

earlier understandings of Ibn Mardanīsh. But it is important to note that there are other marginalized figures even within the history of Ibn Mardanīsh I seek to excavate, doubly invisible for their gender, social status, or servile position. Most important among these for the purposes of this book are the women—wives, concubines and sisters—who appear at the edges of the narrative, mentioned in passing in historical chronicles or on tombstones, where even in death they are left nameless. Ibn Mardanīsh's rise to power was facilitated through alliances cemented by marriage, and the integration of his children into the Almohad elite was similarly aided by the marriage of two of his daughters to the Almohad caliph and his heir. In most cases, these women are referred to simply as the daughter of their father or the wife of their husband, their identities reduced to their relationship to the men around them. Although chronicles rarely offer insights into the lives these women led, the fleeting mentions of their existence suggest their importance in formalizing alliances and in knitting together the empires of former enemies.[14] As D. Fairchild Ruggles has shown, women who bore rulers' children, whether free or enslaved, captured or traded or married across borders, had a profound role in producing the complex culture of al-Andalus.[15] Although these women are not the focus of this book, I endeavor to listen for their presence in the sources, and to speculate about their lives, even when historians have minimized their contributions and omitted their names. Like Ibn Mardanīsh's dynasty more generally, these women are casualties of a "bundle of silences" born from power dynamics at particular moments in the creation of sources, archives, and narratives in the construction of history.[16]

Like the women of Ibn Mardanīsh's family, his regime appears only at the margin of most historical narratives. The dynasty Ibn Mardanīsh founded failed, lasting only as long as he lived and leaving few written

14 Manuela Marín's magisterial volume on women in al-Andalus discusses the importance of weddings as a form of political representation and affirmation. Marín, *Mujeres en al-Andalus,* Estudios Onomástico-Biográficos de al-Andalus 11 (Madrid: Consejo Superior de Investigaciones Científicas, 2000), 442–43.

15 D. F. Ruggles, "Mothers of a Hybrid Dynasty: Race, Genealogy, and Acculturation in al-Andalus," *Journal of Medieval and Early Modern Studies* 34, no. 1 (2004): 65–94. On the anxieties interfaith sex and marriage provoked in medieval Iberia, see also Simon Barton, *Conquerors, Brides, and Concubines: Interfaith Relations and Social Power in Medieval Iberia* (Philadelphia: University of Pennsylvania Press, 2015); David Nirenberg, *Neighboring Faiths: Christianity, Islam, and Judaism in the Middle Ages and Today* (Chicago: University of Chicago Press, 2014).

16 I adapt this framework from Michel-Rolph Trouillot, *Silencing the Past: Power and the Production of History* (Boston: Beacon Press, 1995), esp. 26–27.

sources of its own. Most of the written sources about him come from his Almohad enemies or were compiled centuries after his death, and they often malign him or distort or erase his time in power. There is no chronicle written by Ibn Mardanīsh himself that might explain his beliefs and record his rule. Remaining written sources must be read for their silences; for the faint echoes of a vision of power that once must have been asserted in other sources more clearly. Almohad chancery documents respond to letters from Ibn Mardanīsh now lost, sometimes indicating the major issues at stake in the battle between the two dynasties. Biographical dictionaries show the scholarly men and women the ruler collected in his territory and appointed to administrative and religious posts. Other relevant texts—fragments of what must have been a large body of written material from his territory in Sharq al-Andalus (eastern al-Andalus) itself—must be sought within larger compilations, excavated from sources written by his rivals, and extrapolated from the omissions and interpolations of the narratives that have come down to us. This kind of textual archaeology yields a new understanding of the practice of power in the Islamic Mediterranean.

As later rulers commissioned historical narratives to legitimate their own states, scholars in their employ engaged in historiographic pruning to create linear narratives, emphasizing their ruler's piety, bravery, and God-given right to rule. This later dynastic and nationalist narrativizing excised or simplified earlier periods, often creating teleological frameworks that led, inexorably, to their own moment. Material culture, with its survivals, transformations, and adaptations, offers one potential solution to the problem posed by such chronicles, and it can provide a roadmap for reading written sources. Objects, architecture, and archaeology can expose, through their materials, forms, techniques, and movement, the aspirations and affiliations of those who produced or collected them and, in the process, highlight the routes of people, goods, and ideas. Tracing changes in the built environment and in the goods that were traded and produced can point to the ideals of authority to which rulers aspired, as well as the contingent processes they employed to maintain their power. In the case of Ibn Mardanīsh, a failed ruler whose court's writings are nearly all lost, material culture offers the best evidence of his ideology of authority as a ruler closely attuned to the ideals and norms of authority in the Islamic East.

This book interrogates nostalgic or teleological visions of al-Andalus by excavating the memory of Ibn Mardanīsh across these diverse sources. But I aim for more than historiographic analysis. I believe that reading chronicles against and alongside other kinds of historical sources—chancery documents, inscriptions, and especially material culture—offers access to new perspectives on the construction of Ibn Mardanīsh's dynasty and its importance. What such a reading shows is not only that Ibn Mardanīsh sought to connect himself and his kingdom to explicitly Islamic ideas of authority and to the most powerful courts of his age, but also that the end of his rule did not entail the end of his vision. Rather, the material forms he marshaled to articulate his authority and his opposition to Almohad norms in turn transformed how authority was presented in the Almohad and Castilian contexts. Even as later chroniclers presented increasingly caricatured depictions of his failed dynasty, Ibn Mardanīsh's innovations continued to reverberate in the courts of subsequent rulers.

By examining this wider range of sources together, I find that Ibn Mardanīsh's "failure" is illusory: even as the Almohads presented him as impious and destined to fall, they accorded him the respect due to a fellow king in their sources, and even as they besieged and conquered his territories, they incorporated his children, scholars, and craftsmen into their own elite. The years after Ibn Mardanīsh's death witnessed the subsequent transformation of Almohad and Castilian ruling culture, in many cases on the model of the dead emir. If we follow textual clues and material culture together, as I do to understand Ibn Mardanīsh's construction of power, we discover that much of what was most important in his own court became fundamental to the presentation of power in the courts of both his former enemies and his former allies. This case study also demonstrates how a broader set of written, visual, and material sources can challenge the authoritative narrative of historical chronicles and reveal connections that might subvert the chronicles' ideological aims.

On the surface, this book is narrowly focused on a single ruler and his brief period in power. The goal of this book is not to rehabilitate Ibn Mardanīsh as an important Andalusī ruler but rather to plumb the intractable historical question of how rulers, states, and ideas that fail are remembered or forgotten by others. Through a focus on one man's period in power, it addresses much broader questions of historical memory and why and how certain periods are remembered and others forgotten. Studying Ibn Mardanīsh offers insight into these processes and their links to ideological projects, especially the construction of al-Andalus as the preeminent site of Islamic loss and nostalgia and, later, as a protomodern locus of tolerance in an otherwise bleak European Middle Ages.

Investigating Ibn Mardanīsh as historical actor and a historiographic subject offers an opportunity to examine how, when, and why the categories of race and religion were projected on the past and made to perform particular roles. Ibn Mardanīsh is a useful figure to study precisely because of his slipperiness, or what Dozy saw as the difficulty of classifying him, which directs attention to the ways in which rival rulers and later scholars sought to deploy elements of his history or identity to specific ends. Ibn Mardanīsh's story has been used to argue that blood determines religious identity, that collaboration across religious lines is dangerous, that Spaniards were loyal to nation above all even in the twelfth century, that Islam and secularism are not incompatible, and that medieval people, just like modern ones, were ultimately pragmatic rather than ideologically hidebound. All of these uses of Ibn Mardanīsh echo broader arguments that depict al-Andalus variously as exceptional, as a lost paradise, as the victim of religious intolerance, or as a model for interreligious communities. Behind these constructions of al-Andalus lies the very same classifying impulse discussed above—the need to make sense of the seeming paradox of a European Islam; behaviors that seem modern in the medieval period; and people, ideas, monuments, objects that resist classification according to the established disciplines, civilizations, and periods according to which we organize our knowledge.

As Ernst Gombrich notes in the epigraph at the beginning, none of these means of classifying are part of the "objective world of things." They are, as we university teachers insist to our students, constructions. And yet they are powerful. What vistas might we open up if we tried not only to release these constructions but to strip back the layers they have imposed on our understanding of the world? What if, in Talal Asad's words, we recognized that "the world has *no* significant binary features," and instead of classifying, we found meaning in the relentlessly realigning kaleidoscope of "overlapping, fragmented cultures, hybrid selves, continuously dissolving and emerging social states"?[17]

The book comprises an introduction and seven chapters. The first chapter, "Caliph and *Mahdī*," lays out heated debates among rulers and scholars over new ideas concerning the caliphate and righteous authority at a time of major demographic transition in the Islamic world. As newly Muslim groups began to form dynasties that challenged or supported the Arab caliphate, some military strongmen emerged as sultans

---

17 Talal Asad, *Formations of the Secular: Christianity, Islam, Modernity* (Stanford, CA: Stanford University Press, 2003), 15.

ruling in the name of the caliphate. A class of *ʿulamāʾ*, or legal scholars, also began to systematize and take over the law-giving aspects of governance. Political theories developed by scholars such as al-Māwardī and al-Ghazālī justified these developments in the name of the unity of the umma, or global Muslim community, under a single caliphate. However, new claimants to the caliphate rejected these compromises. In North Africa and al-Andalus, several messianic movements appeared that sought to recenter religious and political power in the hands of a single figure. In the twelfth century, the Almohad movement proclaimed a revolution led by an infallible *mahdī*, a messianic figure who, according to Islamic tradition, would lead the world at the end of time. Upon his death, his successors reformulated the caliphate to mean succession to the mahdī, not to the Prophet Muḥammad. This contest over the meaning of the caliphate forms the nucleus of the conflict between the Almohads and Ibn Mardanīsh.

The second chapter, "Rebel against the Truth," focuses on the Almohad caliphate and its battles with fellow Muslims. Ibn Mardanīsh, as the Almohads' most substantial rival in al-Andalus, fought them for a quarter of a century from his capital in Murcia. Using Almohad chronicles, chancery documents, and poetry, this chapter narrates the history of Ibn Mardanīsh's reign and shows how the Almohads portrayed him and other Muslim rebels against them as the ultimate enemies and the most important targets of jihad. Their Berber-centric, messianic vision of the caliphate departed dramatically from earlier Sunnī understandings of the caliphate, and accordingly Ibn Mardanīsh justified his resistance to the Almohads as an act of fealty to the more conventionally recognized caliphate of the Abbasids in Baghdad. Jihad was a uniquely labile tool that could augment a ruler's religious legitimacy while simultaneously serving as a practical means for eliminating rivals. As the Almohads' chancery documents and chronicles make clear, they cast Ibn Mardanīsh not simply as a political threat but also as an embodiment of the dangers and sins of this world, and his inevitable defeat thus reflected the Almohads' role as enactors of divine justice. Although much contemporary scholarship focuses on medieval battles between Muslims and Christians, this chapter shows that intrareligious conflicts were often even more intense, since competing conceptions of righteous authority were at stake.

The third chapter, "Filiative Networks," uses the lens of genealogy to explore how Ibn Mardanīsh countered Almohad claims through his own program of legitimation. It begins with a discussion of his lineage, which has been debated in scholarship: he is known by the distinctive, non-Arabic name of an ancestor several generations removed (Mardanīsh = Martínez?) and was likely a descendant of an Iberian Christian, but he is also said to belong to an Arab tribe. The chapter situates these tribal claims within the context of post-Umayyad al-Andalus and then turns to the names and titles that appear on objects associated with Ibn Mardanīsh and his family. He minted pure gold dinars, traditionally a prerogative of the caliph, but his coins presented him as an emir ruling the province of al-Andalus in the name of the Abbasid caliph al-Muqtafī (r. 530–55/1136–60). This decision to mint coins in the name of the Abbasid caliph broke with four centuries of Andalusī independence from Baghdad and represented a substantial shift in the ruling culture of the region. The changing inscriptions on Ibn Mardanīsh's coins demonstrate that he responded to Almohad claims by integrating himself increasingly closely with the norms of the Sunnī caliphate in the east. This is also visible in the scholars who fled Almohad conquest to settle in Ibn Mardanīsh's territories, many of whom found work in his government and whose biographies show their integration into scholarly networks that span the Islamic world. These scholars' intellectual genealogies, much like Ibn Mardanīsh's names and titles, made his dynasty the bearer of Sunnī traditions of authority at a moment when the Almohads sought to reformulate the caliphate.

Chapter 4, "Material Genealogies and the Construction of Power," considers the ways in which the rest of Ibn Mardanīsh's cultural programs expressed affiliation with the caliphate in the east, adopting motifs and forms en vogue among the Abbasids and the Fatimids. He built palaces, oratories, and a series of fortifications across his territory at regular intervals, producing spaces and objects that echoed those found in the Islamic East. The iconography of the palace Ibn Mardanīsh constructed in Murcia, Dār al-Ṣughrā, now part of the Monastery of Santa Clara, incorporated highly stylized repetitive Arabic inscriptions that seem to have been adapted from Fatimid *ṭirāz*, as well as paintings of musicians, dancers, and seated drinkers. The Norman palatine chapel (Cappella Palatina) in Palermo, Sicily, constructed at roughly the same time as Ibn Mardanīsh's palace, used a similar cycle of "courtly" images, adapted by the parvenu Normans from Fatimid examples, which were in turn indebted to forms borrowed by the Umayyads and Abbasids from late antique models. This chapter reveals that iconography frequently understood as generic and courtly carried specific ideological weight for Ibn Mardanīsh. These princely images were not simply a means of exhibiting power or a record of the revelry that occurred in his court. They were also a rejection of the Almohads' famous austerity and their prohibition of mixed-gender gatherings, music and dancing, and brightly colored buildings and figural representation. The use of such motifs both articulated resistance to Almohad abstraction and harked back to earlier caliphal and imperial traditions. Although some later scholars took elements such as Dār al-Ṣughrā's figurative paintings as indications of Ibn Mardanīsh's impiety, they are better seen as key components of political culture in the Islamic and Mediterranean worlds and beyond, and thus as expressions of Ibn Mardanīsh's affiliation with these traditions.

The fifth chapter, "Vassals, Traders, and Kings," examines Ibn Mardanīsh's relationships with Christian kings and traders in the context of the western Mediterranean. It surveys Ibn Mardanīsh's treatment in Christian chronicles and treaties, including discussion of his name in Latin and Castilian sources, which often refer to him as Rex Lupus or Rey Lobo, the Wolf King. Archival records indicate that Ibn Mardanīsh traveled regularly to Toledo, home to the child-king Alfonso VIII (r. 1158–1214), whose reign was contested by two Christian noble families, and it seems that he intervened in these debates on behalf of the Castro family. Similar tantalizing evidence suggests that for ten years Ibn Mardanīsh administered Almería on behalf of Castile, after Castile conquered the city with several other Christian kingdoms. Ibn Mardanīsh's own treaties, which established permanent trade delegations for Genoese and Pisan traders in Almería and his other ports, demonstrate his integration in the cultural, political, and economic system of the broader western Mediterranean. Treaties also refer to him as a vassal to Alfonso VIII. It is in the context of this close relationship that we should understand Alfonso VIII's own cultural production, especially the gold dinars that he began to mint in 1174, just two years after Ibn Mardanīsh's death. These coins translated the form, titles, and scriptural passages of Ibn Mardanīsh's coinage from an Islamic to a Christian context while maintaining the use of Arabic—simply replacing the caliph with the pope and the Quran with the Bible. I argue that Alfonso's dinars are not just modeled on Ibn Mardanīsh's gold coins but constitute an attempt to present the Castilian king as the inheritor of Ibn Mardanīsh's anti-Almohad legacy.

Chapter 6, "Resistance and Assimilation after the Almohad Conquest," focuses on the transformation of the Almohad caliphate by its conquest and incorporation of Ibn Mardanīsh's kingdom. Although

Almohad chronicles present Ibn Mardanīsh's death and defeat as a victory, close attention to the material landscape the Almohads inherited and the people they incorporated into their realm shows that his ideologies and the forms that encoded them lived on. The buildings, objects, and legal practices the Almohads promoted after their incorporation of Ibn Mardanīsh's territories were quite different from those that predated their conquest. His sons became governors and military commanders for the Almohads, and his daughters the wives of caliphs. Two generations later, Ibn Mardanīsh's grandson al-Maʾmūn would become the Almohad caliph and renounce the central Almohad doctrine that the dynasty's founder Ibn Tūmart had been the infallible mahdī.

Chapter 7, "Reconquista, a Lost Paradise, and Other Teleologies," looks at how Arabic narratives about Ibn Mardanīsh shifted to conform to teleological explanations for the decline of al-Andalus. Contemporary twelfth-century sources, many of them produced by scholars associated with the Almohads, presented Ibn Mardanīsh in complex ways—as rebellious, impious, and too close to Christians, but nevertheless courageous and skilled on the battlefield. But beginning in the fourteenth century, after the Almohads had been defeated and al-Andalus reduced to the rump state of Granada, dependent on the goodwill of its Castilian patrons, this view began to change. The first part of this chapter concentrates on two historical moments: the fourteenth century, when the Nasrid chronicler Ibn al-Khaṭīb, writing in exile from Granada in Marinid North Africa, began to depict Ibn Mardanīsh as Christianized, and the seventeenth century, when al-Maqqarī, writing about the history of al-Andalus from Cairo, extended this idea and presented Ibn Mardanīsh as a proximate cause for the fall of al-Andalus. In the works of these two exiled historians, al-Andalus began to acquire its mythical frame as a lost paradise. For Ibn al-Khaṭīb, an attack on Ibn Mardanīsh's alliances with Castile served as an oblique critique of his erstwhile Nasrid patrons, who would soon thereafter execute him on charges of heresy. For al-Maqqarī, surrounded by Moriscos who had been forced out of Spain for their "Muslim blood," Ibn Mardanīsh's alliances with Christians seemed to imply a hereditary disposition. I contend that al-Maqqarī's perception of Ibn Mardanīsh and of al-Andalus more generally was also inspired by contemporary Christian narratives of the conquest of al-Andalus as a unified and providential process, defined by conflict between Christians and Muslims. The relationships of Ibn Mardanīsh with his caliph in Baghdad, his Almohad rivals in North Africa, and his kingly lord in Castile began to accrete explanations that made them fit better into the story of an all-consuming battle between Christians and Muslims. Ibn Mardanīsh, criticized as irreligious and reimagined as a crypto-Christian, became a stand-in for the dangers of interreligious alliance.

Chapter 7 ends with an assessment of how nineteenth- and twentieth-century historians used the Arabic chronicles about Ibn Mardanīsh to construct visions of al-Andalus that could support diverse ideological goals. For Spanish scholars seeking to naturalize the Islamic past within the narrative of Christian Spain, figures such as Ibn Mardanīsh offered opportunities to highlight a "nationalist spirit" or a "Hispanified Islam" that made Muslim Andalusīs fundamentally different from their coreligionists in North Africa or the Middle East. Ibn Mardanīsh's figurative art, the plaudits he received for kindnesses to Christians, and his numerous alliances with Christian kingdoms all served as evidence of a special "European Islam" that was more cosmopolitan, flexible, and modern than that found elsewhere. At the same time that this narrative developed in European historiography, scholars working in the Arab Middle East began to focus on the history of al-Andalus as an instructive model for the future of Arab-European interactions. Arab intellectuals participating in the *nahḍa*, the "Awakening," a late nineteenth-century cultural reform movement based in Egypt and the Levant, used the history of Ibn Mardanīsh in particular to argue for the compatibility of Arabness or Islam with modernity and to stake a claim to the heritage of Europe.

The book concludes with a postscript that demonstrates the enduring significance of Ibn Mardanīsh today. He appears as a regional hero in Murcia, as the subject of comic books for schoolchildren, as the leader of a troop of "Moros" in the "Moors and Christians" festival of Murcia, and as a regular subject of columns in both right-wing and left-wing newspapers in Spain. By projecting contemporary visions of secularism and nationalism back across time, scholars have used Ibn Mardanīsh and the history of al-Andalus to fuel arguments about the essence of their countries, their religions, and modernity. The violence he perpetrated against Christian and Muslim rivals is effaced, whereas that of his Almohad rivals is magnified to the extent that they are often referred to as "the ISIS of the Middle Ages." While the Almohads are described as "fundamentalists," deeply rooted in Islamic traditions, Ibn Mardanīsh's efforts to preserve Sunnī ideals of the caliphate and his connections to Baghdad are lost. These narratives continue to legitimate visions of the world as divided between a civilized, secular and/or Christian Europe and a barbaric, violent, and religious Islamic world.

As Wendy M. K. Shaw recently argued in her book-length critique of the distorting effect of Western academic frameworks on our understanding of the art and culture of the Islamic world, "The problem is not the poor fit of categories claiming their own natural and innocent truth, but failure to recognize that the game of categorize and conquer becomes an a priori affirmation of difference and hierarchy."[18] Labels such as "Andalusī" or "Berber" or "North African" or "European," "Maghribī" or "Mashriqī," or "Muslim" or "Christian" are not, themselves, the problem. The problem arises when assumptions about what such labels imply obscure other possibilities. The problem is thinking that being "Andalusī" necessarily means being proto-Spaniard, more secular, more modern, and more "European" than counterparts to the east, and therefore missing how deeply anachronistic this view is.

This book shows both how a medieval upstart constructed his legitimacy in a border society in a time of demographic and political change, and how the complexities of his time have been flattened and distorted in the years since. Attempts to make Ibn Mardanīsh fit into the geographic, political, and religious categories that structure the modern academy have made him emblematic of hierarchies of modernity. His modern iterations—as a secularized, Hispanified, and Christianized Muslim king or as modern, Europeanized, and tolerant Arab ruler—serve to reify visions of European secularism as the model of civilization to which the rest of the world should aspire. According to such visions, al-Andalus, as a European locus of Islamic culture, came close to achieving the flexibility, tolerance, and cosmopolitanism that would become a hallmark of "modernity"; they thus separate it from other Islamic contexts and treat it as superior. These civilizational categories have come to represent racialized hierarchies that privilege the culture and history of the West above the rest. Reintegrating al-Andalus and Ibn Mardanīsh into their broader Islamic and Mediterranean contexts destabilizes such geography-bounded visions of "civilizations" and instead reveals a world of overlapping spheres, bisected by networks of trade and alliance, with no significant binary features.

---

18 Wendy M. K. Shaw, *What Is "Islamic" Art? Between Religion and Perception* (Cambridge: Cambridge University Press, 2019), 39.

Chapter 1

Caliph and *Mahdī*

The Battle over Power in the Islamic Middle Period

At some point in the late eleventh century, Abū Muḥammad Ibn al-ʿArabī (d. 493/1099), the great Andalusī jurist, wrote a letter to his former teacher al-Ghazālī (d. 505/1111) in Baghdad on behalf of the Almoravid emir Yūsuf ibn Tāshufīn (r. 456–500/1065–1106).[1] He described the chaos that had followed the fall of the caliphate of Cordoba, the rise of the party kings (*mulūk al-ṭawāʾif*), and the reaction of the Andalusīs, who had called on the Almoravids to come to al-Andalus help defend them against the Christians. But once the Almoravids had succeeded in scaring off the ambitious Christian armies, which had been hungry for more victories after their conquest of Toledo, the Andalusīs turned back to their old ways, ruling from their own castles and making alliances with their Christian neighbors. According to Ibn al-ʿArabī, Yūsuf Ibn Tashufīn had asked the Andalusīs to join him to wage jihad against the Christians, but they had responded, "We will go to holy war only alongside an imam of the Quraysh, which you are not, or a representative of such an imam, which you are not either." Yūsuf had replied that he served the Abbasid caliph, but they

1 María Jesús Viguera Molíns, "Las cartas de al-Gazālī y al-Ṭurṭūšī al soberano almorávid Yūsuf b. Tāšufīn," *al-Andalus* 42, no. 2 (1977): 351–53; É. Lévi-Provençal, "Le titre souverain des almoravides et sa légitimation par le califat ʿabbaside," *Arabica* 2 (1955): 265–88.

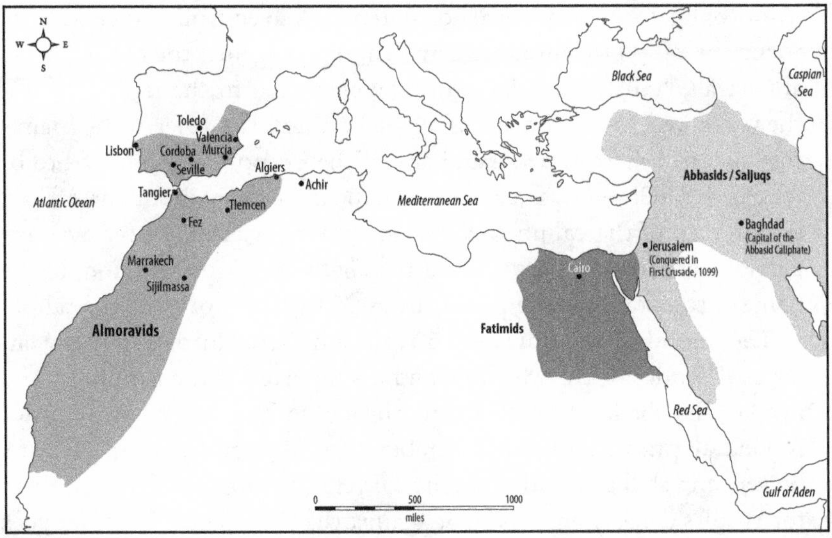

MAP 1.1. The Islamic Mediterranean, circa 1100 CE. Map by Mike Bechthold.

did not believe in his sincerity. So, Ibn al-ʿArabī wrote, could al-Ghazālī indicate what the Almoravids should do? Should they fight the kings who ruled the small city states, or *Taifas*, that had emerged after the collapse of the Umayyad Caliphate of Cordoba, even though they were fellow Muslims? If they did so and defeated them, what should they do with the kings' goods? And could al-Ghazālī get the Abbasid caliph al-Mustaẓhir (r. 487–512/1094–1118) to send to Yūsuf an edict granting the latter permission to rule in his name? After all, Ibn al-ʿArabī reasoned, the Almoravid emir was having Friday prayers said in the Abbasid caliph's name in more than two thousand mosques in the "two Maghribs" (*maghribayn*), al-Andalus and North Africa.

Al-Ghazālī seems to have responded to his disciple's letter with not one but two missives of his own. The first, addressed to Ibn al-ʿArabī, was a fatwa proclaiming that maintaining unity with fellow believers under the Abbasid caliph was obligatory and that anyone with authority, whether in the East or in the West, was required to "decorate his minbars with the invocation of the true imam," the Abbasid caliph, even if he had not been explicitly invested with authority by the caliph.[2] Furthermore,

2 Viguera Molíns, "Cartas de al-Gazālī," 353–56.

it was obligatory for all rivals or potential subjects of a ruler who invoked the caliph to submit to him. "All rebels against the truth," wrote al-Ghazālī, "must, with the sword, be converted to the truth."[3] But if they accepted the authority of the caliph and the ruler in his name, they had to be left in peace and any of their captured goods had to be returned. Al-Ghazālī went on to explain that even without the official recognition of the caliph, any just imam who wielded power over any part of the earth and proclaimed the *khuṭba*, or Friday sermon, in the name of the caliph was implicitly invested with authority by the caliph.

The second letter, addressed to Yūsuf ibn Tāshufīn, describes the latter as defender of the Muslims and a supporter of the caliphate, and invokes the shade of God's divine throne on him on Judgment Day.[4] Al-Ghazālī praises both Ibn al-ʿArabī's knowledge and piety and Yūsuf's bravery and skill as a leader, and he conveys the support of the caliphate for Yūsuf's dynasty and his fight against the Christians. "Whoever goes against your orders," he wrote, "goes against those of the Commander of the Faithful, the descendant of the uncle of the Prophet [al-ʿAbbās], making it obvious that all Muslims must fight him."[5]

These messages from al-Ghazālī to the Almoravid ruler helped the Almoravids to justify their claim to rule al-Andalus and allowed them to present their fight against the Taifa kings as a holy war. The two correspondents–Ibn al-ʿArabī, a Mālikī scholar from Seville seeking justification for the Almoravids' conquest of Taifa al-Andalus, and al-Ghazālī, the great philosopher and legal scholar who served the Abbasid caliph in Baghdad and sought to justify an increasingly decentralized political system–had the common goal of maintaining unity.[6] Al-Ghazālī would be central to the legitimation of both the Almoravid and Almohad dynasties, though in dramatically different ways.[7] The correspondence

---

3 Viguera Molíns, "Cartas de al-Gazālī," 354.

4 Viguera Molíns, "Cartas de al-Gazālī," 356–61.

5 Viguera Molíns, "Cartas de al-Gazālī," 360.

6 There is also evidence that Ibn al-ʿArabī was seeking help from al-Ghazālī and the Abbasid caliph in ingratiating himself with the Almoravid ruler, who had confiscated his family's property in Seville. See Viguera Molíns, "Cartas de al-Gazālī"; Madeline Fletcher, "Ibn Tūmart's Teachers: The Relationship with al-Ghazālī," *Al-Qanṭara* 18, no. 2 (1997): 305–30.

7 In later years, the Almoravids seem to have turned against al-Ghazālī's legal approach and ordered the burning of his books, but this move, too, reflects a deep engagement with his ideas. On the burning of the books, see Delfina Serrano Ruano, "Why Did the Scholars of al-Andalus Distrust al-Ghazali? Ibn Rushd al-Jadd's Fatwā on Awliyāʾ Allāh," *Der Islam* 83 (2006): 137–56; Nora Eggen, "A Book Burner or Not? History and Myth: Revisiting al-Qāḍī ʿIyāḍ and the Controversies over al-Ghazālī in the Islamic West," *Journal of Arabic and Islamic Studies* 18 (2018): 87–109.

sketched above highlights the central question of the Islamic Middle Period (roughly 1000 to 1500 CE): Who should rule the Islamic world? In a time when increasing numbers of newly Muslim, non-Arab groups were asserting their right to rule, scholars such as al-Ghazālī and Ibn al-ʿArabī and powerful military men formed new alliances in order to justify their own power and maintain the symbolic power of the caliphate.

The independent rulers of al-Andalus, the Almoravids, and the Almohads were all deeply invested in the same big theological and political questions as their Saljuq and Ghaznavid counterparts in the east. Through letters like al-Ghazālī's, by commissioning new works of history, legal scholarship, theology, and philosophy, and through other forms of cultural production, these rivals sought to connect themselves to Islamic traditions of authority. Although political histories of the Islamic world frequently depict the Maghrib and al-Andalus as peripheral, and the Almoravid and Almohad periods as a time of stagnancy, decline, or fanaticism, it was a time of transition in which the central ideas of the broader Islamic world were debated and deployed in new ways.

This chapter examines the contestation of authority in the Islamic Middle Period. I begin with a brief outline of ideas about the caliphate in the tenth through twelfth centuries, once new claimants and increasingly powerful military men and scholars had begun to sap the central authority of the Abbasid caliph. I then turn to messianism, focusing on the rise of the Almohads. Deliberately echoing early Islamic tropes, narratives of the life of the Almohad leader Ibn Tūmart cast his movement as a new call to submit to God and equated rivals with pre-Islamic polytheists. The Almohads' efforts to transform their Muslim rivals into infidels demonstrates the fissures within Islam at this time, rooted in a rich debate over what constituted righteous Islamic rule and emerging out of a political system in flux. The third section examines the parameters of the caliphate born of Ibn Tūmart's messianic movement and its parallels to and differences from other visions of caliphal authority.

Political and Religious Authority in the Islamic Middle Period

The rulers who competed with one another in the Islamic West were not simply fighting over territory. They were also fiercely contesting what it meant to be a Muslim ruler at a time when new forms of authority were challenging the primacy of the caliphate. The context of the western Mediterranean, especially the legacy of Umayyad authority in al-Andalus and of Fatimid ideology in North Africa, informed the particularities of the political cultures born in the region. However, the questions with which the rulers grappled were of central importance throughout the Islamic world. First and foremost among them was the role of the caliph, traditionally understood as the successor to the Prophet Muḥammad in ruling the global Muslim community and providing both political and religious guidance. Scholars, soldiers, and rulers all sought to weigh in on the nature of the caliphate and on their own roles in mediating between temporal power and the divine. In the period from the tenth through the twelfth century, as new claimants to the caliphate emerged in Fatimid Ifrīqiya and Umayyad Cordoba and as increasingly powerful military men ruled in the name of the Abbasid caliph, scholars elaborated theories of government that justified or challenged existing structures.

In Baghdad, al-Ghazālī and his predecessor, al-Māwardī (d. 450/1058), another prominent Sunnī legal scholar who wrote for an Abbasid caliph, both elaborated novel theories of the caliphate that sought to preserve the unity of the umma in the face of new challenges to the caliphate. In the Maghrib, the Almoravid dynasty heeded al-Ghazālī's emphasis on maintaining unity, proclaiming allegiance to the Abbasids. But their rival Ibn Tūmart (d. circa 524/1130), founder of the Almohad dynasty, responded to the decreasing power of the Abbasid caliph by reformulating the institution of the caliphate entirely. He presented himself as the mahdī, a messianic figure with a special connection to the divine, and made his successors the caliphs of the Almohad Empire.

Al-Māwardī wrote his work *al-Aḥkām al-Sulṭāniyya* ("The ordinances of government") while serving as a *qāḍī*, or judge, for the Abbasid caliph al-Qāʾim (422–67/1031–75) at a time when the Buyids had taken over much of the practice of power in the Abbasid Empire.[8] The work was therefore concerned with an Islamic empire divided among emirs and sultans, and it sought to delineate the respective spheres of the caliph and the new class of rulers that had recently emerged.

---

8 Al-Māwardī, *Kitāb al-Aḥkām al-Sulṭāniyya*, ed. Aḥmad Mubārak al-Baghdādī (Kuwait: Maktabat Dār al-Qutayba, 1989). See Wafaa Hassan Wahba's English translation, *The Ordinances of Government = Al-Aḥkām al-sulṭāniyya w'al-wilāyāt al-Dīniyya* (Reading: Garnet, 2006), and H. A. R. Gibb, "Al-Māwardī's Theory of the Khilāfah," *Islamic Culture* 11, no. 3 (1937): 291–302, as well as discussion of al-Māwardī's theories in E. I. J. Rosenthal, *Political Thought in Medieval Islam* (Cambridge: Cambridge University Press, 1962), and in Amir H. Siddiqi, *Caliphate and Kingship in Medieval Persia* (Lahore: Shaikh Muhammad Ashraf, 1942).

Al-Māwardī began by stating the two-part function of the caliphate: to preserve religion and to administer the political sphere.[9] A caliph is necessary to fulfill the ideal of a political system rooted in more than reason. A government led by a caliph and based on divine law, he asserted, provides true justice, and helps prepare its subjects for the afterlife. Al-Māwardī used the words *khilāfa* (caliphate) and *imāma* (imamate) nearly interchangeably throughout to refer to the caliphate, starting with the first sentence, in which he wrote that the imamate is *khilāfat al-nubuwwa*, or the successor to prophecy.[10] Though at the time he was writing, both the Fatimids and the Cordoban Umayyads had proclaimed their own caliphs, al-Māwardī asserted that there could not be more than one imam at any time.[11] Indeed, he wrote, the imamate is a requirement described in the Quran, and it serves to replace prophecy as the power that ensures that the world follows divine law.[12] Al-Māwardī indicated that there were two possible ways for the caliph to be chosen: by the consensus (*ijmāʿ*) of his subjects, who pledge allegiance (*bayʿa*) to him, or by designation by the previous caliph (*naṣṣ*).[13] However, since the size of the Abbasid Empire made it impossible for all of the caliph's subjects to pledge their allegiance to him personally, a select group could give bayʿa to the caliph and represent the consensus of his subjects. These electors of the caliph were known as *ahl al-ʿaqd wa-l-ḥāll* ("the people of the binding and the loosening"), and al-Māwardī suggested that the most important members of this group were the ʿulamāʾ, or religious scholars. He thus granted scholars a central role in determining the shape of political power.

Al-Māwardī's description of the qualifications and duties of the caliph is a useful summary of the standard Sunnī understanding of power in the Islamic world in his time. But his treatment of the role of the caliph included one new theory, dealing with the rise of governors who had not been explicitly granted power by the caliph. Diverging from the traditional understanding of the caliph as the arbiter of all power whose permission was required for legitimate rule, al-Māwardī suggested that rulers who conquered their own territories could be emirs of the caliph

9 Al-Māwardī, *al-Aḥkām*, 3.

10 Al-Māwardī, *al-Aḥkām*, 3.

11 Al-Māwardī, *al-Aḥkām*, 10. This view differs from that of al-Māwardī's predecessor al-Ashʿarī, who argued that there could be more than one caliph at once as long as they were separated by a considerable distance.

12 Al-Māwardī, *al-Aḥkām*, 3–4.

13 Al-Māwardī, *al-Aḥkām*, 6.

even if they never won explicit caliphal approval. This idea, called *imārat al-istilāʾ*, or emirate through claiming power, sought to reunify a fragmenting Islamic world under the theoretical authority of the caliph. The strongmen and warriors across the Islamic world who set themselves up as emirs or sultans could be recognized as legitimate rulers on behalf of the caliph, who could grant them ruling titles and other insignia of power.

Al-Ghazālī, who, like al-Māwardī, adhered to the Shāfiʿī school of law, expanded on his predecessor's explanation of the respective roles of the caliph and other power holders. He lived in Baghdad during a period in which Saljuq sultans held military and administrative power in the Levant and the Islamic East and the Fatimids ruled as caliphs in North Africa, and his work reflects these challenges to the caliphate. His *Kitāb al-Mustaẓhirī* was written in support of the authority of the young Abbasid caliph al-Mustaẓhir against internal Shiʿī rivals who supported the Fatimid caliph.[14] In defending the Abbasid caliph against the Fatimid claimants to the position, al-Ghazālī had to acknowledge the power of the Saljuqs, who maintained the Abbasid caliphate. The traditional prerogatives of the caliph, including minting gold coins (*sikka*) and having his name mentioned in the khuṭba, had largely been taken over by Saljuq sultans, who included their own names in sermons and on coins, sometimes alongside that of the caliph.[15] Given this context, al-Ghazālī's defense of al-Mustaẓhir's authority granted extensive freedom to the Saljuqs, moving significantly beyond al-Māwardī's articulation of caliphal power.

Al-Ghazālī's list of qualifications and responsibilities, like al-Māwardī's, was largely drawn from the Quran and the Sunna, and it followed the earlier scholar's framework for the most part. The caliph

---

14 The book was edited by ʿAbd al-Raḥmān Badawī and published as *Faḍāʾiḥ al-Bāṭiniyya wa-Faḍāʾil al-Mustaẓhiriyya* (Cairo: al-Dār al-Qawmiyya, 1383/1964). It was translated into English by Richard Joseph McCarthy as part of *Freedom and Fulfillment: An Annotated Translation of al-Ghazālī's al-Munqidh min al-Ḍalāl and Other Relevant Works of al-Ghazālī* (Boston: Twayne, 1980). For more on al-Ghazālī's book, and especially its treatment of Ismaili thought, see Farouk Mitha, *Al-Ghazālī and the Ismailis: A Debate on Reason and Authority in Medieval Islam* (London: I. B. Tauris in association with Institute of Ismaili Studies, 2001).

15 The military strength of the Saljuqs, their promotion of Sunnī thought, and their support for the caliph resulted in what George Makdisi has called a Sunnī revival and Yasser Tabbaa and others have seen as inspiring the diffusion of a new architectural style as well. I return to the architecture of the Sunnī revival in subsequent chapters. See Makdisi, "The Sunni Revival," in *Islamic Civilisation, 950–1150*, ed. D. S. Richards (Oxford: Cassirer, 1973); Tabbaa, *The Transformation of Islamic Art during the Sunni Revival* (Seattle: University of Washington Press, 2001).

should have the theological knowledge (*ʿilm*) necessary to interpret religious law (*ijtihād*) and the determination and courage (*najda wa-shajāʿa*) to wage jihad against the enemies of the umma. But, al-Ghazālī acknowledged, al-Mustaẓhir lacked these important qualities. Al-Ghazālī nonetheless defended al-Mustaẓhir's suitability for the position by pointing to the religious and military authority held by those under him. He argued that al-Mustaẓhir did not need to perform ijtihād since he had religious scholars to do it for him, and he did not need to exhibit great personal courage since he had Saljuq sultans who buttressed his authority through their force (*shawka*).[16] Instead of these qualities, al-Ghazālī encouraged the caliph to cultivate personal piety (*waraʿ*), and limited his role to one of largely spiritual authority. Al-Ghazālī urged the caliph to delegate practical authority to power holders who would promise allegiance to the caliph.

In his discussion of the appointment of a new caliph, al-Ghazālī allowed that a sultan might designate the caliph—an astonishing recognition and justification of the status quo under the Saljuqs.[17] For al-Ghazālī, like al-Māwardī before him, the benefit of incorporating new forms of power into the framework of the caliphate lay in the continuing unity of the Islamic community. To guarantee public order and maintain at least the image of caliphal authority, al-Ghazālī was willing to grant unprecedented power to wielders of military might.

As illustrated by the anecdote at the start of this chapter, the Almoravids sought to frame their own dynasty as not just supportive of but also authorized by the Abbasid caliphate. Al-Ghazālī's letters granted the Almoravid rulers a potent form of legitimation, both from a leading scholar of the Islamic east and from the caliph himself. The Almoravids minted coins in their own names, as "Commander of the Muslims" (*amīr al-muslimīn*), an otherwise unattested name that echoed the traditional caliphal title "Commander of the Faithful" (*amīr al-muʾminīn*). They did not use the name of the Abbasid caliph on the gold coins they minted, but on the reverse of their coins customarily included "The Imam ʿAbd Allāh, Commander of the Faithful" (*al-imām ʿAbd Allāh amīr al-muʾminīn*), a phrase that had become the standard way of indicating an absent caliph in the coinage of al-Andalus.[18] In the years following the collapse of

16 Rosenthal, *Political Thought*, 41.

17 Rosenthal, *Political Thought*, 42.

18 On the "absent" or "fictive" imam during the Taifa period, see François Clément, *Pouvoir et légitimité en Espagne musulmane à l'époque des taifas (Ve-XIe siècle): L'imam fictif,* (Paris:

the caliphate of Cordoba in 422/1031, as rulers emerged in each city and sought to claim the mantle of the Umayyads for themselves by minting gold coins, this was the way they made obeisance to the idea of a caliph without committing themselves to a specific overlord. The Almoravids continued this tradition, though in a few late coins, they also wrote "the Abbasid" (*al-ʿAbbasī*) at the end of the phrase, in case of any doubt over which distant caliph they acknowledged.[19] This half-hearted solution to the problem of unity under a single caliph would not please all of the Almoravids' subjects, and new approaches enacted by aspiring rulers in al-Andalus and the Maghrib would eventually destroy their empire.

Millenarianism and the Rise of the Mahdī

Al-Māwardī and al-Ghazālī responded to the challenge of increasingly decentralized power by authorizing military men and scholars to take growing roles alongside the caliph. Others sought to recenter religious and political power in a single messianic figure. Messianic ideas had been present among Muslim communities from the rise of Islam, but grew more potent between the tenth and twelfth centuries. Judaism, Christianity, and Islam have interconnected traditions of messianism, though the specifics vary by community. Paralleling Christian ideas, Islam presented Jesus as the Messiah (*masīḥ*), or anointed one, who would return at the end of times to defeat the Antichrist (*dajjāl*) and unify the Muslims under a single rule. In addition to this concept, Islam introduced the idea of the mahdī, "the rightly guided one," who would usher in a period of peace and justice just before the end of the world.[20] The question of whether the masīḥ and the mahdī are one and the same has been continuously debated, with the majority opinion since the earliest period being that they constitute two distinct figures.[21] According to

Harmattan, 1997); Alejandro Peláez Martín, *El califa ausente: cuestiones de autoridad en al-Andalus durante el siglo XI* (Madrid: La Ergástula, 2018); on "the imam ʿAbd Allāh" on coinage specifically, see David Wasserstein, *The Caliphate in the West: An Islamic Political Institution in the Iberian Peninsula* (Oxford: Clarendon Press, 1993), 117.

19 Ronald Messier, *The Almoravids and the Meanings of Jihad* (Santa Barbara, CA: Praeger, 2010), 212.

20 Neither the term nor the concept of the mahdī appears in the Quran, but the term is built on the semantic root *h-d-y*, which appears frequently throughout the text to refer to God's guidance. The concept developed on the basis of various hadith regarding the end of times.

21 According to the eighth-century scholar al-Ḥasan al-Baṣrī, Jesus, and not any living Muslim figure, was the mahdī. By contrast, his contemporary Muḥammad ibn Sīrīn argued that there would be a specifically Muslim mahdī who would rule near the end of times, and

Islamic theology, the time marking the imminent end of the world (and the arrival of the mahdī and the masīḥ) will be defined by disorder and chaos (*malāḥim wa-fitan*). The association of the figure of the mahdī with the restoration of order after a period of disorder and violence has historically made it a particularly potent political symbol for Muslim rulers facing challenges as well as for those attempting to unseat such rulers.

As a divinely guided ruler who will lead the human community at the time of the apocalypse, the mahdī spanned the temporal and spiritual realms.[22] At various moments and places in the Islamic world, those who sought greater religious or political authority were able to claim it by presenting themselves as the mahdī. The ambiguity of the role and its relationship to prophecy allowed rulers and revolutionaries considerable flexibility in suggesting that they enjoyed a direct and intimate relationship with God. The mahdī could fit into the framework of either the Sunnī caliphate or the Shiʿī imamate. But until the twelfth century, Sunnīs and Shiʿīs used the figure of the mahdī in very different ways.[23] For Sunnīs, the mahdī was an exclusively eschatological figure, without political significance except as a *laqab*, or caliphal title. No Sunnī figures claimed to be the messiah-like ruler who had come to rule at the end of times. Instead, Sunnīs responding to Shiʿī challenges often used eschatological language to counter Shiʿī claims. Some rulers, including Umayyad and Abbasid caliphs, used "al-Mahdī" as a regnal title or were referred to as such in panegyric poetry. Such usage implied divine

---

that Jesus would descend from heaven to pray behind him. *Encyclopaedia of Islam,* 2nd ed. (henceforth *EI*[2]), s.v. "Al-Mahdī" (Wilferd Madelung).

22 On the idea of the mahdī, see "Mahdisme et millénarisme en Islam," a special issue of *Revue des mondes musulmans et de la Mediterranée* 91–94 (2000), ed. Mercedes García-Arenal; Mercedes García-Arenal, *Messianism and Puritanical Reform: Mahdīs of the Muslim West* (Leiden: Brill, 2005); ʿAbd al-Majīd Qaddūrī, ed., *Mahdisme: Crise et changement dans l'histoire du Maroc* (Rabat: Université Mohammad V Faculté des lettres et des sciences humaines, 1994); Dominique Urvoy, "La pensée d'Ibn Tūmart," *Bulletin d'études orientales* 27 (1974): 19–44; Patricia Crone, *God's Rule: Government and Islam* (New York: Columbia University Press, 2004), also published as *Medieval Islamic Political Thought* (Edinburgh: Edinburgh University Press, 2004); Abdulaziz Abdulhussein Sachedina, *Islamic Messianism* (Albany: State University of New York Press, 1981). See also discussions of the Fatimid conception of the mahdī in Michael Brett, *The Rise of the Fatimids: The World of the Mediterranean and the Middle East in the Fourth Century of the Hijra, Tenth Century CE* (Leiden: Brill, 2001), and Heinz Halm, *The Empire of the Mahdi: The Rise of the Fatimids* (Leiden: Brill, 1996).

23 For discussion of Sunnī mahdism as opposed to Shiʿī mahdism, see Crone, *God's Rule,* 79–80, 250–52.

guidance and had eschatological associations.[24] But these rulers did not claim to be the mahdī of the end of times.

For Shiʿīs, by contrast, the figure of the mahdī became associated quite early with the final imam in a line of imams descended from the Prophet's nephew and son-in-law ʿAlī. Each branch of Shi'ism identified a different person as this final imam, who would serve as both a spiritual and a temporal ruler in the end of days.[25] In the Islamic West, the Ismaili Shiʿī movement in Ifrīqiya that would become the Fatimid dynasty began with a ruler claiming to be the mahdī. In 910, ʿAbd Allāh Abū Muḥammad proclaimed himself *amīr al-muʾminīn*, "commander of the faithful," and *al-mahdī bi-llāh*, "the one rightly guided by God," and he established the Shiʿī Fatimid dynasty in North Africa. The emergence of the Fatimid dynasty inspired the rise of apocalyptic language among the Umayyads of Cordoba. Fewer than twenty years later, in Cordoba, ʿAbd al-Raḥmān III claimed what he saw as his ancestral right as an Umayyad to the title of *amīr al-muʾminīn*. Although he did not call himself the mahdī, he used a laqab that mirrored that of his Fatimid rival, *al-Qāʾim bi-Amr Allāh*, "he who undertakes the command of God," implying that it was he, not the Fatimid leader, who would bring in the Day of Resurrection (*yawm al-qiyāma*).[26] The word *al-qāʾim* carries semantic ambiguity that allows it to be understood simultaneously as the one who acts on

---

24 On the uses of the laqab al-Mahdī and other messianic references, see Patricia Crone and Martin Hinds, *God's Caliph: Religious Authority in the First Centuries of Islam* (Cambridge: Cambridge University Press, 1986), 36–37 (on the Umayyads), 80–82 (on the Abbasids). For a more detailed study of the centrality of messianism in the Abbasid caliphate, see Hayrettin Yücesoy, *Messianic Beliefs and Imperial Politics in Medieval Islam: The ʿAbbāsid Caliphate in the Early Ninth Century* (Columbia: University of South Carolina Press, 2009). For example, the third Abbasid caliph, Muḥammad b. ʿAbdallah, who provided the foundation for the great flowering of the caliphate, took the regnal title al-Mahdī (158–69/775–85). On context of the first appearance of this laqab on the silver coins minted in Rayy in 145 AH (762–63 CE), see Jere Bacharach, "Laqab for a Future Caliph: The Case of the Abbasid al-Mahdī," *Journal of the American Oriental Society* 113, no. 2 (1993): 271–74.

25 According to Twelver Shiʿīs, their twelfth imam, Muḥammad al-Mahdī, went into occultation in 329/941 and will return before the Day of Judgment to rule alongside Jesus. When the imam of the Zaydī community of Yemen, named al-Mahdī li-Dīn Allāh, died in the eleventh century, his successors refused to call themselves "imam" because they believed he would return to rule once more. Crone, *God's Rule*, 107.

26 The second Fatimid caliph, Abū al-Qāsim Muḥammad (r. 322–44/934–46), took *al-qāʾim bi-amr Allāh* as his regnal title and minted his coins in this name. This laqab also appears on the coins of the Abbasid caliph who ruled from 422–67/1031–75. See Michael Bates, "Names and Titles on Islamic Coins: An Index," Unpublished working paper, American Numismatic Society, updated August 7, 2019, https://www.academia.edu/26072179/Names_and_Titles_on_Islamic_Coins (accessed March 2, 2020). Janina Safran suggests that this title is synonymous with mahdī in Shiʿī contexts, since it is the mahdī who will bring in the Day of Judgment. Safran, "The Command of the Faithful in al-Andalus: A Study in the Articulation of Caliphal Legitimacy," *International Journal of Middle East Studies* 30, no. 2 (1998): 185.

God's command and the one who is lifted up by God's command, thus implying both righteousness and divine election. ʿAbd al-Raḥmān also presented himself as the one following the right path (*hudā*, from the same root as mahdī). For both of these tenth-century challengers to the Abbasid caliphate, eschatological language played a central role in articulating legitimacy and in challenging rivals. Until the twelfth century, however, Sunnī rulers used reference to divine guidance to support their authority without directly proclaiming themselves to be the messianic ruler who would usher in end times.

In the twelfth century, apocalyptic language began to play a central legitimizing role among some Sunnīs in the Islamic West, with several people claiming to be the mahdī on a model much closer to Ismāʿīlī usage. Maribel Fierro has shown that the figure of the mahdī could serve as a means of recentering religious and political authority in one person, reversing the trend toward separating these powers into different realms and offering the leader's subjects religious certainty.[27] Mahdism can be seen as a different response to the same challenge of dispersal of the caliph's religious and political power that, in previous centuries, led al-Māwardī and al-Ghazālī to develop their theories. In the first half of the twelfth century, a new type of Sufi figure appeared throughout al-Andalus, winning followers and sometimes even claiming the imamate himself.[28] One such figure was Ibn Qasī (d. 546/1151), whose movement harnessed Sufi and millenarian ideas to oppose the Almoravids at the end of their rule in al-Andalus. Ibn Qasī, who ruled in Gharb al-Andalus, present-day Portugal, attracted followers with an ideology of seeking union with God. One of his works is extant, and it describes spiritual exercises that help the seeker reach the Truth.[29] The silver coins

27 Maribel Fierro, "The *Qāḍī* as Ruler," in *Saber religioso y poder político en el Islam*, ed. Manuela Marín and Mercedes García-Arenal (Madrid: Agencia Española de Cooperación Internacional, 1994), 110; Maribel Fierro, "Le mahdi Ibn Tûmart et al-Andalus: L'élaboration de la légitimité Almohade," *Revue des mondes musulmans et de la Méditerranée* 91–94 (2000): 107–24; Maribel Fierro, "Spiritual Alienation and Political Activism: The Ġurabāʾ in al-Andalus during the Sixth/Twelfth Century," *Arabica* 47, no. 2 (2000): 247.

28 For example, Ibn Barrajān (d. 536/1141) and Ibn al-ʿArīf (d. 536/1141). On these fascinating figures and the emergence of what José Bellver has called "learned Sufism" in al-Andalus, see Bellver, "'Al-Ghazālī of al-Andalus': Ibn Barrajān, Mahdism, and the Emergence of Learned Sufism on the Iberian Peninsula," *Journal of the American Oriental Society* 133, no. 4 (2013): 659–81. Yousef Casewit's *The Mystics of al-Andalus: Ibn Barrajān and Islamic Thought in the Twelfth Century* (Cambridge: Cambridge University Press, 2017) outlines how Ibn Barrajān, alongside Ibn al-ʿArīf and Ibn Qasī, developed new approaches to the Quran and hadith through engagement with the particular mixture of Neoplatonic and Ismāʿīlī thought circulating in al-Andalus in the twelfth century.

29 Ibn Qasī, *Kitāb khalʿ al-naʿlayn wa-iqtibās al-nūr min mawḍiʿ al-qadamayn*, ed. Muḥammad al-Amrānī (Safi, Morocco: IMBH, 1997). Ibn Qasī's complex theology and its relation to

he minted reveal that he claimed a spiritual authority that impinged on the Almoravids' political rule. The legends on his coins call him *al-imām al-qā'im bi-amr Allāh*, "the imam who undertakes the command of God" (or is raised up by the command of God), the same appellation used by the Cordoban Umayyad caliph ʿAbd al-Raḥmān III to counteract his Fatimid rival.[30] By using this title, Ibn Qasī laid claim to the imamate and also evoked the Day of Judgment. Later, he minted another coin with the legend *Allāh rabbunā wa-Muḥammad nabiyyunā wa-l-mahdī imāmunā*, "God is our Lord and Muḥammad is our Prophet and the mahdī is our imam," a variant of the legend the Almohads would subsequently use on their own coins.[31] Both numismatic and literary evidence show that Ibn Qasī brought together the Shiʿī concept of an infallible imam, the apocalyptic promise of a mahdī, and the Sufi ideal of friendship with God (*walāya*) to justify his political and religious authority.[32] His movement failed, however, and Ibn Qasī eventually submitted to the Almohads, who appointed him as governor of Shilb (Silves, Portugal), where he would be assassinated in 546/1151.

It was in the context of Ibn Qasī's movement in al-Andalus that the Almohads emerged with their own mahdī in North Africa. The first half of the twelfth century saw the people of al-Andalus fighting the Almoravids in two primary ways: first, several cities installed judges as rulers

---

Sufism as well as Ismāʿīlī thought has been elucidated in Michael Ebstein, "Was Ibn Qasī a Ṣūfī?" *Studia Islamica* 110 (2015): 196–232.

30 Ibn Qasī claimed to be an infallible imam and the mahdī. In the centuries after the Almohads, this title continued to hold special power for aspiring leaders launching new political and religious movements, including the founder of the Saʿadī dynasty in sixteenth-century Morocco, who called himself al-Qā'im bi-Amr Allāh, Muḥammad al-Mahdī. For discussion of the Saʿdī use of the concept and the broader history of mahdism in the medieval Maghrib, see Michael Brett, "Le Mahdi dans le Maghreb médiéval," *Revue des mondes musulmans et de la Méditerranée* 91–94 (2000): 93–106.

31 M. Telles Antunes and A. Sidarus suggest that the Almohads copied Ibn Qasī's legend. Their evidence is that Almohad coins use the less grammatically correct legend *Allāh rabbunā wa-Muḥammad rasūlunā wa-l-mahdī imāmunā* ("God is our Lord and Muḥammad is our Messenger and the *mahdī* is our Imam"), which makes Muḥammad seem like the messenger of the Almohads rather than the Prophet of God. This reading implies that the Almohads chose the legend they used in order to differentiate themselves from Ibn Qasī. Antunes and Sidarus, "Mais um quirate cunhado em Beja em nome de Ibn Qasi e Abu Talib al-Zuhri," *Arqueología Medieval* 1 (1992): 221–23. Fierro points out that it is equally likely that Ibn Qasī copied the Almohads' legend, given that the Almohad movement may have been well underway in North Africa by the time of Ibn Qasī's rebellion in Gharb al-Andalus. See Fierro, "Le mahdi Ibn Tûmart et al-Andalus," 109; Fierro, "Spiritual Alienation," 256.

32 Ebstein, "Was Ibn Qasī a Ṣūfī?" 198. Ebstein argues that Ibn Qasī's philosophy was far removed from the Sufism that had developed in the Islamic east and instead had closer connections to Ismāʿīlī thought, with a cosmological approach inspired by Neoplatonism.

in opposition to the Almoravids; and second, the followers (*murīdūn*) of Ibn Qasī proclaimed him the imam. The Almoravids had claimed legitimacy based on their acknowledgment of the Abbasids, their jihad against the Christians, and their Mālikī orthodoxy and respect for the ʿulamāʾ.[33] When successive defeats by the Christians began to undermine their authority and the Almohads weakened their North African base, the ʿulamāʾ whom the Almoravids had maintained in positions of power in al-Andalus took advantage of the vacuum and, in several cases, declared themselves rulers.[34] The Almohads' doctrine of the mahdī and their resistance to the Almoravids' Mālikism allowed the Almohads to respond to both of the political challenges they faced in al-Andalus, undermining the sources of authority relied on by the qāḍīs who claimed power and countering Ibn Qasī's assertion of his role as mahdī with one of their own.[35] Fierro shows that the concept of the mahdī may have emerged relatively late in Almohad history (and that Ibn Tūmart may not have claimed the title for himself), and she suggests that it was only in the context of post–Ibn Qasī al-Andalus that the Almohad doctrine of the mahdī as we now understand it became fully formed.[36] Although it is clear that there were messianic elements to the Almohad movement from the beginning, the specifics of Ibn Tūmart's role as the mahdī, and especially the role of his successors as caliphs, may not have been clearly articulated until after his death.[37]

Revolution and Apocalyptic Ideology in the Islamic Far West

Ibn Tūmart was born around 1080 in the Sūs Valley in what is today southern Morocco, and traveled first to al-Andalus and then to Baghdad seeking religious knowledge.[38] When he returned to the Maghrib after

33 Fierro, "*Qāḍī* as Ruler," 105.

34 Fierro, "*Qāḍī* as Ruler," 105. For a general discussion of the phenomenon in its historical context, see 104–10.

35 Fierro, "Le mahdi Ibn Tûmart et al-Andalus," 107–24, as part of the special issue "Mahdisme et millénarisme en Islam," here 115.

36 Fierro, "Le mahdi Ibn Tûmart et al-Andalus," 116.

37 There is also some evidence of the existence of another messianic figure along with Ibn Tūmart at the rise of the Almohad movement. Bishr al-Wansharīsī, one of Ibn Tūmart's ten closest companions, is described as having been able to perform miracles, and he was known as *al-masīḥ*, the messiah. Maribel Fierro, "The Legal Policies of the Almohad Caliphs and Ibn Rushd's *Bidāyat al-Mujtahid*," *Journal of Islamic Studies* 10, no. 3 (1999): 231n18.

38 The narrative of Ibn Tūmart's early life is contained in the book *al-Ḥulal al-mawshiyya fī dhikr al-akhbār al-Marrākshiyya*. There are reasons to doubt this narrative, and parts of it, such as Ibn Tūmart's ostensible meeting with al-Ghazālī in Baghdad, are certainly myth. See Fierro,

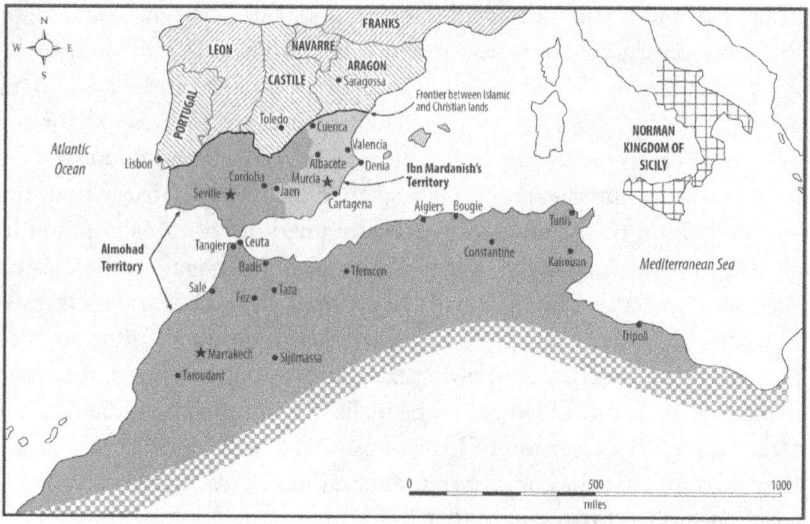

Map 1.2. The western Mediterranean, circa 1150 CE. Map by Mike Bechthold.

years in the east, he began to expound a particular version of *tawḥīd*, or divine unity, that rejected the Mālikī (and Almoravid) understanding of God's attributes. Almohad sources describe the early years of the Almohad movement in ways that are reminiscent of narratives about the life of the Prophet and the birth of Islam. Like the Prophet, Ibn Tūmart meditated in a cave, and when he emerged from his retreat in Igīlīz, he made a speech to his supporters that outlined the characteristics of the mahdī. To his supporters, this speech was a clear indication of his role as the mahdī, sent by God to bring justice to the world at the end of times. According to the anonymous chronicler of *al-Ḥulal al-mawshiyya*, Ibn Tūmart gave his khuṭba, or speech, during the month of Ramadan in 515/1121 and outlined the characteristics of the mahdī foretold by the Prophet Muḥammad as follows:[39]

> And God bless our lord Muḥammad, the Messenger of God, the herald of the Imam al-Mahdī (*al-mubashshir bi-l-imām al-mahdī*),

"El Mahdī Ibn Tūmart: Más allá de la biografía 'oficial,'" in *Política, sociedad e identidades en el Occidente islámico (siglos XI–XIV)*, ed. Miguel Angel Manzano Rodriguez and Rachid El Hour Amro (Salamanca: Ediciones Universidad de Salamanca, 2016), 73–98.

39 Anonymous, *al-Ḥulal al-mawshiyya fī dhikr al-akhbār al-Marrākshiyya*, ed. Suhayl Zukkār and ʿAbd al-Qādir Zamāma (Casablanca: Dār al-Rushshād al-Ḥadītha, 1979), 107. It is unknown when or in what context this narrative was written, but it seems to have been produced in the fourteenth century, likely in a Nasrid context. It may have been based on earlier,

> who will fill the earth with equity and justice (*bi-qisṭan wa-ʿadlan*), just as it had been filled with tyranny and oppression (*kamā malaʿat jawran wa-ẓulman*). God sent him to abolish falsehood with truth and to eradicate tyranny with justice (*wa-izālat al-jawr bi-l-ʿadl*). And the name [*ism*] is the name, the genealogy [*nasab*] is the genealogy and the deed [*fiʿl*] is the deed.[40]

Ibn Tūmart's description of the mahdī echoed discussions of the figure in hadith collections, which foretold a mahdī whose name, like the Prophet's, would be Muḥammad ibn ʿAbd Allāh, whose genealogy would go back to the Prophet, and whose deed would be to fill the earth with justice.[41] The chronicler writes that ʿAbd al-Muʾmin, the future successor to Ibn Tūmart and first Almohad caliph, reported that he and nine other men instantly recognized their leader as mahdī, based on this description. These men, later known as the group of ten, gave bayʿa to him and promised to support his mandate to bring justice to earth just as the Companions of the Prophet Muḥammad had promised to the latter.[42]

In narrating the life of Ibn Tūmart in a way that mirrored the life of the Prophet Muḥammad, early Almohad propagandists reimagined the Islamic West as the Arabian Peninsula, Berber tribes as the most important Arab tribes of early Islam, and Ibn Tūmart as a prophetlike figure.[43] Ibn Tūmart, for his part, followed the model of the Prophet

---

Almohad period sources that have since been lost. Ambrosio Huici Miranda believes the chronicle was compiled by Abū ʿAbd Allāh Muḥammad ibn Abī al-Maʿālī Ibn Sammāk in 783/1381. *EI*², s.v. "Al-Ḥulal al-Mawshiyya" (Ambrosio Huici Miranda). Huici Miranda describes the chronicle as a "curious motley patchwork" of reliable sources and fabricated ones. It is therefore difficult to judge the historical accuracy of any individual part, including the claim that Ibn Tūmart was recognized as the mahdī in 515/1121 or even during his lifetime. The speech is also included in Ibn al-Qaṭṭān al-Marrākushī, *Nuẓum al-jumān li-tartīb mā salafa min akhbār al-zamān*, ed. Maḥmūd Makkī (Beirut: Dār al-Gharb al-Islāmī, 1990), 36.

40 Anonymous, *al-Ḥulal al-mawshiyya*, 107. The translation is adapted from Linda G. Jones's article on the importance of oratory in the Almohad legitimation of power, "The Preaching of the Almohads: Loyalty and Resistance across the Strait of Gibraltar," *Medieval Encounters* 19 (2013): 71–101.

41 On the name and acts of the foretold mahdī, see *Sunan Abī Dāwūd*, hadith number 4282, 4: 507, *Sunan Ibn Māja*, hadith number 4083, 5: 276. See further discussion of the question of genealogy and authority in the following chapter.

42 Anonymous, *al-Ḥulal al-mawshiyya*, 107–8.

43 On the idea that the territory ruled by the Almohads constituted a new Ḥijāz and the resulting prohibition of Jews and Christians in this territory, see Maribel Fierro, "A Muslim Land without Jews or Christians: Almohad Attitudes regarding the 'Protected People,'" in *Christlicher Norden—Muslimischer Süden: Ansprüche und Wirklichkeiten von Christen, Juden und Muslimen auf der Iberischen Halbinsel im Hoch- und Spätmittelalter*, ed. M. Tischler and A. Fidora (Frankfurt am Main: Aschendorff, 2011); also Fierro, "Conversion, Ancestry, and Universal

Muḥammad assiduously, proclaiming that the people of his own tribe, the Hargha, occupied a higher rank than members of other tribes and naming his closest supporters honorary members of the Hargha tribe.[44] Like the Prophet, Ibn Tūmart made *hijra*, or emigrated, to a distant city, in this case, Tīnmallal, which became the base for the consolidation and expansion of Almohad power. After the Almohads moved to Tīnmallal in 518/1124, they welcomed a new tribe, the Hazmīra, into the city and pushed out or killed those Tīnmallalīs who rejected the incorporation of this new group into their city.[45] Ibn Tūmart's bloody purge (*tamyīz*) of those who were seen as insufficiently committed to the Almohad cause echoed the Prophet Muḥammad's purge of Jewish tribes in Medina.[46] But even generally pro-Almohad sources record the purge with ambivalence, indicating the large number of self-declared Almohads who were killed and condemned as "people of hell."[47] Ibn ʿIdhārī (d. after 712/1312) notes that a legal scholar (*faqīh*) from the former Roman province of Ifrīqiya who was a member of the Almohad group of ten, the innermost circle of the mahdī's supporters, objected to the violence of the purge, asking Ibn Tūmart, "How can you kill peoples [*aqwām*] who have pledged allegiance to you [*bāyaʿūka*], who have entered into obedience to you [*dakhalū fī ṭāʿatika*], and whose goods have been distributed [*taqassama amwālihim*]?" Ibn Tūmart responded by ordering that the faqīh be killed and crucified for doubting his infallibility.[48]

It was from Tīnmallal that Ibn Tūmart's forces fought the Almoravids and began to build their new state, based on the teachings of a divinely guided leader. The focus of the early Almohads was the rectification of what they perceived to be major flaws in the interpretation and application of the *sharīʿa*, or divine law, especially under the rule of

---

Religion: The Case of the Almohads in the Islamic West (Sixth/Twelfth–Seventh/Thirteenth Centuries)," *Journal of Medieval Iberian Studies* 2, no. 2 (2010): 155–73.

44 The Hargha here are parallel to the Prophet Muḥammad's tribe, the Quraysh. However, al-Baydhaq reports that Ibn Tūmart also called the Hargha his *anṣār*, or helpers, the name associated with the people of Medina who assisted the Meccan Muslims. See Évariste Lévi-Provençal, *Documents inédits d'histoire almohade* (Paris: P. Geuthner, 1928), 55.

45 Ambrosio Huici Miranda, *Historia política del imperio almohade* (Tetouan: Editora Marroquí, 1957), 1:72–73.

46 Amira Bennison, *The Almoravid and Almohad Empires* (Edinburgh: Edinburgh University Press, 2016), 67; Huici Miranda, *Historia política*, 1:72–73.

47 Ibn ʿIdhārī records that fifteen thousand people were killed as part of this purge. Ibn ʿIdhārī al-Marrākushī, *al-Bayān al-mughrib fī akhbār al-Andalus wa-l-Maghrib*, ed. G. S. Colin and É. Lévi-Provençal (Beirut: Dār al-Kutub al-ʿIlmiyya, 2009), 4:60.

48 Ibn ʿIdhārī, *al-Bayān al-mughrib*, 4:60; Bennison, *Almoravid and Almohad Empires*, 67; Huici Miranda, *Historia política*, 1:72.

the Almoravids.[49] Conflicts among jurists and rulers over the right to interpret—and enforce—the sharīʿa for the masses were present from the Umayyad period onward. The Almoravids' dependence on Mālikī jurists (*fuqahāʾ*) to interpret divine law, their hostility toward philosophically inflected Ghazālian theology, and their opposition to new Sufi movements emerging in al-Andalus meant they were vulnerable to the Almohads' critique.[50] Although it is difficult to determine which sources on the early Almohads are contemporary to the events they purport to describe, it is clear that Ibn Tūmart and his successor ʿAbd al-Muʾmin sought to reframe religious knowledge.[51] They rejected tradition (*taqlīd*) and the legal works (*kutub al-furūʿ*) that guided Mālikī judges and jurists and instead sought a return to the Quran and Sunna of the Prophet, illuminated through logic.[52] Ibn Tūmart's movement sought to reunite certainty regarding religious knowledge, derived from the application of logic to divine texts, with the military and political strength of a state.

A central component of Ibn Tūmart's movement was *ḥisba*, the duty to command the good and forbid the evil (*al-amr bi-l-maʿrūf wa-l-nahī ʿan al-munkar*). This phrase from the Quran became a fundamental individual obligation in Islam and was further elaborated in the concept of ḥisba by al-Ghazālī.[53] As al-Ghazālī described it, those who enacted ḥisba

---

49 The earliest non-Almohad source referring to Almohad doctrine calls it a *madhhab fikr*, or school of religious thought. Abū Yaʿlā Ḥamza ibn Asad Ibn al-Qalānisī, *Tārīkh Abī Yaʿlā Ḥamza Ibn al-Qalānisī: al-Maʿrūf bi-dhayl tārīkh Dimashq*, ed. Hilāl ibn al-Muḥassin Ṣābī and H. F. Amedroz (Beirut: Maṭbaʿat al-Ābāʾ al-Yasūʿiyyīn, 1908), 291; Tilman Nagel, "La destrucción de la ciencia de la *šarīʿa* por Muḥammad ibn Tūmart," *Al-Qanṭara* 18(2) (1997): 295.

50 Delfina Serrano Ruano shows that the attitudes of Andalusī Mālikī fuqahāʿ toward al-Ghazālī's magnum opus, *Iḥyāʾ ʿulūm al-dīn*, varied considerably. While much has been made of the Almoravids' burning of this work, she shows that several Andalusī fuqahāʿ also publicly supported al-Ghazālī. Serrano, "Why Did the Scholars of al-Andalus Distrust al-Ghazali?"

51 Emile Fricaud has written about a process of "Désalmohadisation" that occurred with in histories written in the Marinid period, as particular elements of the early Almohad project were effaced or transformed to correspond to later ideas about Almohadism. Fricaud, "Les *Ṭalaba* dans la société Almohade (Le temps d'Averroès),"*Al-Qanṭara* 18 (1997): 331–88.

52 Saʿīd Aʿrāb, "Mawqif al-Muwaḥḥidīn min kutub al-furūʿ wa-ḥaml al-nās ʿalā al-madhhab al-ḥazmī," *Daʿwat al-Haqq* 249 (1985): 26–30; Fierro, "The Legal Policies of the Almohad Caliphs."

53 This phrase appears in Quran 3:104, 3:110, and 9:71. On understandings of the phrase as it applies to the individual believer, the essential reference is Michael Cook's book *Commanding Right and Forbidding Wrong in Islamic Thought* (Cambridge: Cambridge University Press, 2001), see 427–59 for details on the thought of al-Ghazālī. For the centrality of the ḥisba to Ibn Tūmart and his followers and a selection of narratives about the Almohads' forbidding the wrong, see Bennison, *Almoravid and Almohad Empires*, 247–56.

superseded martyrs of jihad in their holiness.[54] The Andalusī scholar Ibn Ḥazm (d. 456/1064) had described *al-amr bi-l-maʿrūf* as a justification for public revolt against an unjust ruler, and al-Ghazālī later argued that the doctrine should be central to religious and political practice.[55] Ibn Tūmart and his followers extended this concept even further, into what Vincent Cornell has called "a theology of moral and political imperatives," which transformed the individual duty to address mistakes into a call for public action.[56]

Ḥisba thus became the basis for revolutionary violence. As seen in the khuṭba by Ibn Tūmart describing the mahdī above, the messianic figure's central role was to replace injustice with justice, a divine mandate that echoed the individual obligation to forbid evil and command good. Narratives about Ibn Tūmart's life frequently refer to his role as a teller of uncomfortable truths, someone who would remind those around him of their moral duty, even when such statements placed him in danger. Several chroniclers relate a story about Ibn Tūmart's return to the Maghrib aboard a boat on which he angered his fellow travelers by throwing out wine and ordering them to pray.[57] The chronicler ʿAbd al-Wāḥid al-Marrākushī (d. circa 647/1249) writes that Ibn Tūmart so aggravated his boatmates with his enjoining of the good and forbidding of the evil that they threw him overboard; they let him back on board only after seeing him survive miraculously behind the boat for more than half a day, at which point they began to venerate him.[58] The same author also recounts a story about Ibn Tūmart chastising the Almoravid ruler ʿAlī ibn Yūsuf ibn Tāshufīn for his impiety and being exiled for his impudence.[59]

The Almohads considered the Almoravids impious in everything, from their clothing to their food, and claimed the right to "correct"

---

54 Mercedes García-Arenal, "La práctica del precepto de *'al-amr bi-l-maʿrūf wa-l-nahy ʿan al-munkar'* en la hagiografía Magrebí," *Al-Qanṭara* 13, no. 1 (1992): 155.

55 García-Arenal, "La práctica del precepto," passim; on Ibn Ḥazm, see 148.

56 Vincent J. Cornell, "Understanding Is the Mother of Ability: Responsibility and Action in the Doctrine of Ibn Tūmart," *Studia Islamica* 66 (1987): 71–103, here 73.

57 On the variations of this story in different chronicles and its relationship to Quranic and biblical narratives about Jonah, see David Wasserstein, "A Jonah Theme in the Biography of Ibn Tūmart," in *Culture and Memory in Medieval Islam: Essays in Honour of Wilferd Madelung*, ed. F. Daftary and J. Meri (London: I. B. Tauris, 2003).

58 ʿAbd al-Wāḥid al-Marrākushī, *al-Muʿjib fī talkhīṣ akhbār al-Andalus*, ed. Khalīl ʿUmrān al-Manṣūr (Beirut: Dār al-Kutub al-ʿIlmiyya, 2003), 127.

59 Al-Marrākushī, *al-Muʿjib*, ed. al-Manṣūr, 130–32. The same story appears in al-Baydhaq as well; see Lévi-Provençal, *Documents inédits*, 26–29, for the Arabic original and 108–12 for the French translation.

them, through force if necessary. The Almoravids had claimed power on a similar basis, commanding the good and forbidding the wrong among the tribes of North Africa and waging jihad against anyone who resisted as well as against non-Muslims.[60] But the Almohads framed their "struggle in the path of God" even more explicitly around the rejection of evil and the embrace of good and directed their campaign specifically against their coreligionists. Vincent Lagardère has shown that jihad went from a central objective of the state under the Almoravids to an individual obligation under the Almohads, who expected all believers to support it through taking direct action, paying extra taxes, and contributing their wealth, even at the cost of sacrificing their ability to undertake the pillar of pilgrimage to Mecca.[61] Scholarly critics of the Almoravids had questioned the legitimacy of their leadership of jihad given that the Almoravid leader was not a caliph, and the Almoravid emirs had pointed to their support for the Abbasids in order to justify their jihad.[62] By contrast, Ibn Tūmart used his claim to be the infallible imam and the foretold mahdī to authorize his new campaign of jihad without requiring the permission of any distant authority. In the process, he recentered the Islamic world on the Islamic far west, al-Maghrib al-Aqṣā.

Along with developing al-Ghazālī's emphasis on the importance of ḥisba and making it the core of a program of political change and violence, Almohad theology also extended al-Ghazālī's critique of the ʿulamāʾ.[63] Al-Ghazālī harbored reservations about the class of ʿulamāʾ whom he saw gaining significant power and who, he felt, had lost touch with the important aspects of religion.[64] In rooting their caliphate in the

60 García-Arenal, "La práctica del precepto," especially 149–50.

61 Vincent Lagardère, "Le ǧihād almohade: Théorie et practique," in *Los Almohades: Problemas y perspectivas*, ed. Patrice Cressier, Maribel Fierro, and Luis Molina (Madrid: Consejo Superior de Investigaciones Científicas, 2005), 2:617. On Almoravid conceptions of jihad, see also Lagardère, *Les Almoravides, le djihād andalou (1106–1143)* (Paris: L'Harmattan, 1999); Messier, *The Almoravids and the Meanings of Jihad*.

62 Viguera Molíns, "Cartas de al-Gazālī."

63 On Ibn Tūmart's relationship with the thought of al-Ghazālī, see Frank Griffel, "Ibn Tūmart's Rational Proof for God's Existence and Unity, and His Connection to the Niẓāmiyya *Madrasa* in Baghdad," in *Los Almohades*, ed. Cressier, Fierro, and Molina, 2:753–813; Madeleine Fletcher, "The Almohad Tawḥīd: Theology which Relies on Logic," *Numen* 38, no. 1 (1991): 110–27; Fletcher, "Ibn Tūmart's Teachers."

64 See, for example, al-Ghazālī, *Iḥyāʾ ʿulūm al-dīn*, translated by Nabih Amin Faris as *The Book of Knowledge* (Delhi: Islamic Book Service, 1962), sect. 6 ("On the Evils of Knowledge and on Determining the Distinguishing Features of the Learned Men of the Hereafter and Those of the Teachers of Falsehood"), 147–212.

religious knowledge of the infallible mahdī, who could determine divine law through reason and without the involvement of other scholars, the Almohads circumvented the problem of a powerful class of ʿulamāʾ. A manuscript that claims to have been dictated by Ibn Tūmart's successor ʿAbd al-Muʾmin on the basis of notes from Ibn Tūmart's lessons outlines Ibn Tūmart's understanding of religious knowledge.[65] Whereas the approach to jurisprudence (*fiqh*) endorsed by the Almoravids followed the precedent (*taqlīd*) of earlier interpretations of law (ijtihād), Ibn Tūmart believed that the leaders and scholars who had made these interpretations were fallible. For Ibn Tūmart, *ẓann*, or supposition, which was the root of ijtihād, led to error, and only reason could accurately determine divine law. On this basis, his ideology disqualified the customary sources used by Sunnī scholars to determine the law and undermined the traditional science of the sharīʿa.[66] In rejecting the sources of Islamic law, the Almohads moved far beyond al-Ghazālī's critique, but his centrality to their claim to power is reflected in the story that Ibn Tūmart studied with al-Ghazālī while traveling in the Islamic east.[67]

Instead of the traditional approaches to the sharīʿa, Ibn Tūmart relied on reason and on the interdependence of this world and the divine.[68] Ibn Tūmart's vision of God allowed knowledge of the divine to be obtained through reason alone, an Aristotelian approach that would later be reflected in the writings of philosophers supported by the Almohads, such as Ibn Ṭufayl's *Ḥayy ibn Yaqẓān*, not to mention in the extraordinarily

---

65 *Kitāb al-aʿazz mā yuṭlab*, edited by J. D. Luciani as *Le Livre d'Ibn Toumert*, with an introduction by Ignaz Goldziher (Algiers: P. Fontana, 1903). There are many open questions about when this text was written and to what extent it represents the ideas of Ibn Tūmart as opposed to those of ʿAbd al-Muʾmin or later Almohads.

66 Nagel, "La destrucción de la ciencia de la *šarīʿa*," 297. The Almohad rejection of the traditional forms of Sunnī law is captured in the famous anecdote about the Mālikī legal scholar Ibn al-Jadd (d. 586/1190), who tried to explain why there were differences (*ikhtilāf*) among the Sunnī legal schools to an Almohad caliph. The caliph reportedly refused to accept such differences and said that on one side there was only the Quran and the Sunna of the Prophet, and on the other, the sword. Fierro, "Le mahdi ibn Tûmart et al-Andalus," 112; see also Fierro, "Legal Policies of the Almohad Caliphs," 236.

67 Most of the biographies of Ibn Tūmart include mention of a period of time that the future Almohad mahdī spent studying with al-Ghazālī. Modern scholars, like Ignaz Goldziher, have largely rejected this narrative as apocryphal and as the coincidence of Ibn Tūmart and al-Ghazālī in the same city as a chronological impossibility. Madeline Fletcher, on the other hand, believes that Ibn Tūmart and al-Ghazālī likely coincided in Alexandria around 500 AH and that al-Ghazālī would have been eager to meet a figure from Almoravid territories after his correspondence with Ibn al-ʿArabī. See Goldziher, in his introduction to *Le livre d'Ibn Toumert*, 5–12; Fletcher, "Ibn Tūmart's Teachers."

68 Fierro, "Le mahdi ibn Tûmart et al-Andalus," 112.

dynamic tradition in the Latin West known as scholasticism.[69] At the same time, Ibn Tūmart's doctrine made the imam central for religious knowledge. According to him, the imam was "one of the pillars of religion and one of the supports of the sharīʿa, and the maintenance of right in the world [*dunyā*] is guaranteed only by the existence of the imamate [*iʿtiqād al-imāma*] at all times until the Hour of Judgment."[70] Ibn Tūmart presented himself as the latest in a line of imams that went back to Adam, through Noah and Abraham, and as a successor to the prophets, who could thus lead the community in righteousness.[71]

In his own writings Ibn Tūmart does not explicitly call himself the mahdī, although recognizing him as such would later become a crucial element of Almohad ideology.[72] But Ibn Tūmart's works are replete with discussions of the importance of the mahdī and the centrality of his role in humankind's relationship to God. At one point, Ibn Tūmart indicates that the mahdī has already arrived to reestablish God's will on earth, foreshadowing his later claims to be the mahdī.[73]

In some ways, Ibn Tūmart's presentation of the mahdī as the imam followed the older Sunnī model of the caliph. The authority of the mahdī, like that of the caliph, was based on enjoining the good and forbidding the evil, interpreting the divine law, and fighting injustice and unbelievers through jihad. But in other, important ways, Ibn Tūmart's conception of the mahdī went beyond any other political or religious model, except perhaps that of a prophet, because he portrayed the mahdī as absolutely crucial to the salvation of the world. Ibn Tūmart wrote that the mahdī is the figure closest to God and that he supports the sky and the earth, echoing the idea of a holy man as a *quṭb*, or pillar, that upholds the continuity of the cosmos.[74] In Ibn Tūmart's view, belief in the mahdī defines religion:

> Falsehood is removed only by the *mahdī*; truth does not arise except through the *mahdī*; the *mahdī* is known among the Arabs and

69 Fierro, "Legal Policies of the Almohad Caliphs," 228.

70 *Livre d'Ibn Toumert*, 245.

71 This concept echoes theories of righteous authority expounded by Sunnī scholars including al-Māwardī, who called the imamate *khalīfat al-nubuwwa*, or the successor ("caliph") to prophecy in maintaining the faith and administering the world. Al-Māwardī based this idea on his reading of Quran 4:62. Al-Māwardī, *al-Aḥkām*, 3. It is also, of course, closely connected to Shiʿī ideas of the imamate.

72 Huici Miranda, *Historia política*, 1:98–99.

73 *Livre d'Ibn Toumert*, 251.

74 *Livre d'Ibn Toumert*, 252. As Tilman Nagel has shown, this idea parallels the figure of the *quṭb* articulated by Ibn Tūmart's Persian Sufi contemporary ʿAbd al-Qādir al-Jīlānī. Nagel, "La destrucción de la ciencia de la *šarīʿa*," 303.

> the non-Arabs [*al-ʿarab wa-l-ʿajam*], among the nomadic peoples [*al-badū*] and the settled peoples; knowledge [*ʿilm*] is established through him in every place and in every administration [*dīwān*]. . . . Belief in the *mahdī* is obligatory, so anyone who doubts him is an unbeliever.[75]

The mahdī described by Ibn Tūmart provided the certainty in matters of religion that was lacking in a world in which the caliph had lost his central role. The mahdī counteracted the precedent-based Mālikism of the Almoravids and replaced the differences among the Sunnī schools of law with one truth, mediated by a figure whose connection to the Divine was intimate and unknowable.[76]

Ibn Tūmart's description of the mahdī as imam parallels Shiʿī understandings of the imamate. Throughout Almohad texts, Ibn Tūmart is presented as the "the foretold *mahdī* and the infallible imam" (*al-mahdī al-maʿlūm al-imām al-maʿsūm*). The infallibility of the imam was a deeply Shiʿī concept, and by claiming to be infallible, Ibn Tūmart made himself the source of religious certainty, circumventing and replacing the scholars of the Sunnī legal schools, or *madhhab*s. He also claimed descent not only from the Quraysh—a requirement for a caliph—but also from the ʿAlid branch of the Prophet Muḥammad's family, through the line of his grandson Ḥasan.[77] And in presenting himself as the foretold mahdī, Ibn Tūmart counteracted the ideology of the Ismāʿīlī Fatimids and other Shiʿīs who believed their own imams to be the mahdī. The concept of the infallible mahdī as the founder of a new political movement mirrored the founding ideology of the Fatimid dynasty, and like his tenth-century Fatimid predecessor, Ibn Tūmart would inaugurate a caliphate to succeed him.

Reimagining the Caliphate as Succession to the Mahdī

Whereas most writings about the figure of the mahdī presented him as ruling for a set number of years at the end of days, Ibn Tūmart used the

75 *Livre d'Ibn Toumert*, 257.

76 The Almohads maintained a general appreciation for the Mālikī madhhab, arguing that customary practice in Medina, the city of Mālik ibn Anas, the founder of the legal school, was closest to the practice of the Prophet and his companions. For this reason, Nagel and Fierro have called Almohad doctrine "reformed Mālikism." See Fierro, "Le mahdī Ibn Tūmart et al-Andalus," 115n23; Tilman Nagel, "Le mahdisme de Ibn Tūmart et Ibn Qasī: Une analyse phénoménologique," *Revue des mondes musulmans et de la Méditerranée* 91–94 (2000): 125–36.

77 For the standard Almohad depiction of Ibn Tūmart's genealogy, see al-Baydhaq's chronicle, in Lévi-Provençal, *Documents inédits*, 31.

role of the mahdī not to herald the end times but instead to launch a movement that would create a new caliphate. The chronicle written by al-Baydhaq, an early companion of Ibn Tūmart, describes him declaring that ʿAbd al-Muʾmin would be the one to rid the world of sin and calling him the "lamp of the Almohads," even before the former been proclaimed the mahdī. When the younger man protested that he was only interested in the absolution of his own sins, Ibn Tūmart reportedly responded: "The expurgation of your sins will be the rectification of the earth by your hands. . . . The people whom you govern will be happy, and unhappy those who oppose you."[78]

The recognition of ʿAbd al-Muʾmin as the khalīfa, or successor, to Ibn Tūmart transformed the Almohad movement by creating a long-lasting political structure that nonetheless maintained a new form of religious certainty at its core. In the process, ʿAbd al-Muʾmin gained an importance that equaled or even surpassed that of Ibn Tūmart. Michael Brett has shown that Almohad chronicles and panegyric poetry presented ʿAbd al-Muʾmin as the man who was destined to bring the world justice, echoing the biblical parallel of Joshua, who was appointed by Moses to lead people to the Promised Land.[79] Just as Ibn Tūmart's narrative was cast as a new birth of Islam, the Almohad caliphate was presented as the rebirth of the institution, correcting and perfecting earlier models. The caliphate begun by ʿAbd al-Muʾmin consisted not of successors to the Prophet Muḥammad, but rather of successors to the mahdī Ibn Tūmart. The problem posed by the fact that the world had not ended under Ibn Tūmart's watch in spite of the traditional understanding of the mahdī as the person who would usher in the end times was elided in Almohad sources as his messianic role became a stand-in for a new, prophetlike position.

As Sarah Bowen Savant and Helena de Felipe have noted, genealogical claims are frequently used to establish visions of continuity in times of great change and to legitimate religious and political claims through

---

78 Al-Baydhaq, in Lévi-Provençal, *Documents inédits*, 56; translation, 86–87. Very little is known about al-Baydhaq's life outside of what he wrote himself, which survives only partially in a single manuscript at the Escorial Library, discovered and published by Lévi-Provençal in the work cited here.

79 Michael Brett, "Le Mahdi dans le Maghreb médiéval," citing a poem that describes ʿAbd al-Muʾmin as Joshua to Ibn Tūmart's Moses, written by al-Rusafī (d. 572/1177) and preserved in al-Marrākushī's *al-Muʿjib*.

reference to real or imagined ties of kinship.[80] The eleventh through thirteenth centuries in the Islamic West constituted a period of transition in which genealogical arguments served to authorize claims to power. For the Ṣanhāja Berbers who led the Almoravid movement, not claiming the caliphate for themselves avoided the need to invent a Qurayshī lineage.[81] Nevertheless, genealogical treatises and historians asserted that Yūsuf ibn Tashufīn, and indeed all of the Ṣanhāja, were descended from the Yemeni tribe of Ḥimyar, which made them ethnically Arab and thus kin, broadly speaking, to the Prophet.[82] Although this claim was contested by contemporary scholars, Almoravid historians crafted elaborate explanations for why the Almoravid emirs did not speak Arabic in spite of their Arab descent, arguing that they had been acculturated to a Berber identity over centuries of living in North Africa.[83]

The Almohads, who laid claim not only to the caliphate but also to the position of mahdī, had a thornier set of genealogical problems to address. The mahdī, as presented in *al-Ḥulal al-mawshiyya*, corresponded to the messianic figure who would rule at the end of days that had been familiar in the Islamic world for centuries. But it is unclear whether Ibn Tūmart claimed this status for himself and, if he did so, whether it happened in 515/1121 or much later.[84] Even if the fully fledged vision of Ibn Tūmart as the mahdī only emerged after his death, however, it is clear that Arabic names and genealogies were fundamental to the Almohads' claims to power, at the same time that they celebrated Berber lineages and language.[85]

Almohad chroniclers presented the mahdī Ibn Tūmart, a Maṣmūda Berber from Sūs, as a direct descendant of the Prophet via his daughter Fāṭima and his grandson Ḥasan, whose descendant Idrīs had settled in

---

80 Sarah Bowen Savant and Helena de Felipe, "Introduction," in *Genealogy and Knowledge in Muslim Societies: Understanding the Past*, ed. Sarah Bowen Savant and Helena de Felipe (Edinburgh: Edinburgh University Press, 2014).

81 Helena de Felipe, "Berber Leadership and Genealogical Legitimacy: The Almoravid Case," in *Genealogy and Knowledge in Muslim Societies*, ed. Savant and de Felipe, 57.

82 De Felipe, "Berber Leadership and Genealogical Legitimacy."

83 On Ibn Ḥazm's skepticism about these claims, see de Felipe, "Berber Leadership and Genealogical Legitimacy," 61–62, and on the Almoravids' Berber acculturation, see 63.

84 As noted earlier, Fierro has suggested that the claim arose only later in Almohad history. See Fierro, "Le mahdi Ibn Tûmart at al-Andalus," esp. 115–16. As noted above, the date of *al-Ḥulal al-mawshiyya*'s composition and its context are unknown and contested.

85 For the standard Almohad depiction of Ibn Tūmart's genealogy, see al-Baydhaq, in Lévi-Provençal, *Documents inédits*.

Morocco.[86] Similarly, after ʿAbd al-Muʾmin, who was a Zanāta Berber, was proclaimed the first Almohad caliph in 527/1133, his genealogy on both the paternal and the maternal side was connected to various Arab tribes as well as to the mahdī Ibn Tūmart. Traditionally, claimants to the caliphate were expected to be of Qurayshī descent. According to the Almohad *Kitāb al-ansāb* ("Book of genealogies"), ʿAbd al-Muʾmin's mother descended from the Quraysh and was connected to the same Idrīsid line as the mahdī.[87] This matrilineal descent was an unusual assertion of Qurayshī legitimacy for a caliph, since all previous claimants had connected themselves to the Quraysh through their fathers. ʿAbd al-Muʾmin's father, on the other hand, was given a genealogy going back to the northern Arabian tribe of Qays ʿAylān.[88] Earlier and later historians had posited a Qaysī genealogy for North African groups, including the Zanāta, in several cases arguing for the tribe's maternal descent from the Qaysīs.[89] The tribe of Qays ʿAylān had also produced the pre-Islamic prophet Khālid ibn Sinān al-ʿAbsī, whose grandson had settled in Egypt during the Islamic conquests, where his Kāhina Berber clients then "adopted" Khālid ibn Sinān as something of a Berber prophet.[90] By claiming descent from him, the Almohads counteracted claims that they could not be caliphs without belonging to the Quraysh: they were still descendants of an Arab prophet. Subsequently, ʿAbd al-Muʾmin's descendants came to be known as *sayyids*, a term that usually indicated descent from the Prophet but here meant descent from the first Almohad caliph, and only they were deemed eligible to rule.

As Fierro has shown, ʿAbd al-Muʾmin's genealogies in the *Kitāb al-ansāb* "integrated him into a network of excellences and merits that included justice, truth, God's army, prophecy, caliphate, conquest, practice of the licit, religious knowledge, generosity, respect for pious people and those dedicated to religious knowledge, and dominion over not just

86 Maribel Fierro, "Las genealogías de ʿAbd al-Muʾmin, primer califa almohade," *Al-Qanṭara* 24 (2003): 85, citing Ibn al-Qaṭṭān, *Nuẓum al-Jumān*, 111–13.

87 The *Kitāb al-Ansāb*, an anonymous tract likely written in the first half of the thirteenth century, was published by Lévi-Provençal in his *Documents inédits*; the relevant pages here are 22–24 of the edition and 33–35 of the translation. See also Fierro, "Las genealogías de ʿAbd al-Muʾmin," 84–85.

88 Fierro, "Las genealogías de ʿAbd al-Muʾmin," 86–87; Helena de Felipe, "Leyendas árabes sobre el origen de los beréberes," *Al-Qanṭara* 11 (1990): 379–96.

89 Fierro, "Las genealogías de ʿAbd al-Muʾmin."

90 On this fascinating pre-Islamic Arab prophet and his continuing significance in North Africa, see Ella Landau-Tasseron, "Unearthing a pre-Islamic Arabian Prophet," *Jerusalem Studies in Arabic and Islam* 21 (1997): 42–61. On his significance to the Almohads, see Fierro, "Las genealogías de ʿAbd al-Muʾmin."

Arabs but also non-Arabs."[91] They also connected him to important earlier power groups in the Maghrib, including the Fatimids and the Idrisids. The twelfth century was evidently a time of great demographic and political change, in which upstarts seeking to legitimate their power benefited from genealogically minded scholars who could present them as inheritors of the noblest blood.

The first Almohad coins, minted under ʿAbd al-Muʾmin, were undated, implying that the age counted in years since the Prophet Muḥammad's *hijra* had come to an end and a new age had begun.[92] The early Almohad caliphs created an elaborate state bureaucracy peopled by *ṭalaba*, or students, and *ḥuffāẓ*, or memorizers.[93] These terms traditionally referred to people who had studied or memorized the Quran and the Sunna of the Prophet, but what Almohad "students" studied and memorized was the writings and actions of the mahdī Ibn Tūmart.[94] These disciples, steeped in the lessons of the founder of their dynasty, then became advisors to the Muʾminid princes who became governors of the territories the Almohads conquered. The reformulation of religious and political structures extended even to sacred geography, since there are some indications that the Almohads viewed the territory under their rule as the new Islamic heartland. Fierro has suggested that the Almohads'

91 Fierro, "Las genealogías de ʿAbd al-Muʾmin," 102–3: "La genealogía qaysí/muḍarí de ʿAbd al-Muʾmin le integran en una red de excelencias y méritos que incluyen: justicia, verdad, milicia de Dios, profecía, califato, conquista, práctica de lo lícito, conocimiento religioso, generosidad, respeto por las gentes piadosas y dedicadas al saber religioso, dominio tanto sobre los árabes como sobre los no árabes."

92 Maribel Fierro, "Revolución y tradición: Algunos aspectos del mundo del saber en al-Andalus durante las épocas Almorávide y Almohade," *Biografías almohades II*, ed. M. L. Ávila and M. Fierro (Madrid: Consejo Superior de Investigaciones Científicas, 2000), 133.

93 On the Ṭalaba (a plural of the Arabic word *ṭālib*, student), see Fricaud, "Les *Ṭalaba* dans la société Almohade." The Ḥuffāẓ were expected to memorize the compositions of the Mahdī as well as the *Muwaṭṭaʾ* of Mālik. On the elaborate education of these doctrinarians of the Almohad movement, see J. F. P. Hopkins, *Medieval Muslim Government in Barbary until the Sixth Century of the Hijra* (London: Luzac, 1958), 106–8.

94 According to the anonymous chronicler of *al-Ḥulal al-mawshiyya*, the Almohads also required *ṭalaba* to study the *Muwaṭṭaʾ* of Imam Mālik ibn Anas. See Anonymous, *al-Hulal al-mawšiyya: Crónica árabe de las dinastias almorávide, almohade y benimerín*, trans. Ambrosio Huici Miranda (Tetouan: Editora Marroquí, 1951), 179–80. Fierro has suggested that the Almohad emphasis on Mālikism emerged at a later stage of the empire, after the Almohads had conquered al-Andalus and assimilated its largely Māliki elite. Maribel Fierro, "La religión," in *El retroceso territorial de al-Andalus: Almorávides y Almohades siglos XI al XIII*, ed. María Jesús Viguera Molins (Madrid: Espasa Calpe, S.A., 1997), 446–48. See further discussion of the ways in which the incorporation of Ibn Mardanīsh's territories into Almohad territory seems to have changed elements of the Almohads' intellectual and cultural ideologies in chapter 6.

treatment of Jews and Christians—forcing these previously protected "people of the book" to convert, be killed, or emigrate—may have been based on a desire to see their territory as equivalent to the Ḥijāz, the only Islamic territory in which non-Muslims were forbidden to live.[95]

Ibn Tūmart's revolution, based on the model of the rise of the early Islamic state, introduced a novel understanding of the relationship of religious knowledge to political power. It emphasized a new kind of religious learning, focused on the thought of a new kind of leader, one whose position lay somewhere between the temporal and the divine and whose teachings held a status unmatched by any since those of the Prophet Muḥammad. More than a political leader but less than a prophet, the mahdī was mentioned after God and the Prophet Muḥammad on every Almohad coin, all minted after his death, and Almohad diplomatic correspondence opened with formulations praising God, His Prophet, and His mahdī. This central role for the founder of the dynasty reflected a messianic conception of political authority that recast the principles of leadership on spiritual grounds. Ibn Tūmart was portrayed as an infallible leader and the acknowledged mahdī (*al-imām al-maʿṣūm, al-mahdī al-maʿlūm*), phrases usually reserved in the Sunnī context for prophets and in the Shiʿī context for imams. A letter from the Almohad chancery written after his death includes the standard prayers for the mahdī: "We ask [God] to be pleased with the infallible imam, the known mahdī, he who undertakes the cause of God the Most High [*al-qāʾim bi-amr Allāh al-taʿālā*], and the caller to His path [*al-dāʿī ilā sabīlihi*]."[96] With the mahdī leading in the name of God, Ibn Tūmart's movement transformed his actions into the embodiment of God's will, his calls for political submission into calls to God's path, and by extension, his rivals into rivals against God.

But the arrival of Ibn Tūmart did not placate all of his potential subjects who yearned for the ideal of a ruler who would unite the world's Muslims and guide them to righteousness. Some scholars, judges and soldiers rejected Ibn Tūmart's radical new vision of authority and instead asserted themselves as rulers. The mahdī and his Muʾminid successors

---

95 Maribel Fierro, "A Muslim Land without Jews or Christians"; Fierro, "Conversion, Ancestry and Universal Religion"; Fierro, "Spiritual Alienation," 231.

96 This praise for Ibn Tūmart follows forms common to many Almohad writings and inscriptions. Aḥmad ʿAzzāwī, ed., *Rasāʾil Muwaḥḥidiyya: Majmūʿa jadīda* (al-Qunayṭira: Jāmiʿat Ibn Ṭufayl, Kulliyyat al-Ādāb wa-l-ʿUlūm al-Insāniyya, 1995), 2:121.

had to fight Almoravid loyalists and a new crop of Taifa rulers who opposed the Almohad reformulation of political and religious authority. Their most powerful and longest-lasting opponent was Muḥammad ibn Saʿd ibn Mardanīsh, who, like the Almoravids before him, aligned himself with the Abbasid caliph and presented himself as the defender of the unity of believers.

CHAPTER 2

Rebel against the Truth

Almohad Visions of Ibn Mardanīsh

In 548/1153, after the expanding Almohad Empire had conquered most of the Maghrib and al-Andalus, its first caliph, ʿAbd al-Muʾmin, asked his secretary to write a letter to the most powerful of his remaining rivals, an Andalusī named Muḥammad ibn Saʿd ibn Mardanīsh. The letter began:

> From the Commander of the Faithful—may God help him with His victory and support him with His aid—to the Shaykh Abū ʿAbd Allāh Muḥammad ibn Saʿd—may God direct him to the right course and make easy for him that which will be pleasing to Him: peace be upon you and the mercy of God and His blessings.[1]

Following the norms of diplomatic letters, this one opens with respect, calling Ibn Mardanīsh a shaykh and invoking the blessings of God on him. But even in this opening line lurks a call and a warning: it is ʿAbd al-Muʾmin to whom God will grant victory, and Ibn Mardanīsh who must be guided to the right path. The letter—which consists of several pages of elaborate, erudite classical Arabic, much of it in the complex rhymed prose form known as *sajʿ*—combines praise for the

---

1 *Majmūʿat rasāʾil muwaḥḥidiyya min inshāʾ kuttāb al-dawla al-muʾminiyya*, ed. Évariste Lévi-Provençal (Rabat: Maṭbūʿāt Maʿhad al-ʿUlūm al-ʿUlyā al-Maghribiyya, 1931), 35.

messianic founder of the Almohad movement, the mahdī Ibn Tūmart, appeals to the shared Islamic faith of Ibn Mardanīsh and the Almohads, and a warning to heed the call (*da ʿwa*) of the Almohads and submit to their rule.[2] Throughout, the message is clear: anyone who claims to follow the path of God, as revealed to the Prophet Muḥammad, must now follow the infallible imam, the mahdī Ibn Tūmart, who undertakes the command of God. "God gave you the blessing of faith and the virtue of submission and obedience to Him, and in it you find conviction and joy," the caliph's secretary writes, going on to describe how God sent the mahdī as a mercy to His creation, tasking him with guiding people toward Him and transforming sites of calamity and danger into havens of salvation. The letter calls on Ibn Mardanīsh to follow the path of God (*sabīlihi*) more closely by following His mahdī:

> So respond—may God raise you up—to the herald [*dā ʿī*] of God and be happy, and hold fast to the command [*amr*] of the mahdī, may God be pleased with him; direct the reins of your care to take into consideration consequences [*ma ʾāl*] [of your actions] and to reflect on the causes of affliction and of decline, and prepare the way for these matters and the administration of these powers, and know that there is no power except by the powers of God the Most High, for He is the one who has power and might. So do not let deception deceive you about God, for this world [*dunyā*] is a house of deception and a market of artifice.[3]

This call to abandon the temptations of this world and accept the command of the mahdī reflected the goals of the Almohads' revolutionary movement. As seen in the preceding chapter, the Almohad caliphate, born out of Ibn Tūmart's messianic revolution, was based on a radical reformulation of traditional Islamic forms of religious and political authority. It rejected earlier caliphal traditions and (at least at this early stage) the authority of scholars in favor of the infallible teachings of the mahdī, who, the Almohads believed, had ushered in a new age of piety and justice.[4] In urging Ibn Mardanīsh to turn away from the "market of

2 The full letter can be found in *Majmū ʿat rasā ʾil muwaḥḥidiyya*, 35–37.

3 *Majmū ʿat rasā ʾil muwaḥḥidiyya*, 37.

4 From the beginning, it was clear that Ibn Tūmart's followers saw this new beginning as a return not only to the early Islamic period (as discussed further below) but also to biblical times. As Maribel Fierro has noted, this view is reflected in the names of their early chronicles, the names of the first caliphs, and the association of Ibn Tūmart with Jonah, mentioned in the preceding chapter. Fierro, "Conversion, Ancestry and Universal Religion," 166.

artifice" that is this world and toward the path of God as indicated by His mahdī, they were seeking to achieve not just Ibn Mardanīsh's political compliance but also his religious salvation. The Almohad vision of the universe was divided between opposing poles—artifice and reality, deception and truth, danger and salvation, world (dunyā) and religion (*dīn*). The foretold, infallible Mahdī, acting on God's behalf, had called on the world to believe and thereby made any resistance tantamount to disbelief. When Ibn Mardanīsh refused to submit, he became one of the Almohads' preeminent targets of jihad.

Chronicles about Ibn Mardanīsh, many written by Almohad authors or based on their reports, describe him and his kingdom as the antithesis of the Almohads' rule of justice. In their portrayal, whereas the Almohads were endeavoring to create a world centered on salvation, enjoining the good, forbidding the evil, and rejecting and expelling those who would not accept the unity of God (tawḥīd), Ibn Mardanīsh was caught miserably in the artifice of this world. The Almohad sources depict him as routinely engaging in sinful behavior: getting drunk, fixating on sensual pleasures, seeking money, and pursuing close relationships with Christians. Almohad sources and those based on them also emphasize Ibn Mardanīsh's purportedly cruel treatment of his own family members, describing how he ordered the execution of his sister and her children, and suggesting he had been driven mad toward the end of his life, as even his own siblings and children turned against him.[5] Fierro notes that this presentation of Ibn Mardanīsh in Almohad sources echoes their broader treatment of those who rejected their authority. She writes:

> When a revolutionary movement proposes a model of power led by a ruler or *imām* with quasi-divine pretensions—as was the case for the Fatimids and the Almohads—a kind of propaganda is developed that seeks the delegitimation and disqualification of

5 Alfonso Carmona's article constitutes the best overview of the "bad press" Ibn Mardanīsh received in sources written by the Almohads: Carmona, "Represión y abuso de poder en el régimen de Ibn Mardanīš," in *Estudios onomástico-biográficos de al Andalus*, vol. 14, ed. M. Fierro, *De muerte violenta: política, religión y violencia en Al-Andalus* (Madrid, CSIC: 2004). Pilar Garrido has also characterized the general historiographic treatment of Ibn Mardanīsh as "tirano, filocristiano y mal musulmán." Garrido, "Aproximación a las fuentes árabes sobre Abū ʿAbd Allāh Muḥammad b. Saʿd b. Muḥammad b. Aḥmad al-Yudāmī al-Tuyībī, ibn Mardanīš (518/1124-5–567/1172)," in *Rey Lobo: El legado de Ibn Mardanīš, 1147–1172*, ed. Jorge A. Eiroa and Mariángeles Gómez Ródenas (Murcia: Comunidad Autónoma de la Región de Murcia, 2019), 49.

> their enemies, attributing to them an unmitigated violence whose touchstone is the cruel treatment of members of their own family.[6]

As Fierro notes, the Almohad historiographic treatment of Ibn Mardanīsh parallels the way other dynasties sought to delegitimate their rivals and predecessors, including the Trastámara dynasty of Castile, which successfully branded their predecessor King Peter I "the Cruel" through similar propaganda. By presenting Ibn Mardanīsh as impossibly cruel, Almohad chroniclers underlined the contrast between him and the Almohad caliphs, who are described as fair and just. Like the Almoravids before him, Ibn Mardanīsh and his followers appear in these sources as people of Satan, and the fight against them constitutes a holy jihad.

For the Almohads, as for their predecessors and contemporaries, "struggling in the path of God" (*jihād fī sabīl Allāh*) was the primary tool for the articulation of righteous authority and its legitimation. It allowed a ruler to express his vision of the boundaries of good and evil and to demonstrate his piety and martial fitness by fighting for the faith. Jihad functioned as a means of subduing or eliminating rivals and, if successful, as potential evidence of divine favor. In the early years of their mission, the Almohads' primary target was not Christians, though they would later be famous for their battles against the Christian kingdoms of the Iberian Peninsula. From the lifetime of the movement's founder, Ibn Tūmart, until the death of Ibn Mardanīsh in 1172, the Almohads' greatest jihad was against fellow Muslims, waged over the duties of piety, the form of authority, and the shape of the community. On one side of this confrontation was the Almohads' radical reinterpretation of the caliphate, rooted in the teachings of the mahdī Ibn Tūmart, who asserted the corruption of traditional legal and political systems and instead advocated an abstract and rational universe that he, as the infallible guide brought to humankind by God, could illuminate. On the other side were first the Almoravids and then Ibn Mardanīsh, the Almohads' strongest and longest-lasting rival in al-Andalus. He supported the system the Almohads sought to supplant: a single, centralized Sunnī caliphate, with

---

6 Maribel Fierro, "Terror y cambio dinástico en el Occidente islámico medieval," in *Por política, terror social. Reunió Científica XIV Curs d'Estiu Comtat d'Urgell celebrat a Balaguer els dies 30 de Juny i 1i 2 Juliol de 2010 sota la direcció de Flocel Sabaté i Maite Pedrol* (Lleida: Pagés editors, 2013), 112. My translation from the Spanish: "Cuando un movimiento revolucionario propugna un modelo de poder a cuya cabeza se sitúa un líder o *imām* con pretensiones cuasidivinas—como fue el caso fatimí y el almohade—se pone en marcha una propaganda que busca la deslegitimación y la descalifacación de sus adversaries, achacándoles una violencia desmedida cuya piedra de toque es el trato cruel hacia miembros de su propia familia."

ʿulamāʾ and soldiers working to maintain the cohesion and salvation of the umma.

This chapter begins with an overview of the Almohads' jihad against their rivals—first the Almoravids and then others who resisted them. It then provides a brief narrative of Ibn Mardanīsh's life, as recorded in mostly Almohad sources, focusing on his conflict with the Almohads. I rely as much as possible on the earliest Arabic chronicles, from the twelfth century, since, as discussed in chapter 7, later chronicles reflect further processes of mythification. Where the sources disagree, I note the disagreement in the footnotes. Because the way Ibn Mardanīsh is presented underwent a fundamental shift in the fourteenth century, I try in this chapter to avoid the later Arabic chroniclers such as Ibn al-Khaṭīb, Ibn Khaldūn, and al-Maqqarī who are usually the starting point for any discussion of the twelfth century in al-Andalus and the Maghrib but whose writings reflect the later, changed perspective on Ibn Mardanīsh. That means that my primary written sources for understanding Ibn Mardanīsh's time in power were produced at the Almohad court for Almohad audiences. These sources include chancery documents and the chroniclers al-Baydhaq and Ibn Ṣāḥib al-Ṣalā. Unsurprisingly, they present their own challenges to understanding how Ibn Mardanīsh or his followers might have seen his regime. Chronicles written by scholars who worked for Almohad rulers and sought to record the early years of the Almohad caliphate in a hagiographic mode formed an integral part of the dynasty-building project of the Almohads. Chancery documents, too, articulated directly the Almohads' projection of their power and the ways in which they tried to lure Ibn Mardanīsh to their side. Almohad narratives about Ibn Mardanīsh reveal how the Almohads defined their own caliphate against him; they also show, albeit in an allusive and incomplete manner, how he delineated his dynasty against them. I therefore read these sources less for information about Ibn Mardanīsh's character or pastimes and more for their tone, which conveys unexpected respect and admiration for his strength and persistence and transmits fragments of debates between the two powers in phrases articulated across media and across years.

Jihad and Legitimacy from the Almoravids to the Almohads

Like the Almohads would do after them, the Almoravids gained legitimacy as protectors of Islam along the border with Christendom. They were Ṣanhaja Berbers from the foothills of the Anti-Atlas Mountains and the western Sahara who had taken over the lucrative salt and gold trade between Ghana and the Mediterranean and preached a strident Mālikism to the people of northwest Africa. They were also known for using jihad to expand their empire. Especially in the aftermath of their defeat of Alfonso VI of Castile-Leon at the Battle of Zallāqa in 499/1086, the Almoravids were able to present themselves to the people of al-Andalus as the best protectors against the territorial ambitions of their Christian neighbors. The famous fatwa of al-Ghazālī in support of the Almoravids argued explicitly that it was their ability to unify the Muslims of al-Andalus against the threat posed by the Christians that made them righteous.[7] Taifa kings who resisted the Almoravids were enjoined by a series of fatwas from Mālikī jurists to fall in line with the Almoravids, and most of the rulers of the city-states of al-Andalus were defeated, killed, or sent into exile.[8] But with the rise of the Almohads, the Almoravids faced the novel challenge of rivals who preached jihad against them.

By the mid-twelfth century, the Almoravids' power was waning as they lost territory in North Africa and Iberia. Ibn Tūmart and his supporters, many of whom were from his tribe, the Maṣmūda, which was based in the Atlas Mountains, accused the Almoravids of having become accustomed to luxury and of practicing a corrupted Islam, much as the Almoravids had charged the Taifa kings of al-Andalus the century before. The Almohads quickly won support from their fellow mountain tribes. They began to conquer territory and enforce their own authority and religious vision using violence, in an echo of the early Islamic conquests. The early letters of the mahdī Ibn Tūmart reveal his conception of the world as divided between *muwaḥḥidūn*—followers of the form of tawḥīd, or radical monotheism, that he promulgated—and infidels. According to this schema, those who opposed Almohad dogma and refused to submit to the Almohads' authority were infidels, and none more so than the Almoravids.

In a letter written by Ibn Tūmart and addressed to his fellow Almohads, he explained that it was illicit (ḥarām) for the Muslim community to follow a ruler who was rebelling against God, and then explained that the Almoravids contravened the teachings of Islam because they attributed a human form to God (he called them *mujassimūn*, or

7 Viguera Molíns, "Cartas de al-Gazālī."

8 Bennison, *Almoravid and Almohad Empires*, 47.

anthropomorphists).[9] Therefore, he concluded, it was necessary to kill them, and anyone who died fighting them was a martyr and was guaranteed a position in heaven. He compared the faithful Almohads fighting the Almoravids to the Prophet and his Companions, who fought for the religion of God against the infidels.[10] After claiming that God had made the position of their enemies weak and confused and that of the Almohads strong so that the latter may carry out His wish, Ibn Tūmart made another specific reference to the early Muslim conquests.[11] His letter closed with a proverb taken from the first hemistich of a poem by Khālid ibn al-Walīd, the great conqueror of the early Islamic period: "And in the morning, the people will praise the night voyage."[12] Through these explicit references to the formative early conquests, Ibn Tūmart associated himself with the Prophet Muḥammad and the Almoravids with the pagans of pre-Islamic Arabia whom the Prophet fought.[13]

Though depictions of the Almohads generally focus on their fierce battles against the Christians of Iberia, Ibn Tūmart was explicit that the primary target of jihad should be more proximate "infidels." In another letter to his followers, Ibn Tūmart wrote that jihad against the Almoravids and other Muslims who did not follow the Almohads superseded jihad against the Christians:

> Know, may God give you success, that jihad against them is a religious obligation [*farḍ*] upon the noble people [*aʿyān*], for those who are able to fight; so wage jihad against the infidels [*kafara*], the veiled ones [*mulaththimūn*], since the jihad against them is greater by many times than the jihad against the Christians [*Rūm*] and the rest of the infidels, because they have attributed a corporeal form to the Creator—glorified be He—and rejected tawḥīd, and are rebels against the truth.[14]

Like al-Ghazālī's letter to the Almoravids discussed in the previous chapter, Ibn Tūmart's letter framed political submission as acceptance

9 Delfina Serrano, "Porque llamaron los Almohades a los Almoravides antropomorfistas?" in *Los Almohades*, ed. Cressier, Fierro, and Molina.

10 Lévi-Provençal, *Documents inédits*, 2; translation, 3–4.

11 Lévi-Provençal, *Documents inédits*; 4, translation, 6.

12 Lévi-Provençal, *Documents inédits*; 8, translation, 12.

13 On the memory of the early battles of Islam in the Islamic West and their uses in legitimating authority, especially during the Almohad caliphate, see the writings of Javier Albarrán, including "The *Jihād* of the Caliphs and the First Battles of Islam," *al-ʿUṣūr al-Wusṭā* 26 (2018): 113–50.

14 Lévi-Provençal, *Documents inédits*, 9; translation, 15.

of divine truth and rebellion against his state as rebellion against God. Their resistance to Almohad claims to power, alongside the issue of attributing a "corporeal form to the Creator," justified the Almohads' determination that the Almoravids were "rebels against the truth."

The focus in Ibn Tūmart's letters on the question of God's corporeality echoed earlier debates on the topic, especially the *miḥna*, or "inquisition," in ninth-century Baghdad.[15] In this earlier debate, the question of whether God possessed the physical attributes mentioned in the Quran had occupied center stage. Did believing in God's corporeality (i.e., that He sat on a throne, or had a hand) involve *tashrīk*, the belief that God could have an associate—in other words, polytheism? This issue formed the core of the disagreement between the Muʿtazilites and the Ashʿarites.[16] Ibn Tūmart came down forcefully on the side of the Muʿtazilites in arguing that any attribution of a body to God constituted rejection of God's unity and made the person endorsing such a position into a polytheist.[17]

Ibn Tūmart's role as a messianic figure made these debates the basis of full-scale military engagement. In another letter, Ibn Tūmart addressed the Almoravids as people of corruption whom Satan had caused to sin and who had angered God.[18] Philosophical questions as to what constituted the unity of God (tawḥīd) were turned into a cosmic battle between good and evil that played out on the battlefield between two groups of Muslims. In their letters, Ibn Tūmart and his caliphal successors portrayed non-Almohads as heretics and as being under the sway of Satan. An Almohad letter describes how loyal subjects of the Almoravids act: "[They] follow lies and the footsteps of Satan, adhering to customs of ignorance [*jahl*] and dissimulation, eating that which is illicit [ḥarām], committing crimes, persevering in grave sins and debauchery, sacrificing their religion [dīn] for the sake of their material life [dunyā], consuming the goods of people with deception."[19] By presenting other

---

15 On the twelfth-century context of the Almohads' critique of the Almoravids as anthropomorphists and their broader attacks on Almoravid literalism, see Serrano, "Porque llamaron los Almohades a los Almoravides antropomorfistas?"

16 For a full discussion of the relationship of Ibn Tūmart's conception of tawḥīd to both Muʿtazilite doctrine and Neoplatonism, see Fletcher, "Almohad Tawḥīd."

17 In this as in other areas, the Almohads followed transcendentalist impulses in Islamic theology and philosophy. For an overview of the conflict between "anthropomorphist" and "transcendentalist" approaches to understanding God, see EI^2, s.v. "Tashbīh wa-Tanzīh" (J. van Ess).

18 Lévi-Provençal, *Documents inédits*, 12.

19 Lévi-Provençal, *Documents inédits*, 4; translation, 6–7.

Muslims as heretics, the Almohads strengthened their claim to orthodoxy, especially once they defeated these "unbelievers." Heretics, as deviant insiders, play an important role in the formation of orthodoxy, both in shifting the focus of debate and in reinforcing the authority of those who defeat them.[20]

In a letter addressed to the Almoravid ruler ʿAlī ibn Yūsuf, Ibn Tūmart, the letter's ostensible author, explained that God had commanded him to refute the arguments of the oppressors and to invite people to believe once more (*qad amaranī Allāh bi-idḥāḍ ḥujjat al-ẓālimīn, wa-duʿāʾ al-nās ilā al-yaqīn*). He argued that the Almoravids' perverse ideology had placed them beyond the pale of Islam and made their blood licit to spill.[21] According to the letter, God's choice to appoint Ibn Tūmart His instrument had brought forth a new religious movement that enforced the truth through jihad. Yet, even though Almohad sources present this jihad as parallel to the battles of early Islam, which had been directed against the pagans along the edges of the Islamic empire, or people of the book who refused to submit to Islamic authority, it had a new set of targets. By marking the Almoravids as infidels and targets of jihad, the Almohads turned fellow Muslims whose understanding of the corporeality of God differed from their own into infidels.[22] Although many religious scholars criticized the lax religiosity of their peers, most refused to participate in *takfīr*, or calling Muslims unbelievers, following two verses in the Quran that suggest that it is the role of God alone to determine who is faithful and that believers should concern themselves with their

---

20 Lester Kurtz, "The Politics of Heresy," *American Journal of Sociology* 88, no. 6 (1983): 1085–1115.

21 Lévi-Provençal, *Documents inédits*, 11; translation, 17–18.

22 Earlier movements, such as that of the Kharijites, who held that anyone who sinned was no longer a Muslim and could therefore be killed as an apostate, had also attacked fellow Muslims, and many debates between Sunnīs and Shiʿīs likewise featured accusations of unbelief. The Almohads' articulation of jihad against Muslims who would not submit to their authority echoed early Islamic attitudes toward pagans who would not submit politically and religiously to the nascent Islamic empire as well as Umayyad uses of jihad. Much like the Almohads half a millennium later, the Umayyads saw themselves as the divinely guided rulers of the global Muslim community and branded all opponents of their rule infidels to be subdued by the armies of the dynasty. Chancery letters written by Umayyad secretary ʿAbd al-Ḥamīd, in particular, equate rebels against Umayyad authority with Satan and treat them as enemies not only of the dynasty but of all Muslims and of God. See, for example, *ʿAbd al-Ḥamīd al-kātib wa mā tabaqqā min rasāʾilihi*, ed. Iḥsān ʿAbbās (Amman: Dār al-Shurūq, 1988), 234–64, and discussion in Paul Heck, "'Jihad' Revisited," *Journal of Religious Ethics* 32 (2004): 95–128, especially 107–8; Wadād al-Qāḍī, "The Religious Foundation of Late Umayyad Ideology," in *Saber religioso y poder político*, ed. Marín and García-Arenal, especially 253, 266, 273.

own souls.[23] As an infallible and divinely guided ruler, Ibn Tūmart could claim direct access to divine knowledge in his determination of who constituted a Muslim.

Ibn Tūmart's campaign to vanquish the Almoravids was not successful during his lifetime, since he died in 524/1130, just nine years after declaring himself the mahdī. But the Almoravid dynasty was defeated relatively rapidly under his successors, and by the 530s/1140s, the traditional Almoravid Mālikī political system had been replaced in most of the former Almoravid Empire with new Almohad structures. A particularly brutal phase followed the conquest of the former Almoravid capital of Marrakech in 541/1147, when a rebel called Ibn Hūd al-Massī emerged outside the city. He claimed to be a new mahdī and to enjoy divine guidance, and he succeeded in winning followers among the Almohad elite. Suppressing the rebellion took the Almohads two years and prompted another massive purge of the Almohad elite, leading, according to the Almohad chronicler al-Baydhaq, to the execution of 32,780 people.

The threat of violence and the promise of religious certainty succeeded in converting huge swaths of the Maghrib al-Aqsā and al-Andalus to Almohadism. An 1148 letter written by Shelomoh ha-Kohen ha-Sijilmāsī to his father in South Arabia and found in the Cairo Geniza reports the news from the Maghrib that Jews and non-Almohad Muslims were being forced to convert to Almohadism. He writes that in Tlemcen ʿAbd al-Muʾmin had killed "all the people there except those who had converted."[24] Even in this earliest period of Almohad power, however, it was clear that anyone who accepted the tawḥīd of the Almohads would be spared, much like an infidel in early Islamic Arabia who converted to Islam would have been. In this way, too, Ibn Tūmart's daʿwa, issued in an age of ignorance (*jāhiliyya*) like in pre-Islamic Arabia, echoed the previous call of the Prophet Muḥammad.

The Material Culture of a New Regime

Sometime in the first half of the thirteenth century, King Ferdinand III of Castile presented an intricately woven banner to the Monastery of

23 Quran 5:105 reads, "O believers, look after your own souls. He who is astray cannot hurt you, if you are rightly guided"; and 4:94 reads, "O believers, when you are journeying in the path of God, be discriminating, and do not say to him who offers you a greeting, 'Thou art not a believer,' seeking the chance goods of the present life."

24 Amira K. Bennison and María Ángeles Gallego, "Religious Minorities under the Almohads: An Introduction," *Journal of Medieval Iberian Studies* 2, no. 2 (2010): 148–49.

FIGURE 2.1. Banner of Las Navas de Tolosa, Monasterio de las Huelgas, Burgos. *Photo:* Patrimonio Nacional, Monasterio de Santa María La Real de Las Huelgas, 00652193.

Las Huelgas in Burgos. The banner, inscribed with verses from the Quran, may have been captured from the Almohads by his grandfather Alfonso VIII during the iconic Battle of Las Navas de Tolosa in 1212, or perhaps in one of Ferdinand's later engagements with the Almohads, in Jaén, Cordoba, or Seville. It served as a symbol of the Castilian king's victory over the Almohads and became the principal prize of the monastery's treasury. Thus preserved in remarkably good condition, this banner provides insight into the centrality of ideas of jihad and ḥisba to Almohad conceptions of political and religious authority.[25]

25 The provenance of this banner has been much disputed by scholars. For a summary of these debates and an argument that the banner is actually from the Marinid period rather

The banner's inscriptions reveal the Almohad preoccupation with sinfulness and forgiveness. The central medallion is filled with three nested eight-pointed stars, made up of complex gold strapwork. Upon closer examination, the outermost star resolves into Kufic letters, forming two words rotated and repeated again and again: *al-mulk li-llāh*, or sovereignty belongs to God.[26] The long letters and loops that form these words are stretched, wrapped, and connected into a web, making the eight points of the outermost star as well as the lines that cross its interior, delineating two intersecting squares that form another star. The banner is woven of silk and gold-wrapped animal substrate and is predominantly cream, gold, blue, red and green. Around the central medallion's gold straps and Kufic inscriptions, four panels of cursive (*naskhī*) Quranic inscriptions form a square. The verses cited are ayas 10–12 of Sūrat al-Ṣaff (61), "The Ranks," which treats those who refused to follow the ancient prophets and calls on hypocrites and unbelievers to submit to God. The verses on the banner read:

> O believers, shall I direct you to a commerce that shall deliver you from a painful chastisement?
>
> You shall believe in God and His Messenger, and struggle in the way of God [*tujāhidūn fī sabīl Allāh*] with your possessions and your selves. That is better for you, did you but know.
>
> He will forgive you your sins and admit you into gardens underneath which rivers flow, and to dwelling-places goodly in Gardens of Eden; that is the mighty triumph.

Displayed at the forefront of an Almohad army, the inscription on this banner could be seen as a promise to the faithful marching into war: fight in the way of God, and you will enter paradise. One of the unusual design elements of the banner, its reversed script on the two

---

than Almohad, see Miriam Ali-de-Unzaga, "Qur'anic Inscriptions on the 'Pennon of Las Navas de Tolosa' and Three Marinid Banners," in *Word of God, Art of Man: The Qur'an and Its Creative Expressions*, ed. Fahmida Suleman (Oxford: Oxford University Press, 2007). Regardless of whether or not this banner was produced by the Almohads, the Quranic citation which adorns it reflects the Almohad fixation on sinfulness and forgiveness, echoed in their cultural production elsewhere. For an overview of textiles with Arabic inscriptions preserved in Christian contexts in Spain, see María Judith Feliciano, "El corpus epigráfico de los tejidos medievales en Iberia: Nuevas aportaciones," in *Arte y producción textil en el Mediterráneo medieval*, ed. Laura Rodríguez Peinado and Francisco de Asís García (Madrid: Polifemo, 2019), 289–317.

26 Thanks to Prof. Nasser Rabbat for helping me find the second word of this phrase, *li-llāh*, which initially eluded me. The expression *al-mulk li-llāh* is common in Almohad contexts, including on the copper-alloy door of what was their congregational mosque in Seville and is now the Puerta del Perdón of the Cathedral of Seville.

rectangular panels on the sides of the banner, would make these parts of the inscription illegible to those in front of the banner. Although it is impossible to see the back of the banner today, since it was mounted on canvas for conservation, these panels were likely legible to those behind the banner, reminding them of their duty to fight in the path of God and to win paradise in return. Indeed, it is precisely the exhortation to struggle in the way of God and the promise of forgiveness of sins that are reversed on the banner, and would have been legible for those behind it.[27]

Whether the banner was legible simultaneously to those in front of the army and those who followed it into battle, Almohad propaganda of all sorts spoke explicitly to two audiences: their faithful subjects, and those who had yet to submit. Like the letters discussed above, Almohad material culture presented their dynasty as a restoration and a new beginning, which promised salvation to those who submitted and hellfire to those who resisted. Although this banner is venerated today as a trophy of the Christian defeat of the Almohads at the Battle of Las Navas, its inscriptions reflected their earlier project of bringing fellow Muslims into the Almohad fold via jihad—a project whose successful completion, with the defeat of Ibn Mardanīsh, would allow the Almohads to turn toward jihad against Christian armies in earnest. The use of the same inscription on the Qaṣba of the ʿŪdāya, constructed in Rabat around 591/1195, around the time of their great defeat of Christian armies at the Battle of Alarcos, emphasized the Almohads' jihading credentials, reminding the faithful of their duty to struggle in God's path even as it metaphorically equated entering the Almohad city with entering paradise.[28]

---

27 The two panels of mirrored text are, on the right side, the first part of 61:11, "You shall believe in God and His Messenger, and struggle in the way of God with your possessions and your selves," and on the left side, the second part of 61:11 and the first part of 61:12, "That is better for you, did you but know. (beg. 61:12) He will forgive you your sins." The passage begins on the upper panel and finishes on the lower panel. The uppermost inscription on the banner, in the band that runs across the top above the square of inscriptions discussed here, is the *taʿawwudh*, "I take refuge in God from Satan the outcast," discussed further below, though it is here incomplete, as well as the basmala and the beginning of prayers for the Prophet Muḥammad. The missing text at the beginning and the end suggest that at least this panel was cut down from a longer textile, which raises interesting questions about reuse and the life of this object.

28 María Antonia Martínez Núñez has noted that the content of the inscriptions on the banner of Las Navas corresponds exactly to the epigraphy on the door of the Qaṣba of the ʿŪdāya (*taʿawwudh*, *basmala*, and Quran 61:10–12). See Maria Antonia Martínez Núñez, "Ideología y Epigrafía Almohades," in *Los Almohades: Problemas y Perspectivas*, ed. Patrice Cressier,

Almohad inscriptions consistently emphasize their doctrine of righteous warfare against all who would not accept their religious movement and political authority. Much of their early architecture used mud brick, often plastered and unpainted, covered with geometric patterns and a vast number of inscriptions, usually consisting of Quranic words or phrases. Monumental inscriptions had been relatively rare in the decorative programs of their predecessors, but the Almohads revitalized this form, introducing new calligraphic styles to write largely religious inscriptions across a wide range of objects and spaces.[29] Many of these inscriptions focused on the interconnected concepts of ḥisba (enjoining the good and forbidding the evil) and jihad.

The inscriptions often begin with the *taʿawwudh*—the expression *aʿūdhu bi-llāh min al-shayṭān al-rajīm*, "I take refuge in God from the outcast Satan," spoken by Muslims before reciting the Quran or in other ritually significant moments. This phrase was unusual in monumental contexts: previously it had appeared only in a few Eastern inscriptions on madrasas from the eleventh century and on some funerary inscriptions from the Almoravid period.[30] Now it routinely preceded the largely Quranic inscriptions on mosques, gates, textiles, and more, emphasizing the Almohad focus on the Quran itself and urging viewers to recite the verses they used, preceded by the correct phrase. The most common Quranic inscriptions across Almohad objects and architecture are those relating to jihad. Quran 22:77, "O men, bow you down and prostrate yourselves, and serve your Lord, and do good; haply so you shall prosper," frequently used in mihrabs, is followed in the Almohad mosques of Marrakech by 22:78, which exhorts the believers to "struggle for God as is His due" (*jāhidū fī Allāh haqqa jihādihi*):

> Struggle for God as is His due, for He has chosen you, and has laid on you no impediment in your religion, being the creed of your father Abraham; He named you Muslims aforetime and in this, that the Messenger might be a witness against you, and that you might be witnesses against mankind. So perform the prayer, and

---

Maribel Fierro, and Luis Molina, vol. 1, 2 vols. (Madrid: Consejo Superior de Investigaciones Científicas, 2005), 9nn23, 25.

29 Martínez Núñez, "Ideología y epigrafía," 7.

30 Martínez Núñez, "Ideología y epigrafía," 22; on the Eastern inscriptions she mentions from the madrasa of Niẓām al-Mulk at Khardgird and the madrasas of Sultan Ḥasan and Qayt Bey in Cairo, see Sheila Blair, *The Monumental Inscriptions from Early Islamic Iran and Transoxiana* (Leiden: Brill, 2014), 149.

> pay the alms, and hold you fast to God; He is your Protector—an excellent Protector, an excellent Helper.[31]

This passage, like most of the forty-one uses of the root *j-h-d* in the Quran, is not explicitly related to warfare.[32] But through their consistent use of Quranic passages with variations on the theme of struggling for or in the path of God, Almohad writings and inscriptions seem to link this theme to holy war.

On Bāb al-Ruwāḥ—one of the Almohads' portals into the city of Rabat, built in the 580s/1190s—monumental Quranic inscriptions emphasize the duty to command the good and forbid the evil:

> You are the best of peoples, evolved for mankind, enjoining what is right, forbidding what is wrong, and believing in God. If only the People of the Book had faith, it were best for them: among them are some who have faith, but most of them are perverted transgressors. They will do you no harm, barring a trifling annoyance; if they come out to fight you, they will show you their backs, and no help shall they get.[33]

By the time the gate was constructed under the third Almohad caliph Abū Yūsuf Yaʿqūb (r. 580–95/1184–99), the Almohads had turned from their jihad against fellow Muslims to jihad against the Christians of Iberia, and this public inscription about the people of the book may reflect a new emphasis on jihad against Christians. But like earlier letters and inscriptions, this one emphasizes the central elements of the Almohad claim to authority: ḥisba, which, by asserting the evil committed by coreligionists, could turn them into legitimate targets of violence, and jihad, theoretically aimed at non-Muslims but also directed at all

31 Translations of the Quran here and throughout come from A. J. Arberry, trans., *The Koran Interpreted* (New York: Macmillan, 1955). On the uses of these verses in Almohad architecture, see Martínez Núnez, "Ideología y epigrafía," 25, although the numbers of the verses she cites are 22:76 and 22:77.

32 On the concept of jihad in the Quran, see Michael Bonner, *Jihad in Islamic History: Doctrines and Practice* (Princeton, NJ: Princeton University Press, 2008), esp. 21–26. See also Reuven Firestone, *Jihad: The Origin of Holy War in Islam* (Oxford: Oxford University Press, 1999), and Fred Donner, "The Sources of Islamic Conceptions of War," in *Just War and Jihad: Historical and Theoretical Perspectives on War and Peace in Western and Islamic Traditions*, ed. James Turner Johnson (New York: Greenwood Press, 1991), 46–48.

33 The inscription here is Quran 3:110–11. On this and other Almohad urban fortifications, see Patrice Cressier, "Les portes monumentales urbaines Almohades," in *Los Almohades*, ed. Cressier, Fierro, and Molina. On the inscriptions, see Martínez Núñez, "Ideología y epigrafía," 26–29 (though she writes that the verses are 3:106–7).

FIGURE 2.2. Outer façade of the Bāb al-Ruwāḥ gate in Rabat, 580s/1190s. *Photo:* Wikimedia Commons; photo uploaded by Dortiti, licensed under the Creative Commons Attribution-Share Alike 4.0 International (CC BY-SA 4.0) license (https://creativecommons.org/licenses/by-sa/4.0/).

those deemed to be unbelievers because of their unwillingness to follow Almohad doctrine.[34]

Reading the inscriptions alongside early Almohad letters reveals their pointed nature: jihad is primarily a tool to bring recalcitrant Muslims into the Almohad fold, a particularly intense form of commanding the good and forbidding the evil. A letter from Ibn Tūmart offers brotherhood to those Almoravids who accept the invitation to repent but tells his followers, with reference to resisters, that "if they are rebels against the Truth and persist in offering their help to the people of lies and corruption, *kill them wherever you find them and do not take from amongst them any companion or ally*."[35] The italicized part of this sentence is drawn from Quran 4:89 and concerns the Hypocrites (*munāfiqūn*), who withdrew support from Muḥammad after claiming to be believers. In Ibn Tūmart's letter it is directed against anyone who claims to be Muslim without following the mahdī; such people, too, according to Ibn Tūmart, are hypocrites and valid targets of jihad. Striving for God and following his *amr*, or command, requires obedience to the mahdī and his

34 On the interdependence of ḥisba and jihad, see García-Arenal, "La práctica del precepto," 149–50; and on the ways in which ḥisba could lead to takfīr and turn Muslims into targets of jihad, see Martínez Núñez, "Ideología y epigrafía," 28.

35 The italicized text is Quran 4:89, not, as Lévi-Provençal claims, 4:91. Lévi-Provençal, *Documents inédits*, 2; translation, 3.

successors, who will command the good and forbid the evil, with arms ready to enforce compliance.

The period of violence and conversion inaugurated by Ibn Tūmart and completed largely under his successor ʿAbd al-Muʾmin was directed simultaneously against bodies and spaces. The Almohad conquest of Almoravid territories included the destruction of Almoravid structures and the beginnings of their own building programs in Marrakech and beyond. Like their stance toward people who had yet to submit to their political and religious authority, the Almohads' attitude toward the buildings they encountered ranged from conversion and assimilation to annihilation. In fact, the story of Almohad material culture parallels the Almohads' treatment of rebels and their military posture more generally: threats of pious violence followed by a flexible application that sometimes leads to obliteration and other times to integration.

One of the first steps the Almohads took upon their conquest of any territory from other Muslims was the purification of the latter's mosques[36]—a process that indicated, as Fierro has argued, that they did not see non-Almohads as true Muslims, nor their structures as properly Islamic.[37] In some cases, as in the case of the mosque of Carmona after the Almohad takeover of that city from allies of Ibn Mardanīsh in 556/1161, ritually washing the structure with water was enough to make it an Almohad building.[38] In other cases, however, the Almohads saw in the fundamental form of the mosque itself irredeemable impiety, and they demanded its demolition and reconstruction. According to al-Baydhaq's narrative of the conquest of Marrakech, the Almohads refused to inhabit the city because the eastward orientation of its mosques was incorrect in the eyes of the Almohad conquerors:

> [The Almohads declared,] "There should be no deviation or inclination in the orientation of mosques for the people of Muḥammad, upon him be praise. Such deviations are fine for Jews and others,

---

36 On Almohad purification of Almoravid mosques, see Ibn ʿIdhārī, *al-Bayān al-mughrib,* 158–59; Ibn Ṣāḥib al-Ṣalā, *Tārīkh al-mann bi-l-imāma ʿalā al-mustaḍʿafīn bi-an jaʿalahum Allāh aʾimma wa-jaʿalahum al-wārithīn,* ed. ʿAbd al-Hādī Tāzī (Beirut: Dār al-Andalus, 1383/1964), 37, 104, 193, 206. Huici Miranda notes a fascinating reversal of this custom: when Muḥammad ibn Yūsuf Ibn Hūd revolted against the Almohads in thirteenth-century Sharq al-Andalus, he believed that Almohad mosques needed to be purified, since they had been tainted by Almohad superstitions. Huici Miranda, *Historia política,* 2:469.

37 Fierro, "Conversion, Ancestry and Universal Religion," 163.

38 María Jesús Viguera Molíns, "Las reacciones de los Andalusíes," in *Los Almohades,* ed. Cressier, Fierro, and Molina, 2:713–14, citing Ibn Ṣāḥib al-Ṣalā.

> but not for him [the caliph]!" "Therefore," said the *faqīhs*, "the city will be purified, and you may inhabit it." "And how will it be purified?" "The mosques will be demolished and we will construct others."[39]

So, al-Baydhaq continues, many (though, he notes, not all) of the mosques of the city were demolished, and new mosques were constructed.[40] The orientation (qibla) of Almohad mosques was entirely consistent: their prayer niches faced southeast, at a nearly invariable 155–59 degrees, which meant that they faced the Sahara rather than the Kaʿba in Mecca. According to Abbey Stockstill, this orientation was caused by the Almohads' uniform application of an astronomic method of determining the qibla using the rising point of the star known as Suhayl al-Wazn.[41] Stockstill's argument that the orientation of Almohad mosques was determined astronomically is convincing, but it is also worth noting that their orientation would have been correct if Almohad territory had in fact been northwest of Mecca in the Ḥijāz.[42] An orientation of roughly 150 degrees, often arrived at through astronomical calculation, also corresponds to the orientation of the Kaʿba itself.[43] The Almohads' mosque orientation, like their mirroring of tropes, narratives, and language connected to the rise of Islam, may have served to speak in yet another register to their continuation of the prophetic mission.

---

39 Al-Baydhaq, in Lévi-Provençal, *Documents inédits*, 105; translation, 173–74.

40 Al-Baydhaq, in Lévi-Provençal, *Documents inédits*, 105; translation, 174.

41 Abbey Stockstill, "A Tale of Two Mosques: Marrakesh's Masjid al-Jamiʿ al-Kutubiyya," *Muqarnas* 35, no. 1 (2018): 65–82. Almohad mosque orientation is clearly mapped in Michael Bonine, "Sacred Direction and City Structure: A Preliminary Analysis of the Islamic Cities of Morocco," *Muqarnas* 7 (1990): 50–72; see especially the table on page 52 and the map on page 53. David King has written extensively about the methods for calculating the *qibla* in this period, see "The Sacred Direction in Islam: A Study of the Interaction of Religion and Science in the Middle Ages," *Interdisciplinary Science Reviews* 10, no. 4 (1985): 315–28; King, "The Enigmatic Orientation of the Great Mosque of Cordoba," *Suhayl* 16–17 (2018–19): 33–111. As Bonine and King both show, in the case of mosques constructed within preexisting urban infrastructure, street grids and topographic features significantly affected mosque orientation. But Stockstill shows that most Almohad mosques were constructed on the ruins of Almoravid cities and were unconstrained by the urban fabric.

42 As noted earlier, Fierro has argued that the Almohads saw their territory as a new Ḥijāz, and that this idea provided the justification for their expulsion of people of the book. Fierro, "A Muslim Land without Jews or Christians," 231.

43 David King's research on the qibla of early Islamic buildings shows that astronomical calculation yielded mosques oriented like the Kaʿba itself: King, "The Sacred Direction in Islam," 315–28; King, "The Enigmatic Orientation of the Great Mosque of Cordoba," 33–111.

Evidently, the Almohads objected to more than just the Almoravids' mosque orientation. They also destroyed opulent palaces, such as that of the pro-Abbasid Hammadids, the Qalʿat Banī Ḥammād, which, textual sources suggest, once possessed an elaborately painted muqarnas dome and mosaics of painted tile. Early Almohad opposition to polychromy was so well known that the people of Fez are said to have preemptively whitewashed the colorful elements of the Qarawiyyīn Mosque in Fez.[44] The importance that the Almohads attached to public inscriptions is also made clear by their destruction of Almoravid inscriptions, an act that, like their "purification" of Almoravid mosques, typically took place immediately after a city's conquest, including in Fez, Marrakech, and Tlemcen.[45]

Ibn Mardanīsh in Almohad Sources

Ibn Mardanīsh was the Almohads' most significant Andalusī rival for power in the later twelfth century. He fought Almohad armies for nearly thirty years from his capital in Murcia, maintaining his independence until his death, and he also used cultural production to contest the Almohad understanding of Islamic rule. In addition to the political challenge Ibn Mardanīsh posed to the Almohads' hegemony in Iberia, his military victories over them undermined their claim to divinely supported success. Almohad ideology predicated the empire's righteousness on its consistent triumph over foes. In his work *Aʿazz mā yuṭlab*, Ibn Tūmart claimed that one of the signs of his authenticity as mahdī was his ability to conquer the earth, east and west.[46] Therefore, any rebellion or military failure shook Almohad authority to its core.

Almohad depictions of Ibn Mardanīsh tended to focus on his rebellion against God, as demonstrated by his refusal to submit to the rightly

44 Ibn Abī Zarʿ, *Rawḍ al-qirṭās*, trans. Ambrosio Huici Miranda (Valencia: Anubar, 1964), 59–60; Julio Navarro Palazón and Pedro Jiménez Castillo, "La yesería en época almohade," in *Los Almohades*, ed. Cressier, Fierro, and Molina, 1:250. Similarly, perhaps to avoid the fate of the Qalʿat Banī Ḥammād, unknown followers of Ibn Mardanīsh covered the painted muqarnas dome of his palace in Murcia, Dār al-Ṣughrā, with a fine layer of plaster before the arrival of the Almohads.

45 G. Deverdun, *Les inscriptions arabes de Marrakech* (Rabat: Imprimerie de l'Agdal, 1956), ix, 12–14; María Antonia Martínez Núñez, "Ideología y epigrafía almohades," in *Los Almohades*, ed. Cressier, Fierro, and Molina, 1:6.

46 Ibn Tūmart, *Kitāb al-aʿazz mā yuṭlab*. It seems likely that the modern form of this book is the result of significant editing in the later twelfth century, and it is therefore uncertain whether this particular phrase was part of the original message of Ibn Tūmart. See Fletcher, "Almohad Tawḥīd," 110.

guided successors to the mahdī Ibn Tūmart. In presenting him as a sinner, Almohad sources highlighted his alliances with Christian kings against the Almohads and the presence of Christian mercenaries in his armies. The first of the two most important early Almohad sources on Ibn Mardanīsh is al-Baydhaq's partially preserved commentary.[47] It covers the period from the rise of the Almohads to al-Baydhaq's death in the 550s/1160s. The second source is Ibn Ṣāḥib al-Ṣalā's *al-Mann bi-l-Imāma*, also fragmentary, which chronicles the Almohad dynasty from 554/1159 until 568/1172.[48] Both authors emphasize Ibn Mardanīsh's status as a traitor not just against the Almohads but also against God, and Ibn Ṣāḥib al-Ṣalā frequently mentions his Christian allies. Other sources, including letters to Ibn Mardanīsh from the Almohad chancery and diplomatic correspondence among Almohad governors as well as Almohad panegyric poetry, reflect the same focus on the sinfulness of rebellion against the Almohads, particularly when it was accompanied by alliance with Christians. A final source, ʿAbd al-Wāhid al-Marrākushī's *Kitāb al-Muʿjib fī al-Talkhīṣ*, completed in 621/1224 as the Almohad dynasty was beginning to disintegrate, offers a less clearly pejorative depiction of Ibn Mardanīsh and provides important information not available elsewhere.[49] Although al-Marrākushī was educated in Almohad Fez, Seville, and Cordoba, he likely completed his book in Baghdad, perhaps sponsored by the Abbasid caliph al-Nāṣir himself.[50] This may explain the work's generally less hostile approach to Ibn Mardanīsh.

Almohad histories speak little about Ibn Mardanīsh's origin or his rise to power, but later sources give a sense of his early years, presumably based on now-lost chronicles. Muḥammad ibn Saʿd ibn Muḥammad ibn Aḥmad ibn Mardanīsh was born in Peñiscola (Banīshkūla), a small fortified town on the Mediterranean coast between Valencia and Barcelona, in 518/1124–25. His family was famous for its warriors, who

47 Al-Baydhaq's chronicle was partially preserved in the Escorial Library and is included among the several texts published in Lévi-Provençal's *Documents inédits d'histoire almohade*.

48 Ibn Ṣāḥib al-Ṣalā, *al-Mann bi-l-imāma*. Carl Brockelmann records that Ibn Ṣāḥib al-Ṣalā died in 578/1182, though J. F. P. Hopkins writes that he lived until at least 594/1198. See Brockelmann, *Geschichte der arabischen Litteratur*, 2nd ed. (Leiden: Brill, 1937–49), suppl., 1:554; *EI*², s.v. "Ibn Ṣāḥib al-Ṣalāt, Abū Marwān ʿAbd al-Malik b. Muḥammad al-Bādjī" (J. F. P. Hopkins).

49 Al-Marrākushī, *Kitāb al-muʿjib fī al-talkhīṣ*, ed. Muḥammad Saʿīd al-ʿAryān (Cairo: Lajna Iḥyā al-Turāth al-Islāmī, 1962).

50 Al-Marrākushī was, as his name indicates, born in Marrakech in 581/1185 and was educated in Fez, Seville, and Cordoba. He seems to have left the Maghrib permanently in 613/1217 in favor of the east, where he went on *ḥajj* and lived in Egypt and Baghdad. *EI*², s.v. "ʿAbd al-Wāḥid b. ʿAlī al-Tamīmī al-Marrākushī," (E. Lévi-Provençal)

had served first the Taifa kings in the northeast of the peninsula and then the Almoravids.[51] As Aragon conquered this territory in the early twelfth century, the Banū Mardanīsh moved south and entered the service of the Almoravids. Ibn Mardanīsh's father Sa'd was the Almoravid governor of Fraga, a town further inland on the Cinca River, east of Saragossa. According to a fourteenth-century report by Ibn al-Khaṭīb, Sa'd was responsible for the wound that would eventually kill King Alfonso I of Aragon at the Battle of Fraga in 528/1134.[52] At that battle, Ibn Mardanīsh's father and his future father-in-law Ibn 'Iyāḍ, one of the Almoravids' military leaders in Sharq al-Andalus who was then based in Lérida, both led contingents of Almoravid soldiers. Ibn Mardanīsh's brother 'Abd Allāh ibn Sa'd was also known as a fierce fighter and served, briefly, as the independent ruler of Valencia.[53] Ibn Mardanīsh was therefore well situated by virtue of family connections and military skills to take power as Almoravid power frayed.

Facing challenges in North Africa from the rise of the Almohad dynasty, the Almoravids' grip on al-Andalus began to weaken in the late 530s/early 1140s.[54] Ibn Mardanīsh's brother 'Abd Allāh and Sayf al-Dawla Ibn Hūd both profited from this vacuum and declared themselves rulers of Valencia and Murcia, respectively, but after they died in battle in 540/1146 at Albacete (al-Basīṭ), Ibn 'Iyāḍ took control of both cities. Al-Marrākushī, writing a century later, said that on horseback, Ibn 'Iyāḍ was a fierce and unbeatable warrior, whom no one dared to face. The Christians would send one hundred horsemen against him

51 Viguera Molíns has argued that the Banū Mardanīsh were Christians from Navarre who converted to Islam at the hands of the Banū Hūd Taifa rulers of Saragossa and the Upper March (Thaghr al-Aqṣā) and served in their military. M. J. Viguera Molíns, *Los reinos de taifas y las invasions magrebíes* (Madrid: Mapfre, 1992), 197–98.

52 Ibn al-Khaṭīb, *al-Iḥāṭa fī akhbār Gharnāṭa*, ed. Yūsuf 'Alī Ṭawīl (Beirut: Dār al-Kutub al-'Ilmiyya, 2003), 2:70. Christian sources suggest that Alfonso I died several days after the battle at a monastery in Aragon. See the Simon Barton and Richard Fletcher, ed. and trans., *Chronica Adefonsi Imperatoris*, in *The World of the Cid* (Manchester: Manchester University Press, 2000), 188.

53 There is some confusion in the sources about whether this 'Abd Allāh was Ibn Mardanīsh's uncle or his brother. Codera and Dozy refer to him as his uncle, whereas Viguera Molíns calls him Ibn Mardanīsh's brother (*Reinos de taifas*, 195). 'Abd Allāh would be commemorated as the warrior of Albacete (Ṣāḥib al-Basīṭ). Codera, *Decadencia y desaparición*, 53; Ibn al-Abbār, in Reinhart Pieter Anne Dozy, *Notices sur quelques manuscrits arabes* (Leiden: Brill, 1847), 226. J. Bosch-Vilá, in *EI*^{2}, s.v. "Ibn Mardanīsh," suggests that 'Abd Allāh was a lieutenant for Ibn 'Iyāḍ.

54 On the dizzying succession of rulers in Sharq al-Andalus in the period between Almoravid and Almohad rule, see Viguera Molíns, *Reinos de taifas*, 189–201.

and still be unable to defeat him.[55] Ibn Mardanīsh married Ibn ʿIyāḍ's daughter and served him as a lieutenant, carrying his weapons and his goods. By marrying his daughter, Ibn Mardanīsh integrated himself into Ibn ʿIyāḍ's family, formalizing their close relationship and facilitating his eventual succession to the elder ruler. After taking control of Murcia, Valencia, and the rest of Sharq al-Andalus, Ibn ʿIyāḍ made his son-in-law Ibn Mardanīsh his governor in Murcia. The following year, when it became clear that Ibn ʿIyāḍ was dying, the nobles and army leaders came to him to ask who should succeed him. Ibn ʿIyāḍ had a son, and the people pointed to him, but the dying man replied, "I have heard that he drinks wine and neglects his prayers, and if that is true, he is unqualified. So put *him* at your head," pointing to Ibn Mardanīsh. "He has abundant bravery and is very capable, and maybe God will benefit the Muslims through him!"[56] After Ibn ʿIyāḍ's death on Rabīʿ al-Awwal 22, 542 (August 21, 1147), Ibn Mardanīsh stayed in Murcia and made it the capital of Sharq al-Andalus, expanding his territory through battle, strategic alliance, and marriage and ruling it until his death in 568/1172.[57]

Ibn Hamushk was another supporter of Ibn ʿIyāḍ and ruled the town and castle of Segura (Shaqūra) in Ibn ʿIyāḍ's name. After Ibn Mardanīsh acceded to power, he married Ibn Hamushk's daughter as well, cementing a close alliance that would allow the two men to bring a vast territory under their control.[58] Ibn Hamushk, whose full name was Ibrāhīm ibn Muḥammad ibn Mufarraj ibn Hamushk, was also said to come from the region of Saragossa, where his great-grandfather Hamushk is thought to have converted at the hands of the Banū Hūd, the Taifa rulers of that region.[59]

---

55 Al-Marrākushī, *al-Muʿjib*, ed. al-ʿAryān, 3:278.

56 Al-Marrākushī, *al-Muʿjib*, ed. al-ʿAryān, 3:279.

57 Al-Marrākushī, *al-Muʿjib*, ed. al-ʿAryān, 3:279. Ibn al-Khaṭīb records the date of Ibn Mardanīsh's death as 561, and al-Maqqarī as 566. See Ibn al-Khaṭīb, *al-Iḥāṭa*, 2:73–74; Aḥmad ibn Muḥammad al-Maqqarī (d. 1041/1632), *Nafḥ al-ṭīb min ghuṣn al-Andalus al-raṭīb*, ed. Iḥsān Abbās (Beirut: Dār Ṣādir, 1968), 4:379. Bosch-Vilá suggests that Ibn Mardanīsh was pushed out of Murcia by ʿAbd Allāh al-Thaghrī after Ibn ʿIyād's death and had to retreat to Valencia, where he was welcomed and able to build up enough power to take back Murcia (EI^2, s.v. "Ibn Mardanīsh"). A newly discovered coin supports the idea that another ruler, ʿAlī ibn ʿUbayd, briefly held power in Murcia during 542/1147 before Ibn Mardanīsh was able to return from Valencia and defeat him. See Tawfīq Ibrāhīm, "A Dinar of ʿAli ibn ʿUbaid Struck in Murcia," in *XII Congreso Internacional de Numismática* (Madrid, Ministerio de Cultura, 2005), 1593-1597.

58 Marín discusses the importance of Ibn Mardanīsh's marriages in expanding his base of support and his territory. She writes, "se observa en la política matrimonial de la familia mardanīšī, antes y después de la muerte del emir, un recurso sistemático a las alianzas exteriores a la familia." *Mujeres en al-Andalus,* 551.

59 See the editor's footnote, al-Marrākushī, *al-Muʿjib*, ed. al-ʿAryān, 3:280.

The Almohads began to conquer al-Andalus in 540/1145–46, and after a protracted series of battles and rebellions, the majority of the Andalusī rulers who had resisted them traveled to Salé to submit to the Almohad caliph ʿAbd al-Muʾmin in 545/1150. By this time, Ibn Mardanīsh had become the single most important challenger to the Almohads in al-Andalus and the strongest bulwark against Almohad advance for the Christian kingdoms of the north. This position facilitated a series of alliances that would last for the remainder of his reign. The alliances with Alfonso VII of Castile-Leon, Alfonso VIII of Castile, and Ramon Berenguer IV of Barcelona offered the Christian kingdoms the vassalage of Ibn Mardanīsh, with an annual tribute and gifts of fortresses, in exchange for military aid and protection.[60] Arabic chronicles consistently refer to Ibn Mardanīsh's fighters as "the Christians" or "his Christian companions." The extent to which such language reflects the actual religious makeup of his army is unclear, since the Arabic sources that discuss Ibn Mardanīsh's Christian "friends" and army were written for Almohad consumption or were based on Almohad sources, and describing him as close to the Christians served to delegitimate his authority. Christian chronicles and treaties confirm that Ibn Mardanīsh, usually referred to as Rex Lupus, attended Christian courts and was seen as a vassal. With the aid of his Christian allies, Ibn Mardanīsh won all of Sharq al-Andalus, established himself in the major urban centers of Valencia and Murcia, and continuously challenged the Almohads in the cities they held in al-Andalus.

The very first sentence of the surviving volume of Ibn Ṣāḥib al-Ṣalā's chronicle of the Almohad caliphate reveals just how important a rival Ibn Mardanīsh was for the Almohads. It also demonstrates the chronicler's efforts to associate the Almohads' opponents with sinfulness and to emphasize their closeness to infidel Christians.

> In this year, 554 [1159], Muḥammad ibn Saʿd ibn Mardanīsh set out from the city of Murcia with his army and his companions [*aṣḥābihi*], the Christians, may God exterminate them, in his perverse decision to take advantage of what he, in his deviance and impelled by wine, considered an opportunity, in the absence of the Commander of the Faithful ʿAbd al-Muʾmin, to conquer the Almohads—may God help them—on the peninsula of al-Andalus, until he arrived at Jaén, where Muḥammad ibn ʿAlī al-Kūmī agreed

60 These alliances are discussed in greater depth in chapter 5.

to break his recognition [of the Almohads], accommodating his will, with his evil judgment propelling him to rebellion.[61]

ʿAbd al-Mālik ibn Muḥammad Ibn Ṣāḥib al-Ṣalā was an Andalusī from Beja in Gharb al-Andalus, now Portugal. He converted to Almohadism at some point before 560/1165, when he attended lessons on Almohad tawḥīd in Marrakech, and then served as a functionary in the court of Caliph Yūsuf I (r. 558–80/1163–84).[62] His chronicle, *al-Mann bi-l-Imāma*, was originally composed as a three-volume history, but only the second volume, which focuses on the years 554–68/1159–73, survives. It is one of very few works of history composed during the Almohads' reign in Almohad territories, so it offers an important perspective on the period.[63] Given the time period that the surviving volume covers, it is unsurprising that Ibn Mardanīsh's fight against the Almohads and his eventual submission would make up a significant portion of the work. But the ubiquity of Ibn Mardanīsh in the history underlines just how important he was to the Almohad struggle for power and, as discussed in chapter 6, how significantly the submission of his territory transformed the caliphate.

In 554/1159, Ibn Ṣāḥib al-Ṣalā recorded Ibn Mardanīsh's brief success in taking Jaén from the Almohads, as well as his attempts on Cordoba and Seville. The Almohads managed to hold him off with a combination of false letters, spies, and loyal soldiers who guarded the walls of the cities all night, but their fear of dissension within their Andalusī capital at Seville is revealed by their imprisonment of all those suspected of anti-Almohad sentiment.[64] The following year, Ibn Hamushk conquered Carmona and besieged Cordoba again, and this time he managed to kill its governor, an Almohad *ḥāfiẓ*.[65] In 557/1162 Ibn Mardanīsh and

---

61 Ibn Ṣāḥib al-Ṣalā, *al-Mann bi-l-imāma*, 115–16.

62 On Ibn Ṣāḥib al-Ṣalā's biography, see Ambrosio Huici Miranda's preface to his translation of the work, *Al-Mann bil-Imāma: Estudio preliminar, traducción e índices* (Valencia: Anubar, 1969), 5–8.

63 The second volume of the work survives in a single copy at the Bodleian Library at Oxford. It was edited by ʿAbd al-Hādī al-Tāzī in Beirut in 1964 and translated into Spanish by Ambrosio Huici Miranda in 1969. Ibn Ṣāḥib al-Ṣalā's earlier work, *Thawrat al-murīdīn*, a history of the rebels against Almohad power, has been lost, but references to it in later works offer a partial understanding of the text. See also Huici Miranda's preface for more on the "singularity" of the surviving work: *Al-Mann bil-Imāma*, 5–8.

64 Ibn Ṣāḥib al-Ṣalā, *al-Mann bi-l-imāma*, 116–20.

65 On Ibn Hamushk's siege of Cordoba, see Ibn Ṣāḥib al-Ṣalā, *al-Mann bi-l-imāma*, 126–27. In the Almohad context, the term *ḥāfiẓ* (pl. *ḥuffāẓ*) meant not someone who had memorized the Quran but someone who had memorized the central dogmas of Almohad thought and been trained in a special school set up by the first caliph, ʿAbd al-Muʾmin. The *ḥuffāẓ*

Ibn Hamushk, together with a Christian nobleman whom the Arabic sources call Muḍār al-Aqrʿa (Muḍār the Bald) and whom Évariste Lévi-Provençal identifies as Alvar Rodríguez, descended with Christian forces on Seville to try to take it from the Almohads.[66] When the Almohad governor (and future caliph) Abū Yaʿqūb and his army defeated them, Ibn Mardanīsh and his supporters turned to Granada, where they were able to defeat the Almohads and briefly take control of the city.[67] The Almohad capital at Seville was threatened: with Jaén, Granada, and Carmona under their authority, Ibn Mardanīsh and Ibn Hamushk were moving steadily toward the heart of Almohad power in al-Andalus.

In response to the loss of Granada, Caliph ʿAbd al-Muʾmin decided to wage holy war (*ghazw*) on the lands of the Christians (Rūm) on the peninsula of al-Andalus. Al-Marrākushī reports that ʿAbd al-Muʾmin wrote to his followers, encouraging their participation in jihad, and in 558/1163 he gathered a great group of fighters to cross the Strait.[68] This vast army aimed not just to fight the Christians but also to win the remaining territories belonging to Ibn Mardanīsh. According to

constituted a second tier of Almohad power after the *ṭalaba*, who had been trained by Ibn Tūmart himself.

66 Lévi-Provençal, *Documents inédits*, 204. Much research remains to be done about this fascinating figure. If he was indeed Alvar Rodríguez, as Lévi-Provençal and others suggest, he was a very important member of the ruling elite of Castile, Leon, and Asturias. There are two potential Alvar Rodríguezes who flourished in this period in the twelfth century, both of whom were close to the court of Alfonso VII. The first was the son of Rodrigo Fernández de Castro, a Castilian nobleman who served Alfonso VII as an *alférez*, or standard-bearer. His mother was Eylo Álvarez, the daughter Alvar Fañez, a captain of Alfonso VI of Leon who appeared in both the Poema de Almería and the Song of the Cid. Alvar Rodríguez himself was the *alférez* and majordomo of Ferdinand II of Leon. He was also the second husband of Queen Urraca, the illegitimate daughter of Alfonso VII, and after their marriage in 1163, they endeavored to make their territory in Asturias into an independent kingdom. See Concepción Casado Lobato, "¿Un intento de secesión asturiana en el siglo XII?," *Asturiensia medievalia* (Universidad de Oviedo. Departamento de Historia Medieval) 3 (1979): 163–72. This Alvar seems to have lived until at least 1174, when he was recorded as the majordomo of Ferdinand II. The second potential Alvar Rodríguez was the son of Rodrigo Vélaz and Urraca Alvárez, the daughter of Alvár Fáñez, a Galician count who was vassal to Alfonso VII of Castile and also received properties from Ferdinand II of Leon. This second Alvar is recorded as having been present at the Battle of Almería in 1147. He is thought to have died around 1167. See Simon Barton, *The Aristocracy in Twelfth-Century León and Castile* (Cambridge: Cambridge University Press, 1997), 230.

67 Al-Baydhaq, in Lévi-Provençal, *Documents inédits*, 121; translation, 202–4. On this episode, see also Dozy, *Recherches*, 1:364–88.

68 Al-Marrākushī, *al-Muʿjib*, ed. al-ʿAryān, 3:306. Al-Baydhaq writes that this group of soldiers gathered in Salé and then went to Gibraltar, where the Almohads constructed a strong fortress from which to direct themselves to Granada. Lévi-Provençal, *Documents inédits*, 121; translation, 204.

al-Baydhaq, ʿAbd al-Muʾmin led his army across the Strait, causing Ibn Mardanīsh to flee toward the Darro (Ḥadarruh) Valley, Ibn Hamushk toward his fortress at Segura, and Muḍār to the Alhambra (*qaṣr al-ḥamrāʾ*). The Almohads chased Muḍār from Granada and recaptured the city.[69] Ibn Ṣāḥib al-Ṣalā's narrative of the battle emphasizes the Almohads' piety and dedication to holy war in the name of God, and contrasts it with the impiety, rebellion, and confusion of Ibn Mardanīsh, Ibn Hamushk, and their Christian helpers. He says that the bodies of Ibn Mardanīsh's soldiers blackened the river Darro and that Muḍār was defeated and killed, his head cut off, raised on a pike, and displayed on the gate of Alcántara in Cordoba.[70] Ibn Mardanīsh's son-in-law Ibn ʿUbayd was also killed. Ibn Mardanīsh watched, heartbroken, from a neighboring mountain and was forced to flee like a fugitive into the hills.[71]

But in Jumādā II of 558/1163, before he could continue his campaign to the center of Ibn Mardanīsh's power, ʿAbd al-Muʾmin died.[72] His body was transported to Tīnmallal and was buried alongside the tomb of the Almohad mahdī, Ibn Tūmart. ʿAbd al-Muʾmin had designated his eldest son, Muḥammad, as his successor, and the people gave *bayʿa* to him, but, al-Marrakūshī writes, "This one had traits not suitable for the caliphate, such as an addiction to drinking wine, a deficiency of judgment, an excess of frivolity, and personal cowardice, and it is also said that he had a kind of leprosy; but God knows best."[73] Muḥammad ruled a brief forty-five days before relinquishing power to his brothers Yūsuf and ʿUmar, whom al-Marrākushī describes as having good judgment and being capable.[74] Yūsuf, known as Abū Yaʿqūb, would become

---

69 Al-Baydhaq, in Lévi-Provençal, *Documents inédits*, 121; translation, 205.

70 Ibn Ṣāḥib al-Ṣalā's report that this grandson of Alvar Fáñez died in 1162 would suggest that he is not either of the Alvar Rodríguezes discussed in note 65 above. Viguera Molíns also writes that Alvar Rodríguez died in the Battle of Granada in 557/1162, which would indicate that this was neither the Alvar Rodríguez who would continue to serve as majordomo for Ferdinand II of Leon until 1174 nor the Alvar who died in 1167. Viguera Molíns, *Reinos de taifas*, 231.

71 Ibn Ṣāḥib al-Ṣalā, *al-Mann bi-l-imāma*, 198–99.

72 Historians disagree about the date of his death, though they mostly agree on the month and the year. Possible dates include the eighth, tenth, twentieth, and twenty-seventh of the month. Al-Marrākushī, *al-Muʿjib*, ed. al-ʿAryān, 3:306; al-Baydhaq, Lévi-Provençal, *Documents inédits*, 121, trans. 205; Ibn Abī Zarʿ, *Rawḍ al-qirṭās*, 131; ʿAbd al-Raḥmān ibn Muḥammad Ibn Khaldūn, *Kitāb al-ʿibār*, edited and translated as *Histoire des Berbères et des dynasties Musulmanes de l'Afrique septentrionale*, trans. William MacGuckin de Slane, new edition by Paul Casanova (Paris: Geuthner, 1982), Arabic 1:318, French translation, 2:195.

73 Al-Marrākushī, *al-Muʿjib*, ed. al-ʿAryān, 3:306.

74 Al-Marrākushī, *al-Muʿjib*, ed. al-ʿAryān, 3:307–8. Al-Baydhaq presents the transition from ʿAbd al-Muʾmin to Yūsuf as seamless, though he includes a brief note indicating that

the next caliph and would oversee the conquest of Ibn Mardanīsh's territories in the years that followed. In al-Marrākushī's descriptions of Ibn ʿIyāḍ, his son, Ibn Mardanīsh, and the claimants to the Almohad caliphate, sound judgment and ability are contrasted with drinking and irreligiosity, with those who have strong capabilities winning power over their less qualified rivals. For al-Marrākushī in the mid-thirteenth century, Ibn Mardanīsh fell into the category of a good and capable ruler, like the Almohad caliphs, but, as we will see, this vision of him would shift in subsequent centuries.

Almohad writings about Ibn Mardanīsh foretold a divinely sanctioned victory for the Almohads against the infidel. A panegyric for the Almohad caliph Abū Yaʿqūb Yūsuf ibn ʿAbd al-Muʾmin, written by the Andalusī poet Ibn al-Munakhkhal describes Ibn Mardanīsh as a traitor who would pay for his sins on Judgment Day:[75]

> Ibn Saʿd is not a confederate of a good omen [*saʿd*] when he enters upon the morning,
> Sworn ally to the Christians, aiding their dominion [*aḥkāmihim*]
> So he will surely become twisted [*mujaddalan*] in judgment,
> If his soul is not purified of its offenses
> He extends toward unification [tawḥīd] a hand of supplication
> In rebuke of the soul, rinsing its sins [*ajram*][76]
> Why does the traitor elude you, even if he was enthroned
> In the *dār al-mujarrima,*[77] and climbed its stars?
> But oh! Your determination is set free, even if he mounted
> The brightness of the planets and urged forward their Mars.[78]

Muḥammad was taken to Aghmāt and imprisoned—a statement that makes no sense without the information that he had briefly been caliph. Lévi-Provençal, *Documents inédits,* 121; translation, 205–6.

75 ʿAbd Allāh ibn al-Shaykh al-Shāʿir Muḥammad ibn Ibrāhīm Ibn al-Munakhkhal al-Shālibī is said to have recited this poem upon the occasion of the people of Cordoba pledging allegiance (*bayʿa*) to the Almohad caliph Yūsuf I (r. 1163–84). See Ibn Ṣāḥib al-Ṣalā, *Tārīkh al-mann bi-l-imāma,* 457–61.

76 *Ajram* is the plural of both *jurm,* sin, and of *jirm,* celestial body. The whole poem can be seen as an extended metaphor comparing Ibn Mardanīsh to a star, since Saʿd, his father's name, also means a good omen or one of several stars that were known to be good omens.

77 An area of the skies filled with so many stars that they are indistinguishable from each other and appear as a band of white, like the Milky Way. See Ibn Ṣāḥib al-Ṣalā, *Tārīkh al-mann bi-l-imāma,* 460n2.

78 Ibn Ṣāḥib al-Ṣalā, *al-Mann bi-l-imāma,* 460. See discussion of the poem in Fawzī Saʿd ʿĪsā, *al-Shiʿr al-Andalusī fī ʿaṣr al-Muwaḥḥidīn* (Alexandria: al-Hayʾa al-Miṣriyya al-ʿĀmma li-l-Kitāb, 1979), 132–33.

Like the Almoravids, Ibn Mardanīsh is depicted as sinful for refusing to accept tawḥīd and is condemned to torment in Hell. Interestingly, Ibn Mardanīsh's close association with his Christian allies reinforces his infidel status—he is a hypocrite who refuses to heed the Almohad call and instead aids the Christians against the Almohads. Though he reaches his hand toward tawḥīd, here meaning both the Almohad doctrine of God's unity and God Himself, Ibn Mardanīsh is unable to wash away his sins.

Just as writings by the mahdī Ibn Tūmart sought to portray the Almoravids as infidels against whom jihad was even more necessary than it was against the Christians, later Almohad writers devoted significant energy to casting Ibn Mardanīsh and other Muslim opponents as unbelievers. These later sources, written after most of the Almohads' Muslim rivals in North Africa and Iberia had been subdued, reinforced the Almohads' assessment of the rebels' impiety by associating the latter with Christians. Like the author of the poem above, many Almohad writers referred to the Christian friends or allies of their Muslim rivals in nearly every sentence that they wrote about Ibn Mardanīsh and his father-in-law and ally Ibn Hamushk.

Ibn Ṣāḥib al-Ṣalā consistently describes Ibn Mardanīsh and Ibn Hamushk as sinners for their rejection of the Almohads and their close relationships with their Christian allies. Linda Gale Jones's elegant analysis of Ibn Ṣāḥib al-Ṣalā's treatment of Ibn Mardanīsh, Ibn Hamushk, and their Christian "companions" (*aṣḥāb*) demonstrates how the chronicler set up a binary between the pious, righteous, and divinely guided Almohads and their impious, hypocritical, and Satan-led rivals. She shows that Ibn Ṣāḥib al-Ṣalā's language and themes echo Islamic tropes of justice and injustice from the Quran and hadith in order to emphasize the parallels between the Almohads and the early Muslims and to associate the Almohads' Andalusī rivals with the hypocrites of early Islamic Arabia, against whom jihad was sanctioned.[79] Nevertheless, like all propagandistic texts, Ibn Ṣāḥib al-Ṣalā's work overstates its case: although it casts the conflict in cosmic terms, the period's politics were less polarized than his depiction would suggest. In fact, even as Ibn Ṣāḥib al-Ṣalā's greatest criticism against Ibn Mardanīsh relates to his Christian allies, the Almohads' diplomatic letters reveal their efforts to

79 Linda G. Jones, "'The Christian Companion': A Rhetorical Trope in the Narration of Intra Muslim Conflict," *Anuario de Estudios Medievales* 38 (July–December 2008): 793–829.

make their governors accept their new alliance with the Christian city-state of Pisa.[80]

Ibn Ṣāḥib al-Ṣalā's binary language is also responsible for the equation of the Almohads' Andalusī rivals with the Christians alongside whom they frequently fought. Thus, Ibn Mardanīsh was an infidel, just as the Christian mercenaries in his army were. By extension, anyone who fought the Almohads, regardless of religion, became an infidel led by Satan. Although he did not suggest that either Ibn Mardanīsh or Ibn Hamushk was an insincere Muslim (or even mention their potentially Christian roots), Ibn *Ṣāḥib* al-Ṣalā elsewhere points to false conversions as a reason for rebellion against the Almohads. Thus, when describing the conquest of Granada by Ibn Hamushk and Ibn Mardanīsh, he writes that they were helped by members of the former Jewish community of Granada, who had merely pretended to be Muslims after their forced conversion at the hands of the Almohads. The true Muslims of Granada fought against them and were defeated by their perfidious infidel neighbors. In later years, this view of Muslims who fought the Almohads as crypto-Jews or crypto-Christians would change the way in which Ibn Mardanīsh was portrayed in the sources. At the time, however, Ibn Mardanīsh, like the Almoravids before him, could be depicted as an infidel whose blood could be spilled licitly solely because of his opposition to the Almohads. Associating him with Christian companions simply helped underline his impiety.

By portraying the Almohad movement as a new religious daʿwa, the Almohads could represent rejection of their authority as a grave sin and equate all rebels with early Islamic unbelievers, who had to be fought until they submitted politically and religiously. Mirroring the early Islamic attitudes toward infidels, the Almohads permitted any non-Almohad who answered their call and followed their vision of Islamic rule to be fully integrated into society and often even accorded positions of honor and authority. By equating political compliance with religious salvation, the Almohad movement, like early Muslim leaders, could promise the wonders of Paradise to the impious rebels who accepted their call to God's path.

80 See letters concerning these alliances in Aḥmad ʿAzzāwī, *Rasāʾil Muwaḥḥidiyya: Majmūʿa jadīda* (al-Qunayṭira: Jāmiʿa Ibn Ṭufayl, Kulliyyat al-Ādāb wa-l-ʿUlūm al-Insāniyya, 1995), 1:162–66, 173–75, 255–56. For a detailed analysis of a series of bilingual Almohad chancery documents preserved in the Archivo di Stato di Pisa, see Pascal Buresi, "Les documents arabes et latins échangés entre Pise et l'Empire almohade en 596–598/1200–1202," in *Documents et histoire, Islam VIIe–XVIe siècles*, ed. A. Regourd (Geneva: Droz, 2013).

In Almohad chronicles, Ibn Mardanīsh occupies an in-between space: he is treated as recalcitrant, dangerously friendly with Christians, and unequivocally in the wrong in his resistance against the Almohads, but he is presented simultaneously as a legitimate ruler with great military skill. Al-Baydhaq lists the "hypocritical rebels" (*al-thāʾirūn al-munāfiqūn*) of the Maghrib and al-Andalus and records their defeat by God, in His greatness and power.[81] He does not include Ibn Mardanīsh in this group—perhaps because he had not yet been defeated, or because his territory had never been under Almohad rule.[82] But he does portray Ibn Mardanīsh as the Almohads' greatest rival, who could grant protection to the "rebels" they fought. One such rebel, Dardūsh of Carmona, fled the Almohads to Ibn Mardanīsh's territory.[83] Another rebel, Ibn Miqdām, revolted against the Almohads in Purchena (Burshāna); immediately after killing him, the Almohad general Abū Ḥafṣ turned his army against the territories under Ibn Mardanīsh's control. Abu Ḥafṣ won Lorca (Lūrqa), Cartagena (Qarṭajanna), and Velez Malaga (Ballash) for the Almohads, diminishing Ibn Mardanīsh's lands, and retreated with his armies first to Cordoba and then to North Africa. Ibn Mardanīsh arrived to besiege Lorca, and Abū Ḥafṣ came back across the Strait to fight him, along with Caliph Abū Yaʿqūb. At a battle at Faḥṣal-Jallāb outside Murcia in 560/1165, the Almohads killed many of Ibn Mardanīsh's most valuable soldiers, leaving him only a small number of knights.[84]

Ibn Ṣāḥib al-Ṣalā's chronicle, written in Marrakech where he was serving as secretary to Abū Yaʿqūb, records the arrival of the news about the great victory outside Murcia. Ibn Ṣāḥib al-Ṣalā writes that he rose early to go to the antechamber of the court, where he saw a cat devouring a dove. He said to his companions, "Praise God! By God, Ibn Mardanīsh has been defeated!" When his companions asked what he meant, he explained that the cat represented the North African lion and the dove the foreign enemy, so he predicted that the Almohads had defeated their Andalusī rival. At that very moment, soldiers arrived at the entrance to

81 Lévi-Provençal, *Documents inédits*, 122, list continues through 127; translation, 207, the list continues to 216.

82 Al-Baydhaq, in Lévi-Provençal, *Documents inédits*, 122–26; translation, 207–15.

83 Al-Baydhaq, in Lévi-Provençal, *Documents inédits*, 125; translation, 213.

84 Al-Baydhaq, in Lévi-Provençal, *Documents inédits*, 126; translation, 214. This battle at Faḥṣ al-Jallāb, ten miles outside Murcia, is evidently different from the 567/1172 battle also known by the name of al-Jallāb.

the palace carrying the battle standards of Ibn Mardanīsh and bearing news of the Almohads' victory.[85]

Though the Almohad armies had driven Ibn Mardanīsh within the walls of Murcia, they had not defeated him entirely. He and his supporters fought back, attacking Ronda. After this substantial defeat, Ibn Mardanīsh faced new internal challenges, including a series of defections by family members. There is a sense of cosmic justice in al-Baydhaq's narration of the challenges Ibn Mardanīsh faced in the 560s/1160s. He writes that Ibn Mardanīsh lost his mind after the defections of his brother in Valencia, his brother-in-law in Alcira, and his allies Ibn Dallāl in Segorbe and Ibn ʿAmrūs in Játiva, and that he killed his sister (the wife of the ruler of Alcira). Ibn Mardanīsh's eventual acknowledgment of Almohad authority over his sons is cast as inevitable, for traitors can never win out over the righteous.[86] In al-Baydhaq's account, as in all other Almohad chronicles, the success of the Almohads' movement was a foregone conclusion, since they were the enactors of God's will.

On the first day of Ramaḍān in 564/1169, the Almohad caliph Abū Yaʿqūb Yūsuf ibn ʿAbd al-Muʾmin had his secretary write a letter to Ibn Mardanīsh inviting him, as the caliph's father had done sixteen years earlier, to submit. Like the earlier letter, this one invoked the parties' shared faith in the message of the Prophet Muḥammad and encouraged Ibn Mardanīsh to accept Almohad tawḥīd. But this letter closed with a specific and dire warning:

> The most great shaykh Abū Ḥafṣ, may God glorify him, is moving this year with the armies of the Almohads, may God help them, to the Andalusī Peninsula, may God protect it, with the intention of jihad and raiding [*ghazw*]. So we told him that we are thinking of our discussion with you and that he should avoid that side [*jānib*], so that he does not intervene by purpose and so that nothing is revealed to him until your writing arrives, and he seeks to know how you respond to the invitation and its consideration, so hasten your response to this ruling.[87]

85 Ibn Ṣāḥib al-Ṣalā, *al-Mann bi-l-imāma*, 274–76; Viguera Molíns, *Reinos de taifas*, 253–54.

86 Al-Baydhaq, in Lévi-Provençal, *Documents inédits*, 126; translation, 215.

87 The letter was written by Caliph Yūsuf I's secretary Abū al-Ḥasan ʿAbd al-Mālik ibn ʿAyyāsh after Friday prayers on the first of Ramaḍān 564/1169. *Majmūʿat rasāʾil Muwaḥḥidiyya*, 141–49.

Ibn Mardanīsh's response to this letter does not survive, but it was evidently not positive. The Almohad armies did travel to the peninsula in 564/1169, and they attacked the territories of Ibn Mardanīsh. They were aided by the submission of Ibn Mardanīsh's father-in-law and lieutenant, Ibn Hamushk, whose daughter Ibn Mardanīsh had apparently repudiated.[88] Ibn Ṣāhib al-Ṣalā described how Ibn Mardanīsh divorced the daughter and sent her, beaten and in tears, to her father. This indicated the end of the two rulers' longstanding alliance, and Ibn Ṣāhib al-Ṣalā indicated that Ibn Hamushk turned immediately to the Almohads to profess his acceptance of their creed.[89] A later narrative, from Ibn al-Khaṭīb, provides further color to the story of Ibn Hamushk's daughter's departure: he writes that she abandoned her son with Ibn Mardanīsh and fled to her father's land. When someone asked her how she could have left behind her son, Ibn al-Khaṭīb writes that she said, "Son of a dog, puppy of evil, from a dog of evil [*jarū kalb, jarū sūʾ, min kalb sūʾ*]. I don't need him."[90] Although the chronicles do not record the reasons for this rupture, the role of the daughter in holding together Ibn Mardanīsh and Ibn Hamushk's political and military relationship—and eventually pulling them apart—seems clear. Marrying an ally's daughter could facilitate a closer and longer-term relationship, tying together two families socially, legally, and politically. But the interpersonal dynamics of marriage could also risk this alliance. In the case of Ibn Hamushk, the chronicles report that Ibn Mardanīsh's maltreatment of his daughter impelled him directly into the arms of the waiting Almohads. Of course, these are Almohad and later chronicles, so it may be that the daughter's repudiation is yet another polemical story about Ibn Mardanīsh's character, and that Ibn Hamushk simply saw, earlier than Ibn Mardanīsh, that the Almohads were ascendant and it was time to surrender.

Sometime during Ramaḍān 564/May–June 1169, Ibn Hamushk went to Cordoba to submit to Almohad authority. A letter from the Almohad governor of Cordoba to the governor of Granada conveys the good news

---

88 Ibn Ṣāhib al-Ṣalā, *al-Mann bi-l-imāma,* 388–90; Al-Maqqarī, *Nafḥ al-Ṭīb*, 1:443; Huici Miranda, *Historia política*, 1:239.

89 Ibn *Ṣāhib* al-Ṣalā, *al-Mann bi-l-Imāma,* 389.

90 Ibn al-Khaṭīb, *al-Iḥāṭa,* 1:155. Manuela Marín discusses this repudiation and Ibn Hamushk's daughter's response in *Mujeres en al-Andalus,* 518–19.

and describes Ibn Hamushk's shift of political allegiance in spiritual terms as a conversion to tawḥīd:

> The face of His guidance was revealed to the shaykh Abū Isḥāq Ibrāhīm ibn Hamushk, may God grant him success, and he was separated from the watering places of his ignorance, and it was made clear to him that this illustrious power is the vessel of the Savior in which he hastens toward eternal happiness, that which saves and does not delay in error, and without which there is no salvation. So he hurried to enter it in the land of those whose souls were purified and whose hearts bore His love, and he saw that his sins would be eliminated and his crimes forgiven thereby, and he proclaimed and announced the call of the mahdī [*al-da'wa al-mahdiyya*] throughout all of his lands and began to take refuge in His protection and to follow His path, and he came to speak to the Almohads to ask for their protection and to hold their rope [*ḥabl*], trusting and devoted and accepting pure government and trustworthy love.[91]

From the letter's perspective, by accepting Almohad authority, Ibn Hamushk transformed himself from an infidel into a sinless, pure soul. His political surrender meant his absolution as a traitor, companion of Christians, and inciter of rebellion against the Almohads. The following year, Ibn Hamushk moved to North Africa, where he was given a post in the Almohad administration and where he would eventually die.

In 567/1171, Abū Ya'qūb set out to complete his father's mission, crossing into al-Andalus to capture the territories held by Ibn Mardanīsh. He recruited his brother 'Uthmān ibn 'Abd al-Mu'min, who was serving as governor of Granada, to help him in conquering Murcia, "the seat of the kingdom of Muḥammad ibn Sa'd" (*dār mamlakat* Muḥammad *ibn Sa'd*). 'Uthmān and his armies approached Murcia, where they encountered Ibn Mardanīsh's forces at the Battle of al-Jallāb, four miles outside of Murcia.[92] Ibn Mardanīsh charged out of Murcia with a great force consisting mostly of Christians (lit. "Franks," *Ifranj*), because, according to al-Marrākushī, "Ibn Sa'd had requested their aid for his wars

91 *Rasā'il Muwaḥḥidiyya, majmū'a jadīda*, 2:128.

92 Al-Marrākushī, *al-Mu'jib*, ed. al-'Aryān, 3:321–22. Whether this al-Jallāb is the same site as that of the abovementioned Battle of Faḥṣ al-Jallāb in 560/1165, described by al-Baydhaq as being ten rather than four miles from Murcia, is an open question.

and took them as his soldiers and helpers [*anṣār*]."[93] He decided to do so, al-Marrākushī claims, after he perceived the difference between his own goals and those of his military leaders as well as his subjects' disapproval of him. So, al-Marrākushī reports, he killed many of his military leaders whom he suspected in various ways, including by building a wall around some and leaving them captive until they died of hunger and thirst, and by beating others to death. He then brought in Christian soldiers, divided the goods of the military leaders he had killed among the Christians, and forced residents out of Murcia so he could lodge the Christians in their houses.[94]

This story, echoed in many later sources, paints Ibn Mardanīsh as the oppressor of his Muslim, Murcian subjects and suggests that the compensation he offered his Christian mercenaries went beyond the customary payment of wages and veered into preferential treatment. Al-Marrākushī narrates this story in midst of the narrative about the Battle of al-Jallāb, although it presumably took place several years earlier, since the sources speak consistently about Ibn Mardanīsh's "Christian helpers" from the earliest period of his reign. This placement serves to cast the whole battle that followed as a chance for the distribution of divine justice against Ibn Mardanīsh and his corrupt Christian companions.

Ibn Mardanīsh and his troops encountered the Almohads and were crushed. All of the Christian nobles (*aʿyān al-Rūm*) were killed, and Ibn Mardanīsh fled to Murcia to prepare for a siege.[95] Without further explanation, Ibn Ṣāḥib al-Ṣalā includes a strange narrative about how Ibn Mardanīsh and his two viziers locked up the official in charge of criminal justice (*ṣāḥib al-maẓālim*) without food or water in a tower, where he stayed until he consumed his clothes out of desperation.[96] Abandoned by his brother, his sons-in-law, and others, Ibn Mardanīsh left Murcia to try to take Alcira del Júcar (Jazīrat al-Shūqar) from his son and designated successor Hilāl, who had taken control of it and proclaimed his support for the Almohads.[97] When Ibn Mardanīsh arrived, he asked his brother Abū al-Ḥajjāj Yūsuf to help him win back the territory, but even together they were unable to do so and eventually broke their siege in

93 Al-Marrākushī, *al-Muʿjib*, ed. al-ʿAryān, 3:322.

94 Al-Marrākushī, *al-Muʿjib*, ed. al-ʿAryān, 3:322.

95 Al-Marrākushī, *al-Muʿjib*, ed. al-ʿAryān, 3:322.

96 Ibn Ṣāḥib al-Ṣalā, *al-Mann bi-l-imāma*, 470. This narrative is slightly different in Ibn ʿIdhārī, *Bayān al-mughrib*, who suggests that it was the two viziers who were locked up, not the *ṣāḥib al-maẓālim*; see 86.

97 Ibn Ṣāḥib al-Ṣalā, *al-Mann bi-l-imāma*, 471.

disappointment. In the aftermath, Abū al-Ḥajjāj counseled his brother to accept the authority of the Almohads. Realizing the truth of his doomed situation, Ibn Mardanīsh's health failed him, and he died on the Rajab 10, 567/March 8, 1172. Al-Marrākushī writes that the Almohads had encircled him and were still besieging him when he died a natural death.

His death was concealed until his brother Yūsuf ibn Saʿd, known as al-Raʾīs (the leader), had arrived from Valencia, which he was ruling in the name of Ibn Mardanīsh. Yūsuf consulted with Ibn Mardanīsh's eldest children, and after exhausting all other possibilities, they decided that they should place their fates in the hand of the Almohad caliph Abū Yaʿqūb and submit to him.[98] Ibn Mardanīsh's shaykhs and military leaders and his son Hilāl all expressed their formal recognition of the Almohad caliph. Nearly a month later, in late April, Hilal set off for Seville to demonstrate his community's submission in person.[99] Al-Marrākushī reports that he knew the names of eight of Ibn Mardanīsh's surviving sons—Hilāl, which means crescent moon, with the *kunya* Abū al-Qamr (father of al-Qamr, or the moon), the eldest of the sons and Ibn Mardanīsh's successor; Ghānim; al-Zubayr; ʿAzīz; Nusayr; Badr; Arqam; and ʿAskar—but not the names of his younger sons.[100] He does not mention a son named ʿAbd Allāh, even though Ibn Mardanīsh was called Abū ʿAbd Allāh Muḥammad ibn Saʿd on his coinage and in Almohad chancery documents.[101] In addition, al-Marrākushī records at least two daughters, one named *Ṣafiya*, who married the future caliph Abū Yūsuf Yaʿqūb, and another of unknown name who married the caliph Abū Yaʿqūb Yūsuf.

Those who refused to accept the Almohads' authority and were overrun by Almohad armies faced terrible fates. The story of Ibn Ḥassūn of Malaga (d. 548/1153) is illustrative. Ibn al-Khaṭīb, the fourteenth-century Nasrid polymath, described in his book *Aʿmāl al-Aʿlām* the brutal end of Ibn Ḥassūn, who had resisted the Almohads after the fall of

---

98 Al-Marrākushī, *al-Muʿjib*, ed. al-ʿAryān, 3:322–23. This narrative of Yūsuf's decision to submit to the Almohads differs from others, in which a dying Ibn Mardanīsh himself was responsible for the decision to submit.

99 Ibn *Ṣāḥib* al-*Ṣalā*, *al-Mann bi-l-imāma*, 471.

100 Al-Marrākushī, *al-Muʿjib*, ed. al-ʿAryān, 3:323.

101 *Kunyas*, names typically derived from *Abū*, "father of," or *Umm*, "mother of," plus the name of their eldest son, were not always based on offspring. A Quran in the Istanbul University Library (Ms. A 6755), dated to 538/1143–44 and produced in Cordoba for a Murcian patron on the occasion of the birth of his son, refers to the newborn as "Abū ʿAbd Allāh Muḥammad," though the child clearly could have had no son of his own. Many thanks to Umberto Bongianino for the reference.

the Almoravids. Knowing that his daughters were likely to become Almohad slaves or concubines and that he would be killed if his resistance failed, he tried, unsuccessfully, to kill his daughters and himself by starting a fire in his castle, by poisoning himself, and then by trying to spear himself through the chest. When the Almohads broke through his defenses and entered the castle, they found him bleeding on the floor, but it took him two more days to die. The Almohads enslaved his daughters, who became concubines of military commanders in the Almohad army, and Ibn Ḥassūn's body was beheaded and crucified after his death as a warning to would-be rebels.[102]

It was perhaps the difference in the respective fates of Ibn Hamushk and Ibn Ḥassūn that led Ibn Mardanīsh or his brother to counsel his children to submit to the Almohads. After Ibn Mardanīsh died in 567/1172, his children indeed surrendered to the Almohads. His sons became Almohad governors for their Andalusī territories. His daughters' marriages to the Almohad caliph Yūsuf and his successor, the future caliph Yaʿqūb, and the linking of their two families helped turn public sentiment toward the Almohads.[103] The daughters subsequently gave birth to future caliphs. Following D. F. Ruggles, one wonders what the songs and stories these mothers soothed their babies with might have been like, and if, in the privacy of their own quarters, they regaled their children with stories of Ibn Mardanīsh's heroism.[104] Ibn Mardanīsh's offspring were fully integrated into the highest echelons of Almohad society. This, too, echoed the narratives of the rise of Islam, in which several of the most powerful enemies of the early Muslim community became important Muslim leaders following their conversion.

---

102 Ibn al-Khaṭīb, *Aʿmāl al-aʿlām*, ed. É. Lévi-Provençal, 2nd ed. (Beirut: Dār al-Makshūf, 1956), 254–55. It is worth noting that this source postdates the events it purports to describe by two centuries, and it is possible that its narrative has been colored by later attitudes and agendas. I am grateful to Emily Silkaitis for the reference to this story. Maribel Fierro also mentions it in "Violence against Women in Andalusi Historical Sources (Third/Ninth–Seventh/Thirteenth Centuries)," in *Violence in Islamic Thought from the Quran to the Mongols*, ed. Robert Gleave and Istvan Kristo-Nagy (Edinburgh: Edinburgh University Press, 2015).

103 The marriage ceremonies are described in the late thirteenth-century work of Ibn ʿIdhārī al-Marrākushī, *al-Bayān al-mughrib fī akhbār al-Andalus wa-l-Maghrib: Qism al-Muwaḥḥidīn*, ed. M.I. al-Kattānī, M. Ibn Tāwīt, M. Znaybar, and ʿA. Q. Zamāma (Beirut: Dār al-Gharb al-Islāmī, 1985), 135; fourteenth-century work of Ibn al-Khaṭīb, *Aʿmāl al-aʿlām*, ed. Sayyid Kasrawī Ḥasan (Beirut: Dār al-Kutub al-ʿIlmiyya, 2003), 2:240–41, as well as in the seventeenth-century compilation of Maqqarī, *Nafḥ al-ṭīb*, 1:445. While these narratives are likely based on earlier sources, they often encode later biases, as I discuss further in chapter 7.

104 Ruggles asks, "In what language were the lullabies that she sang to her children? What games did they play together?" "Mothers of a Hybrid Dynasty," 75.

At the same time that the Almohads publicly celebrated and incorporated Ibn Mardanīsh's children into their ruling elite, they also effaced traces of his rule and began the process of marginalizing the memory of his long rebellion against them. Many of his fortresses had been demolished during Almohad sieges of his territory, and subjugation of the landscape he had ruled became evidence of the triumph of the Almohads' righteous authority. Like the ruins of old, Ibn Mardanīsh's palaces came to stand in for the victory of "true" Islam over the decadence of past rulers. The thirteenth-century poet al-Qarṭājannī refers to Qasr ibn Saʿd, Ibn Mardanīsh's castle in Monteagudo, in his poem "Qaṣīda Maqsūra." The poem was recited at the Hafsid court, which carried on the caliphate rooted in the authority of Ibn Tūmart after the fall of the Almohads.

> And what a short time we granted ourselves in happiness [*wa kam qaṣarnā zamānan li-l-saʿd*] in the Qaṣr Ibn Saʿd, in joy and bliss
> We wandered through haloes of moons; their beauty effaced the destruction of the passage of time
> And we held back our gaze from the castle [*qaṣr*] within it; time has preserved it as a warning [*ʿibra*] for those left behind
> Like al-Ḥīra the White. If [Qaṣr ibn Saʿd] was compared to it, al-Hīra's splendor would scarcely compare.[105]

In the poem, al-Qarṭājannī reflects on the loss of Sharq al-Andalus to Castile and Aragon and mentions the region's iconic sites. He compares the ruins of Qaṣr ibn Saʿd to the legendary white palace of al-Ḥīra in Mesopotamia, which had been constructed by the pre-Islamic Christian Lakhmid dynasty allied with the Sasanians.[106] The Lakhmids' ruined palace was a topos in Abbasid poetry. Like the poetic laments for the ruined palace and city of al-Ḥīra, al-Qarṭājannī's poem seems simultaneously to be mourning the passage of time and the loss of beauty and celebrating the arrival of Islam.[107] But in this case, reflecting the Almohad conception of religion, the poet compares Ibn Mardanīsh's castle to one

105 al-Qarṭājannī's "Qaṣīda Maqṣūra" appears in Mahdī ʿAllām, *Dirāsāt adabīyah* (Al-Qāhirah: Maktabat al-Shabāb, 1984), 100–210. This passage is on page 146.

106 For an analysis of this poem, see E. García-Gómez, "Observaciones sobre la 'Qaṣīda Maqṣūra' de Abū-l-Ḥasan Ḥāzim al-Qarṭāyannī," *al-Andalus* 1 (1933): 81–103. The lines that refer to Qasr Ibn Saʿd are 289–98.

107 For more on the Ubi Sunt genre and the importance of al-Ḥīra for Arabic poems in this mode, see Adam Talib, "Topoi and Topography in the Histories of al-Ḥīra," in *Historian and Identity in the Late Antique Near East*, ed. Philip Wood (Oxford: Oxford University Press, 2012).

built by pre-Islamic Christians, later displaced by the rise of Islam. Al-Qarṭājannī's poem thus praises the castle's beauty while also suggesting the inevitability of its destruction by a righteous dynasty—one that happened to be the predecessor of the rulers to whom he recited his poem. Yet by the time he recited this poem in Tunis to the Hafsid caliph al-Mustanṣir, al-Qarṭājannī's native region, where he had spent his youth, had been conquered and divided by the kingdoms of Castile and Aragon. The castle of Ibn Saʿd therefore served as a cautionary tale—once splendid, twice conquered, and a warning to observers about the inevitability of time's destruction.

Chapter 3

Filiative Networks

Lineage and Legitimacy in Sharq al-Andalus

In his biographical dictionary of notable scholars, litterateurs, and leaders, written in the mid-thirteenth century in Cairo and Damascus, the judge and scholar Ibn Khallikān wrote about the death of "Abū ʿAbd Allāh Muḥammad ibn Saʿd, who was called Ibn Mardanīsh and was at that time ruler of Sharq al-Andalus." Suggesting that he had been poisoned by his mother and outlining how his death and the subsequent submission of his children to the Almohads facilitated the expansion of the Almohad Empire and allowed it to concentrate on fighting the Christian kingdoms, Ibn Khallikān paused to discuss the ruler's unusual name. "*Mardanīsh* is derived from the Romance [*lughat al-Franj*, lit. language of the Franks] word for human excrement [*ʿadhira*]."[1] According to Ibn Khallikān, this ruler in the lands of the distant West was known by a name derived from the local Romance word *mierda*, a name that highlighted his proximity to Christians and their language while also seeming to pass judgment on him.

Ibn Mardanīsh's many names reflect the interplay of ideas about his origins and lineage with concepts of righteous authority. Few

1 Ibn Khallikān, *Wafayāt al-Aʿyān*, ed. Ihsān ʿAbbās (Beirut: Dār al-Thaqāfa, 1971), 7:130–38, biography no. 845 ("Yūsuf b. ʿAbd al-Muʾmin, ṣāḥib al-Maghrib").

contemporary sources call him Ibn Mardanīsh, but as Ibn Khallikān's biography indicates, by the century after his death the appellation was widespread enough as a shorthand for his full name to have reached the Islamic East. The monikers Rex Lupus (Wolf King) and Emir Muḥammad ibn Saʿd were both in regular usage during his own lifetime. These multiple names reflect his complex identities, as he fulfilled different roles for his largely Muslim subjects and his Christian overlords, and hint at how he was perceived by supporters and rivals in his time and remembered by different audiences after his death.

Ibn Khallikān implies and later scholars would state outright that Ibn Mardanīsh's familial origins on the Iberian Peninsula determined his anti-Almohad position. But scattered evidence from Ibn Mardanīsh's own court shows that he, his family members, and the scholars he employed consciously developed and presented genealogies that connected them to the Islamic east and the Arabian Peninsula in particular. They constructed identities (genealogical, intellectual, cultural) that emphasized their rootedness in the very Islamic traditions under attack by the Almohads. These identities were in some cases ones that carried particular Andalusī importance, and in others ones that expressed filiation with the earliest Islamic periods or contemporary centers in the east. None express an anachronistic sense of loyalty or connection to a Spanish state that did not yet exist.

Much modern scholarship on this period has imagined static ethnic and cultural identities with substantial differences between "Andalusīs" and North African "Berbers." But these identities were constantly reformulated in relation to one another, and as Ramzi Rouighi has recently shown, the very idea of a singular, coherent Berber identity was invented in al-Andalus, to apply to those living on the Peninsula and in proximate North Africa.[2] Furthermore, the complex cultural admixtures that proliferated in al-Andalus, from the mass conversions of the ninth century to the regular intermarriage of Arabs, Berbers, Christians, and Jews, undermined any claim to an unsullied identity. During the *shuʿūbiyya* controversies of the eleventh century (a literary movement juxtaposing the virtues of Arab versus non-Arab lineage), claims to noble descent from kings of old were the basis for competition among rulers, but beyond poetic sparring, geographic origins rarely figured into discussions

2 Ramzi Rouighi, *Inventing the Berbers*. See Introduction, note 8, for further discussion of the problematic nature of the term Berber.

of power.[3] Genealogy, however—and specifically, claims to descent from an Arab tribe—played a central role in the literature of political and religious legitimacy. That is, even though later writings, discussed further in chapter 7, explained Ibn Mardanīsh's resistance to the Almohads in ethnic, racial, or nationalist terms, Ibn Mardanīsh legitimated himself by connecting his dynasty to the defunct Almoravid regime and to the centers of power in the Islamic east.

In this and the following chapter, I use genealogy to explore Ibn Mardanīsh's time in power. By genealogy, I mean not just Ibn Mardanīsh's lineage, although that is part of what this chapter addresses, but also cultural genealogies—how Ibn Mardanīsh affiliated himself, through his cultural production, to ruling cultures distant in time and space in order to legitimate himself. The chapter focuses on claims about Ibn Mardanīsh's lineage and what can be gleaned from inscriptions on tombstones and coins about how he presented himself, both genealogically and in relation to the broader political and theological issues of the day. It also addresses how the scholars who flocked to Ibn Mardanīsh's territories as the Almohads won the rest of al-Andalus presented their intellectual networks, and how their chains of connection to scholars across time and space supported Ibn Mardanīsh's claim to rule. Throughout, I endeavor to be sensitive to the problems posed by the sources and to practice a kind of textual archaeology, understanding and highlighting the biases of the authors and reading the visual and the material alongside (and sometimes against) the written.

Ibn Mardanīsh's Names and Lineages

Ibn Mardanīsh, like his Almohad rivals, sought to situate himself within an Islamic tradition that valued Arab descent but at the same time to celebrate the particulars of his context. For Ibn Mardanīsh, this meant

3 The famous *shuʿūbī* letter of al-Andalus, written by Ibn García, a Basque convert to Islam who worked for the *saqlabī* (formerly enslaved Northern European) ruler of Denia in the later eleventh century, argued for the superiority of non-Arab Muslims (including European converts and Berbers) over Arabs. The letter was addressed to an Arab working in the court of Ibn Sumādiḥ of Almería and sought explicitly to undermine the authority of a rival Taifa ruler. See Göran Larsson, *Ibn García's Shuʿūbiyya Letter: Ethnic and Theological Tensions in Medieval al-Andalus* (Leiden: Brill, 2003). On the earlier *shuʿūbiyya* movement in the Islamic East, see H. A. R. Gibb, "The Social Significance of the Shuʿūbiyya," in *Studies on the Civilization of Islam*, ed. S. J. Shaw and W. R. Polk (London: Routledge, 1962); Roy Mottahedeh, "The Shuʿūbīyyah Controversy and the Social History of Early Islamic Iran," *International Journal of Middle East Studies* 7, no. 2 (1976): 161–82.

crafting a distinctly Andalusī genealogy and ruling culture that also referenced the Islamic East, especially Abbasid Baghdad, to counteract the new messianic conception of the caliphate being advanced by the Almohads. Later debates about Ibn Mardanīsh's name and genealogy among medieval and modern scholars alike reveal anxieties about identity and religion in the changing political context of the twelfth-century Iberian Peninsula.[4] Ibn Mardanīsh's conflicting genealogies reflect attempts to augment or undermine his authority and, among later scholars, to make sense of his long-standing alliances with Christians in a period increasingly marked by interreligious conflict.[5]

Later scholars' fascination with Ibn Mardanīsh's roots begins with his name. Ibn Mardanīsh's full name was Abū ʿAbd Allāh Muḥammad ibn Saʿd ibn Muḥammad ibn Aḥmad ibn Mardanīsh al-Judhāmī or, according to some authors, al-Tujībī. The conflicting *nisba*s indicate different Arab tribal roots: al-Judhāmī would mean that he was from the North Arabian tribe of Judhām, whereas al-Tujībī suggests that he belonged to the Tujīb clan within the South Arabian tribe of Kinda. Each of these nisbas could indicate descent from the tribe or conversion at the hands of a *mawlā*, or patron, who belonged to the tribe.[6] Both tribes played very important roles in early Islamic history and in al-Andalus, and using either nisba situated Ibn Mardanīsh within a lineage with distinguished roots in early Islamic Arabia and Iberia.

The Tujīb clan had been prominent in the conquest of North Africa, helping to establish the city of Fustat (in today's Cairo) and occupying one of its most important medieval neighborhoods.[7] The Tujībīs were also very important in Iberia, ruling Saragossa as Taifa princes before the rise of the Banū Hūd. The Judhāmī tribe, too, was influential in Iberia; the Banū Hūd of Saragossa—successors to the Banū Tujīb—belonged to it. The Banū Hūd constituted one of Ibn Mardanīsh's

4 Similar kinds of anxieties are visible in the debates in Almohad contexts about the sincerity of converts' belief in Islam. See Fierro, "Conversion, Ancestry and Universal Religion," esp. 160–65.

5 The question of heredity and religion, as it was formulated in later centuries, is addressed in chapter 7.

6 Fierro's onomastic study of three biographical dictionaries from the tenth and twelfth centuries demonstrates that a growing number of scholars adapted Arabic nisbas over time: in the early dictionaries, about 30 percent of scholars have an Arabic nisba, but in the later dictionary 48 percent have such a nisba. Maribel Fierro, "Mawālī and muwalladūn in al-Andalus," in *Patronate and Patronage in Early and Classical Islam*, ed. Monique Bernards and John Nawas (Leiden: Brill, 2005).

7 S. D. Goitein, *A Mediterranean Society* (Berkeley: University of California Press, 1983), 4:17–18.

primary rivals for power in Sharq al-Andalus. His predecessor as ruler of the region in the years of declining Almoravid power was Sayf al-Dawla Ibn Hūd al-Judhāmī. Sayf al-Dawla, known in Christian sources as Zafadola, had been vassal to King Alfonso VII of Castile-Leon and had been present at his imperial coronation in 1135. It was fighting alongside Sayf al-Dawla that Ibn Mardanīsh's brother ʿAbd Allāh had been killed.[8] The Judhāmī clan therefore held a significant position in Sharq al-Andalus in the twelfth century, and the Tujībīs had been their predecessors and rivals in Saragossa. Both nisbas were thus closely connected to the region known as the Upper March (*al-thaghr al-aqṣā*), which is likely where Ibn Mardanīsh's family originated.[9] Perhaps Ibn Mardanīsh's supporters sought to cover his bases by linking him with both tribes, one South Arabian and one North Arabian, paralleling the northern and southern Arabian genealogies claimed by the Almohads and the Almoravids, respectively. Constructing his genealogy on the basis of these two distinct tribal roots could bolster his appeal to supporters of the Banū Hūd, the Tujībīs, or the Berber groups that claimed descent from northern or southern tribes.[10] Modern scholars, however, have seen the existence of the two nisbas as evidence that Ibn Mardanīsh was not truly of Arab descent, since genuine uncertainty about one's patrilineal descent from a particular tribe would have been unlikely.[11]

There is further confusion about his name because of the unusual—and clearly not Arabic—name by which he is known, Ibn Mardanīsh. Modern scholars are divided on the root of his name but have generally

8 Ibn al-Abbār, in Dozy, *Notices*, 226.

9 María Jesús Viguera Molíns argues that the Banū Mardanīsh were Christians from Navarre, living near a waterway known as Merdanix, before converting to Islam. This is discussed further below. See Viguera, "Sobre el nombre de Ibn Mardanīš," *Al-Qanṭara* 17 (1996): 231–38; Viguera, *Los reinos de taifas y las invasions magrebíes* (Madrid: Mapfre, 1992), 197–98.

10 The tension between the northern tribes of Qays and the southern tribes of Yaman played an important role in several early conflicts in the Islamic East. Khalid Blankinship notes that the Berbers who accepted Islam and were fully inducted into the early Arab armies that were then largely responsible for the conquest of al-Andalus were granted honorary membership in Yamanī or Muḍarī tribes. This honorary adoption may be at the root of Almoravid and Almohad genealogical claims. See Khalid Yahya Blankinship, *The End of the Jihād State: The Reign of Hishām Ibn ʿAbd Al-Malik and the Collapse of the Umayyads* (Albany: State University of New York Press, 1994), 68.

11 Viguera Molíns sees the two nisbas as another indication that Ibn Mardanīsh was a descendant of a convert from Christianity, since she deems it highly unlikely that someone of Arab descent would confuse or change their nisba. See María Jesús Viguera Molíns, "Sobre el nombre de Ibn Mardanīš," 238. In this she follows Dozy, *Recherches*, 1:365.

settled on his patrilineal descent from an Iberian Christian.[12] For most of the modern era, scholars have assumed that *mardanīsh* was the Arabic corruption of a Christian name, whether Castilian, Latin, or Greek, and that this name belonged to the first family member to convert to Islam.[13] It is important to note that in all of the Almohad sources I have consulted, Ibn Mardanīsh is known as Muḥammad ibn Saʿd (as, indeed, he presented himself on his coins, discussed below), and there is no mention of his potentially Christian roots. There is no indication that Ibn Mardanīsh's parentage or his ancestor's potential conversion from Christianity was of interest to his contemporaries. Ibn Khallikān's commentary, written in thirteenth-century Cairo, is the earliest surviving source that suggests the name is related to a non-Arabic origin—but he made no mention of the possibility that this meant Ibn Mardanīsh was descended from Christians.[14] In the twelfth and thirteenth centuries, no one seems to have cared about a Muslim's Christian great-great-great grandfather. Although genealogical scholars sought to trace lineages back to noble Arab tribes and rulers claiming power associated themselves with ancient prophets and holy families, the lack of an Arab lineage had no bearing on perceptions of piety. The Almohads, in particular, deemed anyone who did not accept their authority an infidel, whereas anyone who accepted their vision of tawḥīd was instantly absolved of all sins.

---

12 Scholars such as Codera, Dozy, and Viguera Molíns believe that the first Muslim member of Ibn Mardanīsh's family was likely either Mardanīsh himself or his son Aḥmad, which would place the conversion in the tenth century, at the time of mass conversions to Islam. See Bulliet's estimate of rates of conversion in Iberia, based on the name changes in biographical dictionaries: Richard W. Bulliet, *Conversion to Islam in the Medieval Period: An Essay in Quantitative History* (Cambridge, MA: Harvard University Press, 1979). For a critique of Bulliet's estimates for al-Andalus, see Alwyn Harrison, "Behind the Curve: Bulliet and Conversion to Islam in al-Andalus Revisited," *Al-Masāq* 24:1 (2012): 35–51.

13 Dozy believed that Mardanīsh was an Arabic corruption of the Latin Martinus or the Castilian Martínez and further suggested that this meant Mardanīsh had been the first member of a Christian family to convert to Islam. Dozy, *Recherches*, 1:365. Codera was dissatisfied with the changes in vocalization between Martínez and Mardanīsh that Dozy's explanation entailed and instead suggested that the name was an Arabization of the Byzantine Mardonius, positing that Ibn Mardanīsh may have descended from a Byzantine family still present in Cartagena. Codera y Zaidín, *Decadencia y desaparición*, 63–66. More recently, Jorge Eiroa and Mariángeles Gómez Ródenas have argued that this emphasis on his Christian descent constitutes part of the "black legend" the Almohads created around Ibn Mardanīsh, in "El emirato de Ibn Mardanīš: Un breve síntesis interpretiva," in *Rey Lobo: El legado de Ibn Mardanīš, 1147–1172*, ed. Jorge A. Eiroa and Mariángeles Gómez Ródenas (Murcia: Comunidad Autónoma de la Región de Murcia, 2019), 16–41, here 20.

14 Ibn Khallikān, *Wafayāt al-Aʿyān*, 7:130–38, biography no. 845 ("Yūsuf b. ʿAbd al-Muʾmin, ṣāḥib al-Maghrib").

Ibn Mardanīsh's ally and father-in-law Ibn Hamushk, whose submission to the Almohads was discussed in the previous chapter, also had an unusual name that has been explained with reference to a Romance root. His full name was Ibrāhīm ibn Muḥammad ibn Mufarraj ibn Hamushk, and like Ibn Mardanīsh would eventually be, he was known by the distinctive and non-Arabic name of his ancestor. Ibn Hamushk's name was attributed to the Arabization of a bizarre Romance phrase, *He mochico*, a commentary on his great-grandfather's tiny ear (*mocho*) that had been cut in battle.[15] Modern scholars have assumed the names Hamushk and Mardanīsh to mark the first member of each familial line to convert to Islam, and in modern writings, as in later medieval ones, discussion of these unusual names often precedes mention of likely Christian roots. These sources therefore discount Ibn Mardanīsh's Arab nisba as pure fabrication.[16] But in spite of the name's strangeness, it is possible that Mardanīsh is not an Arabization of a Christian name that accompanied conversion to Islam but an unusual name that entered the genealogy through other means. It has been argued that both Mardanīsh and Hamushk are toponyms—"Mardanīsh" denoting the waterway Merdanix in Navarre, and "Hamushk" the village of Hamusco (now Amusco) in the province of Palencia.[17] This theory would complicate a religious or even linguistic explanation for these names, since the use of places as names has no clear-cut association with religion or language.

How did Ibn Mardanīsh himself present his genealogy? Two tombstones from his time offer some clues. The first of these, preserved in the Museo Arqueológico de Murcia, is a marble gravestone that belonged to a female member of the Banū Mardanīsh family who died in 557/1162. She may well have been Muḥammad ibn Saʿd ibn Mardanīsh's sister.[18]

---

15 This suggestion appears in Ibn al-Khaṭīb, *Iḥāṭa*, ed. Ṭawīl, 1:151–52. It is repeated in Codera y Zaidín, *Decadencia y desaparición*, 116–17. Mariano Gaspar Remiro notes, however, that there is no evidence of the origins of this name or any awareness of its potentially Romance roots in Latin sources: *Historia de Murcia musulmana* (Saragossa: Tip. de Andrés Uriarte, 1905), 186–87.

16 See, for example, *EI*², s.v. "Ibn Mardanīsh" (J. Bosch-Vilá): "While a more fully documented and convincing philological study remains to be made, it is certain that, despite his nisba, Ibn Mardanī<u>sh</u> was a *muladí* (*muwallad*) descended from a Spanish Christian family."

17 On Mardanīsh, see Viguera Molíns, "Sobre el nombre de Ibn Mardanīš"; on Hamushk, see Gaspar Remiro, *Historia de Murcia musulmana*, 186–87.

18 Museo Arqueológico de Murcia, inv. no. 210. The inscription is transcribed, translated to Spanish, and analyzed in María Antonia Martínez Nuñez et al., *Epigrafía Árabe: Catálogo del gabinete de antigüedades* (Madrid: Real Academia de la Historia, 2008), 169, no. 64. My reading of the inscription is much indebted to both the transcription and the suggestions of the authors regarding the barely legible final word (which they read as raḥimahu). The

The gravestone is inscribed with an epitaph in simple Kufic script carved in relief. The text starts with a citation from the Quran (31:34) and continues as follows:

> This is the grave of the free, noble [*al-ḥurra al-fāḍila*] daughter of him of the two viziers [*dhū al-wizāratayn*], the illustrious leader [*al-qāʾid al-ajall*], the warrior [*mujāhid*] Abū ʿUthmān Saʿd ibn Mardanīsh ibn Muḥammad, may [God] have mercy on him . . . the year 557.

This inscription indicates that Saʿd ibn Mardanīsh, the father of Muḥammad ibn Saʿd, was known (at least in 557/1162) as "he of the two viziers" and as a *qāʾid* and a *mujāhid.*[19] These were all common honorifics in the Almoravid period, and as the ruler of Fraga during the Almoravid period, Saʿd may well have used them. The inscription also suggests that Mardanīsh was not the first family member to convert to Islam, because it claims that he was the son of a Muḥammad.[20] Finally, this woman of the Mardanīsh family died in 557/1162, in the middle of Muḥammad ibn Saʿd's time as ruler of Sharq al-Andalus. But there is no mention of her powerful brother (or, perhaps, half-brother) on her gravestone. The phrase used to describe her, "free and noble [woman]" (*al-hurra al-fāḍila*), was traditionally used to refer to women of Almoravid ruling families.[21] Her status as a noble free woman may have been determined by her brother's position as ruler; it may also reflect

---

suggestion that the deceased may be the sister of Muḥammad ibn Saʿd ibn Mardanīsh is made in footnote 534. Virgilio Martínez Enamorado also discusses this tombstone as that of a sister of Ibn Mardanīsh in "Poder y epigrafía Mardanīšíes: Confirmando (otra vez) a Ibn Jaldūn," in *Rey Lobo: El legado de Ibn Mardanīš, 1147–1172*, ed. Jorge A. Eiroa and Mariángeles Gómez Ródenas (Murcia: Comunidad Autónoma de la Región de Murcia, 2019), 104–15.

19 Saʿd ibn Mardanīṣh died in 528/1134. There is some confusion about names here, however, since Muḥammad ibn Saʿd ibn Mardanīsh is usually referred to in chronicles as Muḥammad ibn Saʿd ibn Muḥammad ibn Aḥmad ibn Mardanīsh—with two more generations separating him from the ancestor Mardanīsh. Since Saʿd's death date is appropriate for the father of Muḥammad, one can assume that in a short inscription carved into stone the craftsman responsible shortened the name to Saʿd ibn Mardanīsh, as many others would shorten Muḥammad ibn Saʿd to Ibn Mardanīsh later. It is nonetheless unusual to include the ancestor before Mardanīsh (Muḥammad) while leaving out intermediate generations. Perhaps this reflected a conscious effort on the part of Muḥammad ibn Saʿd, then ruling in Murcia, to invent a longer Muslim genealogy for himself, or perhaps the craftsman made an error in placing Muḥammad after Mardanīsh rather than before it.

20 Nearly all modern scholars, including Codera, Dozy, and Viguera Molíns, have assumed that either Mardanīsh or his son Aḥmad converted to Islam from Christianity in the mid-tenth century. See Dozy, *Recherches*, 365–66; Codera, *Decadencia y desaparición*, 63–66; Viguera Molíns, "Sobre el nombre de Ibn Mardanīsh." Jābir Khalīfa Jābir's book about the Banū Mardanīsh has a chapter dedicated to this question, and he also concludes that they were of Christian descent. See Jābir, *Banū Mardanīsh*, 41–47.

21 *EA*, 169, n. 533.

FIGURE 3.1. Tombstone of al-ḥurra al-fāḍila bint Saʿd ibn Mardanīsh, 557/1162. *Photo:* Museo de Santa Clara, Murcia.

her father's role as a supporter of the Almoravids. Ibn Mardanīsh may have used terms familiar from the Almoravid period for his family to imply a continuation of Almoravid social forms under his rule. Such usage suggests that Ibn Mardanīsh saw his status as comparable to that of the Almoravid leaders who preceded him.

Another Mardanīshī funerary inscription is preserved in the Museo Arqueológico Nacional in Madrid and shows a further adaptation of Almoravid terminology.[22] Also in marble with a simple Kufic inscription in relief, this gravestone commemorates a Murcian leader from the time

22 Museo Arqueológico Nacional de España, inv. no. 572; see *EA*, 170–71, no. 65. I follow here the transcription of the authors of *EA*, which depends on a drawing of the inscription held in the Real Academia de la Historia that was completed in 1862, before the stone was fractured. There are several anomalies in the spelling of both this and the earlier inscription, and the authors of the *EA* disagree in some respects with the readings of earlier scholars, including Lévi-Provençal (see, for example, their different reading of the phrase *barrada ḍarīḥahu*). I find the readings of the authors of the *EA* most convincing. For Lévi-Provençal's reading, see his *Inscriptions arabes d'Espagne* (Leiden: Brill, 1931), no. 103, pl. 24. See also Martínez Enamorado, "Poder y epigrafía," 112.

of Ibn Mardanīsh. The inscription begins with a quotation from the Quran (35:5, although it is incomplete and could also be 61:9) and then continues with many of the titles seen in the first gravestone:

> This is the grave of him of the two viziers [*dhū al-wizāratayn*], the illustrious leader [*al-qāʾid al-ajall*] Abū ʿImrān Mūsā ibn Yaḥyā, called Ibn al-Azraq al-Fihrī. He died, may God have mercy upon him and look upon his face with favor [*naẓẓara wajhahu*] and sanctify his soul [*qaddasa rūḥahu*] and refresh his tomb [*barrada ḍarīḥahu*], in the middle of the night on Wednesday . . . of Jumādā . . .

FIGURE 3.2. Tombstone of Abū ʿImrān Mūsā ibn Yaḥyā, qāʾid of Ibn Mardanīsh. *Photo:* Museo Arqueológico Nacional. Inv. 50572. Photographer: Ángel Martínez Levas.

in the year 566, and he was giving testimony . . . and He sent His Messenger with guidance [quotation from Quran 9:33].[23]

Here, one of Ibn Mardanīsh's military rulers is commemorated with exactly the same terminology used to describe Ibn Mardanīsh's father on the other tombstone: *dhū al-wizāratayn* and *al-qāʾid al-ajall*. The use of the same titles suggests that Ibn Mardanīsh cast himself as the equivalent of an Almoravid *amīr al-muslimīn*. This title ("Commander of the Muslims," rather than the traditional caliphal name *amīr al-muʾminīn*, "Commander of the Faithful") had allowed the Almoravids to associate themselves with the caliphate without claiming it themselves. Though his territory was dwarfed by that of the former Almoravid Empire, and his administration was far smaller, Ibn Mardanīsh adapted the symbols and terminology of the earlier dynasty for his own rule in order to legitimate the latter.

Scholars, Judges, and Secretaries in the Service of Ibn Mardanīsh

Ibn Mardanīsh's administration, like his claimed titles and genealogies, connected him, through long chains of masters and students, to the most important scholars and religious leaders of both al-Andalus and the Islamic East. Biographical dictionaries offer insight not otherwise available into the administration and ideology of Ibn Mardanīsh's kingdom. Although relatively few biographical entries explicitly mention Ibn Mardanīsh (and those that do always call him Muḥammad ibn Saʿd), many more indicate that the scholars they treat were present in Ibn Mardanīsh's territories. Analysis of this group of scholars, done by Alfonso Carmona and Victoria Aguilar, yields fascinating data. Aguilar assembled a list of ninety-six scholars residing in the city of Murcia between 541/1147 and 568/1172. This group constitutes more than one quarter of all the ʿulamāʾ whom biographical dictionaries associate with

23 The use here of the Quranic verse 9:33 ("It is He who has sent His Messenger with the guidance and the religion of truth, that he may uplift it above every religion, though the unbelievers be averse") has parallels in a number of other twelfth-century funerary contexts as well as on Almoravid coinage, and has been associated by Kassis with a hardening attitude toward Jews and Christians in the eleventh and twelfth century. However, there is no evidence that its use on the tombstone of a vizier of Ibn Mardanīsh reflects such an attitude. Hanna Kassis, "Muslim Revival in Spain in the Fifth/Eleventh Century: Causes and Ramifications," *Der Islam* 67 (1990): 78–110, here 103; see also Carmen Barceló, "Estructura textual de los epitafios andalusíes (siglos IX–XIII)," in *Homenaje a Manuel Ocaña Jiménez* (Cordoba: Junta de Andalucía, 1990), 50–51.

Murcia across all five centuries of Islamic rule.[24] Dominique Urvoy has also confirmed the extraordinary concentration of scholars in Murcia between 1150 and 1170, writing that the city housed more scholars in this twenty year period than did either the Andalusī Almohad capital of Seville or Granada.[25] Carmona's article focuses on forty 'ulamā' in Ibn Mardanīsh's territories during his rule, including some outside the city of Murcia.[26] Of the biographical entries for these forty scholars, eleven explicitly mention Muḥammad ibn Sa'd.[27] Some served him as judges, members of a consultative council (*shūrā*), or secretaries. Others lived under his authority but held no official role, in some cases refusing to serve the government and preferring a life of asceticism and teaching.

The majority of these scholars originated from the region under Ibn Mardanīsh's rule, but some moved to his territory in response to the Christian or Almohad conquests of their cities. Many studied in the East, receiving certificates (*ijāza*s) that authorized them to teach the *Muwaṭṭa'* of Mālik, the seven canonical readings of the Quran, or the hadith collection of al-Bukhārī or Muslim. While the Almohads valued learning about these works as well, giving such significant importance to Mālik's *Muwaṭṭa'* that the Almohad *ṭalaba* had to memorize it, they rejected the standard Mālikī approach to legal works (*furū'*) in favor of a return to the sources and logical reason.[28] In this, they echoed the attitude of the Andalusī scholar and proponent of the Ẓāhirī school Ibn Ḥazm (d. 456/1064), who had also rejected deductive analogy (*qiyās*) and supposition (*ra'y*) on the part of an individual jurist, in favor of a

---

24 Victoria Aguilar, "Identidad y vida intelectual en la Murcia de Ibn Mardaniš," in *Política, sociedad e identidades en el occidente islámico (siglos XI–XIV)*, ed. M. A. Manzano and Rachid El Hour (Salamanca: Ediciones Universidad Salamanca, 2016), 31.

25 Urvoy's count of scholars in Cordoba yields a roughly similar number as that in Murcia. He also notes that in the decade that followed (after Ibn Mardanīsh's death), Murcia lost this high concentration. Dominique Urvoy, *El mundo de los ulemas andaluces del siglo V/XI al VII/XIII: Estudio Sociológico,* trans. Francisco Panel (Madrid: Ediciones Pegaso, 1983), 162.

26 Alfonso Carmona, "El saber y el poder: Cuarenta biografías de ulemas levantinos de época de Ibn Mardaniš," in *Estudios onomástico-biográficos de al-Andalus,* ed. Ávila and Fierro, vol. 10, *Biografías almohades II* (Madrid: Consejo Superior de Investigaciones Científicas, 2000). Unsurprisingly, the scholars listed by Aguilar and Carmona overlap in many cases.

27 Carmona, "El saber y el poder," 58.

28 On the differences between Almoravid and Almohad attitudes toward law, and how the latter situated themselves in relation to the Mālikīs and Ẓāhirīs, see Dominique Urvoy, *Pensers d'al-Andalus: La vie intellectuelle à Cordoue et Seville au temps des Empires Berberes (fin Xie siècle–début XIIIe siècle)* (Toulouse: CNRS, 1990), 80–89; Fierro, "The Legal Policies of the Almohad caliphs." The anecdote that the *ṭalaba* had to study the *Muwaṭṭa'* comes from Anonymous, *al-Hulal al mawšiyya*, trans. Ambrosio Huici Miranda, 179–80.

literal and logical reading of the Quran.[29] Almohad descriptions of the existing religious elite Ibn Tūmart encountered in the Maghrib present them as hidebound, ignorant, and hostile to the dialectical theology the Mahdī presented to them.[30] The Almohad movement succeeded in winning over some religious scholars, like Ibn Rushd, known in Latin as Averroes, who brought together the Almohads' emphasis on logical reasoning and a Mālikī-inflected attitude toward legal works.[31] But other legal scholars, who continued to value the ability to make personal supposition, adjudicate on the basis of analogy, or root their opinions in collections of earlier legal decisions, sought new places to practice. Ibn Mardanīsh's territory seems to have become a center for the transmission of such knowledge at precisely the moment that the Almohads were undermining these traditional roots of the Islamic legal system.[32]

In the Almoravid period and the years that followed, scholars and judges, in particular, held significant political power. Rachid El Hour has shown how vital judges and scholars were to the Almoravids in their administration of al-Andalus, often exceeding in importance the governors under whom they served. El Hour demonstrates that sometimes scholars were able to oust governors whom they saw as corrupt or inefficient through direct appeal to the Almoravid emir. He sees this as evidence of their immense local influence, which would have posed a significant threat to any Almoravid ruler who did not acquiesce to the demands of their judges.[33] In the transitional period between the Almoravids and the Almohads, a number of autonomous qāḍī rulers emerged, including the famous Qāḍī ʿIyāḍ (r. 542–43/1147–48), who had been a judge under the Almoravids and became the de facto ruler of Ceuta as Almoravid power collapsed. He rebelled against the Almohads and even minted a dinar with anti-Almohad legends before he surrendered, accepted tawḥīd, and was brought to Marrakech, where he would die in 544/1149.[34]

---

29 Maribel Fierro, "Why Ibn Ḥazm became a Ẓāhirī: Charisma, Law and the Court," *Hamsa* 4 (March 2018): 1–21.

30 Bennison, *The Almoravid and Almohad Empires,* 250–52.

31 Fierro, "The Legal Policies of the Almohad Caliphs."

32 On Almohad attitudes toward *sharīʿa,* see Nagel, "La destrucción de la ciencia de la *šarīʿa.*"

33 Rachid El Hour, "The Andalusian Qāḍī in the Almoravid Period: Political and Judicial Authority," *Studia Islamica* 90 (2000): 67–83; see also Fierro, "*Qāḍī* as Ruler."

34 On ʿIyāḍ's coinage, see Hanna Kassis, "Qadi Iyad's Rebellion against the Almohads in Sabta (A. H. 542–543/A. D. 1147–1148): New Numismatic Evidence," *Journal of the American Oriental Society* 103 (1983): 505–14; Maribel Fierro, "Sobre monedas de época Almohade: El

In Sharq al-Andalus, too, scholars and judges served as leaders in this period of transition. Biographical dictionaries, especially Ibn al-Abbār's *Takmila* and Ibn ʿAmīra al-Ḍabbī's *Bughyat al-Multamis*, offer insight into the elite families that occupied Sharq al-Andalus in this time. They also provide important information about the administration of Ibn Mardanīsh's kingdom and about the scholarly lineages that connected his court to centers of power in al-Andalus and the Islamic East. Al-Ḍabbī (d. 599/1202–3) was likely from Murcia and was educated there by many of the scholars whose life and works he describes in his book. Ibn al-Abbār (d. 658/1260) lived in the following century but also originated from Sharq al-Andalus, and he began his *Takmila* ("Completion," of the earlier biographical dictionaries of Ibn al-Faraḍī and Ibn Bashkuwāl) while serving in the court of Ibn Mardanīsh's great-grandnephew Zayyān ibn Mardanīsh, who ruled Valencia and then Murcia when the Almohad caliphate was collapsing.[35] Both scholars therefore offer perspectives on Sharq al-Andalus that are considerably closer to Ibn Mardanīsh's court than are the largely Almohad sources discussed in the previous chapter. As biographical dictionaries, however, they provide not a cohesive narrative of Ibn Mardanīsh's time in power but instead a series of brief intellectual biographies of distinguished scholars, some of whom were in his employ.

Ibn Mardanīsh enjoyed many advantages granted by his family and marriages, but he had not been born in Murcia and consequently needed the support of local elites. Scholars provided this support and created the administrative structure on which he would rely. Of the ninety-six scholars studied by Aguilar, seventy-two (80 percent) came from territories under Ibn Mardanīsh's control, and most belonged to local elite families.[36] Aḥmad ibn Muḥammad ibn Ziyādat Allāh al-Thaqafī, known as Ibn al-Ḥallāl, was the most important of the scholars living in Sharq al-Andalus under Ibn Mardanīsh at the beginning of the latter's reign. Ibn al-Abbār describes him as a scholar of *fiqh*, inclined toward *raʾy* (legal reasoning) and *masāʾil* (questions to and answers from a scholar), who had also studied literature (*adab*). He was born in Murcia and had served as a member of the city's shūrā, or consultative assembly, as well as the

dinar del cadí ʿIyāḍ que nunca existió. Cuándo se acuñaron las primeras monedas almohades y la cuestión de la licitud de acuñar moneda," *Al-Qanṭara* 27, no. 2 (2006): 457–76.

35 On Zayyān, see Emilio Molina López, "El gobierno de Zayyān b. Mardanīsh en Murcia (1239–1241)," *Miscelánea Medieval Murciana* 7 (1981): 159–88; A. Balbale, "Affiliation and Ideology at the End of the Almohad Caliphate," *Al-Masāq* 30, no. 3 (2018): 266–83.

36 Aguilar, "Identidad y vida intelectual," 16.

judge of Orihuela, but he fell into disgrace under Ibn ʿIyāḍ and was removed from power.[37] Ibn Mardanīsh rehabilitated him and returned him to power, making him the *qāḍī quḍāt al-Sharq*, or the judge in charge of all judges in his territory.[38] In this capacity, he appointed a number of other judges throughout Sharq al-Andalus and seems to have overseen most aspects of the legal and religious life of the region. According to Ibn al-Abbār, Ibn al-Ḥallāl appointed his close companion Ibn al-Aṣfar (d. 564/1168) to the shūrā in Murcia and promoted him to the post of qāḍī of both Játiva and Orihuela, for example.[39]

Ibn al-Ḥallāl had studied with the great scholar Abū ʿAlī al-Ṣadafī (d. 514/1120), and he came from a local family of noble scholars and leaders that, according to al-Ḍabbī, was known for being welcoming to strangers.[40] As the second most important person in Sharq al-Andalus in the first decade of Ibn Mardanīsh's rule, Ibn al-Ḥallāl seems to have imported a large number of scholars and teachers from elsewhere and acted as their patron.[41] One such figure was the *wāʿiẓ*, or preacher, al-Salāwī, whose full name was Yaḥyā ibn Muḥammad ibn ʿAbd al-Raḥmān ibn Baqī. Ibn al-Ḥallāl brought al-Salāwī from the North African city of Salé to Sharq al-Andalus, where Ibn Mardanīsh granted him a paid post. Ibn ʿAbd al-Mālik Al-Marrākushī reported that al-Salāwī continued his preaching in Sharq al-Andalus, devoting his time to teaching and moral exhortation (*waʿẓ wa-tadhkīr*).[42] But Ibn al-Ḥallāl was eventually denounced for injustice, and Ibn Mardanīsh imprisoned him, confiscated his goods, and then executed him in 554/1159.[43] The scholars he had supported, including al-Salāwī, mostly seem to have lost their official positions in the aftermath of his disgrace but nonetheless remained in Sharq al-Andalus. Al-Salāwī began to practice medicine and managed to support himself through this work while continuing to teach students.[44] Ibn al-Ḥallāl's protégé

37 On the fascinating council known as the shūrā, see Manuela Marín, "Sūrā et ahl al-sūrā dans al-Andalus," *Studia Islamica* 62 (1985): 25–51.

38 Ibn al-Abbār, *Kitāb al-Takmila li-Kitāb al-Ṣila: Complementum Libri Assilah (dictionarium Biographicum)*, ed. Francisco Codera y Zaidín (Madrid: Romero, 1886–89), no. 174; Carmona, "El saber y el poder," 75–77.

39 Ibn al-Abbār, *Takmila*, ed. al-Abyārī, 101, no. 189; Carmona, "El saber y el poder," 92.

40 Aḥmad b. Yaḥyā b. ʿAmīra al-Ḍabbī, *Bughyat al-Multamis fī Tārīkh Rijāl Ahl al-Andalus*, ed. al-Hawarī (Beirut: Dār al-Kutub al-ʿIlmiyya, 2005), 708–9, no. 367.

41 Carmona, "El saber y el poder," 60.

42 Ibn ʿAbd al-Mālik al-Marrākushī, *Kitāb al-Dhayl wa-l-Takmila*, ed. Muḥammad Bencherifa (Beirut: Dār al-Thaqafa, n.d.), 8:413, no. 199; Aguilar, "Identidad y vida intelectual," 28.

43 On his "injustice," see Ibn al-Abbār, *Takmila*, 92–93; Ibn ʿAbd al-Mālik al-Marrākushī, *Dhayl*, 1:426.

44 Al-Ḍabbī, *Bughyāt al-Multamis*, no. 1464; Carmona, "El saber y el poder," 91.

Ibn al-Aṣfar was imprisoned for several months before he was eventually cleared, returned to his judgeship in Orihuela, and placed in charge of administering the shūrā.[45]

Not all of the scholars who served in Ibn Mardanīsh's administration were local elites, however. Of the forty scholars Carmona discusses, at least five came to Murcia from other cities in the aftermath of the unrest (*fitna*) that accompanied the end of Almoravid rule in 539–40/1145.[46] Several more—at least four, by Carmona's count—left Almería following the Christian conquest of that city in 1147 and settled in Ibn Mardanīsh's kingdom. The biographies of other scholars show movement into and out of Ibn Mardanīsh's territories, with some going to North Africa for a while and then returning.[47] Some of the scholars who came to Sharq al-Andalus left Almohad lands; others departed from territories recently conquered by Christians. Carmona notes the intriguing case of the Granadan scholar Abū Muḥammad Ibn Sahl, who seems to have moved to Baeza after the Christians conquered it in 541/1146 and stayed there until they left in 552/1157, apparently teaching logic and mathematics to Christian scholars who journeyed there from Toledo to study with him.[48] Ibn al-Khaṭīb wrote about Ibn Sahl, "He acquired great fame in the science of logic (*manṭiq*), in mathematics, and in the other ancient sciences; his importance grew because of this knowledge, and his fame reached so far that Muslims, Christians, and Jews alike agreed that no one in his time equaled him."[49] When the Christians left, Ibn Sahl moved first to Ibn Hamushk's territories and then to Murcia, where Ibn Mardanīsh placed him in charge of his son's education.[50]

The scholars of Ibn Mardanīsh's realm who appear in biographical dictionaries are overwhelmingly associated with the teaching of Mālikism and are often presented as having mastered *Muwaṭṭa'* of Mālik or the *Mudawwana* of Sahnūn, the two most important Mālikī texts. Many scholars in these dictionaries traveled to Mecca to perform the pilgrimage and stayed to learn from Mālikī scholars

45 Ibn al-Abbār, *Takmila*, ed. al-Abyārī, 101, no. 189; Carmona, "El saber y el poder," 93.

46 Carmona, "El saber y el poder," 61.

47 Carmona, "El saber y el poder," 63–64.

48 Carmona, "El saber y el poder," 64; Ibn al-Khaṭīb, *Iḥāṭa*, 3:404–5.

49 Ibn al-Khaṭīb, *Iḥāṭa*, 3:404–5.

50 Ibn al-Abbār, *Takmila*, ed. Codera, 484–85, no. 1392; Carmona, "El saber y el poder," 106–7. Ibn Sahl died in Murcia in 571/1176.

in the holy cities; an example is Muḥammad ibn Yūsuf ibn Sa'āda (d. 565/1170), from Valencia, who studied with the *imām* of the Mālikī school in Mecca.[51] Interestingly, however, 20 percent of the biographies of scholars who worked in Sharq al-Andalus under Ibn Mardanīsh also mentioned the great Shāfi'ī scholar and traditionist al-Silafī (d. 576/1180) in Alexandria.[52] Some scholars, such as Khalaf ibn Muḥammad ibn Khalaf ibn Sulaymān ibn Khalaf ibn Muḥammad ibn Fatḥūn (d. 557/1162), seem to have received an ijāza from al-Silafī by corresponding with him in writing.[53] Others, such as Ibn Sa'āda, studied with al-Silafī in person in Alexandria after leaving Mecca. Another scholar, 'Abd Allāh ibn Mūsā Ibn Burṭuluh (d. 563/1167–68), who was born in Murcia, went on the pilgrimage in 510/1116–17 and then stayed in the East to study with al-Silafī as well as other famous scholars in Egypt, including al-Ṭurṭūshī (d. ca. 520/1126), before returning to his native city.[54] Ibn Burṭuluh became imam of the great mosque of Murcia during the Almoravid period and married the daughter of his local teacher, the important scholar Abū 'Alī al-Ṣadafī, who had also taught Ibn al-Ḥallal.[55] The daughter, named Khadīja or Fāṭima, according to conflicting reports, was herself a scholar.[56] Although his biography does not mention the name

---

51 Carmona, "El saber y el poder," 94. For more on this figure, who would eventually serve as one of Ibn Mardanīsh's judges in addition to teaching hadith and fiqh, see Ibn al-Abbār, *Takmila*, ed. Codera, 223–26, no. 746.

52 Of the forty scholars Carmona discusses, eight have biographies that mention al-Silafī, making him the most commonly named Eastern scholar. See Carmona, "El saber y el poder," 69.

53 Ibn al-Abbār, *Takmila*, ed. Codera, 52–53, no. 174; Carmona, "El saber y el poder," 77–78. On the practice of receiving ijāzas based on correspondence, see J. A. C. Brown, *Hadith: Muhammad's Legacy in the Medieval and Modern World* (Oxford: Oneworld, 2009).

54 Ibn al-Abbār, *Takmila*, ed. Codera, 479–81, no. 1384; Carmona, "El saber y el poder," 87–89. On this fascinating figure and the family of the Banū Burṭuluh in Murcia, see Victoria Aguilar, "Tres generaciones y varios siglos de historia: Los Banū Burṭuluh de Murcia," in *Estudios onomástico-biográficos de al-Andalus*, ed. Manuela Marín and Helena de Felipe, vol. 7, *Homenaje a José María Fórneas* (Madrid: Consejo Superior de Investigaciones Científicas, 1995).

55 For more on the 315 scholars in biographical dictionaries recorded as having studied with him and the works they transmitted, see Aguilar, "Identidad y vida intelectual," 22; Cristina de la Puente, "Obras transmitidas en al-Ándalus por Abū 'Alī al-Ṣadafī," *Al-Qanṭara* 20 (1999): 195–200.

56 For more on Fatima and other female scholars living under Ibn Mardanīsh's authority, see Victoria Aguilar, "Fatima, Amat al-Rahman y otras mujeres en el mundeo del saber de Murcia en el siglo XII," in *Mujeres de letras pioneras: En el arte, el ensayismo y la educación*, ed. María Gloria Ríos Guardiola, María Belén Hernández González, and Encarna Esteban Bernabé (Murcia: Comunidad Autónoma de la Región de Murcia, 2016), 27–45.

of Ibn Mardanīsh, Ibn Burṭuluh continued to live in Murcia under Ibn Mardanīsh's rule until his death, and a number of the other important scholars of Murcia studied with him.

In the aftermath of Ibn al-Ḥallāl's downfall, Ibn Mardanīsh seems to have replaced him with a group of important scholars, who shared responsibilities and moved throughout the region. Most of these scholars had already been prominent in the Almoravid and early Mardanīshī periods, but their official roles now grew. The abovementioned Ibn Fatḥūn, from Orihuela, had been his city's judge under Ibn ʿIyāḍ and had also served as an emissary to Marrakech. After Ibn al-Ḥallāl's disgrace, Ibn Mardanīsh reappointed Ibn Fatḥūn judge of Orihuela once more. Ibn al-Abbār writes,

> The emir Abū ʿAbd Allāh Ibn Saʿd distinguished him [Ibn Fatḥūn] above any other of his men, a privilege he had well earned, because he was a loyal official and a subordinate always in his post, in addition to being one of the most notable personalities of his age for his equanimity and majesty, his words always in accordance with the truth and his actions always in conformance with it, too.[57]

Like many of his contemporaries in Sharq al-Andalus, Ibn Fatḥūn came from a family of scholars. He had studied with a long list of important locals and had also corresponded with important scholars in the East, including al-Silafī in Alexandria.

Ibn Saʿāda, who had studied with al-Silafī in Egypt after completing the pilgrimage, subsequently returned to Sharq al-Andalus, where he taught hadith, Quran, and law.[58] According to Ibn al-Abbār, Ibn Saʿāda inclined toward Sufism (*taṣawwuf*). Upon his return to Murcia, he served on the city's shūrā and as a preacher at the great mosque of Murcia. After the fall of the Almoravids, he was named judge of Murcia, and then of Játiva as well. After Ibn al-Ḥallāl's death, Ibn Saʿāda shared the duty of giving the sermon of the Friday prayer in the three major cities of Sharq al-Andalus—Murcia, Valencia, and Játiva—with two other important scholars, Abū ʿAlī Ibn ʿArīb (discussed further below) and Ibn Ḥubaysh (d. 584/1188). Ibn Ḥubaysh was from Almería and left his city after the Christian conquest in 542/1147, settling in Ibn

57 Carmona, "El saber y el poder," 78; Ibn al-Abbār, *Takmila*, ed. Codera, 52–53, no. 174.
58 Carmona, "El saber y el poder," 93–98.

Mardanīsh's territory in the town of Alcira, where he worked as imam, preacher (*khaṭīb*), and inspector of judgments (*ṣāḥib al-ahkām*) for twelve years.[59] Like Ibn Saʿāda, Ibn Ḥubaysh saw his importance grow in the years after Ibn al-Ḥallāl's death, and he became known as the greatest traditionist of the Islamic West.[60] Fierro has highlighted an intriguing story about how Ibn Ḥubaysh managed to escape Almería's conquest in 542/1147 without having to pay a ransom. The narrative, attested only in Arabic sources, suggests that it was the scholar's knowledge of Mediterranean history and genealogy that facilitated his escape: it was after reciting to Alfonso VII of Castile-Leon his lineage back to the Byzantine emperor Heraclius that Ibn Ḥubaysh was released.[61] This isolated narrative does not prove that the aspiring emperors of Castile-Leon sought to connect themselves to imperial forebears. But it does show that knowledge of ancient and eastern forebears was universally valued among the rulers of the western Mediterranean. Ideas about nobility and about what constituted a glorious lineage sometimes seem to have superseded the particular genealogies associated with specific religions. Pre-Islamic and pre-Christian heroic figures were venerated in both Christian and Muslim contexts, as evidenced by the circulation of narratives about figures such as Alexander the Great.[62]

59 Carmona, "El saber y el poder," 110–11; Ibn al-Abbār, *Takmila*, ed. Codera, 573–75, no. 1617. On the fascinating position of *ṣāḥib al-ahkām*, the post-Umayyad version of the earlier *ṣāḥib al-shurṭa*, or administrator in charge of the police and market inspectors, see Christian Müller, who describes this position in the eleventh century and beyond as a kind of non-qāḍī judge: Müller, "Administrative Tradition and Civil Jurisdiction of the Cordoban *Ṣāḥib al-Aḥkām*," *Al-Qanṭara* 21, no. 1 (2000): 57–84. On the Almoravid use of this institution, see Rachid El Hour, "Le *ṣāḥib al-aḥkām* à l'époque almoravide," *Al-Andalus Magreb* (Universidad de Cadiz) 8–9 (2000–2001): 49–64.

60 Ibn al-Abbār, *Takmila*, ed. Codera, 573–75, no. 1617.

61 Maribel Fierro, "Heraclius in al-Andalus," in *The Study of al-Andalus: The Scholarship and Legacy of James T. Monroe*, ed. Michelle Hamilton and David Wacks (Cambridge, MA: Harvard University Press, 2018). Ibn Ḥubaysh settled in Ibn Mardanīsh's territory after 542/1147 and moved to Murcia in 556/1161, where he became one of the imams of the main mosque and a regular khaṭīb. Ibn al-Abbār called him "the last of the great traditionist imams of the Maghrib." After the Almohad conquest of Murcia, the Almohads appointed him the city's chief judge; see Victoria Aguilar, "Identidad y vida intelectual," 22. Eventually, he was incorporated into the Almohad scholarly elite, writing books commissioned by the Almohad caliph, and the future Almohad caliph al-Rashīd gave the oration at his funeral. One is left wondering what lost works a scholar of such talent and evident political flexibility might have authored for Ibn Mardanīsh during his twenty-five years in the latter's territory.

62 On medieval European visions of Alexander across genres, see George Cary, *The Medieval Alexander*, ed. D. J. A. Ross (Cambridge: Cambridge University Press, 1956); on the idea of

Like the religious scholars discussed above, men of letters both within and outside Ibn Mardanīsh's government in Sharq al-Andalus connected themselves to the greatest figures of the Maghrib and the Islamic East through chains of scholarly transmission. Biographies indicate that in many cases, scholars of literature and poets were also religious scholars and that the same men who composed verses at parties also transmitted hadith. Biographical dictionaries mention two men who served as secretary (*kātib*) for Ibn Mardanīsh. Muḥammad ibn Aḥmad ibn ʿĀmir al-Balawī, known as al-Sālimī (d. 559/1164), transmitted hadith, wrote about religious sciences and history, and also composed poetry, including a few verses preserved in Ibn al-Khaṭīb's *Iḥāṭa* that were composed at one of Ibn Mardanīsh's drinking parties.[63] ʿAbd al-Raḥmān ibn Muḥammad ibn Muḥammad al-Sulamī, known as al-Miknāsī (d. 571/1176), was a talented scholar and writer described as "the seal of eloquence in al-Andalus." He, too, worked as a secretary to Ibn Mardanīsh "and other emirs," according to Ibn al-Abbār.[64]

The biography of one of the scholars who served as a khaṭīb in Ibn Mardanīsh's territory gives a sense of the scholarly lineages and networks that facilitated and legitimated knowledge in this period. Ḥusayn ibn Muḥammad ibn Ḥusayn ibn ʿAlī ibn ʿArīb al-Anṣārī, born in Tortosa, studied Quranic readings, fiqh, Arabic lexicography, adab, and hadith in Saragossa. Ibn al-Abbār notes that he was a disciple of the poet Abū al-ʿArab al-Ṣiqillī (the Sicilian), whom he met in Tortosa when the poet was close to one hundred years old, and that Ibn ʿArīb was able to study Ibn Qutayba's *Adab al-Kuttāb* with him. According to Ibn al-Abbār, Abū al-ʿArab had received this book through an exceedingly rare chain of transmitters only five people long, beginning with the author, Ibn Qutayba, himself.[65] Ibn ʿArīb also had ijāzas in teaching the Quran, and

---

Alexander in Islamic and Persianate contexts, see Richard Stoneman, Kyle Erickson, and Ian Netton, eds., *Alexander Romance in Persia and the East* (Groningen: Barkhuis, 2012).

63 Ibn al-Khaṭīb, *Iḥāṭa*, 2:123; Carmona, "El saber y el poder," 80; Aguilar, "Identidad y vida intellectual," 22. This figure is discussed in Ibn al-Abbār, *Takmila*, ed. Codera, 213, no. 725.

64 Carmona, "El saber y el poder," 105–6, no. 29; Ibn al-Abbār, *Takmila*, ed. Codera, 567–68, no. 1605. See chapter 6 for further discussion of this figure and his service to the Almohads after Ibn Mardanīsh's death.

65 Ibn al-Abbār, *Takmila*, no. 83; Carmona, "El saber y el poder," 83–84. Ibn Qutayba (d. 276/889 in Baghdad) was of Persian descent, served the Abbasids as a judge, and wrote more than sixty books on grammar, lexicography, religious sciences, and legal theory. *Adab*

he taught Quranic readings and led the prayer in the great mosque of Almería until the Christian conquest of that city in 542/1147, at which point he moved to Murcia. Ibn Mardanīsh put him in charge of leading prayers and preaching in the great mosque of Murcia, where he alternated with Ibn Ḥubaysh and Ibn Sa'āda. Ibn'Arīb educated students in literature (adab) alongside Arabic lexicography and, most of all, in the recitation of the Quran, a skill in which Ibn al-Abbār notes he was unsurpassed in his time.

Like Ibn Qutayba, the ninth-century polymath who had served as a judge under the Abbasid caliph and whose guide for secretaries he studied, Ibn'Arīb was educated in grammar, literature, and the religious sciences and taught these subjects to new generations of scholars. For a ruler such as Ibn Mardanīsh, collecting men of knowledge like Ibn'Arīb and incorporating them into the administrative structure of his realm offered important benefits—augmenting the prestige of his houses of worship, turning his cities into centers of learning, and connecting his regime to the broader intellectual networks of al-Andalus and the East. A few intriguing hints also suggest that Ibn Mardanīsh incorporated the teaching and learning of traditional Islamic sciences into his own family. In addition to hiring the scholar Ibn Sahl to oversee Ibn Mardanīsh's son's education, mentioned above, Ibn Mardanīsh seems to have had a woman in his household who taught a canonical reading of the Quran to other learned women. Very little is known about this woman beyond her teknonym (kunya), Umm Mu'affar, and that she lived in the women's quarters of Ibn Mardanīsh's palace, but Aguilar speculates that she could have been a slave and mother to one of Ibn Mardanīsh's children.[66]

Coinage and Legitimacy

For Muslim rulers, the standard vehicles for proclaiming their authority were the khuṭba—having their names as rulers announced during the Friday prayer sermon—and *sikka*—the minting of coins in their own name. Following this pattern, Ibn Mardanīsh began minting

al-Kuttāb was addressed to secretaries and outlined all of the grammatical knowledge and skills required of a man of letters.

66 Aguilar, "Fatima, Amat al-Rahman y otras mujeres," 35.

gold dinars in 542/1147, shortly after the Almoravids left Sharq al-Andalus.[67] Coinage is an inherently conservative medium, with a bias toward continuity. Any change in the pattern of coinage is therefore significant, since it reflects the conscious choice of the ruler to present himself and his rule in a particular way. Until the rise of the printing press, coinage was one of the primary means of propaganda, and it therefore constitutes a vital source for understanding religious and political ideology.[68]

Ibn Mardanīsh's dinars began as near-duplicates of earlier Almoravid coinage, but as he developed a ruling ideology, the inscriptions on his coins changed to articulate more overt opposition to the Almohads. Although many other medieval Iberian rulers also minted gold coins, the right to do so was generally reserved for the caliph. Thus, the Umayyad emirate of Cordoba did not mint dinars until 316/929, when ʿAbd al-Raḥmān III declared himself the one true caliph of the Islamic world. A warrior prince in a small region outside of the main centers of power in al-Andalus minting his own gold coins, and especially ones as pure and heavy as Ibn Mardanīsh's, was a forceful expression of power.[69] For more than twenty-four years, he minted gold dinars and silver coins

---

67 For discussion of Ibn Mardanīsh's coinage, see Carolina Doménech-Belda, "Moneda y poder en tiempos de Ibn Mardanīš," in *Rey Lobo: El legado de Ibn Mardanīš, 1147–1172*, ed. Jorge A. Eiroa and Mariángeles Gómez Ródenas (Murcia: Comunidad Autónoma de la Región de Murcia, 2019), 116–33; Hanna Kassis, "The Coinage of Muḥammad ibn Saʿd (Ibn Mardanīsh) of Mursiya: An Attempt at Iberian Islamic Autonomy," in *Problems of Medieval Coinage in the Iberian Area*, ed. Mário Gomes Marques (Santarém, Portugal: Instituto Politécnico, 1988). Ibn Mardanīsh's coins are also presented in J. J. Rodríguez Lorente, *Numismática de la Murcia musulmana* (Madrid: Distributed by Carlos Castán, 1984), 59–79, as well as in José Ferrandis Torres, "Tesorillo de dīnāres almorávides hallado en la Alcazaba de Almería," *al-Andalus* 11 (1946): 389–94. They are all also included in Antonio Vives y Escudero's magisterial work on Andalusī numismatics, *Monedas de las dinastías Arábigo Españolas* (Madrid: Juan R. Cayón, 1893). Below I refer to the coins by the numbers assigned to them by Vives. Most of the coins discussed here are also shown in high resolution photographs on the website of the Tonegawa Collection, Madrid: http://www.andalustonegawa.50g.com/almoravids_taifas.htm.

68 See discussion of the importance of numismatic sources for political history in Jere L. Bacharach, "Signs of Sovereignty: The Shahada, Qur'anic Verses, and the Coinage of ʿAbd al-Malik," *Muqarnaṣ* 27 (2010): 1–30.

69 See the chart of the average weights of Ibn Mardanīsh's issue in Kassis, "Coinage," 223–25. Most of his dinars remained consistently close to four grams of gold, though they weighed progressively less in what Kassis calls the second and third phases of his reign, corresponding to the decline of his power. Kassis also notes that in all three phases, dinars were minted in two distinct weights, and he speculates that the slightly lighter dinars were used for paying tribute to the Christian kings of Iberia.

continuously, and Ibn Mardanīsh's production was prolific and well circulated. For generations after Ibn Mardanīsh's death, his coins remained a currency of record: ʿAlī ibn Yūsuf al-Ḥakīm, writing during the reign of Marinid sultan Abū ʿInān Fāris (r. 749–59/1349–58), two hundred years after Ibn Mardanīsh's death, reported that Ibn Mardanīsh's dinars were among the five most commonly used currencies in circulation.[70] Christian archival documents frequently refer to coins called *morabetinos lupinos*, meaning Almoravid-style gold coins of the wolf, referring to Rex Lupus. These coins were a key international currency and were commonly used to settle debts among rulers.[71] Financial agreements signed by Alfonso II of Aragon with Berenguer Reverter and Guilhem VII of Montpellier fixed the prices in morabetinos lupinos, as did an agreement with the Templars.[72]

The numismatist Hanna Kassis, whose systematic work on the coinage of this period has illuminated many of its most interesting characteristics, calls Ibn Mardanīsh the last example before the Nasrids of an Andalusī Islamic ruler who identified more closely with Iberian Christians than with North African Muslims.[73] Although Ibn Mardanīsh and other rulers who allied with Christians against North Africans have traditionally been portrayed as Iberian loyalists, Ibn Mardanīsh's coinage demonstrates justifications for power that are more complex than regional pride. In fact, by pledging allegiance to the current Abbasid caliph by name, Ibn Mardanīsh's coins broke with a four-hundred-year tradition of Iberian independence from the caliphate in Baghdad. Far from endorsing Andalusī regionalism, these inscriptions reveal an engagement with the central questions of religion and authority in an Islamic context and a willingness to transform the traditional Andalusī model to counteract the new ideology of the Almohads.

---

70 ʿAlī ibn Yūsuf al-Ḥakīm, "al-Dawḥa al-mushtabika fī ḍawābit Dār al-Sikka," ed. Hussein Mónes, *Revista del Instituto de Estudios Islámicos en Madrid* 6, no. 1–2 (1958): 121; Kassis, "Coinage," 219.

71 Felipe Mateu y Llopis, "Morabetinos lupinos y alfonsinos desde Ramón Berenguer IV de Barcelona a Jaime I de Aragón (1131–1276): Datos documentales sobre su curso en Navarra, Aragón, Barcelona, Lérida y Valencia con referencias a otras especies monetarias de igual valor," in *II Jarique de Numismatica Hispano-Árabe* (Lleida: Quaderns de l'Institut d'Estudis Ilerdencs, 1990).

72 T. N. Bisson, *Fiscal Accounts of Catalonia under the Early Count-Kings (1151–1213)* (Berkeley: University of California Press, 1984), 2:72–75, 78–81, 87–88.

73 Kassis, "Coinage," 210.

A study of Ibn Mardanīsh's coinage also shows that he presented his authority in ways that echo Almoravid norms while asserting a shift in power. Minted over the course of his rule, his coins also demonstrate his flexibility in responding to new challenges. The inscriptions on the coins indicate that although his earliest conceptions of his rulership were indebted to the Almoravids, he did not aspire to the Almoravid ruling titles. Later, as the Almohad threat grew, Ibn Mardanīsh became more overt in his opposition to the Almohads' authority, pledging explicit allegiance to the Abbasid caliph and aligning himself with the person of the caliph and the Sunnī traditions of the caliphate. Toward the end of his rule, he minted coins in the name of his successor, a practice that was in contemporaneous use throughout the Islamic world.

Ibn Mardanīsh's coinage provides evidence of both the name and the title he used and constitutes one of the most direct responses he offered to the Almohads' claim to authority. The Almoravids, like the Taifa kings before them, had acknowledged a vague "Imām ʿAbd Allāh" as the caliph on their coins. In the later years of their reign, as the Almohads emerged as rivals, the Almoravids inserted "al-ʿAbbāsī" after "al-Imām ʿAbd Allāh," to indicate their loyalty to the Abbasid caliphate. Ibn Mardanīsh would take this one step further, in a direct rebuttal of Almohad claims to the caliphate, by inserting the name of the Abbasid ruling caliph al-Muqtafī, although he misspelled the name as al-Muktafī in the first several rounds of coins he minted.[74]

Ibn Mardanīsh, his predecessors, and his rivals laid claim to varied tribal genealogies that would maximize their nobility and assert their holiness. The mahdī Ibn Tūmart and his caliphal successors linked themselves to Fatimid as well as Abbasid ancestors, northern as well as southern Arabian tribes, and both Berber and Arab forebears. Ibn Mardanīsh's supporters, too, seem to have granted him two Arab tribal affiliations, as seen earlier, and his Christian allies called him by a Latin name as well as his Arabic one. On his coinage and the tombstones of his subordinates and sister, Ibn Mardanīsh used language that

---

74 On the references to "Imām ʿAbd Allāh" in Taifa contexts, see David Wasserstein, *The Caliphate in the West: An Islamic Political Institution in the Iberian Peninsula* (Oxford: Clarendon Press, 1993), 117. It was not until 547/1152–53 that Ibn Mardanīsh's coins began calling the Abbasid caliph by his correct name, Abū ʿAbd Allāh Muḥammad al-Muqtafī (with a *qāf* rather than a *kāf*).

simultaneously borrowed Almoravid titles, portrayed him as an equal of the Abbasid caliph, and challenged the authority of the Almohads. By associating himself with the widest possible range of genealogies, a ruler could set himself up as the inheritor of every good value and every kind of holy authority—one capable of leading his followers to a perfect world.

Ibn Mardanīsh's early coins were nearly duplicates of earlier Almoravid coins, some of which were also minted in Murcia. As such, these coins declared Ibn Mardanīsh's allegiance to the (recently defeated) Almoravid regime and to the Abbasid caliph.[75] They include the testament of faith, a reference to the caliph, and the name of the ruler under whom the coins were minted—in this case, Muḥammad ibn Saʿd (Ibn Mardanīsh), who is referred to as an emir. The central legends are as follows:

Obverse:

Lā ilāha illā Allāh	There is no god but God
Muḥammad rasūl Allāh	Muḥammad is the Messenger of God
Ṣallā Allāh 'alayhi wa-sallam	Peace and blessings of God upon him
al-amīr Muḥammad	the emir Muḥammad
ibn Saʿd	Ibn Saʿd[76]

Reverse:

al-imām	the imam
ʿAbd	ʿAbd
Allāh	Allāh
amīr al-muʾminīn	Commander of the Faithful[77]

75 Hanna Kassis calls the period 542–46/1147–52 the first phase of Ibn Mardanīsh's coinage; his coins maintained basically the same form through these years. See Kassis, "Coinage," 211–12.

76 Ibn Mardanīsh minted coins with this legend and a small variation, with *Allah* above the testament of the faith, from 542/1147–48 until 546/1151–52 in Murcia and Valencia: Vives, *Monedas*, nos. 1931–1939; Ferrandis Torres, "Tesorillo," 333–34; Fuat Sezgin, *Coins and Coinage of al-Andalus* (Frankfurt am Main: Institute for the History of Arabic-Islamic Science at the Johann Wolfgang Goethe University, 2003), 93–94.

77 This legend is identical to that found on Almoravid coinage. Like Almoravid coins, Ibn Mardanīsh's coins sometimes included the letters *lām* and *kāf* under the second legend. One of his dinars, minted in Murcia in 543, has these letters (Vives, *Monedas*, no. 1933; Ferrandis Torres, "Tesorillo," 334), as does an Almoravid dīnār minted in Seville in 517/1123–24 (Vives, *Monedas*, no. 1659; Ferrandis Torres, "Tesorillo," 330).

FIGURE 3.3A-B. Ibn Mardanīsh's gold dinar of 547/1152. *Photo:* Abigail Krasner Balbale. Tonegawa Collection, Madrid.

Although Ibn Mardanīsh's coins follow the example of earlier Almoravid coinage closely, the terminology used in the legends differs in one important way. On the obverse, Ibn Mardanīsh calls himself simply *al-amīr*—prince or governor. The coins minted by the Almoravids referred to their ruler as *amīr al-muslimīn*, commander of the Muslims, a term that echoed the title used for the Abbasid caliph, *amīr al-muʾminīn*, commander of the faithful. By this linguistic trick, the Almoravids were able to present themselves as universally important while refraining from claiming the caliphate itself. Ibn Mardanīsh mirrored the language of Almoravid coinage but without claiming this specific title, settling instead for plain emir (*amīr*), which, without the second part of the *iḍāfa* construct, had no universal meaning.[78]

78 The term *amīr* has different meanings in different contexts. Used on its own, it is usually translated as prince or governor. Derived from the root *a-m-r*, it literally means someone who has authority to command or give orders. When used in the phrase *amīr al-muʾminīn*, it denotes the caliph. The latter is a title first used by the Rashīdūn caliphs in the first Islamic century, and it remained in use until the end of the Ottoman Empire. *Amīr al-muslimīn*, by contrast, was a term invented by the Almoravids, and it did not have the same long life as did the earlier term. Interestingly, the second Almohad caliph, Abū Yaʿqūb Yūsuf (r. 558–80/1163–84) used the term *amīr al-muslimīn* for the first five years of his reign, because he had usurped the throne from a brother and was not universally supported. It was only after his army's defeat of Ibn Mardanīsh at the Battle of al-Jallāb in 560/1165 and the consolidation of broader support in North Africa that Yūsuf took the caliphal title in 563/1168. See *EI*², s.v. "Abū Yaʿḳūb Yūsuf" (Ambrosio Huici Miranda).

The coin's reverse, which in Islamic coinage generally includes the name of the caliph, here has only a perplexingly vague name: "The imam ʿAbd Allāh, Commander of the Faithful." At the time, Abū ʿAbd Allāh Muḥammad al-Muqtafī li-Amr Allāh (r. 530–55/1136–60) was the reigning Abbasid caliph, and if Ibn Mardanīsh's coins were referring to him, they should have been inscribed with "al-Muqtafī." But all of Ibn Mardanīsh's coins minted between 542–46/1147–52 read "ʿAbd Allāh" instead. It was not until 547/1152–53 that Ibn Mardanīsh's coins began to name the Abbasid caliph explicitly. In minting his coins with reference to a vague ʿAbd Allāh as the imam, Ibn Mardanīsh was following earlier precedents. As David Wasserstein has shown, Taifa rulers began the practice of using such ambiguous references as a means of acknowledging a higher religious authority without explicitly pledging allegiance to the Abbasids in Baghdad. Earlier scholars believed that ʿAbd Allāh denoted a specific ruler with that name, but Wasserstein argues convincingly that the Taifa kings meant simply "a slave of God," the literal meaning of the name, and therefore used it to indicate the imam without staking an ideological claim. By such means, Wasserstein concludes, these rulers continued a tradition of allegiance to the caliphate, "but they omitted all mention of any name that might commit them to any particular dynasty or individual."[79] When the Almoravids gained power in al-Andalus, they continued minting dinars with the title ʿAbd Allāh instead of the name of the Abbasid caliph, although, unlike their Taifa predecessors, they explicitly pledged allegiance to the Abbasid caliph elsewhere.

The form of Ibn Mardanīsh's coins, too, is nearly identical to Almoravid coins, with central inscriptions in Kufic script confined within a circle and Quranic passages filling the space between the central legend and the edge of the coin. The Quranic inscriptions on the obverse were the same on both Almoravid and Mardanīshī coins. They include a passage from Quran 3:85, which reads: "Whoso desires another religion other than Islam, it shall not be accepted of him; in the next world he shall be among the losers." By including this traditional Almoravid inscription on his coins, Ibn Mardanīsh presented himself as a pious Mālikī in the tradition of the Almoravids.

79 Wasserstein, *The Caliphate in the West*, 117.

FIGURE 3.4A-B. Almoravid dinar, minted 490/1096–97, Murcia. *Photo:* Tonegawa Collection, Madrid.

In 547/1152, Ibn Mardanīsh minted a coin in Murcia that diverged slightly from the usual formula, adding the customary prayer after the name of the Prophet Muḥammad and—for the first time in al-Andalus—giving the name of the Abbasid caliph (though misspelling his *laqab* as al-Muktafī rather than al-Muqtafī).

Obverse:

Lā ilāha illā Allāh	There is no god but God
Muḥammad rasūl Allāh	Muḥammad is the Messenger of God
ṣallā Allāh ʿalayhi wa-sallam	May God honor him and grant him peace
al-amīr Abū ʿAbd Allāh	the emir Abū ʿAbd Allāh
Muḥammad ibn Saʿd	Muḥammad ibn Saʿd

Reverse:

al-imām	the imam
Abū ʿAbd Allāh	Abū ʿAbd Allāh
Muḥammad al-Muktafī [*sic*]	Muḥammad al-Muktafī [*sic*]
li-Amr Allāh amīr	li-Amr Allāh, the Abbasid
al-muʾminīn al-ʿAbbāsī	Commander of the Faithful

This coin marks the beginning of what Kassis calls the second phase of Ibn Mardanīsh's coinage (547–63/1152–68), in which he moved to "an active attack on the religious (and political) claims of the Almohads."[80] In this phase, unlike the earlier one, Ibn Mardanīsh's coins identified the imam and *amīr al-muʾminīn* he was acknowledging as the Abbasid caliph. This move to differentiate the Abbasid caliph from Fatimid or Almohad claimants to the office followed the increasing territorial expansion of the Almohads. The first five years of Ibn Mardanīsh's rule saw the Almohads rapidly conquering much of North Africa and Iberia, and in 545/1150 a delegation of Iberian emirs traveled to North Africa to pledge allegiance to the Almohad caliph ʿAbd al-Muʾmin.[81] Shortly after his compatriots' delegation submitted to the Almohads, Ibn Mardanīsh began including the Abbasid caliph's name and title on his coins.

Ibn Mardanīsh's acknowledgment of the Abbasid caliph's authority over him indicates the changing political landscape he faced in Iberia. The new legend on coins minted after nearly all of Ibn Mardanīsh's fellow Andalusī rulers had accepted the Almohads' sovereignty sent a clear message to the Almohads that he was unwilling to acquiesce to their rule and that he instead recognized the supreme authority of the Sunnī tradition embodied by the current Abbasid caliph. Given al-Andalus's long tradition of independence from the Abbasid caliphate, and the fact that even the pro-Abbasid Almoravids never included the name of the Abbasid caliph on their coins, Ibn Mardanīsh's decision to include the caliph's full name demonstrates an unprecedented and dramatic shift in the ideology of independent rulership in al-Andalus.[82]

On the new dinars, the inscription on one side praised the Prophet Muḥammad and named the minting ruler as "the emir Abū ʿAbd Allāh Muḥammad ibn Saʿd." The other side displayed a new legend, "the imam Abū ʿAbd Allāh Muḥammad al-Muktafī [*sic*] li-Amr Allāh, the Abbasid Commander of the Faithful." Though the inscription

80 Kassis, "Coinage," 214.

81 *EI*², s.v. "Al-Muwaḥḥidūn" (Maya Shatzmiller).

82 Kassis sees this use of the caliph's name and the term *al-ʿAbbāsī* as "merely symbolic." He notes that the name of the current Abbasid caliph was al-Muqtafī but stops short of asserting that Ibn Mardanīsh was indicating his support for the Abbasid caliphate. He acknowledges that the name Abū ʿAbd Allāh Muḥammad al-Muqtafī disappeared from Ibn Mardanīsh's coinage after the death of this particular Abbasid caliph in 555/1160 but seems reluctant to posit that this is the first example of an independent Andalusī ruler minting coins in the name of an Abbasid caliph. See Kassis, "Coinage," 214–15, on the appearance of the term *al-ʿAbbāsī*.

did not quite get the caliph's name right, it clearly asserted its issuer's affiliation with the Abbasid caliph in Baghdad. The addition of the teknonym (*kunya*) "Abū ʿAbd Allāh" to Ibn Mardanīsh's name in the first legend and the inclusion of both the kunya and the given name of the caliph in the second legend were significant: the combination of the two legends emphasized the shared names of the ruler and the caliph, both of whom were known as "Abū ʿAbd Allāh Muḥammad," and implied that both ruled in the name of and by the grace of God. The shared name also echoes the name of the Prophet Muḥammad, son of ʿAbd Allāh, and the name of the foretold mahdī, Muḥammad ibn ʿAbd Allāh—though in these cases ʿAbd Allāh is the father of Muḥammad, not the son as suggested by the kunya Abū ʿAbd Allāh. The Almohad mahdī Ibn Tūmart also claimed that his name was Muḥammad ibn ʿAbd Allāh. By stressing that he and the Abbasid caliph had the same names—one that mirrored but inverted the name associated with the mahdī—Ibn Mardanīsh may have been responding to Ibn Tūmart's claim. Ibn Mardanīsh's use of the kunya Abū ʿAbd Allāh would traditionally suggest that his eldest son was named ʿAbd Allāh, but none of the discussions of his children mention such a son. As noted in the previous chapter, al-Marrākushī explicitly stated that his heir Hilāl was his eldest son.[83] Its use here may have been purely ideological—a means of highlighting commonalities between the Andalusī emir and the commander of the faithful, while simultaneously echoing the earlier tradition of referring to the caliph as ʿAbd Allāh.

At some point during 547/1152, Ibn Mardanīsh's authority was challenged by two rebellions in quick succession. Little is recorded about these rebellions or about what the issues at stake may have been, but the biography of the scholar Ibn al-Faras (d. 567/1172), who would serve as one of the three rotating preachers in the great mosque of Murcia in the following decade, mentions that he left Valencia for the period 546–47/1151–52 because of these rebellions and the tremendous damage they caused the city.[84] Perhaps it was in the aftermath of the suppression of the rebellions

83 Al-Marrākushī, *al-Muʿjib*, ed. al-ʿAryān, 3:323.

84 Ibn al-Abbār, *Takmila*, ed. Codera, 227–29, no. 750; Carmona, "El poder y el saber," 103. Ibn al-Abbār's biography of Ibn al-Faras mentions two figures who rebelled against Ibn Mardanīsh: Ibn Ḥamīd and ʿAbd al-Mālik ibn Salbān (Silbān?). Huici Miranda discusses the implications of Ibn al-Abbār's brief notice of the rebellions in Valencia and suggests that Ibn Mardanīsh and Ibn Hamushk had to ask Ramon Berenguer IV for help in subduing

FIGURE 3.5. Ibn Mardanīsh's gold dinar in the name of the Abbasid caliph, 548/1153, Murcia. *Photo:* Tonegawa Collection, Madrid.

later the same year that Ibn Mardanīsh added a new phrase to the central legends of his coins, emphasizing his role as the unifier of the Muslim community.

Obverse:

Lā ilāha illā Allāh	There is no god but God
Muḥammad rasūl Allāh	Muḥammad is the Messenger of God
Yaʿtaṣimu bi-ḥabl Allāh	The emir Abū ʿAbd Allāh
al-amīr Abū ʿAbd Allāh	Muḥammad ibn Saʿd, whom
Muḥammad ibn Saʿd ayyadahu	God supports,
Allāh	holds fast to the rope of God

Reverse:

al-Imām	the imam
Abū ʿAbd Allāh	Abū ʿAbd Allāh
Muḥammad al-Muqtafī	Muḥammad al-Muqtafī
li-Amr Allāh amīr	li-Amr Allāh, the Abbasid
al-muʾminīn al-ʿAbbāsī	Commander of the Faithful

Valencia in exchange for tribute, and that this was the basis of their agreement in the same year. Ambrosio Huici Miranda, *Historia musulmana de Valencia* (Valencia: Ayuntamiento de Valencia, 1970), 3:138–39.

The new elements that Ibn Mardanīsh inserted into his coinage reflect an engagement with historical and contemporary approaches to Islamic rulership. After the testament of faith, the coins contain a phrase that ties Ibn Mardanīsh to a broad tradition of Islamic rulership and that associates him with the caliphate. The sentence, "He holds fast to the rope of God" (*yaʿtaṣimu bi-ḥabl Allāh*), is a reference to Quran 3:103, which exhorts believers to hold fast to the rope of God in order to avoid division within the umma:

> And hold you fast to God's bond [*wa-aʿtaṣimū bi-ḥabl Allāh*], together, and do not scatter, remember God's blessing upon you when you were enemies, and He brought your hearts together, so that by his blessing you became brothers. You were upon the brink of a pit of Fire, and He delivered you from it; even so God makes clear to you his signs; so haply you will be guided.[85]

The rope of God, as depicted in this Quranic verse, transformed enemies into brethren, and offered salvation to those on the edge of Hell. Unsurprisingly, this potent image was often used in close association with the caliphate. Patricia Crone and Martin Hinds have shown that Umayyad caliphs were frequently described in poetry as the embodiment of God's rope, connecting the believers to God.[86] As they suggest, the appropriation of this image in a political context implies that the believers must hold fast to the person of the ruler in order to avoid division and straying from the straight path. Thus, "whoever holds fast to this rope is saved, whoever 'scatters' loses the paths of guidance."[87] The Quranic phrase, urging the community to maintain unity through God and to avoid fragmentation, remained important politically through the Abbasid period.[88] It was also a frequent reference in Shiʿī discussions of the imamate as well, where the Prophet's cousin and

85 Quran 3:103, trans. Arberry.

86 Crone and Hinds, *God's Caliph*, 39–40.

87 Crone and Hinds, *God's Caliph*, 40.

88 The root ʿ-ṣ-*m* produced the name of the Abbasid caliph al-Muʿtaṣim ("the one who holds fast") as well as of the last Abbasid caliph, al-Mustaʿṣim ("the one who tries to hold fast").

son-in-law ʿAlī and his heirs were presented as the rope connecting God and the believers.[89]

Ibn Mardanīsh incorporated this phrase into his coin legend immediately before his name and in the third person singular indicative form, suggesting that he was the one holding fast to the rope of God. He was not claiming, as Umayyad panegyric poetry did, that he as the ruler was the rope of God; rather, he was reminding his subjects (and rivals) of his piety and of their duty to avoid division amongst themselves. In using this phrase alongside an expression of support for the Abbasid caliph, Ibn Mardanīsh was highlighting his position as a defender of the caliphate, even if he lacked official recognition from Baghdad. In doing so, he echoed the efforts of sultans and emirs across the Islamic world to justify their power through the religious aura of the caliphate, even (or perhaps especially) when separated from Baghdad by thousands of miles.

Such diffusion of power had already been theorized by al-Māwardī in his work *al-Aḥkām al-Sulṭāniyya*, written at a time when power in the Abbasid Empire was divided between the largely symbolic authority of the caliph and the practical sphere controlled by Buyid sultans. To accommodate the new political reality within the empire while ensuring the continuing unity of the community, al-Māwardī developed the concept of *imārat al-istīlāʾ*, the emirate of taking power. This theory validated all rulers who had successfully seized control over a territory as governors ruling on behalf of the caliph, regardless of whether the caliph had appointed them.[90] Two centuries later, with much of the Abbasid territory governed by a series of sultanic dynasties in the name of the caliph, this mode of taking power had become standard operating procedure. Ibn Mardanīsh's use of a phrase derived from the Quranic exhortation to remain united reveals his understanding of himself as a governor acting for the broader Muslim community, unified under the caliph. He was thus adapting a phrase with deep historical roots in the Islamic political tradition to support his reign.

Ibn Mardanīsh did not claim to be the rope of God, but by asserting that in his resistance to the Almohads he was holding fast

89 See, for example, the *ʿUyūn al-akhbār* of Idrīs ʿImād al-Dīn (d. 872/1468), discussed in Daniel De Smet, "The Prophet Muḥammad and His Heir ʿAlī: Their Historical, Metahistorical and Cosmological Roles in Ismāʿīlī Shīʿism," in *The Presence of the Prophet in Early Modern and Contemporary Islam*, ed. Denis Gril, Stefan Reichmuth, and Dilek Sarmis (Leiden: Brill, 2022), 1: 299–326.

90 Al-Māwardī, *al-Aḥkām*, 40–46. See also Crone, *God's Rule*, 232–33.

to God's rope and safeguarding the unity of the believers he was presenting himself as the bulwark of traditional caliphal power and religious authority in the Islamic West. This presentation also reminded his subjects that rebellion against him, like that which had recently occurred in Valencia, constituted rejection of the divinely mandated unity of the Muslim community under the guidance of the Abbasid caliph. The letter sent by the Almohad caliph ʿAbd al-Muʾmin to dissuade Ibn Mardanīsh from persisting in his resistance (discussed at the beginning of chapter 2) is clearly in conversation with Ibn Mardanīsh's new coinage, and we can read in the letter's urging to "hold fast to the command [*amr*] of the *mahdī*" an alternative vision of authority, according to which it is not the caliph in the East who will stop division in the umma but rather the mahdī in the West.[91] Similarly, inscriptions on the mihrabs of Almohad Marrakech included a passage from Quran 22:78, "Hold you fast to God, He is your Protector" (*wa-iʿtaṣimū bi-llāh hūwa mawlākum*), which suggested that following their rule equated to following God. What was at stake in the conflict between the Almohads and Ibn Mardanīsh was not simply territory but dueling visions of righteous authority and of the Islamic tradition.

The new inscription on Ibn Mardanīsh's coins can also be seen as a response to Almohad gold and silver coins. The use of the name of the Abbasid caliph, al-Muqtafī li-Amr Allāh, parallels and counteracts a similar name for the mahdī Ibn Tūmart that appeared on Almohad dinars and silver dirhams. Ibn Mardanīsh's coins directly challenged the conception of authority presented on Almohad coinage, and although both sets of inscriptions were largely rooted in the Quran, their respective understandings of political power and its relationship to God were

---

91 Kassis suggests that it was the dinar minted in 547/1152 that inspired the letter from the Almohad caliph ʿAbd al-Muʾmin, discussed at the beginning of chapter 2, which called on Ibn Mardanīsh to "abide by the cause of the *mahdī*, for by following in his path you shall be guided." See "Coinage," 214. It is important to note that a different word is used to mean "hold fast" in the two contexts. In the phrase "Hold fast to the rope of God" that appears in Quran 3:103, in the coinage of Ibn Mardanīsh, and in Umayyad panegyric as well as the Quranic inscriptions mentioned below, the verb is *iʿtaṣama*. In the Almohad letter, the verb used is *tamassaka*. The latter word is also Quranic, appearing in 7:171, where it refers to those who hold fast to the book, i.e., the Quran (*wa-lladhīna yumassikūna bi-l-kitāb*). Both words denote following God, but the different wording choices of the Almohads and Ibn Mardanīsh suggest differing visions of how one should follow God's precepts.

very different.[92] The central legends on the earliest Almohad gold dinars and half dinars read as follows:[93]

Obverse:

Lā ilāha illā	There is no God but
Allāh Muḥammad	God; Muḥammad is
rasūl Allāh	the Messenger of God

Reverse:

al-Mahdī imām	The Mahdī is the imam
al-umma al-qā'im	of the umma, the enactor
bi-amr Allāh	of God's command

The obverse of the dinar begins with the standard testament of faith, and the reverse declares the mahdī Ibn Tūmart to be the imam of the umma and the enactor of God's command (*al-qā'im bi-amr Allāh*). This phrase, much like a regnal title in its form, parallels the names of earlier

FIGURE 3.6A-B. Early Almohad "square in circle" gold half-dinar, minted by 'Abd al-Mu'min (r. 524–58/1130–63). *Photo:* Tonegawa Collection Madrid.

92 In studying the iterations of early Islamic coinage under Umayyad caliph 'Abd al-Mālik, Bacharach shows that the use of specific Quranic verses reflected deliberate choices on the part of rulers and thus carried important meaning. "Signs of Sovereignty," 1.

93 In addition to the half dinar pictured here, see the earliest dinar minted by 'Abd al-Mu'min ibn 'Alī (524–58/1130–63). See Miguel Vega Martín, Salvador Peña Martín, and Manuel C. Feria García, *El mensaje de las monedas Almohades: Numismática, traducción y pensamiento islámico* (Cuenca: Ediciones de la Universidad de Castilla La Mancha, 2002), 179–82.

caliphs, but its meaning transcends the traditional role of the caliph. It portrays Ibn Tūmart as enacting the will of God in inaugurating the Almohad dynasty and the caliphs who followed him as gaining their authority through his divinely sanctioned revolution. But the regnal title of the Abbasid caliph, al-Muqtafī li-Amr Allāh, also referenced God's command (*amr Allāh*), and by mentioning him explicitly, Ibn Mardanīsh's coins undermined the Almohads' claims through reference to the standard Sunnī vision of the caliphate. By using the Abbasid caliph's name, Ibn Mardanīsh was challenging the Almohads on both a political and an ideological basis.[94]

The Almohads' starkly monotheist millenarianist movement rejected many aspects of Sunnī traditionalism in favor of a literal reading of the Quran. Unlike the Almoravids, whose coinage quoted Quran 3:85, a verse commonly used by Mālikī scholars to encourage submission to God's law as propagated by the legal scholars, the Almohads inscribed on their dirhams a simple phrase that placed authority firmly in the hands of the Almohad mahdī: *Allāh rabbunā,* Muḥammad *rasūlunā, al-mahdī imāmunā*—"God is our Lord, Muḥammad is our Messenger, the mahdī is our imam."[95] In the Almohads' tripartite vision of authority as presented on their silver coins, God is first, the Prophet Muḥammad second, and the founder of the Almohad state third. In contrast to the traditional structures of the Islamic caliphate, which in the Abbasid context saw the caliph as successor (*khalīfa*) to the Prophet of God, Almohad theology presented the Almohad caliphs as successors to the mahdī, who had ushered in the Almohad revolution. Almohad coins therefore reflect an alternate vision of Islamic authority, one rooted in three levels of divine knowledge (God, Prophet, mahdī), which then legitimate the rule of the successor or caliph. This hierarchy places the ultimate authority for interpretation in the hands of the caliph.[96]

---

94 On the Quranic concept of *amr* and its meanings in Almohad contexts, see Salvador Peña Martín, "El término de origen coránico Amr Allāh ("Disposición de Dios") y el linguocentrismo trascendente islámico, en torno al siglo XII," *Anaquel de Estudios Árabes* 22 (2011): 197–224.

95 See, for example, the Almohad dirham minted in Murcia in Rodriguez Lorente, *Numismática*, 83.

96 Vega, Peña, and Feria point out, in *Mensaje de las monedas Almohades*, 267, that these three phrases could also be seen as invocations of "God, our Lord, Muḥammad, our messenger, and the *mahdī*, our imam," rather than as statements of fact. They suggest that such invocations echo repetitive Sufi *dhikrs*.

Like Almohad coinage, Ibn Mardanīsh's new inscription focused on God, ending nearly every sentence of the obverse legend with an invocation of the name of God. But the specific phrases that make up this invocation differ dramatically in Almohad versus Mardanīshī coins. Whereas Almohad dirhams included the inscriptions *al-Amr kulluhu li-Llāh* or *Lā quwwa illā bi-Llāh* ("The whole matter belongs to God"; "There is no power except in God"),[97] Ibn Mardanīsh's coins read, "[The emir] holds fast to the rope of God." These are all Quranic phrases,[98] but their implications are different, particularly on coinage. In his choice of words, Ibn Mardanīsh was referring to the traditional idea of the Sunnī caliphate as holding the community together under God, while the Almohad legend emphasized the power of God and the Almohads' direct connection to him through the mahdī and thus justified the reorganization of politics under this new form of authority.[99]

The Abbasid caliph al-Muqtafī died in 555/1160, but Ibn Mardanīsh's coins continued to refer to him by name until 557/1161–62, when the legends on his coins reverted to the earlier model, pledging allegiance to an "Imām ʿAbd Allāh, *amīr al-muʾminīn*" but now adding "al-ʿAbbāsī," as on the coins with al-Muqtafī's name, to specify that it was still the Abbasid caliph whom Ibn Mardanīsh recognized as the imam, even if he did not identify the caliph by name.[100] Given the two-year delay, it is possible that Ibn Mardanīsh did not initially know the name of the new caliph; alternatively, he may now have seen a vague allegiance to the Abbasids, in the style of his Taifa and Almoravid predecessors, as a sufficient counterpoint to the Almohads' caliphal claim.

In 564/1168–69, Ibn Mardanīsh began issuing coins in the name of his son Hilāl. These coins inaugurated what Kassis calls the third and final phase of Ibn Mardanīsh's coinage, which would last until his death in 567/1172. In these last years of his reign, Ibn Mardanīsh's dinars became debased, weighing closer to two grams than to the usual four.[101]

97 See the example in Rodriguez Lorente, *Numismática,* 83.

98 The first Almohad phrase is from Quran 3:154, the second from 18:13.

99 Vega, Peña, and Feria devote several chapters to the meaning of *al-amr* in Almohad numismatic inscriptions. Among other explanations, they suggest that *al-amr kulluhu li-Llāh* constitutes both a synthesis of the revolution, with its basis in the Quran, and an expression of the Almohad dynasty's ambitions for universal justice under God. See *Mensaje de las monedas Almohades,* chaps. 2 and 4, especially 159.

100 Vives, *Monedas,* nos. 1952 and 1956; Rodriguez Lorente, *Numismática,* nos. 68–75, 62–63; Kassis, "Coinage," 222.

101 Kassis, "Coinage," 225.

On both his dinars and his dirhams, the obverse legend returned to an earlier pattern, starting with the testament of the faith, omitting any reference to the rope of God, and ending with the following: "The emir Muḥammad ibn Sa'd, his heir [*walī 'ahdihi*] Hilāl."[102] This phrase indicated that Ibn Mardanīsh designated Hilāl as his successor. The phrase had been used in earlier periods of Islamic history to identify the future caliph while his predecessor was still living. Beginning in Umayyad Damascus, future caliphs were described on coins as *walī al-'ahd*, "the holder of the pact of allegiance" (bay'a), and the same general language appeared on the coins of the dying dynasty at the time of the dissolution of the Umayyad caliphate of Cordoba.[103] It was somewhat less common for an emir to designate his successor in this way. Indeed, since few emirs minted gold dinars in their own name before the twelfth century, few had the opportunity to declare their successors in that medium. Even once powerful noncaliphal leaders began to mint their own coins in the waning years of the Abbasid caliphate, the practice of naming a successor remained relatively rare, since it seemed to underline the monarchical, hereditary inheritance of power for which the Umayyads were most frequently criticized. But, like in many other aspects of Ibn Mardanīsh's coinage, there was Almoravid precedent for this choice: 'Alī ibn Yūsuf ibn Tashufīn, Almoravid ruler from 500–37/1106–43, indicated on a coin minted in Almería in 537/1142 that his son Tashufīn would succeed him by adding a line to his standard inscription, "his heir, the prince Tashufīn" (*walī 'ahdihi al-amīr Tashufīn*).[104]

---

102 This legend was used on coins minted in Murcia between 564–66/1168–71. See Vives, *Monedas*, nos. 1964, 1965, 1966, 1967, 1968; Rodriguez Lorente, *Numismática*, nos. 76–80, 64–65; Kassis, "Coinage," 222.

103 For a number of examples, see José Lafuente Vidal, "El tesoro de monedas árabes de Elche," *Boletín de la Real Academia de la Historia* 96 (1930): 846–56. On pp. 850–51, Lafuente mentions the coin of the Cordoban caliph Sulaymān (r. 400–407/1009–16), minted in al-Andalus and Madīnat al-Zahrā' in 400/1009–10, which authorized his son Muḥammad as his heir (*walī al-'ahd*). See images and discussion of the same coins in Antonio Medina Gómez, *Monedas hispano-musulmanas* (Toledo: Instituto Provincial de Investigaciones y Estudios Toledanos, 1992), 145–47. The same phrase was also used by the puppet-caliph Hishām II (r. 366–99/976–1009, 400–403/1010–13) to appoint his son Yaḥyā as his successor (see Lafuente, "Tesoro," 852), and by the Hammudid governor of Ceuta, 'Alī, pretender to the Cordoban Umayyad caliphate in 407/1016 (Medina Gómez, *Monedas*, 148–51). These cases seem to follow the pattern of the same phrase being used on Damascene Umayyad coins and Abbasid coins.

104 Almoravid gold dinar, minted in Almería, 537/1142. National Museum of Antiquities and Islamic Art, Algiers, inv. no. II.N.268.

Figure 3.7. Late dirham of Ibn Mardanīsh, without caliph's name, and with his heir Hilāl (564–67/1168–72). *Photo:* Tonegawa Collection, Madrid

In the years immediately preceding Ibn Mardanīsh's introduction of *walī ʿahdihi*, this phrase was also in use on the other side of the Islamic world, in Saljuq Iraq. In the 550s/1150s, the Saljuq ruler of Iraq minted coins that pledged allegiance to the Abbasid caliph al-Muqtafī and referred to the emir's successor as *walī ʿahdihi.*[105] Ibn Mardanīsh picked up the phrase in his coinage in the 560s/1160s, but from the first coins he minted with his son Hilāl's name, he dropped the specific name of the Abbasid caliph and returned to the generic title "ʿAbd Allāh" that he had used for the caliph on his earlier coins. His coins thus reverted to the form of Almoravid and Taifa coinage, but with an added suggestion of universal authority. Like the Umayyad caliphs of yore, the Almoravid *amīr al-muslimīn*, and the Saljuq sultans to the east, Ibn Mardanīsh felt confident enough in his power to designate his son as his successor and the recipient of a future bayʿa. One rare coin survives that shows that Ibn Mardanīsh may have turned to Almohad models in his last years as well: a silver dirham, inscribed like his gold dinars with the name of his successor Hilāl, but without any mention of the Abbasid caliph, and in the form familiar from Almohad dinars. A circle with a square balanced within, the dinar's form incorporates the star and beaded ornament of many

105 Coins minted in Iraq in the 550s/1150s designate the future governor of Iraq as *walī ʿahdihi*. See *EI*², s.v. "Saldjūḳids" (R. E. Darley-Doran).

of Ibn Mardanīsh's gold coins, but with its simple Kufic inscription "God, there is no god but [he], Muhammad is the Messenger of God," seems to echo Almohad coins.[106] Perhaps it was at this point that Ibn Mardanīsh began to contemplate the submission of his children to the Almohads, and sought, through this coin, to signal a rapprochement with his rivals.[107]

Ibn Mardanīsh's coins articulated a direct challenge to the Almohad vision of society. They staked an ideological claim that countered the increasing power of the Almohad caliphate, incorporated very early Islamic conceptions of political power (such as the concept of the rope of God), and undermined the Almohads' assertion of universal authority through reference to the Abbasid caliph. Ibn Mardanīsh's coins designated his successor in language used by caliphs and emirs on the other side of the Islamic world. By continuing the use of the Almoravid motto (Quran 3:85), Ibn Mardanīsh located himself in a Mālikī tradition with deep roots in the Maghrib. But his later coins presented him explicitly as a ruler fighting for God and supported by God—claims that went beyond those implied in Almoravid coinage. By adopting a characteristically Almoravid legend as well as the Almoravids' support of the Abbasids while simultaneously associating himself with the authority of the caliph as one who holds fast to the rope of God, Ibn Mardanīsh both perpetuated and surpassed Almoravid political forms. His coins show that he adapted elements of the Islamic tradition to craft his own ideological claim to power.

Like many other scholars of the period, Kassis presents Ibn Mardanīsh as a protonationalist who prioritized his regional identity over Islam. Kassis writes that Ibn Mardanīsh "placed his highest priority . . . on the preservation of his Andalusian identity, even at the cost of allying

106 The star motif that appears on many of Ibn Mardanīsh's coins may be a play on his name, Muḥammad ibn Saʿd, since *saʿd* means a star that is a good omen. Stars also appear on the earliest coins minted in early Islamic al-Andalus, perhaps as a reference to Hesperis, the evening star, which the Romans associated with Iberia. The connection between the symbol of the star and Ibn Mardanīsh's regime is emphasized on his tiny fractional dirhams, known by the Almoravid term *quirate*. On an undated half-quirate coin held at the Tonegawa collection, a six-pointed star adorns the obverse and an inscription that reads "The Emir Muhammad ibn Saʿd" is on the reverse. A tiny, undated quarter-quirate in the same collection has the same six pointed star, but on the obverse says simply "Saʿd."

107 Tonegawa Collection, Madrid.

FIGURE 3.8A-B. Almohad style silver dirham of Ibn Mardanīsh (undated). *Photo:* Tonegawa Collection, Madrid.

himself with the Christians against non-Andalusian Muslims."[108] Although Kassis sees Ibn Mardanīsh's articulation of political power as focused on the primacy of al-Andalus rather than the umma, Ibn Mardanīsh's coins reveal an engagement with the broader question of who had the right to lead the Muslim community. He broke with Andalusī precedent to support the Abbasid caliph and challenged the Almohads not along regional or ethnic lines but on the basis of their religious and political ideology. He did so by using legends borrowed from the Almoravids, another North African Berber regime—an unlikely move had his motivation been primarily regional. In this context, the alliances with Christians that supported Ibn Mardanīsh against the Almohads, discussed in chapter 5, can be seen not as evidence of the triumph of an Iberian regional identity but instead as one more

108 Kassis, "Coinage," 217. On this nineteenth- and twentieth-century Spanish nationalist reading of Ibn Mardanīsh and other Andalusī rulers, see chapter 7. Kassis argues that this regionalism was also visible in the works of Ibn Ḥazm (d. 456/1064) and Ibn Bassām al-Shantarīnī (d. 543/1147), and that it was opposed by important judges such as Abū al-Walīd al-Bājī (d. 474/1081). However, the regional pride in al-Andalus that can be seen in the works of these scholars is not equivalent to nationalism, an entirely modern concept, nor to a rejection of Islam, a suggestion that would have scandalized these scholars and judges. Kassis in fact refutes the claims by other modern-day scholars that Ibn Mardanīsh was not Muslim or held Christian loyalties, but sees regional or "Andalusian" pride as central to his opposition to the Almohads.

means of attacking the ideology of the Almohads. In a universe with multiple claimants to supreme religious and political authority, it was often easier to make alliances across religious lines than with coreligionist rivals. For Ibn Mardanīsh, Christian support was crucial in his quest—visible in the shifting inscriptions on his coins—to counter the Almohads' new vision of the caliphate with a return to the Sunnī traditions of the Umayyad and Abbasid dynasties.

Chapter 4

Material Genealogies and the Construction of Power

Al-Dhahabī, writing in the fourteenth century but drawing on a report from a twelfth-century author, said that Ibn Mardanīsh "was busy bringing together those who could make machines of war, buildings, and delicate works of adornment, and he dedicated himself to constructing amazing citadels and great paths and gardens."[1] Many of these buildings, works of adornment, citadels, and gardens have survived to the present day, albeit in partial form, and they offer their own perspective on Ibn Mardanīsh's ruling culture. Like his genealogical claims, Ibn Mardanīsh's material culture related him to powerful predecessors in al-Andalus and beyond. And like the scholars he assembled in his cities, his architecture expressed an authority derived through chains of transmission that linked the Islamic West and East. Constructing buildings and transforming the landscape provided Ibn Mardanīsh with an immediate way to present his authority to his subjects and to distinguish himself from his rivals, the Almohads. The particularities of the conflict between the Almohads and Ibn Mardanīsh, especially their differing attitudes toward earlier caliphal traditions and their theological arguments over materiality and

1 Muḥammad b. Aḥmad al-Dhahabī, *Siyar aʿlām al-nubalāʾ*, ed. Shuʿayb al-Arnāʾūṭ (Beirut: Muʾassasat al-Risāla, 1985), 20:240–42, no. 156.

abstraction, meant that the built environment became a crucial ideological tool for both sides in the battle.

The western Mediterranean in the twelfth century was full of upstarts and parvenus who sought to legitimate their power through elaborate building projects, and it is in this context that Ibn Mardanīsh's massive cultural programs should be seen. Later references to the violence on which his building projects depended, such as Ibn al-Khaṭīb's fourteenth-century narrative about a man forcibly conscripted into building for Ibn Mardanīsh after being unable to pay his extralegal taxes, should be read critically.[2] But such narratives reflect the later perception that Ibn Mardanīsh's building projects were massive in scale and that they must have cost vast sums of money and required considerable labor. In the fourteenth century, surveying the constructed landscape of his native North Africa and beyond, Ibn Khaldūn would conclude that the monuments of a dynasty are proportionate to the dynasty's power, geographic reach, and magnificence.[3]

Ibn Mardanīsh's Almohad rivals were engaged in a similar process, constructing mosques and fortifications in the cities they conquered in North Africa and al-Andalus. So, too, were his contemporaries in Castile and in Sicily. All of these building projects elaborated on representations of power that were in use in the western Mediterranean and introduced new combinations of materials and motifs to articulate their makers' own claim to sovereignty. In collaboration and competition with one another, the new dynasties and rulers of the twelfth century created gardens, waterways, palaces, and houses of worship that would transform the landscapes and architecture of their regions. In the next two chapters, I explore how these forms could travel via alliances or by conquest, expressing affiliation or resistance. In this chapter, I focus on Ibn Mardanīsh's cultural program of legitimation. It is vital to remember that his project competed with similar construction projects throughout the western Mediterranean and often explicitly alluded to them, or to the luxury objects traded from distant places in his ports.[4] In their

2 Ibn al-Khaṭīb, *al-Iḥāṭa,* 2:70–74.

3 Ibn Khaldūn, *The Muqaddimah: An Introduction to History—Abridged Edition,* trans. Franz Rosenthal (New York: Pantheon Books, 1958) chap. 16, "The Monuments of a Given Dynasty Are Proportionate to Its Original Power," 143–46.

4 As Margaret Graves has recently shown, portable objects frequently explicitly alluded to architecture, and vice versa, and may have served as a conduit for the transmission of motifs. See Graves, *Arts of Allusion: Objects, Arts, and Ornament in Medieval Islam* (Oxford: Oxford University Press, 2018).

forms, techniques, and materials, these buildings advanced arguments about the performance of rulership, the relationship between religious and temporal authority, and the legitimacy of earlier caliphal traditions.

In assessing the architecture and cultural production of Ibn Mardanīsh's court, one is faced with several problems. The first is the challenge of working with archaeological sites in varied states of conservation and with fragmentary materials, many excavated decades ago and dispersed to numerous regional and national collections. Ibn Mardanīsh's structures have been relatively understudied, in part because of their poor state, but the pioneering work of Julio Navarro Palazón and Pedro Jiménez Castillo in excavating Ibn Mardanīsh's sites and reconstructing elements of his structures from earlier excavations and museum collections has made further study of them possible.[5] It is perhaps because of these challenges that the art and architecture of Ibn Mardanīsh are often assimilated into those of his predecessors, successors, and rivals. Manuel Casamar Pérez called Ibn Mardanīsh's Castillejo de Monteagudo "the finest example of Almoravid architecture" on the Iberian Peninsula, even though, as will be shown, its most particular features are shared only by other Mardanīshī buildings.[6] Similarly, scholarship on the Qurans produced by the Banū Ghaṭṭūs family largely under Ibn Mardanīsh's authority (though the family endured later under the Almohads as well) categorizes their work as Almohad, and discussions of "Almería silks" tend to classify these silks as Almoravid, even though many of these textiles were created long after the end of the Almoravid

---

5 My debt to Navarro and Jiménez's excavations and publications will be clear from the footnotes throughout this chapter. Among their many publications, two overviews of Ibn Mardanīsh's architecture are worth noting at the outset: Julio Navarro Palazón and Pedro Jiménez Castillo, "Arquitectura mardanisí," in *La arquitectura del Islam occidental*, ed. Rafael J. López Guzmán and Pierre Guichard (Barcelona: Lunwerg, 1995); Julio Navarro Palazón and Pedro Jiménez Castillo, "La arquitectura de Ibn Mardanīš: Revisión y nuevas aportaciones," in *La Aljafería y el arte del Islam occidental en el siglo XI*, ed. Gonzalo Borrás Gualís and Bernabé Cabañero Subiza (Saragossa: Institución Fernando el Católico, CSIC, 2012). In addition, the recent exhibition of over two hundred pieces associated with Ibn Mardanīs at the Museo Arqueológico de Murcia ("Rey Lobo: El Legado de Ibn Mardanish," June–November 2019), curated by Jorge A. Eiroa and Mariángeles Gómez Ródenas, produced a magisterial catalogue with information about all of the fragments usually dispersed across multiple institutions and essays by archaeologists, art historians and textual scholars. *Rey Lobo: El legado de Ibn Mardanīš, 1147–1172*, ed. Jorge A. Eiroa and Mariángeles Gómez Ródenas (Murcia: Región de Murcia, 2019).

6 Manuel Casamar Pérez, "The Almoravids and Almohads: An Introduction," in *Al-Andalus: The Arts of Islamic Spain*, ed. J. D. Dodds (New York: Abrams, 1992), 76–77.

dynasty.[7] Scholars have recently argued that the vast number of archaeological sites associated with Ibn Mardanīsh in the region of Murcia would be difficult to construct in his relatively brief rule, and have argued they should be attributed to a wider time period.[8]

How, then, are scholars to assess the art and architecture associated with Ibn Mardanīsh in relation to his Almoravid predecessors and his Almohad successors? All three regimes used craftsmen and architects trained in the same places, and all existed in the same cultural milieu of the interconnected western Mediterranean. As early as 1949, in his survey of the art of the Iberian Peninsula, Leopoldo Torres Balbás noted that in the late twelfth and early thirteenth centuries, al-Andalus and North Africa formed "an artistic unity, as well as a political one."[9] In spite of their different ideologies, the Almohads continued many of the forms of their Almoravid predecessors, using muqarnas domes, cursive inscriptions, and scallop shells alongside densely carved stucco panels in their palaces and mosques. The same craftsmen likely worked for each dynasty, moving between cities and facilitating artistic and cultural continuity across the Strait of Gibraltar. Given the relative ease of perpetuating earlier forms and the inertia of cultural expectations regarding what a mosque or a palace should look like, the ruptures that exist are significant.

Focusing on these ruptures offers fascinating insights into how architecture and material culture could express theological and political ideas. The differences between the buildings constructed by the Almohads and those of Ibn Mardanīsh, discussed further below, reflect their distinct attitudes regarding materiality, representation, the caliphate, and the behaviors and forms that are licit for a Muslim ruler. I aim to integrate a specific and contextualized vision of the material culture

7 On the Banū Ghaṭṭūs, see Élisabeth Dandel, "Ibn Gaṭṭūs: Une famille de copistes-enlumineurs à Valence (Espagne)," *Histoire de l'art* 24 (1993): 13–24. On "Almería silks," see D. G. Shepherd, "A Treasure from a Thirteenth-Century Spanish Tomb," *Bulletin of the Cleveland Museum of Art* 65, no. 4 (1978): 111–34; Cristina Partearroyo, "Almoravid and Almohad Textiles," in Dodds, *Al-Andalus*. The problem of Almería and its silks, as well as the "Almohad" Qurans of the Banū Ghaṭṭūs, are discussed further in chapters 5 and 6.

8 Alfonso Robles Fernández, for example, argues that the architecture attributed to Ibn Mardanīsh should be reassessed as belonging to a much broader period stretching from the early twelfth century under the Almoravids to the period of the Castilian protectorate in the later thirteenth century. See "Estudio arqueológico de los palacios andalusíes de Murcia (ss. X–XV): Tratamiento ornamental e influencia en el entorno" (PhD diss., Universidad de Murcia, 2016).

9 Leopoldo Torres Balbás, *Ars Hispaniae: historia universal del arte hispánico*, vol. 4, *Arte Almohade, Arte nazarí, Arte mudéjar* (Madrid: Plus-Ultra, 1949), 14.

of Ibn Mardanīsh's realm into an examination of his ruling project. Placing his architecture in local, regional, and broader Islamic frameworks enables moving beyond traditional center-periphery models of the art history of al-Andalus and North Africa, instead highlighting the many networks along which goods, ideas, and people circulated. This circulation, in turn, provided possible forms and ideologies that an upstart such as Ibn Mardanīsh seeking to assert his power could deploy. The resulting cultural program constituted a visual genealogy, legible to varying degrees to those who visited his court, that connected the ruler to local forebears, distant leaders, and political and religious ideologies.

I begin with the material culture of the Almoravids and its commonalities with other dynasties seeking power through connection to the Abbasids during the time of the "Sunnī revival," a name given to this historical period, when new groups of non-Arab Muslims emerged in support of the Abbasids.[10] The art and architecture produced during the Sunnī revival of the eleventh and twelfth centuries featured remarkably similar forms across the expanse of the Islamic world, and Almoravid art shares important commonalities with the art of the late Abbasids, the Ghaznavids, the Saljuqs, and their successors in the East, including the use of complex geometric patterns, cursive inscriptions, and muqarnas.[11]

Ibn Mardanīsh inherited—and transformed—precisely this visual model and ideological project from the Almoravids. I turn to Ibn Mardanīsh's architecture, focusing specifically on the fragmentary remnants of Ibn Mardanīsh's smaller palace, Dār al-Ṣughrā, and the most exceptional surviving element of his architectural program, its painted muqarnas ceiling. I explore some of the objects and spaces around the Mediterranean that may have inspired this palace's form and the

---

10 The term *Sunnī revival*, from the Arabic *iḥyā al-Sunna*, was coined by George Makdisi in his 1973 chapter "The Sunnī Revival." More recently, scholars such as Jonathan Berkey have suggested that this period should instead be understood as one of Sunnī "homogenization." See Berkey, *The Formation of Islam* (Cambridge: Cambridge University Press, 2003), 189–202.

11 For studies of the art-historical dimensions of this period, see Tabbaa, *Transformation of Islamic Art*; Gülru Necipoğlu, *The Topkapı Scroll: Geometry and Ornament in Islamic Architecture; Topkapı Palace Museum Library MS H. 1956* (Santa Monica, CA: Getty Center for the History of Art and the Humanities, 1995), 101. Most recently, Stephennie Mulder has argued against a dichotomous view of Sunnī versus Shiʿī architecture and has highlighted the flexibility and multivalence of architecture produced by the Sunnī dynasties of the eleventh and twelfth centuries for both Sunnī and Shiʿī subjects. See Stephennie Mulder, *The Shrines of the ʿAlids in Medieval Syria: Sunnis, Shiʿis and the Architecture of Coexistence* (Edinburgh: Edinburgh University Press, 2014).

content of its paintings. But this chapter is not only about iconography and its movement across time and space. It is also about affiliation, and about how connections to rulers and dynasties near and far facilitated the transmission of art, architecture, objects, people, and ideas. Just as Ibn Mardanīsh minted coins that made his support for the Abbasid caliph in Baghdad explicit, he embarked on building projects that incorporated more eastward-looking iconography than any earlier structures had. I argue that his architecture should be seen not only as an expression of allegiance to the Abbasid East but as a visual marker of the broader structure of power in the eleventh- to twelfth-century Islamic world.

Instead of seeing the art and architecture associated with the Sunnī revival as radiating from the centers to the peripheries, I argue we should read these forms, which appear first on the edges of the Islamic world, as evidence of the wealth and power of the newly Muslim peoples who mobilized to support the Abbasid caliphate. In other words, power flowed from the edges to the imperial center, granting the Abbasid caliphate a resurgence. The architecture of this power is reflected across the Islamic world, and it destabilizes the paradigm of center and periphery through which it has usually been understood.

Muqarnas, Baghdad, and the Question of the Sunnī Revival

The Abbasids faced significant challenges in the eleventh century. The Fatimid caliphate in Cairo was growing increasingly powerful, espousing a Shiʿī vision of authority and becoming the economic center of the Mediterranean world and beyond. In the Abbasid imperial heartlands of Iraq and Iran, the likewise Shiʿī Buyid family administered the empire in the caliph's name but in practice divested the caliphate of much of its real power. The Abbasid caliph regained significant authority in the century that followed, as newly Muslim groups asserted their Sunnī legitimacy by extending military and ideological support to the caliphate. After more than a century of declining Abbasid power, the Almoravids, like their counterparts to the east, thus helped make the Abbasid caliph relevant again.

The Almoravids, like the Ghaznavids and Saljuqs, were upstarts and relative newcomers to Islam. Affiliating themselves with the Abbasids served to legitimate their authority. Their coins made reference to "the Abbasid Imām ʿAbd Allāh," and as we saw in chapter 1, they sought official permission to rule in the name of the Abbasid caliph.[12] They also employed a series of architectural innovations that has been connected to support for the Abbasid caliphate. Yasser Tabbaa and Gülru Necipoğlu have both made the case that muqarnas, monumental cursive inscriptions, and knotted strapwork patterns served as symbolic links to Baghdad. In the eleventh century, as non-Arab dynasties sought to establish their Sunnī legitimacy, a remarkably uniform set of motifs spread across the Islamic world. For the Almoravids, much as for the Saljuqs in the east, using these hallmarks of cutting-edge architecture may have constituted a visual pledge of allegiance to the imperial center.[13] In Necipoğlu's words, "It was as if the ideological alliance between the Abbasids and the semi-independent Sunni rulers of the decentralized medieval Islamic world was expressed through the rapid dissemination from Baghdad of emblematic signs that acted as a semiotic bond visually uniting distinct regions."[14]

In the section that follows, I will focus on muqarnas in the Islamic west, in order to suggest the possibility that these symbols of Abbasid power may have moved in more than one direction. That is, rather than moving from the imperial center to the peripheries of the Islamic world, these symbols, and the power they encoded, may have ebbed and flowed from multiple centers, to and from the caliph in Baghdad. Like the theories developed by al-Māwardī and al-Ghazālī, discussed in chapter 1, that changed the concept of the caliphate to accommodate the newly powerful scholars and military men who asserted themselves in the Islamic Middle Period, perhaps the art and architecture of the Abbasids was transformed by the newly powerful centers in the far east and far west of the Islamic world.

The widespread presence of the architectural hallmarks of the Sunnī revival in far-flung regions of the empire such as North Africa where new dynasties pledged fealty to the Abbasids suggests an inversion of the traditional way of understanding this architecture: rather than radiating out from Baghdad to the edges of the empire, these signs appear to have traveled from edge to center as part of the ideological support provided by non-Arab dynasties for the tradition of the caliphate. The fact that

12 Lévi-Provençal, "Titre souverain"; Viguera Molíns, "Cartas de al-Gazālī."

13 Tabbaa, *Transformation of Islamic Art*; Necipoğlu, *Topkapı Scroll*. For further discussion of Almoravid art in this context, see A. Balbale, "Bridging Seas of Sand and Water: The Berber Dynasties of the Islamic Far West," in *A Companion to Islamic Art and Architecture*, ed. F. B. Flood and G. Necipoğlu (Hoboken, NJ: Wiley-Blackwell, 2017).

14 Necipoğlu, *Topkapı Scroll*, 108.

these forms are found on the eastern and western edges of the empire at a very early date implies rapid dissemination across the whole empire, no doubt including the imperial center, perhaps even mobilized by actors in Baghdad. But in a period in which the edges of the empire clearly transformed the imperial center in countless other ways, as, for example, through the Saljuqs' drive to construct madrasas, one cannot assume that the direction of architectural innovation could only be from Baghdad to North Africa, and not the reverse.

In fact, the earliest known examples of muqarnas are from the edges of the Islamic world, and from North Africa in particular. Scholars have suggested that the progenitors of muqarnas were the tripartite squinches used beginning in the tenth century at the interior corners of buildings in Iran to mediate between square walls and a dome.[15] In the eleventh century, these forms began to be deployed as a freestanding architectural element, separate from the wall, forming complex layered series of stalactite-like shapes that could fill a vault or dome. The very earliest uses of muqarnas cells have been documented in the Manār palace of the Qalʿat Banī Ḥammād in central Algeria (ca. mid-eleventh century), in excavations of late-eleventh-century Nishapur, and in the carved stucco dome of the mausoleum of Imām Dūr in Samarra (ca. 478/1085).[16] Scholars have argued about the geographic origin of this architectural form, but its early diffusion illustrates the interconnections of the broader Islamic world, implying that craftsmen or instructions for the construction of muqarnas traveled vast distances in a short period of time.[17] Whether muqarnas originated in Nishapur or North Africa or traveled there after being invented in Abbasid Baghdad, it is clearly an architectural innovation that spread rapidly across thousands of miles and had important early uses in North Africa.[18] The Almoravid domed kiosk in Marrakech, the Qubbat al-Barudiyyīn (constructed 1117),

---

15 Michel Écochard, *Filiation de monuments grecs, byzantins et islamiques: Une question de géométrie* (Paris: P. Geuthner, 1977), 65–76.

16 Alicia Carrillo Calderero, "Architectural Exchanges between North Africa and al-Andalus: The Introduction of Muqarnas," *Journal of North African Studies* 19 (2014): 68-82; Necipoğlu, *Topkapı Scroll*, 107, 120, 349; Yasser Tabbaa, "The Muqarnas Dome: Its Origin and Meaning," *Muqarnas* 3 (1985): 61–74.

17 Vicenza Garofalo argues that craftsmen proficient in producing muqarnas must have traveled through the Islamic world in this earliest period of the architectural form's use. Vicenza Garofalo, "A Methodology for Studying Muqarnas: The Extant Examples in Palermo," *Muqarnas* 27 (2010): 357–406, on the movement of craftsmen, 383.

18 On the geographic origins of muqarnas and their spread, see Tabbaa, "Muqarnas Dome"; Alicia Carillo Calderero, "Origen geográfico de los muqarnas: Estado de la cuestión," *Al-Mulk: Anuario de estudios arabistas* 5 (2005): 33–48. As early as 1931, Louis Hautecoeur argued

FIGURE 4.1. Qubbat al-Barudiyyīn, Marrakech, exterior (1117 CE). *Photo:* Abigail Krasner Balbale.

which was perhaps built over an ablutions fountain outside the Almoravids' since destroyed congregational mosque, is among the

---

that it was in North Africa that muqarnas was first developed in its fully fledged form, see "De la trompe aux 'Mukarnas,'" *Gazette des Beaux-Arts* 6 (1931): 26–51, esp. 46.

earliest surviving structures with muqarnas vaults.[19] Muqarnas would become one of the central architectural forms of the Almoravids. In the first half of the twelfth century, the Almoravid ruler ʿAlī ibn Yūsuf also used muqarnas over the central aisle of the Mosque of al-Qarawiyyīn in Fez (renovated between 528–37/1132–43) and at the base of a dome in front of the mihrab in the Great Mosque of Tlemcen (530/1136).

The Qubbat al-Barudiyyīn's cubelike structure has one or two open doorways on each side, surmounted by a series of multilobed-, keyhole-, or horseshoe-arched windows. On the top of the structure, triangular merlons like those on the roof of the Umayyad Great Mosque of Cordoba and the Fatimid al-Azhar Mosque in Cairo surround a dome that rises from the center. The inside is covered with deeply carved stucco, creating a dome that seems to hang like a canopy from the center. The dome rises from eight points, each of which is adorned with a scallop shell and rests on dense foliage of palm and acanthus leaves and pinecones. At the corners of the structure, which are not connected to the central dome, four smaller domes made of muqarnas squinches rise. A cursive (*naskhī*) inscription praising the patron, ʿAlī ibn Yūsuf (r. 500–537/1106–43), and pledging obedience to the Abbasids once ran around all four interior walls, but the Almohads largely destroyed it and only fragments survive.[20] Some elements of this structure's architecture recall earlier Andalusī and Maghribī forms, like the scallop shells and the ribbed dome, which echo the dome behind the mihrab of the Great Mosque of Cordoba, and the carved stucco vegetal ornamentation that parallels both the Qalʿat Banī Ḥammād and Taifa buildings.[21] Although some elements of this structure, such as the carved stucco vegetal ornamentation, the ribbed dome, and the scallop shells, are closely related to earlier Andalusī examples, other elements—including the muqarnas and cursive inscriptions as well as the use of four framing domes around

---

19 There is debate about the original function of the structure. Jonathan Bloom and others have argued that it was an ablution fountain for the demolished Almoravid congregational mosque, whereas Yasser Tabbaa has pointed out that its location (more than eighty feet from the mihrab wall of the mosque) makes this explanation relatively unlikely. See Bloom, "The Minbar from the Kutubiyya Mosque," in *The Minbar from the Kutubiyya Mosque*, ed. Jonathan M. Bloom et al. (New York: Metropolitan Museum of Art, 1998); Tabbaa, "Andalusian Roots and Abbasid Homage in the Qubbat al-Barudiyyin in Marrakech," *Muqarnas* 25 (2008): 133–46.

20 Tabbaa, "Andalusian Roots," 140.

21 Mariam Rosser-Owen has observed similarities between the Qubba's dome and the ribbed dome above the mihrab of the Great Mosque of Cordoba, as well as similarities in the carved stucco ornamentation; see "Andalusi Spolia in Medieval Morocco: Architectural Politics, Political Architecture," *Medieval Encounters* 20 (2014): 152–98, here 172–73.

FIGURE 4.2. Qubbat al-Barudiyyīn, Marrakech, interior of dome (1117 CE). *Photo:* Abigail Krasner Balbale.

a central dome—are new and may have been adapted from the Abbasid East.[22]

Yasser Tabbaa has argued that the Qubbat al-Barudiyyīn echoes a no longer extant dome built by the Abbasids in Mecca, known as the Bāb

22 On the eastward-looking elements, see Necipoğlu, *Topkapı Scroll*, 101; Tabbaa, "Andalusian Roots."

Ibrāhīm.[23] Drawing on a description of the Bāb Ibrāhīm by the Andalusī traveler Ibn Jubayr (d. 614/1217), Tabbaa contends that in its apparent imitation of the Abbasid dome in Mecca, the Qubba was a "symbolic homage to the Abbasid caliphate."[24] Given the Almoravids' desire for recognition from the Abbasids as rulers in their name, muqarnas may have been a central component of the Almoravids' visual articulation of their support for the Abbasids and their endorsement of Sunnī ideals. But the Almoravid use of muqarnas also followed the earliest known uses of these forms, in the Maghrib and al-Andalus, precisely the territories they would come to rule. An architectural description of the palace of the Taifa king of Almería, al-Muʿtaṣim (r. 443–84/1051–91), in the geographical work of al-ʿUdhrī (d. 478/1085) mentions an enormous reception hall with muqarnas.[25] Felix Arnold has argued that if al-ʿUdhrī's description is correct, al-Muʿtaṣim's palace incorporated the second-earliest usage of muqarnas in the Islamic world, and that the style was likely imported from North Africa, where the Qalʿat Banī Ḥammād features the oldest known use of muqarnas.[26] The Almoravids ruled Almería for half a century, beginning in 484/1091, turning it into one of their most important trading centers.[27] The elaborately ornamented

---

23 Tabbaa, *Transformation of Islamic Art.*

24 Tabbaa, *Transformation of Islamic Art*, 127.

25 Jacinto Bosch Vilá, "¿Mocárabes en el arte de la taifa de Almería?" in *Cuadernos de Historia del Islam* (Universidad de Granada) 8 (1977): 139–60; Basilio Pavón Maldonado, "El maylis del taifa al-Muʿtasim de la alcazaba de Almería: Muqarnas = muqarbas = mucarnas = almocárabes = mocárabes en el arte hispanomusulmán," *Revista del Instituto Egipcio de Estudios Árabes en Madrid* 32 (2000): 221–59.

26 Felix Arnold, *Der islamische Palast auf der Alcazaba von Almería* (Wiesbaden: Reichert, 2008), 41–50; Arnold, *Islamic Palace Architecture in the Western Mediterranean: A History* (Oxford: Oxford University Press, 2017), 161. Maurizio Massaiu's fascinating article, "The Use of *Muqarnas* in Ḥammādid Architecture: Some Preliminary Observations," in *Mapping Knowledge: Cross-Pollination in Late Antiquity and the Middle Ages,* ed. Charles Burnett and Pedro Mantas-España (Cordoba: CNERU/Oriens, 2014), 209–30, argues that the traditional dating of the muqarnas in the Qalʿat Banī Ḥammād is based in an understanding of the fall of Ḥammādids promulgated by Ibn Khaldūn, later, that is not supported by archaeological evidence and other sources. He argues the muqarnas at the Qalʿa may be as late as the Almoravid period.

27 The importance of Almería in the political and economic life of the Almoravid empire is evidenced by the number of gold dinars minted in that city. Research by Harry Hazard shows that the mint at Almería produced more dinars, in several varieties each year, during the time it was functioning, than any other mint in the Almoravid Empire. Over the entire period of Almoravid power, only the mint at Sijilmāsa, the gate to the gold routes of the Almoravids, produced more dinars. Hazard, *The Numismatic History of Late Medieval North Africa* (New York: American Numismatic Society, 1952), 15; John Hunwick, "Gao and the Almoravids: A Hypothesis," in *West African Cultural Dynamics: Archaeological and Historical Perspectives,* ed. B. Swartz and R. Dumett (The Hague: De Gruyter Mouton, 1980), 424.

Taifa palace in the city could scarcely have gone unnoticed. Even if muqarnas carried a particular association with the Abbasids, and using such forms in their own architecture served as part of the Almoravids' ideological support of Abbasid legitimacy, they also carried important local meanings.

The Almoravids were the first dynasty in the far west since the ninth-century Aghlabids to support the Abbasid caliphate, and their loyalty to the caliphate in Baghdad was all the more striking because it followed the Fatimids' and Iberian Umayyads' claiming of the caliphate for themselves. Almoravid authority was based on a strident Sunnī traditionalism, which explicitly pledged allegiance to the Abbasids and urged jihad against the Christians. The cultural production of the Almoravids, like that of semi-independent Sunnī dynasties in the East, reflected their rejection of Shiʿī power and their embrace of the Abbasids. At the same time that the Almoravids introduced forms associated with the Abbasids, they also laid claim to the heritage of the Umayyads of Cordoba through their use of spolia taken from the Umayyad monuments of al-Andalus.[28]

Almoravid architecture is often described as a fusion of North African, Andalusī, and Abbasid forms, but the traditions the Almoravids drew on were already hybrids in themselves: the art and architecture produced under ʿAbd al-Raḥmān III (d. 355/961), for example, reflected both contemporary Abbasid and Fatimid models.[29] The Taifa kings who had ruled al-Andalus shortly before the rise of the Almoravids had also produced structures that innovated on earlier traditions and contemporary rivals. The Almoravids carved stucco more deeply than previous dynasties seem to have done, as can be seen in the lower levels of the Qubba as well as in the Great Mosque of Tlemcen and the Qarawiyyīn Mosque in Fez, thus creating what Jonathan Bloom has called the "three-dimensional style," although he suggests that the style was imported from a no longer extant Cordoban tradition.[30] The Almoravids adapted and trans-

28 Mariam Rosser-Owen, "Andalusi Spolia in Medieval Morocco."

29 On the Abbasid models, see D. Fairchild Ruggles, "The Mirador in Abbasid and Hispano-Umayyad Garden Typology," *Muqarnas* 7 (1990): 73–82; see also F. Gabrieli, "Omayyades d'Espagne et Abbasides," *Studia Islamica* 31 (1970): 93–100. In ʿAbd al-Raḥmān's construction and naming of Madīnat al-Zahrāʾ, the Umayyads' palatine city, there are clear parallels to the names the Fatimids gave their mosques and palaces, based on the root z-h-r, meaning brightness, and particularly associated with Fāṭima, the Prophet's daughter, for whom their dynasty was named. Later, in Cairo, Fatimid caliph al-ʿAzīz (r. 365–86/975–96) would name his palatine complex al-Quṣūr al-Zahira. See Janina Safran, *The Second Umayyad Caliphate: The Articulation of Caliphal Legitimacy in al-Andalus* (Cambridge: Harvard University Press, 2000), 59.

30 Bloom, "Minbar from the Kutubiyya Mosque," 23.

formed the materials and techniques they encountered to best articulate their own claim to power, creating visual languages that responded to local precedents and affiliated them with distant powers. María Marcos Cobaleda has described the Almoravids' drive to create a distinct aesthetic "that would transmit all of [their] values, and that would develop into a mark of identity and of differentiation from the 'other.'"[31]

Similarly, Ibn Mardanīsh's architecture, indebted to the Almoravids, the Umayyads, the Taifa kings, and adapted from objects and spaces with origins farther afield as well, continued local traditions and incorporated the most cutting edge, international court styles. His program, like that of the Almoravids, consciously articulated his values and relationships and differentiated him from his rivals. Several of the elements employed by the Almoravids, including the deeply carved style of stucco, the use of muqarnas, and cursive inscriptions, would continue in Ibn Mardanīsh's cultural production. Ibn Mardanīsh's smaller palace in Murcia, the Dār al-Ṣughrā, includes the earliest surviving use of muqarnas on the Iberian Peninsula, a form that would become widespread in Andalusī architecture in the centuries that followed.[32] Ibn Mardanīsh's adoption of these forms is significant: like his coinage, which adapted

31 " Pudiéndose hablar de una intencionalidad clara a la hora de configurar una estética propia que transmitiera todos estos valores, y que se convertiría en un signo de identidad y de diferenciación frente al 'otro.'" María Marcos Cobaleda, "En torno al arte y la arquitectura almorávides: Contribuciones y nuevas perspectivas," in *al-Murābiṭūn (los almorávides): Un Imperio islámico occidental. Estudios en memoria del Profesor Henri Terrasse*, ed. María Marcos Cobaleda (Granada: Junta de Andalucía, 2018), 314–44, here 335–36.

32 Eiroa and Gómez argue that the Dār al-Ṣughrā was an Almoravid-period palace that Ibn Mardanīsh inherited and renovated, "El emirato de Ibn Mardanīš," 35–36. In the same volume, Alfonso Robles Fernández argues that both the Dār al-Ṣughrā and the larger palace that housed the oratory now beneath the church of San Juan de Dios were constructed under the Almoravids, since he believes Ibn Mardanīsh's military priorities took precedent over new construction during his early years in power. Robles, "Los programas ornamentales de los palacios reformados y fundados por el emir Ibn Mardanīš (1147-1172)," in *Rey Lobo: El legado de Ibn Mardanīš, 1147–1172*, ed. Jorge A. Eiroa and Mariángeles Gómez Ródenas (Murcia: Región de Murcia, 2019), 52. Robles participated in archaeological excavations in the early 2000s that have led him and his collaborators to posit at least three stages of construction at Dār al-Ṣughrā; see Indalecio Pozo Martínez, Alfonso Robles Fernández, and Elvira Navarro Santa-Cruz, "Arquitectura y artes decorativas del siglo XII: el alcázar menor de Santa Clara, Murcia (Dār aṣ-Sugra)," in A. Robles Fernández, ed., *Las artes y las ciencias en el Occidente musulmán: sabios mursíes en las cortes mediterráneas* (Murcia, Ayuntamiento de Murcia, 2007), 203–33. The debate over which buildings should be attributed to Ibn Mardanīsh is ongoing. Regardless of whether or not there was a late Almoravid building on the site, I see the decorative cohesion of remnants of the figurative paintings on muqarnas at Dār al-Sughrā and the paintings at the Oratory of San Juan de Dios as consistent with a single period of construction under Ibn Mardanīsh, and therefore follow Navarro Palazón and Jiménez Castillo's dating.

and elaborated on Almoravid models to make an even clearer show of support for the Abbasids, Ibn Mardanīsh's use of muqarnas tied him to the symbols of power in the East. At the same time, the muqarnas reflected local languages of power that would have carried more immediate resonances as well. Ibn Mardanīsh's own usage of muqarnas therefore mediates between the regional and the international, employing the most advanced architectural techniques of his day to create structures that evoked the finest local precedents and the increasingly unified international flavor of courtly culture.

In Ibn Mardanīsh's Dār al-Ṣughrā, muqarnas are used as the base for figurative painting that has connections to North Africa, Samarra, and points further east, and the architecture also incorporates deeply carved stucco with Almoravid and Abbasid precedents. Tracing the movement of these motifs across time and space, especially in the twelfth century, when scholars have found international impulses in the art of the Fatimids and the Ayyubids and have seen echoes of particular dynasties travel immense distances, yields ever-expanding spheres of influence and connection.[33] The spaces and objects that individuals built or commissioned reflected these individuals' known world and the people, places, and ideas with which they sought to express affiliation.

Palace Paintings and the Courtly Cycle

During the excavation of Ibn Mardanīsh's palace Dār al-Ṣughrā in the 1980s, Julio Navarro Palazón and Pedro Jiménez Castillo found fragments of a muqarnas ceiling, which, underneath a thin covering of plaster, contained colorful tempera paintings of figures: a woman playing a *mizmār*, or flute; a horse's head; a man with a turban, bare legs moving as if in dance; the breasts of a woman draped in red fabric; and a bearded man.[34] Hundreds of fragments were recovered, many in such

33 On the idea of an "international style of the twelfth-thirteenth century," see Sophie Makariou, "Introduction: L'Orient de Saladin" and Oleg Grabar, "L'art sous les Ayyoubides" in *L'Orient de Saladin: L'Art des Ayyoubides*, ed. Makariou (Paris: Institut du Monde Arabe, 2001). Makariou argues that Ayyubid art is deliberately international in its influences, and Grabar sees international impulses in the parallels between Sicilian and Andalusī art in the same period. Richard Ettinghausen also discussed the internationalism of art in the twelfth century in his article, "Painting in the Fatimid Period: A Reconstruction," *Ars Islamica* 9 (1942): 112–24.

34 Julio Navarro Palazón and Pedro Jiménez Castillo, "La arquitectura mardanisí," in *La arquitectura del Islam occidental*, ed. Rafael López Guzmán, (Barcelona: Lunwerg Editores/El Legado Andalusí, 1995); Navarro Palazón and Jiménez Castillo, "Casas y palacios de al-Andalus:

small pieces that any identification of figures is impossible. These fragments suggest that there was once a muqarnas dome in the central hall of Ibn Mardanīsh's lesser palace and that the interior of several of the muqarnas cells contained figures associated with what is usually called the "courtly cycle," a series of images of feasting, music, dancing, or hunting associated with the refined life of the court. The dome may once have risen above Ibn Mardanīsh's throne room or perhaps covered an open-sided pavilion in his courtyard garden.[35] This astonishing discovery made Ibn Mardanīsh's palace the site of the earliest surviving use of muqarnas on the Iberian Peninsula and one of few extant examples of figural wall paintings in Islamic architecture.[36]

The fragments that survive, like puzzle pieces, suggest lively scenes that engage with each other. Was the mizmār player, whose bold dark eyes gaze intently toward the left as her hand holds her instrument to her mouth, her cheeks painted with perfect circles of blush, looking toward the dancer whose breasts dressed in red survive? Or perhaps those legs, also surrounded by red fabric but bare to the knee, one leg lifted, belonged to another dancer? The red-turbaned man whose upper head is visible, with dark hair peeking from beneath his turban and a strong brow, looks to the left, and the other bearded man, who holds a long object in one hand, looks in three-quarter view to the right. Did they look toward each other, or toward other figures?

Siglos XII–XIII," in *Casas y palacios de al-Andalus*, ed. Julio Navarro Palazón (Granada: El Legado Andalusí, 1995).

35 The fragments of muqarnas were excavated from an area that had been the center of Ibn Mardanīsh's palace's courtyard garden, but Navarro Palazón argues that the fragments were dumped there when Ibn Mardanīsh's successor, Ibn Hūd, was constructing his own palace on the site in the thirteenth century. See J. Navarro Palazón, "La Dār aṣ-Ṣugrà de Murcia: Un palacio andalusí del siglo XII," in *Colloque international d'archéologie islamique, IFAO, le Caire, 3–7 février 1993*, ed. Roland-Pierre Gayraud, 107. For further discussion of the significance of this use of muqarnas, see the writings of Alicia Carillo Calderero, especially "Decoración tridimensional en Al-Ándalus: Introducción y uso de mocárabes," *Boletín del Museo e Instituto Camón Aznar* 104 (2009): 47–74 and "La decoración de mocárabes de la *Dār al-Ṣughrā* en Murcia: orientalismo en el arte de Ibn Mardanīš," in *Rey Lobo: El legado de Ibn Mardanīš, 1147–1172*, ed. Jorge A. Eiroa and Mariángeles Gómez Ródenas (Murcia: Comunidad Autónoma de la Región de Murcia, 2019), 68–81. Carillo Calderero speculates that the muqarnas dome fragments with figurative paintings initially surmounted a throne hall for Ibn Mardanīsh, while the muqarnas fragments with vegetal ornamentation were used in a garden pavilion from the Almoravid period, "Decoración de mocárabes," 78.

36 See further discussion of the "courtly cycle" and its use in Islamic palaces below. The most significant examples are the paintings in the so-called Umayyad "desert palaces," especially Quṣayr ʿAmra and Khirbat al-Mafjar; the Abbasid palaces at Samarra; the Fatimids' Western Palace in Cairo; and the Norman Cappella Palatina in Palermo. Later, wall paintings appear in the Alhambra and in numerous buildings in the Persianate world.

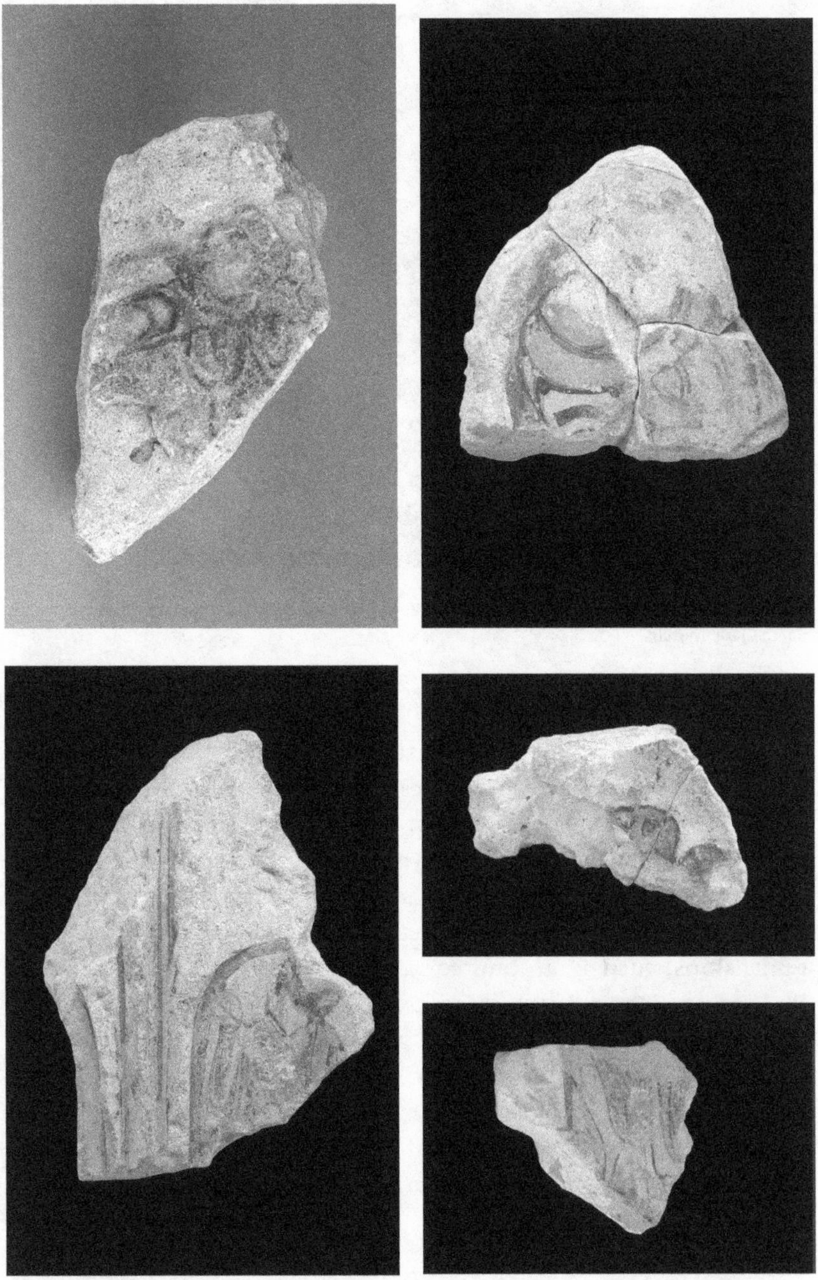

FIGURE 4.3A-E. Fragments of figural painted muqarnas from Dār al-Ṣughrā, Murcia. *Photo:* Museo de Santa Clara, Murcia.

FIGURE 4.3F. Fragment of figural painted muqarnas from Dār al-Ṣughrā, Murcia. *Photo:* Museo de Santa Clara, Murcia.

The background behind the largest human figures, like the turbaned man and the mizmār player, is a cerulean blue, and their features are outlined with a bold black brush. Other figures appear on a creamy ground, outlined with a light brown line, like the bearded man and the dancing legs, and both appear to be enclosed within a red arch. Other fragments show that the architectural structure incorporated three dimensions, curving around corners and surmounted by structures like cornices above the painted areas. Individual muqarnas cells are framed by black ribbons adorned with large white pearls. Some fragments contain no figural imagery, but instead feature creamy vegetal ornamentation arrayed across a rich red ground. Just enough of this imagery survives to gesture toward a cycle frequently called courtly or princely, defined by scenes of leisure, feasting, and hunting that rulers and their courts enjoyed.[37]

37 For an analysis of the Dār al-Ṣughrā paintings and their muqarnas support, see Alicia Carrillo Calderero, "Decoración de mocárabes;" Fatma Dahmani, "Remarques sur quelques

The technical virtuosity of the muqarnas ceiling and the vibrant paintings that would have greeted anyone entering Dār al-Ṣughrā's throne hall would have been striking to what Michael Baxandall has called a "period eye."[38] Few comparably complex cycles of imagery survive in architectural contexts from the medieval Mediterranean, and constitute a potent assertion of his court's importance. Elements of his palace's paintings find parallels in other contexts that range widely across time and space. The pearled borders that surround the interiors of the muqarnas niches in Dār al-Ṣughrā can also be found in an eleventh-century Fatimid fragment from a bathhouse in Fustat, surrounding a painting of a prince wearing a turban drinking in an arch.[39] Pearled borders are also used to frame images in palaces in ninth-century Abbasid Samarra and, moving backward in time and eastward in space, in the palaces of the Sogdians, masters of the silk roads in what is now Afghanistan, perhaps reflecting (or presaging) a lost tradition of Sasanian palace painting. Does this mean that Ibn Mardanīsh, or his architect, sought to emulate the palaces of the Sogdians, five centuries earlier, in distant Afrasiab? Surely not. But pearled borders, especially in roundels or frames that surround figurative scenes, seem to have functioned as a long-lasting imperial language, adapted from Central Asia by the Byzantines, Umayyads, and Abbasids, and deployed across much of the Afro-Eurasian landmass from the sixth century through the fourteenth. They appear on silks produced in Central Asia, Byzantium, and

---

fragments de peinture murale trouvés a Murcie," *Tudmir: Revista del Museo Santa Clara, Murcia* 1 (2009): 163–75. In the recent exhibition in Murcia in which these fragments were displayed, the curators suggested that the bearded man fragment and the dancing legs belong to the same figure, since their scale is similar and the red arch around them both seems to line up. They argue that the legs are bare and one is lifted to indicate that the figure is seated. See Carrillo Calderero, "Decoración de mocárabes," 73–75.

38 Michael Baxandall, "The Period Eye," in *Painting and Experience in Fifteenth Century Italy: A Primer in the Social History of Pictorial Style* (Oxford: Oxford University Press, 1988), 29–57.

39 The Fustat fragment is likely from before 530/1136; the Museum of Islamic Art, Cairo, inv. no. 12880. For discussion of the Fatimid tradition of painting, see Ettinghausen, "Painting in the Fatimid Period;" Ernst J. Grube, "A Coloured Drawing of the Fatimid Period in the Keir Collection," *Rivista degli studi orientali* 59, Fasc. 1/4 (1985): 147–74. Carrillo Calderero also outlines several of the buildings that use similar pearled borders, see "Decoración de mocárabes," 73. Carillo argues, against the common attribution of the painting style as Fatimid, that this tradition of courtly painting should be associated with the Abbasid east, brought to Ifrīqiya in the context of the Aghlabids and then used across the western Mediterranean in the twelfth century (80).

FIGURE 4.4. Painted fragment from a bathhouse in Fusṭāṭ, Fatimid Period, eleventh century. Museum of Islamic Art, Cairo, inv. no. 12880. *Photo:* Museum of Islamic Art, Cairo.

Islamic contexts, including those that survive from al-Andalus, and which circulated throughout Europe and Asia.[40]

Figural scenes of courtly activities, especially hunting, music making, and feasting, often framed by pearled borders, thus link courts across a broad swath of time and space, and seem to have been deployed especially frequently in throne rooms. Early scholarship on these images sought to trace their origins, often attributing them to "Eastern" (i.e., Sasanian) or "Western" (i.e., Roman) traditions, as part of the effort to

40 Knowing the precise origins of such textiles is often difficult, given common iconography, weave structures, materials, and the consistent and widespread exchange of such goods. See, for example, Leslie Brubaker, "The Elephant and the Ark: Cultural and Material Interchange across the Mediterranean in the Eighth and Ninth Centuries," *Dumbarton Oaks Papers* 58 (2004): 175–95, esp. 189–94. Víctor Rabasco García has shown that such textiles could serve as modes of transmission of motifs across vast geographies and highlights the use of these motifs in other media, including architecture, in al-Andalus. Rabasco García, "El arte textile y su impacto en la cultura visual de los Reinos de Taifas," in *Arte y producción textile en el Mediterráneo medieval,* 479–99.

situate Islamic art in the lineage of Western Art History.[41] But as Eva Hoffman has shown in the case of the Abbasid wall paintings from Samarra, using such images was potent precisely because of their wide-ranging and ancient precedents, which allowed rulers to situate themselves within a community of rulers. This cycle of images served as a visual marker of a ruler's position in a fellowship of kings that "collapsed boundaries of time and space, bringing together a continuum of great rulers, past and present, East and West, interweaving mythological, biblical, historical, and contemporary monarchs throughout ancient and medieval realms."[42]

Unfortunately, Ibn Mardanīsh's ceiling survives only in fragments, and a systematic analysis of its design and iconography is impossible.[43] Nevertheless, the pieces that survive reveal continuities with Andalusī, Maghribī, and Mediterranean models and demonstrate that their imagery constituted a potent language of power. Such images appear most frequently on portable objects: ceramics, carved reliefs, and textiles. The ubiquity of such images on portable objects produced and traded across the Mediterranean has made locating their origins difficult. Hoffman has suggested that networks of circulation and viewership formed a shared Mediterranean visual and material culture between the tenth and the twelfth century.[44] Following Hoffman, I argue that is precisely the circulation and widespread use of courtly images similar to those that appear in the ceiling of Dār al-Ṣughrā that constitutes their power. Although muqarnas ceilings with courtly scenes painted on them were rare, the ubiquity of objects decorated with similar scenes, produced

41 See, for example, Grube, "A Coloured Drawing of the Fatimid Period," which assesses the "hellenistic" form of a fragmentary drawing from the Keir collection but concludes, "It is essential to recognize, at this point, that all the scenes considered here are rendered in a style and manner clearly derived from the eastern and Abbasid, rather than the western, hellenistic tradition. . . . The debt of Fatimid painting to the painting of the Abbasid court is too well known to need further emphasizing, but it is perhaps useful to realize that what could appear as new, paying attention to the 'real life of the people,' is actually deeply rooted in an ancient tradition, and one that is eastern rather than western, and courtly rather than popular" (163).

42 Eva Hoffman, "Between East and West: The Wall Paintings of Samarra and the Construction of Abbasid Princely Culture," *Muqarnas* 25 (2008): 107–32, 123.

43 Carrillo Calderero's 2019 "Decoración de mocárabes" offers the most in depth and complete analysis of the fragments yet completed. She finds evidence of at least two workshops that produced the figurative paintings, which she believes were produced at the same time. She also argues that the vegetal decoration originally belonged to a separate part of the building from the figural paintings of the muqarnas cupula, and agrees with Robles that the vegetal ornaments could originate in an earlier, Almoravid phase of building. See 77–78.

44 Eva Hoffman, "Pathways of Portability: Islamic and Christian Interchange from the Tenth to the Twelfth Century," *Art History* 24 (2001): 17–50.

locally and traded across the sea, would have made the ceiling legible as a statement of power both local and international. Such a ceiling signified cosmopolitanism, internationalism, tradition. In evoking objects that moved, Ibn Mardanīsh's ceiling functioned as a visualization of the networks that linked courts distant in space and time.

Images of seated rulers, dancers, and musicians appear across different media, and in the tenth to thirteenth centuries are particularly associated with the Fatimids in North Africa and the Taifa kingdoms in Iberia. An early Fatimid object, a marble bas-relief from Mahdiyya, the first Fatimid capital in today's Tunisia, shows a female musician playing a mizmār for a prince.[45] The eyes of the female musician are inlaid with a silver metal that is also embedded like jewels in the prince's turban, its shimmer creating a sense of movement and liveliness within the marble, which would once have been painted for greater verisimilitude. After the Fatimids moved their capital to Egypt, such depictions of courtly entertainment continued. Their palaces in Cairo were destroyed and only fragments remain, but what survives shows scenes of hunting, feasting, dancing, and music.

In the eleventh and twelfth centuries, Fatimid shallow bowls, made using a lusterware technique that had been imported to Egypt only in the tenth century, frequently depicted similar scenes. These ceramics were of the highest value in the Mediterranean world and were used as *bacini*, or decorations, on the exteriors of Pisan churches. Lustered bowls with similar themes were also manufactured in Ibn Mardanīsh's territory. In the mid-eleventh century, the Abbadid Taifa rulers of Seville seem to have imported the technique (and perhaps craftsmen) of lusterware from Egypt, making al-Andalus the first region in Europe to master this complex process, as an explicitly royal craft.[46] Ibn Mardanīsh's territory seems to have continued this tradition, producing and exporting highly valued lusterware.[47] Some Italian bacini have been identified

45 "Bas Relief with a Prince and a Flute Player," produced in Mahdiyya, Tunisia, in the tenth or eleventh century; Museum of Bardo, Tunis, inv. no. E 16.

46 Recently excavated lusterware included inscriptions indicating that they had been produced at the command of Abbadid rulers in royal workshops in Seville, offering incontrovertible proof of a local lusterware center in al-Andalus beginning in the mid-eleventh century. See Anja Heidenreich and Carmen Barceló, "El inicio de la loza dorada autóctona en la península ibérica: Una aproximación desde sus epígrafas," in *Las artes en al-Andalus y Egipto: Contextos y intercambios*, ed. Susana Calvo Capilla (Madrid: La Ergástula, 2017), 85–110.

47 Julio Navarro Palazón, "Nuevas aportaciones al estudio de la loza dorada andalusí: el ataifor de Zavellá," in *Les illes orientals d'al-Andalus (V Jornades d'Estudis Històrics Locals), 28–30 noviembre 1985*, ed. Guillem Rosselló-Bordoy (Palma de Mallorca: Institut d'estudis Baleàrics,

Figure 4.5. Marble bas-relief with inlaid metal eyes, seated ruler and female mizmār player, Mahdiyya, Tunisia, tenth and eleventh centuries. Museum of Bardo, Tunisia, inv. no. E16. *Photo:* Abigail Krasner Balbale.

as Murcian in origin, reflecting the established trading relationship between Pisa and Sharq al-Andalus.[48] The parallels in the techniques and motifs of these ceramics are so strong that prominent Spanish archaeologists have suggested that many more of the bacini attributed to Fatimid Egypt may in fact be of Murcian manufacture.[49] Many of the lusterware bowls of the twelfth century Mediterranean depict dancers, musicians, and seated rulers, in forms similar to the fragments from Ibn Mardanīsh's ceiling.

1987), 225–38; Silvia Yus Cecilia and Mariángeles Gómez Ródenas, "El repertorio cerámico del siglo XII en la Medina *Mursiya*," in *Rey Lobo: El legado de Ibn Mardanīš, 1147–1172,* ed. Jorge A. Eiroa and Mariángeles Gómez Ródenas (Murcia: Comunidad Autónoma de la Región de Murcia, 2019), 82–93.

48 On Andalusī bacini in Pisa, see Karen Mathews, "Plunder of War or Objects of Trade? The Reuse and Reception of Andalusi Objects in Medieval Pisa," *Journal of Medieval Iberian Studies* 4:2 (2012): 233–58. As Mathews notes, the Pisan use of bacini wove between triumphalist representations highlighting the city-state's military skill in engagements like the conquest of Almería and luxurious demonstrations of its great economic power as a trading partner.

49 Navarro Palazon and Jiménez Castillo, "La Producción cerámica medieval de Murcia," in *Spanish Medieval Ceramics in Spain and the British Isles,* ed. C. M. Gerrard, A. Gutiérrez and A. Vince (Oxford: Tempus Reparatum, 1995).

Similar figures are also found on earlier Andalusī objects, especially from the Taifa period. A monumental marble basin discovered in Játiva within the region of Valencia, which would have been under Ibn Mardanīsh's authority, depicts many of the same motifs, carved into the sides in a series of lively vignettes.[50] Eva Baer has argued that these scenes—men in turbans carrying food, seated men in turbans drinking, an *'ūd* player, other musicians—should be seen as "secular" and as depictions of local rural festivities.[51] Jerrilynn Dodds, by contrast, contends that the basin follows an ancient iconographic tradition in which emblematic scenes of feasting and hunting represent sovereignty.[52] Certainly, the similarity in iconography stretching back to ancient monuments built explicitly to honor emperors suggests hunting and feasting themes served as shorthand for dominion over land and, by extension, for authority.[53] Dodds notes that the image of a naked nursing mother on the basin parallels a similar motif on the Ara Pacis (the Roman altar to the goddess of peace, consecrated in 9 BCE), where it represents the abundance of the earth. The procession of men bearing food also has parallels in the Persianate world that go back to the stone reliefs at Achaemenid Persepolis. As Dodds writes, "Profuse and literal figural imagery in the arts of al-Andalus is nearly always bound to abstract notions of power by virtue of its connection to the Roman and Sasanian past."[54] The Játiva basin is usually dated to the eleventh century, a time when first the 'Āmirid rulers of the late Umayyad period and then the Taifa kings who ruled after its collapse produced large numbers of objects with similar depictions.[55] The juxtaposition of images of feasting, hunting, and wrestling seem to suggest a range of activities associated with the court.[56] Indeed, the ubiquity of this imagery in palace contexts,

---

50 Museo del Almudin, Játiva, inv. no. A25. 16 1/2 × 66 7/8 × 26 3/8 inches. Al-Andalus catalog no. 49, 261–63.

51 Eva Baer, "The 'Pila' of Játiva: A Document of Secular Urban Art in Western Islam," *Kunst des Orients* 7 (1970–71): 142–66.

52 Dodds, "Jativa Basin," in Dodds, *Al-Andalus*, 261–63.

53 André Grabar discussed this as the "landowner's cycle" in his *Christian Iconography: A Study of Its Origins* (Princeton, NJ: Princeton University Press, 1968), 51–54.

54 Dodds, "Jativa Basin," 263.

55 Mariam Rosser-Owen has written about the marble basins of similar scale and with comparable images adorning them that have inscriptions connecting them to the 'Āmirids, in "Poems in Stone: The Iconography of 'Āmirid Poetry, and its 'Petrification' on 'Āmirid Marbles," in *Revisiting al-Andalus: Perspectives on the Material Culture of Islamic Iberia and Beyond* (Leiden: Brill, 2007), 83–98.

56 Although Baer argues that the Jativa basin's representations of wrestlers and dancers with sticks seem to belong to a lower social class than what would typically appear within a

FIGURE 4.6. Játiva Basin, eleventh century, carved marble, 16 ½ x 66 ⅞ x 26 ¾ inches. Museo de Almudí, Xàtiva, inv. no. A25. *Photo:* Abigail Krasner Balbale.

FIGURE 4.7. Játiva Basin, detail: seated man in turban, musicians, dancers. Museo de Almudí, Xàtiva, inv. no. A25. *Photo:* Abigail Krasner Balbale.

in textiles, and on ceramics in the eleventh–twelfth centuries points to a growing number of claimants to power, who, in Dodd's indelible words, were "stockpiling . . . princely symbolism."[57]

These activities, and representations of them in courtly settings, were ubiquitous in most of the Andalusī courts that followed the fall of the caliphate of Cordoba. Cynthia Robinson has shown that late

court, Ernst Grube notes that they constitute military exercises that are depicted in Fatimid contexts as courtly. See Grube, "A Coloured Drawing," 149n2. The wrestlers depicted on the basin, pulling one another's beards, parallel paintings on the ceiling of the Cappella Palatina. On this motif in particular, see Alison Stones, "A Note on the Beard-Pulling Motif: A Meeting between East and West, or a Northern Import?" in *Early Medieval Art and Archaeology in the Northern World: Studies in Honour of James Graham-Campbell*, ed. Andrew Reed and Leslie Webster (Leiden: Brill, 2013), 877–92.

57 Dodds, "Jativa Basin," 263.

FIGURE 4.8. Gathering in a garden, from the *Ḥadīth Bayāḍ wa Riyāḍ*. Vatican Library, Rome. *Photo:* Wikimedia Commons/The Yorck Project.

tenth-century ʿĀmirid cultural production emphasized the ideals of courtly love, depicting drinking companions, musicians, and heart-sick lovers arrayed in gardens, and that these ideals reverberated in the eleventh-century courts of the Taifa kingdoms and beyond.[58] An illuminated manuscript of the love story *Bayāḍ wa-Riyāḍ*, which Robinson argues was produced in the thirteenth century in one of the anti-Almohad kingdoms of Sharq al-Andalus, portrays similar themes in strikingly similar ways with drinkers and musicians in mixed gatherings. Robinson sees this unique text as a product of both Abbasid literary traditions and nascent European traditions of courtly love, which collided in al-Andalus beginning in the ʿĀmirid and Taifa periods and produced

58 Robinson, *Medieval Mediterranean Courtly Culture in al-Andalus: Ḥadīth Bayāḍ wa-Riyāḍ* (London: Routledge, 2006).

objects and texts with a new emphasis on love, music, and drinking in paradisiacal gardens.

Did objects with courtly themes carry meanings connected to the court? For the upper middle-class consumer who purchased a lusterware bowl depicting a dancer, would it have evoked their ruler's palace, the interior of which they were never likely to see? In seeking to explain the proliferation of these courtly motifs in the ceramics of the twelfth century, Oleg Grabar argued that they must have been dispersed in the aftermath of the sacking of Fatimid palaces by mobs of angry, unpaid soldiers. He imagined luxurious vessels, silks, and fragments of wood carving carried off and sold on the open market, which created broad appetite for more of these motifs.[59] This cinematic explanation for the spread of these motifs across so many media has not found widespread purchase among scholars of the Fatimids or the Mediterranean. But it reflects understandable confusion: if these are supposed to be courtly motifs, why did they circulate so widely? The diffusion of such images may reflect the changing political context of the eleventh to thirteenth centuries, marked by the emergence of new dynasties that sought to gain legitimacy through association with the caliphate, or it may simply be evidence of the burgeoning commerce of the Fatimid period, when Genoese and Pisan merchants competed with North African traders to dominate Mediterranean trade.[60] Even the tiniest city-states could use the symbols of sovereignty that adorned the palaces of the Abbasids, the Umayyads, the Romans, and the Sasanians. Like the eleventh-century Taifa princes "stockpiling" courtly motifs, the competing Mediterranean rulers of the twelfth and thirteenth centuries sought to secure the services of the painters, weavers, architects, and craftsmen who could present them as most powerful.

Given the popularity of figural representations of seated rulers, hunters, dancers, and musicians across objects and spaces throughout the

59 Oleg Grabar, "Imperial and Urban Art in Islam: The Subject-Matter of Fatimid Art," in *Early Islamic Art, 650–1100*, vol. 1, *Constructing the Study of Islamic Art* (Hampshire: Ashgate, 2005), 235: "It is our contention that this dumping of a huge mass of expensive objects and works of art on to the public market was a revolutionary one in affecting the taste of large numbers of people in Fatimid Egypt."

60 On trade, circulation, and transmission in the Mediterranean in this period and its art-historical effects, see Eva Hoffman, "Pathways of Portability;" on trade in the Western Mediterranean, see O. R. Constable, *Trade and Traders in Muslim Spain: The Commercial Realignment of the Iberian Peninsula, 900–1500* (Cambridge: Cambridge University Press, 1994).

Mediterranean in the twelfth century, such images were clearly deemed suitable for decorating luxurious settings. But their absence from any other surviving architectural context that is close to Ibn Mardanīsh either in geography or in time highlights the importance of this artistic choice for his palace. It was precisely the rarity of the figurative cycle in Andalusī architecture, and particularly on a muqarnas dome, that made its message so potent. On silks and ceramics, in architecture and in illustrated books, scenes of banquets and hunts and of otherworldly creatures abounded. They were, simultaneously, the most common and the most deluxe of motifs, ubiquitous in the most expensive techniques and materials of the Mediterranean world. Reintegrating these themes into an architectural context, especially on a muqarnas dome, the cutting-edge architectural form of the day that was used only by the most successful rulers in their own palaces, would have been an awe-inspiring demonstration of wealth and virtuosic craftsmanship. Visitors to his palace would have recognized them as expressions of a ruling tradition with local roots and international associations.

Carved stucco served as an important medium for the adornment of these palaces, and in many cases included forms that also appeared in wall paintings. Dār al-Ṣughrā contained elaborate stucco depictions of stylized animals and vegetal designs. Carved stucco was cheap, relatively easy to work, and well suited to the geometric and vegetal forms en vogue in the Islamic world, and it had thus become the standard material for the walls of Islamic palaces. Ibn Mardanīsh's palaces contained stucco fragments with lotus flowers, pinecones, and palmettes curling around each other.

The depth of the carving in this stucco and the frequent use of pinecones and palmettes have parallels in surviving Almoravid stucco in, for example, the Qubbat al-Barudiyyīn and the Qarawiyyīn Mosque in Fez. But the stucco at Dār al-Ṣughrā also incorporates figurative elements, including the bottom half of a bird or a harpy with a band of roundels across its wing, in a pattern reminiscent of textiles. Although birds appear frequently in the carved ivories and marble plaques of Umayyad al-Andalus, the relative absence of zoomorphic elements in earlier and contemporary carved stucco makes this instance striking. The closest precedents to the birdlike figure in Dār al-Ṣughrā are found in the palaces of Taifa al-Andalus, like the mythical creatures carved onto the wall of the Taifa palace of Toledo, or a fragment from the eleventh-century Taifa palace of Balaguer, which depicts a harpy with the body

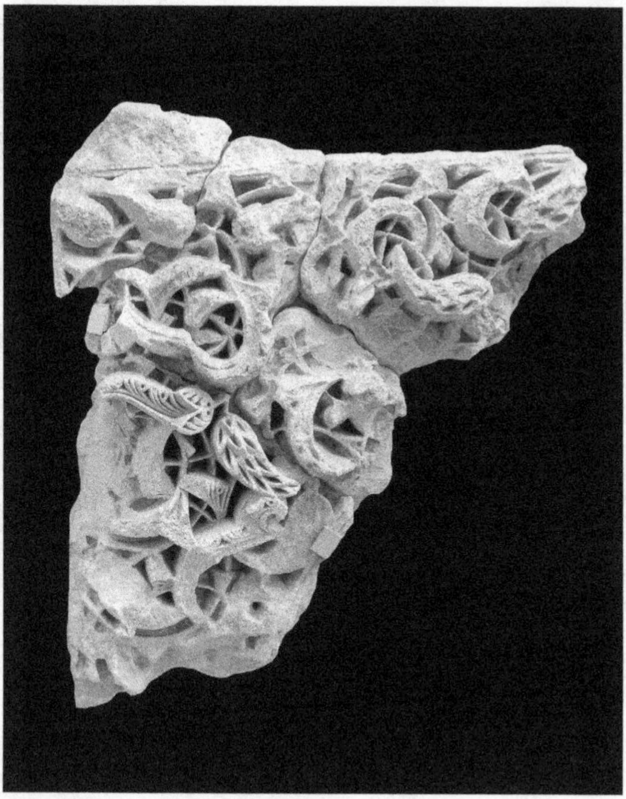

FIGURE 4.9. Carved stucco from Dār al-Ṣughrā, featuring pinecones and palmettes. *Photo:* Museo Arqueológico de Murcia.

of a bird and the hands and head of a woman.[61] The stucco fragments from Balaguer suggest that the palace might have incorporated painted stucco that recalled the themes and motifs of the Fatimid Western Palace.[62] One of the fragments of wood carving attributed to the Fatimid

61 On the Taifa palace of Toledo, found within the Convent of Santa Fé, see F. Monzón and C. Martín, "El antiguo convento de Santa Fe de Toledo. Recuperación de algunas dependencias de época musulmana," *Revista del Instituto de Patrimonio Histórico Español y Bienes Culturales* 6 (2005): 53–76. The excavated fragments of the palace of Balaguer are now held in the Museu de la Noguera in Balaguer, in the province of Lleida. Víctor Rabasco García sees both the harpies at Balaguer and Toledo as drawn from textile motifs, see "El arte textile y su impacto en la cultura visual de los Reinos de Taifas." Navarro Palazón first noted the parallels between the harpy of Balaguer and the bird/harpy of Dār al-Ṣughrā after excavating it, see "La Dār aṣ-Ṣugrà de Murcia," 113.

62 Robinson notes that such international echoes may have relied on lost intermediaries. Robinson, "The Arts of the Taifa Kingdoms," in Dodds, *Al-Andalus*, 59. On Taifa architecture

FIGURE 4.10. Carved stucco from Dār al-Ṣughrā, featuring the bottom half of a bird or harpy. *Photo:* Museo Arqueológico de Murcia.

palaces also includes a harpy, enclosed in a multilobed frame, next to a scene of a seated musician and dancer.[63] As Robinson has noted, the use of such imagery implies that Taifa kings looked to the broader Islamic and Mediterranean contexts as well as their local forebears and contemporary rivals in crafting their own courtly image.[64] Susana Calvo Capilla emphasizes the immense vitality of the artistic and cultural production under the Taifa kings, even as they operated in within the challenging circumstances of political fragmentation and threats from all sides. She suggests "courtliness," developed through art, architecture and literature, enabled rulers' to consolidate and visualize their own power.[65] The use of similar motifs in Ibn Mardanīsh's court indicates that he, too, participated in this Andalusī tradition.

The paintings on the muqarnas in Dār al-Sughrā, though fragmentary, seem to follow the themes visible in fragments from Samarra, in the Umayyad palaces at Khirbat al-Mafjar and Qusayr ʿAmra, and in the period most proximate to Ibn Mardanīsh himself, in the Fatimid

more generally, see also Susana Calvo Capilla, "El arte de los reinos taifas: tradición y ruptura," *Anales de Historia del Arte* 69, no. 2 (2011): 69–92.

63 Museum of Islamic Art, Cairo, eleventh century, inv. no. 12880.

64 Robinson, "Arts of the Taifa Kingdoms," 59–60.

65 Calvo Capilla, "Arte de los reinos taifas," 69.

FIGURE 4.11. Carved stucco from Taifa palace of Balaguer in the form of a harpy, Museu de la Noguera, Balaguer, Lleida. *Photo:* Abigail Krasner Balbale.

Western Palace and the Norman Cappella Palatina in Palermo. The Fatimid Western Palace was destroyed, but carved wooden beams depicting hunters, dancers, and musicians that survived in the Mamluk Mausoleum of the Sultan Qalawūn are thought to have been reused elements of the Fatimid palace.[66] Alongside other Fatimid material culture, like the lively vignettes that appear on carved ivory plaques and ceramics, the carved beams seem to point to a series of courtly themes used by the Fatimids in their lost palace.[67]

66 These are now displayed in the Museum of Islamic Art, Cairo. See also the wooden carvings excavated from under Mamluk palace sites that are similarly assessed to have been from Fatimid palaces, like the one held at the Louvre, inv. no. OA 4062.

67 Carved ivory plaques, with seated rulers, musicians, dancers, hunters, and soldiers superimposed on deeply carved vegetal arabesques, survive in three major collections: the Museo Nazionale del Bargello, Florence, inv. no. 80c 1–6; Museum für Islamische Kunst, Berlin, inv.

The Norman king Roger II commissioned the construction of the Cappella Palatina with a wooden muqarnas ceiling adorned with paintings of fantastic animals, hunting, dancing girls, musicians, and banquets. Although themes of hunting and feasting were widespread throughout the ancient Mediterranean, the relative dearth of such imagery surviving in contexts outside of the Fatimid sphere in the twelfth century has led scholars to connect the Cappella Palatina's painted ceilings, and perhaps the muqarnas substructure itself, to the Fatimids, and have suggested they were produced by artists visiting from the Fatimid court.[68] More recently, scholars have found Almoravid predecessors for the ceiling and the floor of the Cappella Palatina.[69]

The ceiling of the Cappella Palatina, completed in 1144 just before Ibn Mardanīsh took power, is in its muqarnas form and the courtly paintings that adorn it the closest parallel to the ceiling of the Dār al-Ṣughrā in Murcia. But rather than seeking the origin of Ibn Mardanīsh's use of muqarnas and courtly painting in Palermo, and the roots of the Cappella Palatina's ceiling in Fatimid Cairo, I follow Hoffman in recognizing the "synthetic cultural mix" that produced both of these structures.[70] The architects and craftsmen who produced these structures drew on the objects, spaces, and techniques available to them to create a locally contextualized and meaningful vision of power for their patrons,

---

no. I 6375; Musée du Louvre, Paris, inv. no. OA 6266. The function of these unusual objects and their "princely" themes have been discussed by Ernst Kühnel, *Die Islamischen Elfenbeinskulpturm, VIII–XIII Jahrhundert* (Berlin: Deutscher Verlag für Kunstwissenschaft, 1971); Eva Hoffman, "A Fatimid Book Cover: Framing and Re-framing Cultural Identity in the Medieval Mediterranean World," in *L'Egypte fatimide: son art et son histoire*, ed. Marianne Barrucand (Paris: Presses de l'Université de Paris-Sorbonne, 1999), 403–19; Anna Contadini, "Fatimid Ivories within a Mediterranean Culture," in *The Ivories of Muslim Spain: The Journal of the David Collection*, ed. K. von Folsach and J. Meyer, eds., 2, no. 2 (2005): 226–47.

68 The best resource for understanding these paintings is the book edited by Ernst Grube and Jeremy Johns, *The Painted Ceilings of the Cappella Palatina* (Genova: Bruschettini Foundation for Islamic and Asian Art, 2005). For further discussion of the origins of the painters and the iconography, see William Tronzo, *The Cultures of His Kingdom: Roger II and the Cappella Palatina in Palermo* (Princeton, NJ: Princeton University Press, 1997); Jeremy Johns, "Muslim Artists and Christian Models in the Painted Ceilings of the Cappella Palatina," in *Romanesque and the Mediterranean*, ed. Rosa Maria Bacile and John McNeill (Leeds: British Archaeological Association, 2015); and for a more recent reading of some of the scenes, see Lev Kapitaikin, "David's Dancers in Palermo: Islamic Dance Imagery and Its Christian Recontextualization in the Ceilings of the Cappella Palatina," *Early Music* 47, no. 1 (2019): 3–23.

69 Jonathan Bloom, "Almoravid Geometrical Designs in the Pavement of the Cappella Palatina in Palermo," in *The Iconography of Islamic Art: Studies in Honour of Robert Hillenbrand*, ed. Bernard O'Kane (Edinburgh: Edinburgh University Press, 2005); David Knipp, "Almoravid Sources for the Wooden Ceiling in the Nave of the Cappella Palatina in Palermo," in *Die Cappella Palatina in Palermo: Geschichte, Kunst, Funktionen*, ed. T. Dittelbach (Künzelsau: Swiridoff, 2011).

70 Hoffman, "Between East and West," 122.

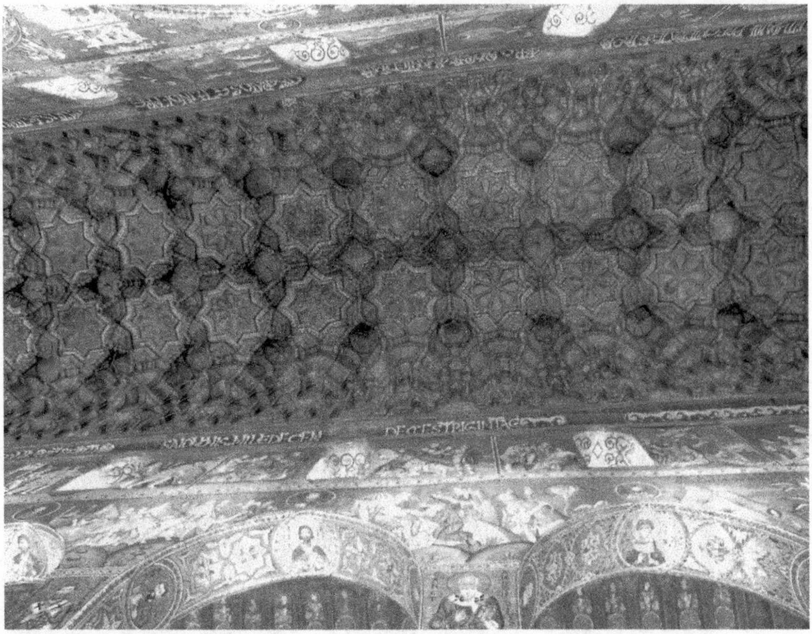

FIGURE 4.12. Ceiling of the Cappella Palatina, Palermo, ca. 1144, constructed for Norman King Roger II. Gypsum and tempera on a wooden substructure. *Photo:* Wikimedia Commons; photo uploaded by CarlesVA, licensed under the Creative Commons Attribution-ShareAlike 3.0 Unported (CC BY-SA 3.0) license (https://creativecommons.org/licenses/by-sa/3.0/).

which simultaneously created a distinct visual identity for the ruler's regime and connected them to their forebears and contemporaries. Both Roger II and Ibn Mardanīsh were upstarts who sought to create new dynasties and constructed buildings that demonstrated their imperial ambitions. Both had ceilings above spaces that might have served as their throne rooms covered with figures dancing, playing instruments, feasting, and drinking. Although Ibn Mardanīsh's palace survives in fragments, and scholars can only hypothesize about its complete form, remarkable parallels between the figures represented in Murcia and Palermo suggest a common iconographic program. As Fatma Dahmani has shown, the red-draped breasts of a dancer on a fragment from Dār al-Ṣughrā mirror almost exactly the torso of a scarf dancer in the Cappella Palatina, as do the wide-legged pants of another fragment and the bearded figure holding a plant or flower.[71]

71 Fatma Dahmani, "Remarques sur quelques fragments de peinture murale trouvés a Murcie."

FIGURE 4.13. Detail from the ceiling of the Cappella Palatina, Palermo, depicting a seated ruler. *Photo:* Wikimedia Commons/The Yorck Project.

The Cappella Palatina's muqarnas are constructed out of wood whereas Ibn Mardanīsh's, likely completed just a few years later, are made of plaster, so in spite of their visual similarity, they were products of two different building traditions.[72] Like his contemporary Roger II, Ibn Mardanīsh was seeking to articulate a new claim to power through his architecture and to counteract the claims of his rivals by building palaces and fortresses that spoke with an imperial voice. Dār al-Ṣughrā's muqarnas ceiling, with its scenes of music and dancing, tied him explicitly to earlier Islamic courts (many of which had used such images in

72 Basilio Pavón Maldonado, "La decoración monumental: Maderas y mocárabes," in *Arquitectura y decoración en el Islam Occidental: España y Palermo* (self-published online, 2011), http://www.basiliopavonmaldonado.es/Documentos/EspanapalermoI.pdf, 123–49 (accessed March 3, 2020).

palaces explicitly designed for caliphs). It also placed him in the realm of kings and emperors—those who, like Roger II, could afford to import craftsmen, materials, and forms from afar to create cosmopolitan spaces that expressed their cultural and military reach.

This courtly iconography constituted a program recognizably linked to imperial power and to caliphal sovereignty. It also may have served to represent the very kinds of gatherings that would have taken place within these settings. The images of dancers and musicians in Ibn Mardanīsh's Dār al-Ṣughrā parallel and echo poetic descriptions of courtly gatherings across the western Mediterranean. Ibn Ḥamdīs (d. 527/1132–33), an Arab poet in Sicily, wrote the following evocative lines:

> As one cradles a lute [ʿ*ūd*], another kisses a flute [*mizmār*].
> A dancer raises her leg,
> to the beat of the tambourine [*ṭār*].[73]

The figures Ibn Hamdīs describes—a dancer raising her leg, a female musician kissing a flute—are the same as those depicted on Ibn Mardanīsh's ceiling, and one must assume that ʿ*ūd* and *ṭār* players once appeared alongside them. Many scholars who write about the paintings in Dār al-Ṣughrā follow their descriptions with a quotation from Ibn al-Khaṭīb, the fourteenth-century Nasrid historian, who claimed that Ibn Mardanīsh reserved two days a week to drinking with his boon companions, including his military commanders, and that the ruler used the songs of his singing slave girls (*qiyān*) to win "control over the hearts of the army." Ibn al-Khaṭīb also mentioned the ruler's great love for wind instruments and dancing.[74] By making reference to this later description of Ibn Mardanīsh's drinking, womanizing, and merry making, modern scholars suggest that the ceiling's courtly cycle constituted an illustration of Ibn Mardanīsh's impiety. But seeing Ibn

73 Ibn Ḥamdīs, *Dīwān*, ed. I. ʿAbbās (Beirut: Dār Bayrūt, 1960), 182, no. 110; translation of J. Johns, G. van Gelder, and M. Hammond quoted in Kapitaikin, "David's Dancers in Palermo."

74 Ibn al-Khaṭīb, *al-Iḥāṭa*, ed. Ṭawīl, 2:71. In chapter 7, I consider some of the potential biases of this fourteenth-century source. Its depiction of the activities at Ibn Mardanīsh's court may be a later invention aiming to malign its subject, but the portrayal of such activities on the walls of the palace nonetheless suggests that Ibn Mardanīsh's court was, at minimum, not explicitly opposed to music and dancing. See discussions of the parties in Ibn Mardanīsh's court in García Avilés, "Arte y poder en Murcia en la época de Ibn Mardanish (1147–1172)," in *El Mediterráneo y el arte español : actas del XI Congreso del CEHA, Valencia, septiembre 1996*, ed. Joaquín Bérchez, Mercedes Gómez-Ferrer Lozano, and Amadeo Serra Desfillis (Valencia: Comité Español de Historia del Arte, 1998), 31.

Mardanīsh's palace as evidence of libertinage and its paintings merely as depictions of pleasurable pursuits is, at its core, Orientalist.[75] Like the wall paintings of dancers and musicians that Ernst Herzfeld discovered in Samarra a century ago, which were ascribed to the Abbasid "harem," these paintings slip too easily into an Orientalist vision of the sensual pleasures of the east, instead of a serious component of political culture.[76] This is a problem that extends more broadly into considerations of what constitutes the "Islamic," a framework that in academic contexts has been formulated, as Shahab Ahmed has shown, as predominantly legalistic.[77] By making law Islamic and not poetry or figurative art, the academic study of Islam has created strange contradictions that obscure or make irrelevant broad swaths of the life and culture of Muslims. In the study of Islamic architecture, Nadia Ali observes, "The aniconic mosque has been taken as the normative model for early Islamic art with the result that the palaces–instead of being used to challenge and complicate the normative–are read as deviant, decadent and anthropomorphic."[78]

No scholar working on the Cappella Palatina has suggested that Roger II wanted the interior of his ceiling adorned with scenes of hunting, dancing, and musicians because he liked to have a good time. Instead, they take the iconography seriously, assume that it seeks to convey a message, and debate its possible meanings.[79] By contrast, Islamic art historians have largely interpreted the frequently sensual imagery of dancers, musicians, and hunts in Umayyad desert castles and Abbasid

75 As Nadia Ali has shown, similar Orientalist impulses led to readings of Umayyad figural painting as representations of a debauched lifestyle. Nadia Ali, "The Royal Veil: Early Islamic Figural Art and the *Bilderverbot* Reconsidered," *Religion* 47, no. 3 (2017): 425–44.

76 The wall paintings Herzfeld excavated at Samarra, which included semi-nude women and scenes of feasting and hunting, were long referred to as the "harem paintings." The part of the palatine complex was later called the Jawsaq al-Khaqānī and has most recently been called the Dār al-Khilāfa, or central palace. This renaming reflects the growing scholarly consensus that the area with these paintings constituted the central locus of power in the Abbasid palatine complex. As Eva Hoffman has argued, the Samarra paintings represented the Abbasid caliphs as inheritors and continuers of earlier princely and imperial traditions. Hoffman, "Between East and West."

77 Shahab Ahmed, *What Is Islam? The Importance of Being Islamic* (Princeton, NJ: Princeton University Press, 2016).

78 Nadia Ali, "The Road from Decadence: Agendas and Personal Histories in the Study of Early Islamic Art," in *Empires of Faith in Late Antiquity: Histories of Art and Religion from India to Ireland*, ed. Jaś Elsner (Cambridge: Cambridge University Press, 2020), 119.

79 See, for example, the debate over the extent of the Norman court's emulation of Fatimid ceremonial and aesthetics between William Tronzo in *Cultures of His Kingdom* and Jeremy Johns in *Painted Ceilings* and "Muslim Artists and Christian Models."

Samarra as illustrations of the irreligious and decadent lives of early princes and rulers. In the case of the Umayyads of Syria, such readings were facilitated by historical chronicles that described the raucous parties, full of drink and sex, that the Umayyads hosted. However, the history of the Umayyads, like that of Ibn Mardanīsh, was largely written by their successors, and descriptions of irreligiosity on the part of their predecessors were one way in which these successors legitimated their own rule.[80] In recent years, scholars have turned away from the assumption that paintings on palace or bathhouse walls were bawdy celebrations of the joys of women and wine and have instead begun to consider such iconography in its specific context. They have revealed the literary sources and astrological conceptions with which the artists engaged and traced the ways in which programs of wall paintings served to represent new conceptions of Islamic authority. These analyses show that the so-called courtly cycle can carry specific, contextual, and significant messages that go far beyond generic illustrations of the indolent life of the palace harem. They can refer to literary sources, encode astrological meanings, and evoke specific objects and spaces.[81]

For Ibn Mardanīsh's court, both courtly gatherings that incorporated singing slave women, musicians, and dancers as well as representations of them constituted vital elements of his ruling culture, rooted in a long Islamic tradition of authority and sharpened by the Almohads' rejection of such activities. Dwight Reynolds has shown that gatherings with music and singing slave girls (*qiyān* or more generically *jawārī*) were a hallmark of late-Umayyad and Taifa courts in al-Andalus and into the Almoravid period.[82] Highly educated and trained performing slaves moved across the Mediterranean as diplomatic gifts and valuable commodities, and gatherings at which they performed music and recited

---

80 Referencing later sources' stories about the sensual pleasures and love of drink of the Umayyad caliphs, Robert Hillenbrand noted, "Such stories might encourage a fallacy that most Umayyad caliphs were libertines. The truth is, of course, more complex." Hillenbrand, "La Dolce Vita in Early Islamic Syria: The Evidence of the Later Umayyad Palaces," *Art History* 5 (1982): 4. There is a considerable body of poetry from the Umayyad period that has similar themes, but concluding that this poetry and the images on palace walls were faithful representations of the pastimes of the caliphs—or that surrounding himself with singing slave girls or holding drinking parties would make the caliph an irreligious libertine—is a significant leap.

81 For contextualized readings of the paintings of the Umayyad palace Quṣayr ʿAmra alone, see Nadia Ali, "Royal Veil"; Garth Fowden, *Quṣayr ʿAmra: Art and the Umayyad Elite in Late Antique Syria* (Berkeley: University of California Press, 2004); Hana Taragan, "Constructing a Visual Rhetoric: Images of Craftsmen and Builders in the Umayyad Palace at Qusayr ʿAmra," *Al-Masāq* 20 (2008): 141–60.

82 Dwight Reynolds, *The Musical Heritage of al-Andalus* (New York: Routledge, 2021).

poetry became the opportunities for rulers to demonstrate their wealth, power, and importance.[83] The rise of such gatherings, called *majālis al-uns* in Arabic, became widespread in al-Andalus starting in ʿĀmirid period, and are described in texts throughout the eleventh and twelfth centuries.[84] These gatherings should not be imagined as celebrations of libertinage or as "secular," however. A report from a Taifa court of the mid-eleventh century describes a *qayna*, or singing slave woman, purchased by a prince for the vast sum of three thousand dinars who could speak knowledgeably about grammar, medicine, anatomy, and natural history, and who could perform the arts of swordsmanship, along with her musical skills.[85] The same slave women who performed music and recited poetry also were trained in recitation of the Quran, and would often open gatherings at court with recitation from the holy book.[86] Such gatherings served as opportunities for rulers to reinscribe themselves in the cultural matrix of Islamic authority. Whether they were kings of a tiny city-state in al-Andalus or caliphs in Baghdad, majālis could demonstrate to courtiers and guests a ruler's ability to connect his court to tradition—Classical Arabic poetry, music, grammar—and to the most cutting-edge science and literature of the day.

Ibn Mardanīsh's palace's paintings thus engage with a mode of performing authority that has deep roots. In the face of the dramatic ruptures—theological, legal, political, and aesthetic—instituted by the Almohads, I see Ibn Mardanīsh's turn toward an Islamic (and ultimately ancient Mediterranean) tradition of images of feasts and music as a counterargument in favor of the continuity of a ruling culture under threat. This expression of support for tradition, and the images

---

83 On singing slave girls in the Abbasid context, and their roles in caliphal courts as well as in gatherings of litterateurs, see Kristina Richardson, "Singing Slave Girls (*Qiyan*) of the ʿAbbasid Court in the Ninth and Tenth Centuries," in *Children in Slavery through the Ages,* ed. Gwyn Campbell, Suzanne Miers, and Joseph C. Miller (Athens, OH: Ohio University Press, 2009) 105–18.

84 Cynthia Robinson has written extensively about the importance of such gatherings (*majālis al-uns*) in ʿĀmirid and Taifa contexts. She describes the *majlis al-uns* as "a versatile social and cultural institution, one which might house activities ranging from 'serious' religious, exegetical, philosophical or intellectual debate to 'frivolous' or amusing poetic recitation and composition, singing, wine-drinking and an ostentatious enjoyment of leisure in the company of witty and elegant 'beautiful people.'" Robinson, *In Praise of Song: The Making of Court Culture in al-Andalus and Provence, 1005–1134 AD* (Leiden: Brill, 2002), here 74–75. See also Robinson, *Medieval Mediterranean Courtly Culture in al-Andalus,* as well as her more recent article "Love in the Time of Fitna: 'Courtliness' and the 'Pamplona' Casket," in *Revisiting al-Andalus.*

85 Ibn Bassām, describing a slave girl of Hudhayl ibn Razīn (d. 1044/5) of Sahla in Aragon, quoted in Reynolds, *Musical Heritage of al-Andalus,* 194–95.

86 Reynolds, *Musical Heritage,* 195–96.

themselves, also would have been seen by courtiers and guests as a direct attack on the Almohads' architectural austerity. Although their preference for unadorned walls softened in later years, the Almohads never used figural paintings or zoomorphic stucco in their buildings. Where it did incorporate ornament, Almohad architecture used geometric and vegetal stucco designs very similar to those in Ibn Mardanīsh's palace. Ibn Mardanīsh, however, used these designs to frame girls dancing for princes—images that were directly opposed not only to Almohad artistic norms but also to their famously rigid attitudes toward music, dancing, and mixed-gender gatherings. Numerous examples throughout Almohad writings describe Ibn Tūmart breaking musical instruments and dispersing gatherings with men and women together.[87] By hosting such gatherings and by representing them within his palace, Ibn Mardanīsh was expressing continuity with Taifa, Umayyad, Fatimid, and Abbasid visions of authority and rejecting the Almohads' ruling culture.

The Almohads' notorious disapproval of colorful architectural ornament and figural representation, which led the people of Fez to preemptively whitewash their congregational mosque the night before the Almohad caliph's arrival, may have impelled a similar transformation of Dār al-Ṣughrā. Someone, whether before or after Ibn Mardanīsh's children went to submit to the Almohad caliph in Seville, covered the paintings on the muqarnas dome with a thin coat of plaster. As discussed in chapter 6, this maneuver seems to have been sufficient to make the building acceptable to the Almohad elite, who stayed there and in Ibn Mardanīsh's other palaces for a month of celebration after their triumphant entrance into the city.

Architecture and Landscape

Three of the surviving nine buildings identified by Julio Navarro Palazón and Pedro Jiménez Castillo as Mardanīshī are palaces: the Dār al-Ṣughrā, or smaller palace in Murcia; a palace at Pinohermoso in Játiva; and the Castillejo at Monteagudo, part of a rural estate (*munya*) outside Murcia. Three fortresses survive in whole or in part. One is the Castillo at Monteagudo, part of the same rural estate that contains the Castillejo; another lies just on the other side of Murcia from Monteagudo in

87 Al-Baydhaq describes Ibn Tūmart and his followers breaking all the instruments in the market at Fez, in Lévi-Provençal, *Documents inédits*, 64; translation, 100–101. For other examples, see discussion in Bennison, *The Almoravid and Almohad Empires*, 248–49.

FIGURE 4.14. Mihrab of the oratory of al-Qaṣr al-Kabīr, Conjunto Monumental de San Juan de Dios, Murcia. *Photo:* Wikimedia Commons; photo uploaded by Gregorico, licensed under the Creative Commons Attribution-ShareAlike 3.0 Unported (CC BY-SA 3.0) license (https://creativecommons.org/licenses/by-sa/3.0/).

Asomada, and the third consists of the remaining defensive walls of the city of Lorca. Only one religious structure remains, the tiny private oratory that likely once belonged to Ibn Mardanīsh's large palace in Murcia, al-Qaṣr al-Kabīr.[88]

The Oratory of al-Qaṣr al-Kabīr, excavated under the church of San Juan de Dios in the early 2000s, is a small square room facing a mihrab,

88 Navarro and Jiménez, "La arquitectura de Ibn Mardanīš." In addition to the above structures, there are two structures that Navarro and Jiménez classify as Mardanīshī but whose significance and original usage are unknown; these are located at Los Alcázares, on the seashore in Murcia province, and in Portazgo. At least two other structures are mentioned in literary sources but remain unknown archaeologically.

which leads to a diminutive room with a dome.[89] It was constructed within the palace, alongside the southern wall of the city, and just next to the oratory is what appears to be a royal pantheon, with remains suggesting this was the final resting place for members of the ruling family. The oratory immediately recalls both Umayyad and Taifa precedents. The mihrab is a horseshoe arch with segmented voussoirs of different colors, like the tenth-century mihrab of the Great Mosque of Cordoba. But unlike that mihrab, which was famously made of Byzantine-style mosaic, this one, like the walls of the Dār al-Ṣughrā, is made of carved and painted stucco. The voussoirs are carved in relief and then painted, mostly in reds and blues, and they end in curves along the upper edge of the mihrab's arch, creating a polylobed effect like the voussoirs of the Almoravid mihrab in Tlemcen. The intrado of the arch is similarly carved and painted, with an eight-pointed star at its center. Behind the mihrab is a tiny room surmounted by a ribbed dome. Each of the dome's ribs, as well as the pendants that support the dome, are edged with black ribbons with white pearls. Some of the interior surfaces still show vine scrolls and palmettes, creamy on a red base, that evoke the vegetal elements of the Dār al-Ṣughrā.

As Susana Calvo Capilla has noted, its closest parallel is the oratory that survives from the Taifa Aljafería palace of the Banū Hūd in Saragossa.[90] Like the oratory in Murcia, the one within the Aljafería uses painted carved stucco to create a mihrab in the form of a multicolored horseshoe arch that echoes caliphal Cordoba. Both oratories include similar motifs, with eight-pointed stars and vine scrolls contained within pearled ribbons, and both contain ribbed domes. It would make sense for Ibn Mardanīsh to emulate the palace oratory of the Banū Hūd, both as one of the finest palaces of the previous century and as one connected to his own family. The Banū Hūd were an important Judhāmī family who had ruled the Upper March (*thaghr al-aqṣā*) during the Taifa period. This is the same region in which the Banū Mardanīsh likely originated, and María Jesús Viguera Molíns suggested the Banū Hūd may have been the sponsors of his family's conversion to Islam, which would have given them the honorary nisba al-Judhāmī.[91] Furthermore, one of Ibn Mardanīsh's

89 Archaeologists J. A. Sánchez Pravia and L. A. García Blánquez published their discovery in "Fulgor en el alcázar musulmán de Murcia: El conjunto religioso-funerario de San Juan de Dios," in *Las artes y las ciencias en el Occidente musulmán*, ed. M. Parra Lledó and A. Robles Fernández (Murcia: Museo de la Ciencia y el Agua, 2007), 234–51.

90 Susana Calvo Capilla, "Arte de los reinos taifas," 80–82.

91 M. J. Viguera Molíns, *Reinos de taifas*, 197–98.

Figure 4.15. Oratory in Aljafería Palace, Saragossa. *Photo:* Abigail Krasner Balbale.

predecessors in Murcia was the ruler Sayf al-Dawla ibn Hūd, alongside whom his brother fought and died.

But Ibn Mardanīsh's architecture at the oratory and elsewhere echoed the Aljafería and other Taifa buildings for more reasons than personal connection. Like the earlier Taifa kings, Ibn Mardanīsh drew together inspiration from caliphal Cordoba and the east to craft the most potent articulation of his legitimacy. Much has been written about the "oriental" elements of Taifa art and architecture. Ibn Mardanīsh continued the Taifa model of drawing from both local and distant models to create new forms. Ibn Mardanīsh presented himself as a righteous Muslim ruler, attuned to the forms of power current in the Islamic East and the Mediterranean world. In his transformation of the landscape, his palatial constructions, and the ornaments and inscriptions on their walls, Ibn Mardanīsh was arguing against the Almohad conception of the caliphate and in favor of Sunnī traditions of authority.

One important element of his articulation of power over the landscape was its visibility and breadth. Excavations and research have suggested that Ibn Mardanīsh may have constructed a series of castles (*quṣūr*) at equal distances from each other across the length of his territory.[92] Such construction would mirror the project of the Umayyad caliph ʿAbd al-Raḥmān III, as reported by the medieval geographer al-Bakrī (d. 487/1094), to create a chain of castles that connected Algeciras on the southern coast with the Sierra de Guadarrama mountain range north of present-day Madrid.[93] The castles of ʿAbd al-Raḥmān III are thought to have acted as a central roadway along which official business was conducted, and a line of castles may have served the same function for Ibn Mardanīsh.

All of the structures constructed under Ibn Mardanīsh share stylistic elements, such as sharp, geometric angles and towers, and common materials.[94] The castles attributed to his reign are characterized by doubled salient towers at the corners, an unusual and distinctive form for castle walls that would have been visible from some distance.[95] This form—like two rectangular boxes jutting out from the corners of castles at right angles to one another—has no clear military advantage to the more traditional single towers at the corners of fortifications, but it would have marked Ibn Mardanīsh's new constructions as distinct from those of his predecessors and rivals. The consistent visual form of his castles and city walls would have demonstrated his power over a vast landscape and reminded his subjects of the strength and extent of his regime. His focus on defensive fortifications points to the realities of his day, since he was constantly at war with the Almohads and other rivals, but it also demonstrates his broader image of himself as a warrior seeking to unify al-Andalus under his rule. By following ʿAbd al-Raḥmān III's pattern of constructing castles at regular intervals along the length of his territory, Ibn Mardanīsh created an infrastructure that could serve both military

---

92 María Jesús Rubiera Mata, "El Rey Lobo de Murcia, Ibn Mardanîs (1147–1172), promotor de la construcción de alcázares viales," in *Imágenes y promotores en el arte medieval: Miscelánea en homenaje a Joaquín Yarza Luaces*, ed. María Luisa Melero Moneo et al. (Bellaterra: Universidad Autónoma de Barcelona, 2001).

93 Félix Hernández Jiménez, "Travesía de la Sierra de Guadarrama en el acceso a la raya musulmana del Duero," *Al-Andalus* 38, no. 1 (1973): 69–186.

94 Navarro and Jiménez, "Arquitectura mardanisí."

95 See discussion of this form in Navarro and Jiménez, "Arquitectura mardanisí."

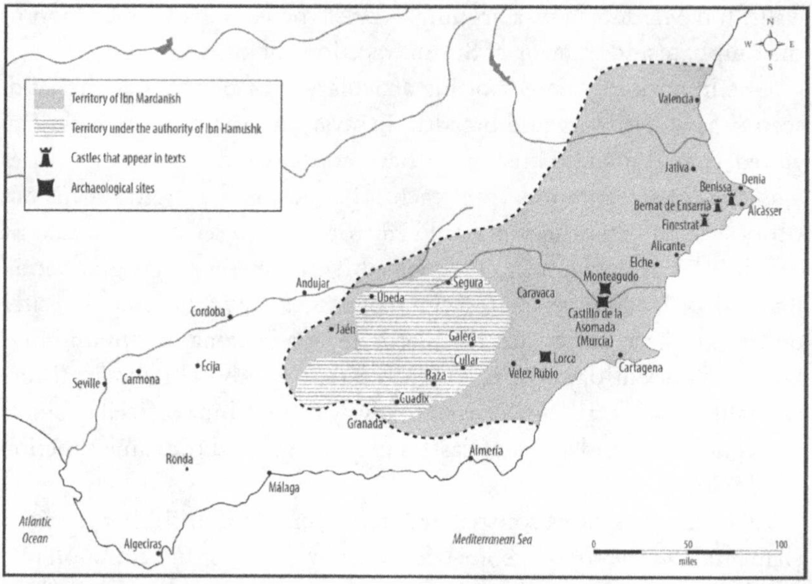

Map 4.1. The fortifications of Ibn Mardanīsh's territory. Map by Mike Bechthold.

and administrative ends. From the summit of the ruined castle of La Asomada on top of a mountain on the southern outskirts of Murcia, the contemporary viewer can still see the mountaintop Castillo de Monteagudo twelve miles to the north, on the opposite side of Murcia. These castles at regular intervals would have facilitated communication and the movement of troops. They also would have served as both military fortifications and palaces, punctuating the landscape with assertions of his power and offering locations for him to practice itinerant kingship by moving from one to another with his entourage and staying for extended periods.

Ibn Mardanīsh's castles, including the one he renovated in Monteagudo (the Castillejo de Monteagudo or Qaṣr Ibn Saʿd) and the nearby castle in Larache (Ḥiṣn al-Faraj) as well as a series of fortifications along the road between Murcia and Cartagena,[96] continued to be important military outposts for Christian armies in the years after the conquest of Murcia, though little remains of them beyond their footprints.[97]

96 Julio Navarro Palazón and Pedro Jiménez Castillo, "El Castillejo de Monteagudo: Qasr ibn Saʿd," in *Casas y palacios de al-Andalus*, ed. Navarro Palazón.

97 José A. Manzano Martínez, "Arquitectura defensiva: Delimitación de entornos y documentación histórica de 20 torres y castillos," *Memorias de Arqueología* 10 (1995): 662–71; José

FIGURE 4.16. Walls of the Castillo de Monteagudo, northeast outskirts of Murcia. *Photo:* Abigail Krasner Balbale.

FIGURE 4.17. View from summit of La Asomada, south of Murcia, across Murcia toward Qaṣr ibn Saʿd (Castillejo) in Monteagudo. *Photo:* Abigail Krasner Balbale.

Almohad sources, including Ibn Ṣāḥib al-Ṣalā, discuss the destruction of Ibn Mardanīsh's palaces and gardens at Monteagudo in the Almohad attacks of 560/1165, and the poet Ṣafwān ibn Idrīs (d. 598/1201) relates his discovery, during a trip he took in 588/1191, of two ruined fortified palaces that had been built by Ibn Mardanīsh. These sources also explicitly mention a rural palace called Ḥiṣn al-Faraj, which is likely the fortress now known as Larache, near Monteagudo. This fortress, within sight of the Castillo and the Castillejo and perhaps once part of Ibn Mardanīsh's palatial landscape in the suburbs of Murcia, nevertheless lacks the stylistic markers of most of his other fortifications, and some scholars have consequently attributed it to a later period.[98] Along with the fortification at Cabezo de Torres, Larache and the Castillejo form a straight line that extends for just under a mile. Even if the structures now at Larache and Cabezo de Torres come from a later period, it is likely that this whole territory comprised a palatial zone, like the productive rural palatial landscape of the Umayyads at Madīnat al-Zahrā', and that small castles were used for Ibn Mardanīsh's family and for honored companions or guests. These rural estates were both productive agricultural areas and sites of royal leisure.[99]

Ibn Mardanīsh's palatial complex in Monteagudo incorporated elaborate waterworks, gardens, and multistory palaces with vistas across the gardens. Andrés Sobejano Alcayna initially excavated Monteagudo in 1924, but information about the site was published only in 1932–33 by Torres Balbás, who attributed the structures to Ibn Mardanīsh on the basis of references in Arabic sources.[100] After their

---

García Anton, "Castillos musulmanes que dominaban la vía Cartagena-Murcia," in *Historia de Cartagena*, ed. Julio Mas García, vol. 5 (Murcia: Mediterráneo, 1986).

98 José A. Manzano Martínez and Francisca Bernal Pascual, "Un palacio fortificado musulmán en la huerta de Murcia: El Castillo de Larache; Estado actual de la investigación," *Verdolay* 4 (1993): 153–66; Manzano Martínez, "Fortificaciones islámicas en la huerta de Murcia: Sector septentrional; Memoria de las actuaciones realizadas," *Memorias de Arqueología* 7 (1992, rev. 1998): 389–441.

99 On the importance of such estates (*munya,* pl. *munan*) in al-Andalus more generally, see D. F. Ruggles, *Gardens, Landscape, and Vision in the Palaces of Islamic Spain* (University Park: Pennsylvania State University Press, 2000); Glaire Anderson, "Villa (*munya*) Architecture in Umayyad Córdoba: Preliminary Considerations," in *Revisiting al-Andalus: Perspectives on the Material Culture of Islamic Iberia and Beyond,* ed. Anderson and M. Rosser-Owen (Leiden: Brill, 2007). Navarro and Jiménez's analysis of archaeological evidence suggests that the eastern edge of the city of Murcia was interspersed with orchards and productive spaces that led to the *munan* around Monteagudo. See Navarro and Jiménez, "Evolution of the Andalusi Urban Landscape: From the Dispersed to the Saturated Medina," in *Revisiting al-Andalus*, 142.

100 Leopoldo Torres Balbás, "Paseos arqueológicos por la España musulmana. Murcia," *Boletín de la Junta del Patronato del Museo Provincial de Bellas Artes de Murcia* 11–12 (1933).

FIGURE 4.18. Monumental complex of Monteagudo: the Castillejo in the foreground, Castillo in background. *Photo:* Abigail Krasner Balbale.

excavation, the palaces were left open; the site was eventually planted as an orchard and then used as a reservoir, destroying all elements of the structure that were not sent to archaeological museums. The carved stucco and other architectural decorations ended up in the collections of the Museo Arqueológico Nacional and the Museo Arqueológico de Murcia. The meticulous work of Navarro and Jiménez, based on the objects in archaeological museums and photographs from the early excavations as well as surveys of the exterior, has revealed new information about these palaces and confirmed their attribution to Ibn Mardanīsh.[101]

The two major structures, known as the Castillo de Monteagudo and the Castillejo or Qaṣr Ibn Saʿd, used a noria, or waterwheel, and pipes, canals, and aqueducts to carry water throughout the palaces and gardens.

In 1934, he published a more extensive article on the same topic: Leopoldo Torres Balbás, "Crónica arqueológica de la España musulmana," *Al-Andalus* 2/2 (1934): 337–91. Henri Terrasse published some of the fragments in *L'Art Hispano-Mauresque des origines au XIIIe siècle* (Paris: Van Ouest, 1932). Following Torres Balbás, Georges Marçais published the Castillejo's plan and associated it with Ibn Mardanīsh's palace in Murcia as well as the Qalʿa of the Banū Ḥammād and the Cuba in Palermo: Georges Marçais, *L'Architecture musulmane d'Occident. Tunisie, Algérie, Maroc, Espagne et Sicile* (Paris: Arts et Métiers grafiques, 1954).

101 Navarro and Jiménez, "El Castillejo de Monteagudo."

FIGURE 4.19. Reconstruction of Castillo and Castillejo of Monteagudo by Antonio Almagro Gorbea. Inventory no. AA-301_i02, "Arquitectura de Al-Andalus," Academia Colecciones, Real Academia de Bellas Artes de San Fernando, Madrid.

New excavations under Navarro, begun in 2018, have revealed that the waterworks were significantly larger than was initially thought and incorporated a massive *alberca*, or water reservoir. They followed earlier Cordoban Umayyad models: Ruggles has shown that the Castillo, built on a platform made of buttress towers on top of a steep hill, and the lower Castillejo, built around a cross-axial courtyard with fountains and pools, constituted an intermediate form between Umayyad-period palaces such as Madīnat al-Zahrā', itself modeled on Abbasid Samarra, and the Nasrid Alhambra.[102] Like these earlier and later structures, Ibn Mardanīsh's castles incorporated elaborate waterworks and gardens as symbols of his cultivated kingdom and vistas of the landscape from on high as representations of his sovereignty.[103]

Like the muqarnas ceiling of Dār al-Ṣughrā, his country castle/palaces display similarities with the Norman buildings constructed in Sicily at roughly the same time. Like the Cuba in Norman Palermo (completed 1180), the design of the castles at Monteagudo included thick walls with projecting towers along each façade, surrounded by verdant gardens. The Castillejo was constructed with a central porticoed

102 Ruggles, *Gardens, Landscape and Vision*, 161–62.

103 Ruggles, "The Mirador in Abbasid and Hispano-Umayyad Garden Typology," *Muqarnas* 7 (1990): 73–82.

patio that led to a reception hall and multiple alcoves, some of which likely contained miradors over the cultivated landscape. The same model would be used in the Zisa palace of Norman Palermo, and later, in the Alhambra. The interior of the Castillejo, like the remnants of late Almoravid architecture and the interior decorations of the Zisa and the Cuba, was defined by carved stucco, fragments of which survive in museums in Murcia and Madrid. All of Ibn Mardanīsh's buildings continue the elaborate decorative forms of Almoravid carved stucco, especially the geometricized vegetal forms, particularly doubled palmettes and pinecones, known in Spanish as *ataurique*.

Ibn Mardanīsh's buildings seem to hark back to Umayyad, Abbasid, and—even more frequently—Almoravid examples, but they also constitute the earliest articulations of many forms that would become ubiquitous in Nasrid and mudejar art and architecture after him. One compelling example of his influence, presented by Navarro Palazón and Jiménez Castillo, is that Ibn Mardanīsh was among the first to popularize anthropomorphic elements in carved vegetal stucco ornamentation, as in a panel from the Castillejo covered with deeply carved and overlapping vines that converge on a single point at the bottom, where one can just make out three fingers of a hand clasping the plant. A similar example in the synagogue known as el-Transito in Toledo (built in the third quarter of the fourteenth century) has been explained with reference to the Hebrew Bible, but Navarro and Jiménez argue that the motif found in both places is an image of the ruler's hand holding abundance in the form of a leaf or palmette, which symbolizes his power and the fertility of his land.[104] Later palaces, including the Castilian Alcazar of Seville and the Nasrid Alhambra, also incorporated what Navarro and Jiménez call the "hand of abundance" as a symbol of sovereignty. Recalling Ibn Mardanīsh's argument with the Almohads, visible in his coins and their letters to him, over what constitutes "holding fast" to the rope of God also hints at the tantalizing possibility that the hand motif constituted a visualization of this theological ideal. However, even if Ibn Mardanīsh or his architects intended this tiny hand holding onto a long, flourishing vine to serve as a visual marker of his loyalty to the Umayyad and Abbasid ideal of the caliph as an embodiment of the unity of believers, it certainly did not continue to carry this meaning in subsequent centuries.

---

104 Navarro Palazón and Jiménez Castillo, "Arquitectura de Ibn Mardanīš," 89–90.

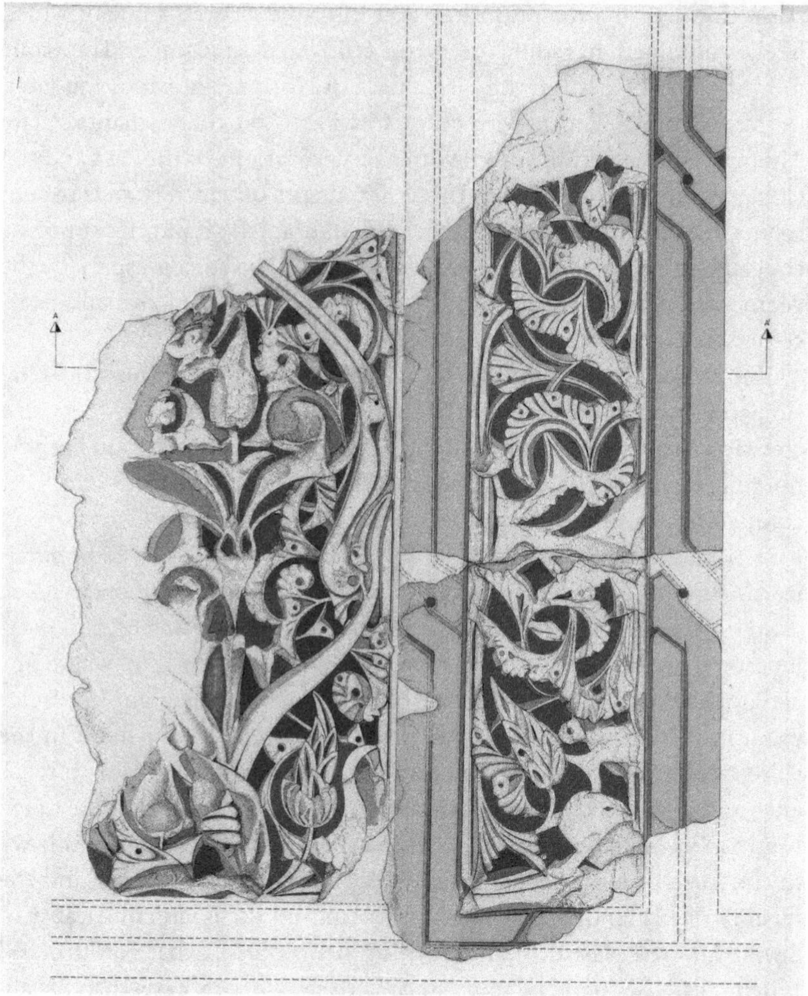

FIGURE 4.20. Drawing by Julio Navarro Palazón and Pedro Jiménez Castillo of the "Hand of abundance" in carved stucco from the Castillejo de Monteagudo. Original pieces in Museo Arqueológico Nacional and Museo Arqueológico de Murcia.

Ibn Mardanīsh also introduced a particular phrase, ubiquitous in the carved stucco of all of his buildings: *al-yumn wa-l-iqbāl*, "good fortune and prosperity," formed in bands of cursive, or *naskhī*, script. This phrase, which seems to have functioned as a Mardanīshī motto like the Nasrid's *wa lā ghālib illa Allāh* ("there is no victor but God"), appears in Dār al-Ṣughrā, Pinohermoso, and the Castillejo, carved into the

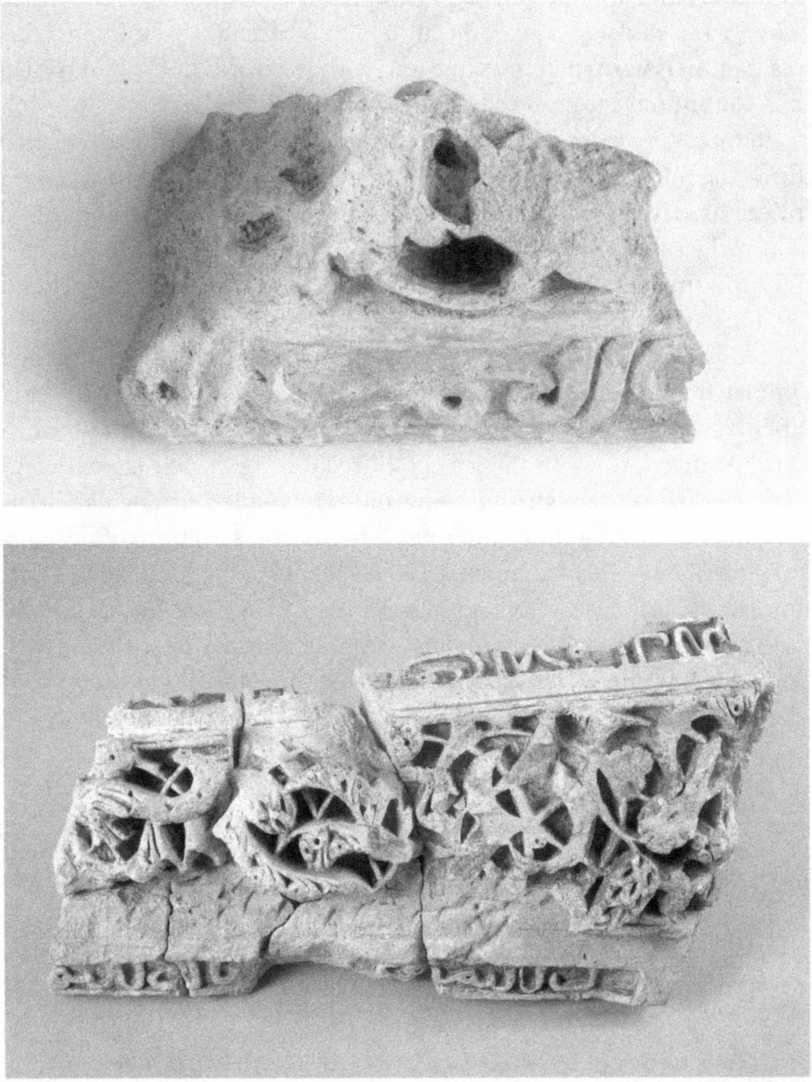

FIGURE 4.21A-B. Carved stucco with inscriptions "good fortune and prosperity" (al-yumn wa-l-iqbāl) from two of Ibn Mardanīsh's palaces. *Top*: Fragment from the Castillejo in Monteagudo, Museo Arqueológico Nacional, Madrid. Photo: Museo Arqueológico Nacional. Inv. 1925/46/16. Photographer: Ángel Martínez Levas. *Bottom*: Fragment from Dār al-Ṣughrā, Murcia. Museo Arqueológico de Murcia. Inv. SC-95/203/231A.

stucco in a loose, barely legible repeating pattern.[105] The inscriptions on these structures share both a function—surrounding doors, windows, or arches—and also an unusual orthography (floating *wāw*, malformed *mīm*, "swan-necked" *nūn*).[106] In all of Ibn Mardanīsh's buildings, this inscription is written in the same way, with the words in the same order, in a continuous repeating ribbonlike band.

In its cursive form and its generic content, the inscription is unusual for an architectural context.[107] Both the script and the phrase echo pieces of eleventh- and twelfth-century metalwork, which were often adorned with long lists of benedictory phrases directed to the owner.[108] Like this inscription, which in Ibn Mardanīsh's buildings wraps around arches, windows, and doors, such inscriptions on metalwork often encircled the body or lip of a vessel, suggesting an protective function. Similar form and content also appear in the tapestry woven silk and linen tiraz textiles being produced in Fatimid Egypt in the mid-twelfth century. Inscriptions on these tiraz shifted during the late eleventh and early twelfth centuries from being mostly executed in angular Kufic script and including the caliph's name to *naskhī* inscriptions of benedictory repeated words or phrases—i.e., *baraka*, blessing, or *al-mulk li-llāh*, sovereignty belongs to God, often accompanied by more figural decoration.[109] Scholars have suggested that this shift may be due to the decreasing power of caliph. The wide dispersal of these textiles indicates that they were highly prized outside of Egypt. Mostly made of yellow and

105 Martínez Enamorado says the profusion of this inscription across so many buildings makes the Mardanīshī dynasty "la dinastía del *al-yumn wa-l-iqbāl*." See "Poder y epigrafía," 114.

106 Robles, "Los programas ornamentales," 55.

107 The Arabic inscriptions on the ceiling of the Cappella Palatina are similarly brief well wishes, though they exhibit more variety than those found in Ibn Mardanīsh's buildings. Jeremy Johns has explored the function of this aphoristic and largely illegible program of Arabic inscriptions in the Cappella Palatina in "Arabic Inscriptions in the Cappella Palatina: Performativity, Audience, Legibility, and Illegibility," in *Viewing Inscriptions in the Late Antique and Medieval Mediterranean*, ed. Antony Eastmond (Cambridge: Cambridge University Press, 2015).

108 Anna Contadini has recently shown that the Pisa Griffin and Mari-Cha Lion, which are adorned with similar inscriptions, are both products of eleventh-twelfth century al-Andalus. See Contadini, "The Pisa Griffin and the Mari-Cha Lion: History, Art and Technology," in *The Pisa Griffin and the Mari-Cha Lion. Metalwork, Art and Technology in the Medieval Islamicate Mediterranean*, ed. Anna Contadini (Pisa: Pacini Editore, 2018). For metalwork with similar inscriptions from the eastern Islamic world, see Boris I. Marshak, "An Early Seljuq Silver Bottle from Siberia," *Muqarnas* 21, Essays in Honor of J. M. Rogers (2004): 255–65; A. S. Melikian-Chirvani, *Islamic Metalwork from the Iranian World, 8th-18th Centuries* (London: H.M. Stationery Office, 1982).

109 Sheila Blair, *Islamic Inscriptions*, 167.

red thread, many of these twelfth century tiraz include the very same inscription: *al-yumn wa-l-iqbāl*.

On tiraz, the inscriptions are positioned in long bands of repetition that traverse the width of the textile, often two or three times, separated by bands of rhombuses or images of birds or rabbits. Many of these textile inscriptions present consistent irregularities in their script, with unusual ligatures between *alifs* and *lāms*, malformed *mīms*, and the same swan-necked *nūn* familiar from Ibn Mardanīsh's architectural contexts. These unusual features, along with the frequent role of textiles as vectors of transmission for iconography, suggest it was Fatimid tiraz that served to bring this inscription to Ibn Mardanīsh and his craftsmen.[110] The use of this inscription made Ibn Mardanīsh's palace walls look like they were draped with the most luxurious textiles of Fatimid Egypt. Perhaps in using these inscriptions that echoed those on Fatimid textiles Ibn Mardanish was simply imitating these highly valued objects. Or perhaps this inscription's placement, like those words carved into the rims of bowls or woven onto bands worn along the shoulders of a body, indicates that it was seen as having apotropaic power. The inscription became a leitmotif in all of his palace architecture—carved into stucco or painted onto walls, always framing arches and windows, sometimes alongside other cursive or Kufic inscriptions. Surviving Fatimid tiraz are largely excavated from funerary contexts, showing these textiles were in great demand for use as shrouds.[111] Jochen Sokoly argues that the funerary use of tiraz was due to a belief that its connection to the caliph imbued it with special spiritual powers, even if it did not include the name of the caliph.[112] In Islamic funerary contexts, textiles were positioned so that the inscription band, seen as being the most holy part, was over the face of the deceased.

The same inscription would appear on later objects and buildings on the Iberian Peninsula, including the thirteenth-century palace built on the ruins of Dār al-Ṣughrā by Muḥammad Ibn Hūd as well as a number

---

110 Rabasco García, "El arte textil"; Eva Hoffman, "Pathways of Portability"; Annabelle Simon-Cahn, "The Fermo Chasuble of St. Thomas Becket and Hispano-Mauresque Cosmological Silks: Some Speculations on the Adaptive Reuse of Textiles," *Muqarnas* 10 (1993): 1–5.

111 On the debates over fine shrouds and the number a pious person should use (3 for men, 5 for women), see Leor Halevi, *Muhammad's Grave: Death Rites and the Making of Islamic Society* (New York: Columbia University Press, 2007).

112 Jochen Sokoly, "Textiles and Identity," *A Companion to Islamic Art and Architecture*, ed. Gulru Necipoğlu and Finbarr Barry Flood (New Jersey: Wiley-Blackwell, 2017); Sokoly, "Between Life and Death: the Funerary Context of Tiraz Textiles," *Riggisberger Berichte*, 5 (Bern: Abegg Stiftung, 1997), 71–78.

FIGURE 4.22. Tapestry woven silk textile with inscription "good fortune and prosperity," Fatimid Egypt, Victoria and Albert Museum.

of Castilian churches and the abovementioned synagogue in Toledo. These buildings are discussed further in chapter 5. But the movement of this inscription from a luxurious portable object from the eastern Mediterranean to the walls of a palace in the western Mediterranean—and from there to a series of buildings throughout cities and kingdoms on the Iberian Peninsula—demonstrates that Ibn Mardanīsh's kingdom functioned as a kind of hinge, bringing in and redistributing goods, ideas, and motifs.

Much of Ibn Mardanīsh's architecture echoes earlier Umayyad Cordoban, Abbasid, and Almoravid models with a scale and geographic breadth that reveals broad ambition. Like his coinage, which appealed to earlier Islamic traditions to counteract growing Almohad influence,

Ibn Mardanīsh's Dār al-Ṣughrā drew on a long history of Islamic figurative art with courtly themes to challenge Almohad attitudes about art and culture. Many of his structures, including the complex of buildings and gardens at Monteagudo, were destroyed by Almohad armies, but the palace at Dār al-Ṣughrā and its throne room were not demolished after Ibn Mardanīsh's death. Instead, someone—whether one of his sons, preparing for his surrender to the Almohads, or an Almohad functionary—carefully covered the figurative imagery with a thin coat of white plaster. In chapter 6, we will see how the Almohads, in turn, began to use muqarnas, more elaborate stucco, and cursive inscriptions in a wide range of buildings after taking over Ibn Mardanīsh's territory. Such adoption was possible only after the "conversion" of his children, followers, and buildings, which enabled their incorporation into the Almohad Empire.

Instead of seeking the "roots" of the architectural elements Ibn Mardanīsh's buildings incorporated, I have focused on the "routes" traveled by these styles and forms in order to visualize the paths of contact and circulation that they reveal.[113] Material culture, perhaps even more than genealogy, which had to aspire to linearity, could lay claim to multiple, overlapping, and even contradictory inheritances. Ibn Mardanīsh's palaces, like his genealogies and like the material culture of his rivals, invoked local precedents, ambitious contemporaries, and distant forebears, real and imagined. He gathered together the rich possibilities offered by these sources of inspiration—the polychrome mihrab of the Aljafería, the muqarnas domes of Almería and Marrakech, the well-spaced fortresses of ʿAbd al-Raḥmān III, the cultivated gardens and pavilions of Madīnat al-Zahrāʾ, the gold morabetinos and deeply carved stucco of the Almoravids, the silks of Cairo—and redeployed them anew. Their geographic and chronological scope and the distances they traveled to reach him served to demonstrate his power and strength and articulate his imperial ambitions. In the routes they took and the virtuosity of their execution, the motifs and techniques deployed in Ibn Mardanīsh's landscapes and objects made a forceful argument for the continuing importance of Islamic and Mediterranean traditions of authority. At the same time that these forms gestured to distant and local

113 In this, I follow the approach of Finbarr Barry Flood, whose work on India, another region whose Islamic past has been highly contested in the context of modern nationalisms, has been foundational to how I think about the circulation of goods, people, and motifs. See Flood, *Objects of Translation: Material Culture and Medieval "Hindu-Muslim" Encounter* (Princeton, NJ: Princeton University Press, 2009).

forebears, their assimilation and redeployment created an aesthetic that would have been instantly recognizable to his subjects, rivals, and neighbors. By using these forms and objects to counteract the Almohads, Ibn Mardanīsh created an aesthetic that would be adopted by his Muslim and Christian successors as a readymade portfolio of forms for expressing cosmopolitan power.

Chapter 5

Vassals, Traders, and Kings

Economic and Political Networks in the Western Mediterranean

In the Museo Diocesano in Fermo, Italy, lies one of the Cathedral of Fermo's greatest treasures: an embroidered chasuble thought to have once belonged to the English saint Thomas Becket (d. 1170). It is a large semicircle, evidently constructed from panels of a larger cloth, woven of blue and white silk, and embroidered in red and gold thread with a dazzling series of roundels containing figurative scenes: eagles attacking quadrupeds, a sphinx, winged lions, elephants carrying howdahs, a falconer on horseback, and seated rulers with attendants. Each roundel is framed by a ribbon edged with gold pearls along a red ground. At the cardinal points of each roundel, smaller roundels intersect with this ribbon, displaying proud animals in profile: colorful plumed peacocks, slender gazelles, rampant lions, and addorsed eagles. Floating among these roundels are eight-pointed stars with pearled borders containing more regal birds. Geometricized tendrils branch from four of the stars' points and appear throughout the textile's negative spaces, gently curving around the images as additional frames. At its center, the chasuble includes a scroll with an Arabic inscription in floriated Kufic, which has been read as connecting the textile to the city of Almería, and to the year 510/1116.[1]

1 This inscription's reading has been much contested. Originally deciphered as reading "In the name of God, the Merciful, the Compassionate, the kingdom is God's . . . greatest

FIGURE 5.1. Detail from the Chasuble of Thomas Becket. *Photo*: Gaetano Apicella, in *The Chasuble of Thomas Becket: A Biography*. Courtesy of The Bruschettini Foundation for Islamic and Asian Art.

Many questions surround this piece, including whether it really was produced in Almería in the twelfth century, if it ever truly belonged to Thomas Becket, and if so, how it arrived in Fermo. But its imagery, with its clear parallels to the painting cycles of the Cappella Palatina, the Dār al-Ṣughrā, and the textiles known as Almería silks, situate it in the elite culture of the western Mediterranean. The textile's movements,

blessing, perfect health and happiness to its owner . . . in the year 510 in al-Mariyya," it has since been evaluated as illegible, due to the difficulty of the script and the degradation of the embroidery. For more on this fascinating textile, see D. S. Rice, "The Fermo Chasuble of St. Thomas a Becket Revealed as the Earliest Fully Dated and Localised Major Islamic Embroidery Known," *Illustrated London News*, October 3, 1959, 356–58; Annabelle Simon-Cahn, "The Fermo Chasuble of St. Thomas Becket and Hispano-Mauresque Cosmological Silks: Some Speculations on the Adaptive Reuse of Textiles," *Muqarnas* 10 (1993): 1–5; and most recently, the whole book devoted to the object, Avinoam Shalem, ed., *The Chasuble of Thomas Becket: A Biography* (Munich: Hirmer/The Bruschettini Foundation, 2017).

now obscured, from an Islamic context to a Christian one, suggest the ways in which portable objects could trace the economic, diplomatic, and cultural connections among rulers and their courtiers in the twelfth century. In their movement, such objects visualize human connections across time and space. But the objects were not inert; instead they acted on those who gifted, traded, purchased, or captured them. They could transform the worlds of those who possessed them, changing how they held their bodies or moved through space, making them envision nobility or wealth or piety in their image, and altering how they would perceive others.[2]

Although recent research suggests the Fermo chasuble's connection to Thomas Becket may be invented, and new readings of the inscription bring into question the textile's attribution to Almería, in the section that follows, I speculate about one potential path this textile could have taken from Almería to Thomas Becket in England. The details of this path and of this textile's life are ultimately unknowable, but the story I trace below shows the intimate links between Ibn Mardanīsh, his Christian neighbors, and ideas of sovereignty and power in the twelfth-century western Mediterranean. Inserting this object into fragmentary written histories integrates it not only into a "shared culture of objects" but also into the lives of individual people, who used such objects to generate their own identities: personal, political, and even imperial.[3] I use this textile to begin an investigation of what Ibn Mardanīsh and his kingdom meant to the Christians who allied with him, and how his bid for power continued to transform their ruling culture even after his death.

Thomas Becket was born in London around 1120, just about the same time Ibn Mardanīsh was born in Peñiscola. These two men—ambitious, intelligent, born noble enough to aspire to higher station—would both, by the time they died around fifty, have played important roles in political and religious changes in their kingdoms. Both would be remembered as noble and honorable by Pope Alexander III after their deaths. Thomas Becket was assassinated in 1170 after a disagreement with King Henry II (1133–89) over how much power the clergy and the papacy should have,

2 See Arjun Appadurai, "Introduction: Commodities and the Politics of Value," in *The Social Life of Things: Commodities in Cultural Perspective*, ed. Appadurai (Cambridge: Cambridge University Press, 1986), 3–63; Igor Kopytoff, "The Cultural Biography of Things: Commoditization as Process," in *The Social Life of Things*, 64–91.

3 Oleg Grabar, "The Shared Culture of Objects," in *Byzantine Court Culture from 829 to 1204*, ed. Henry Maguire (Washington, DC: Dumbarton Oaks, 2004).

and was canonized in 1173. Ibn Mardanīsh was praised in two letters from Pope Alexander III, one in or around 1167 and another in 1174, after his death, both for his nobility and his kind treatment of Christians.[4] As praise from the pope indicates, these two men were not only contemporaries but also actors in the same spheres.

Before he came into conflict with Henry II, indeed, before he even became a priest, Thomas Becket had been a trusted advisor. He was Lord Chancellor to Henry II from 1155 until 1162, serving as the king's primary advisor. At the same time he was serving in that role, Ibn Mardanīsh was building a network of alliances with his Christian neighbors, sending coins and gifts and offering fortresses and military assistance to the kings of Castile and the count-kings of Barcelona in exchange for aid against the Almohads. Ibn Mardanīsh and Henry II were both involved in the internecine conflicts among the Christian kings of the Iberian Peninsula, as will be further discussed below. Perhaps it was Thomas, in his capacity as Lord Chancellor, who received the gifts Ibn Mardanīsh sent to Henry. Henry had become king of England in 1154 and by the early 1160s was also ruling the western half of France. In 1162, he and Louis VII of France fought each other so bitterly that Alexander III had to intervene to make peace between them.[5] In the same year, according to the chronicler Robert of Torigni,[6] "Lupus, King of Valencia and Murcia, although he is a gentile and a Hagarene, gives great gifts of gold and silk, of other kinds, and of horses and camels to Henry, King of England, great things; and he will receive the same in return." Did Thomas ceremonially receive this caravan of camels and horses carrying rich gifts of gold and silk? These goods—silks, gold, camels—were the highest luxuries of the Islamic Mediterranean, universally coveted among Europeans to the north. The gifts reflected a relationship based in a brotherhood among kings, in which, as the chronicle above

4 The first letter is included in the compilation of Latin texts relating to the history of British kings and churchmen held at the Bibliothèque Nationale de France (Latin, 6238, 17v-18r); both letters are also included in Ralph of Diceto's (d. 1202) *Ymagines historiarum,* published as *Radulfi de Diceto decani Lundoniensis opera historica: The Historical Works of Master Ralph de Diceto, Dean of London, edited from the original manuscripts* by William Stubbs (London: Her Majesty's Stationery Office, 1876), vol. 1, 390, 429.

5 Graeme J. White, *Restoration and Reform, 1153–1165: Recovery from Civil War in England* (Cambridge: Cambridge University Press, 2000), 10.

6 "Leupus, rex Valentiae et Musciae, licet gentilis et Agarenus, munera ingentia in auro et serico et in aliis speciebus et in equis et camelis mittet Henricus, regi Anglorum, grandia et ipse ad eodem recepturus." *Chronique de Robert de Torigni, abbé du Mont-Saint-Michel*, ed. Léopold Delisle (Rouen: Le Brument, 1872–73), 341.

describes, a king of one territory offers great gifts to the king of another and receives gifts in return. One can imagine the textile that would become Thomas Becket's chasuble included in this litany of luxury: a textile, adorned with gold embroidery of courtly scenes, and produced at a scale large enough to function as architectural decoration.[7] It would be a fitting gift for a king to give another king.

If, as the inscription suggests, the textile was produced in Almería in 1116 CE, this would only have augmented its prestige for a king to the north of the Pyrenees. As discussed further below, the silks of Almería were known in the nascent Romance literatures of Europe as the peak of fashion, universally sought by the elite. The survival of such silks, often decorated with roundels containing figures of animals or courtly scenes, in royal burials and in reliquaries throughout Europe, show the widespread use of these textiles in palaces and churches. Thomas Becket was known for his luxurious taste in textiles. The chronicler Roger of Hoveden described how he slept on a bed covered with "cloths of silk, embroidered on the surface with gold wrought therein," and how he wore, over his hair shirt, "outer garments remarkable for their splendour and extreme costliness, to the end that, thus deceiving human eyes, he might please the sight of God."[8]

Perhaps after Henry II received the gifts of silk and gold from Ibn Mardanīsh, he had one textile made into a clerical garment, a chasuble, for his loyal advisor Thomas, who was ordained as a priest and then as archbishop of Canterbury that summer. Such a chasuble would be an expression of the king's trust in his new archbishop, just as it had been an expression of royal fellowship as a gift from Ibn Mardanīsh. In the Canterbury Cathedral, peacocks and elephants glittering in gold on the cloak of the passing archbishop, like the Arabic inscription that ran down the center of the back, would have evoked the wealth and power of the Mediterranean world, and of the king who could grant such an item to his archbishop. Although Thomas would not, in the end, offer the loyalty Henry had hoped for, and would end up murdered by the

7 The original cloth would have been at least six feet by nine feet, according to Annabelle Simon-Cahn, and she and Avinoam Shalem have both argued that it could have originally been intended for use as a tent or canopy. Simon-Cahn, "Fermo Chasuble," 3; Shalem, "Architecture for the Body: Some Reflections on the Mobility of Textiles and the Fate of the So-Called Chasuble of Saint Thomas Becket in the Cathedral of Fermo in Italy," in *Dalmatia and the Mediterranean*, ed. Alina Payne (Leiden: Brill, 2014).

8 Roger of Hoveden, *The Annals*, trans. Henry T. Riley (London: H. G. Bohn, 1853), 1:332; Simon-Cahn, "Fermo Chasuble," 2–3.

king's knights, the chasuble would go on to have a long life as a relic of the saint who might once have worn it.

Objects on the Move

Like the chasuble itself, its place of production in Almería served to link kings, popes, and craftsmen in webs of interdependence that traverse geographies, languages, and religions. Almería, as a city, a port, and a center for the production of textiles, was central to the layered and complex relationships between Ibn Mardanīsh, his Christian neighbors and their shared Almohad enemy. Narratives about the golden age of Almería's textile production indicate that it came to an end after 542/1147, when the city was conquered by Alfonso VII (r. as king of Galicia from 1111, as king of Castile-Leon from 1126 to 1157) with aid from Navarre, Barcelona, Genoa, and Pisa. This battle, officially part of the Second Crusade that was also being waged in the Holy Land, was supported by the pope and offered participants remission of their sins. The crusaders took advantage of the disorder in Sharq al-Andalus that accompanied the decline of the Almoravids and the rise of the Almohads, much as Ibn Mardanīsh had.

Evidence suggests that it was with the help of Ibn Mardanīsh that Alfonso VII and his allies managed to conquer Almería. The Castilians ruled Almería for ten years before the Almohads conquered it in turn. In 1149, Ibn Mardanīsh signed treaties with the major trading centers of Genoa and Pisa. These treaties stipulated that he pay a yearly tribute and establish houses of commerce for Genoese and Pisan merchants in the ports of Valencia and Denia, as well as provide the merchants a free weekly bath.[9] He also promised to protect Genoese and Pisan subjects in Tortosa and Almería—cities ostensibly under the control of Castile-Leon. In exchange for his protection of Genoese and Pisan trade, Ibn Mardanīsh received a ten-year peace treaty from each city.[10] These

9 These houses of commerce, known as "factories," were most likely permanent trade delegations for the Genoese and the Pisans in the ports of Sharq al-Andalus. Such institutionalization of trade was common in medieval Europe, particularly in cross-cultural circumstances. Philip Curtin, a historian of global trade and diasporas, has shown how these formal trade institutions helped regulate the cross-cultural encounter. See Curtin, *Cross-Cultural Trade in World History* (Cambridge: Cambridge University Press, 1984), 4.

10 *I diploma arabi del R. Archivio Fiorentini*, ed. Michele Amari (Florence: F. Le Monnier, 1863), 239–40; *Codice diplomatico della repubblica di Genova*, vol. 1, ed. Cesare Imperiale di Sant'Angelo (Rome: Tipografia del Senato, 1936), 247–49.

treaties are among the earliest references to the merchants' guesthouses known in Arabic as *fanādiq* (sing. *fundūq*) and in Italian as *fondacos,* which would proliferate for Christian merchants across the Islamic world in the following century.[11] Why, if Almería was a Castilian territory, were the Genoese making pacts with Ibn Mardanīsh to protect their traders and offer them baths and guesthouses? This treaty suggests that Ibn Mardanīsh administered the city in Alfonso's name after the conquest, and that it was with him those seeking to operate within the city had to negotiate.[12]

Did Ibn Mardanīsh stay in Almería in those ten years he administered the city for the Castilians? Was it visits to the Taifa palace of the city, with its muqarnas domed reception hall, and being surrounded by local silks, that inspired him to construct Dār al-Ṣughrā's muqarnas-mounted hall? The paintings and carved stucco of Dār al-Ṣughrā contain similar iconography to the silks of Almería, which also present fantastical creatures and scenes of feasting, surrounded by borders of pearls. The adaptation of these motifs into architecture may have been inspired by silks once hung on palace walls.[13] And the movement of these motifs in architecture in turn suggests the circulation of goods that bore them and trace the alliances that linked kingdoms. That is, just as Ibn Mardanīsh's palace architecture presented him as the standard-bearer of caliphal tradition by referring to local and distant precedent, creating, in the particular combination of forms that adorned his palace, a distinct visual aesthetic, so too could the use of particular goods and motifs in

11 Olivia Remie Constable, *Housing the Stranger in the Mediterranean World: Lodging, Trade, and Travel in Late Antiquity and the Middle Ages* (New York: Cambridge University Press, 2003), 126–27. Interestingly, Constable notes that the earliest treaty establishing a *fondaco* for Italian merchants is from 1146, between the Castilian king Alfonso VII and the Genoese, promising the latter the continued use of a fondaco in Almería if they help Alfonso take the city from the Muslims. Recent excavations of seven *fanādiq* in Denia suggest that some of these structures may be the factories built for the Genoese or Pisans under Ibn Mardanīsh's authority. See a news report about these excavations here: "Una investigación detecta 7 'hoteles' de época islámica en Dénia, más que en ninguna otra ciudad del país," *La Marina Plaza,* 10 February 2020, https://lamarinaplaza.com/2020/02/10/una-investigacion-detecta-7-hoteles-de-la-era-islamica-en-denia-mas-que-en-ninguna-otra-ciudad-del-pais/ (accessed April 29, 2020).

12 *Codice diplomatico della repubblica di Genova*, 1:248–49.

13 There is a substantial literature on the interplay between textiles and architecture in Islamic contexts. See Lisa Golombek, "The Draped Universe of Islam," in *Content and Context of Visual Arts in the Islamic World: Papers from a Colloquium in Memory of Richard Ettinghausen*, ed. Priscilla Soucek and Carol Bier (University Park: Pennsylvania State University Press, 1988); more recently, see the special issue of the *Textile Museum Journal* (vol. 45, 2018) edited by Patricia Blessing, "Draping, Wrapping, Hanging: Transposing Textile Materiality in the Middle Ages."

the courts of his Christian neighbors carry meaning. As the Muslim vassal administering an Islamic city for a coalition of Christian kings in the aftermath of a crusade, Ibn Mardanīsh built close mercantile and military relationships with Christian neighbors that facilitated the ongoing transmission of material and forms from his territories to points north. This was a world in which people and things moved constantly, tracing trajectories that often contravened the religious or political ideologies they espoused. Kings could pledge to conquer the territories of all the Saracens one month and then travel, in person, to aid a Muslim ally the next—and return weighed down with rich gifts of thanks that would become signs of royal wealth and glory for generations.

Some of these Almería silks that such kings received as gifts or tribute spoke in a explicitly eastern voice. The shroud enclosing San Pedro de Osma, a Cluniac monk who died in 1109, was removed from his tomb at the church of Burgo de Osma in 1968.[14] It was a *jubba*, or cloak, of elaborate figured silk, with doubled bands of pearled roundels surrounding two lions biting two harpies. Between the bands of pearls, in the circle framing the central image, sit four men, each holding two griffins. At the cardinal points of these double circles are smaller doubled roundels, with rosettes at their center, and an inscription that runs in a band through the pearled borders: "This is from what was made in the city of Baghdad, may God protect it."[15] The material was designed with green, red, and yellow silk woven on a cream background, with its most important elements brocaded in gold. Early scholars puzzled over

---

14 Dorothy Shepherd used the death date of the saint to argue that the cloak was produced in the early twelfth century. It is important to note, however, that the saint was disinterred and reinterred in a new sarcophagus in 1250, and as adding textiles to the tombs of saints seems to have been a custom, it is entirely possible that this textile was produced later. See Shepherd, "A Dated Hispano-Islamic Silk," *Ars Orientalis* 2 (1957): 373–82; on adding silks to tombs, see María Judith Feliciano, "Muslim Shrouds for Christian Kings? A Reassessment of Andalusi Textiles in Thirteenth Century Castilian Life and Ritual," in *Under the Influence: Questioning the Comparative in Medieval Castile*, edited by Cynthia Robinson and Leyla Rouhi (Leiden: Brill, 2005).

15 *Hādhā mimmā ʿumila bi-madīnat Baghdād ḥarasahā Allāh*. See Florence Day, "The Inscription of the Boston 'Baghdad' Silk: A Note on Method in Epigraphy," *Ars Orientalis* 1 (1954): 191–94. For more on the textile, now held at the Boston Museum of Fine Arts (no. 33.371), see Partearroyo, "Almoravid and Almohad Textiles." Thomas Glick argues that Abbasid goods were imitated with considerable regularity in Almería and elsewhere in al-Andalus, *Islamic and Christian Spain in the Early Middle Ages* (Princeton, NJ: Princeton University Press, 1979), 277. Feliciano also shows how "the fine art of knocking-off luxury goods" was well known throughout the Mediterranean; see "Medieval Textiles in Iberia: Studies for a New Approach," in *Envisioning Islamic Art and Architecture: Essays in Honor of Renata Holod*, ed. D. J. Roxburgh (Leiden, The Netherlands: Brill, 2014), 52.

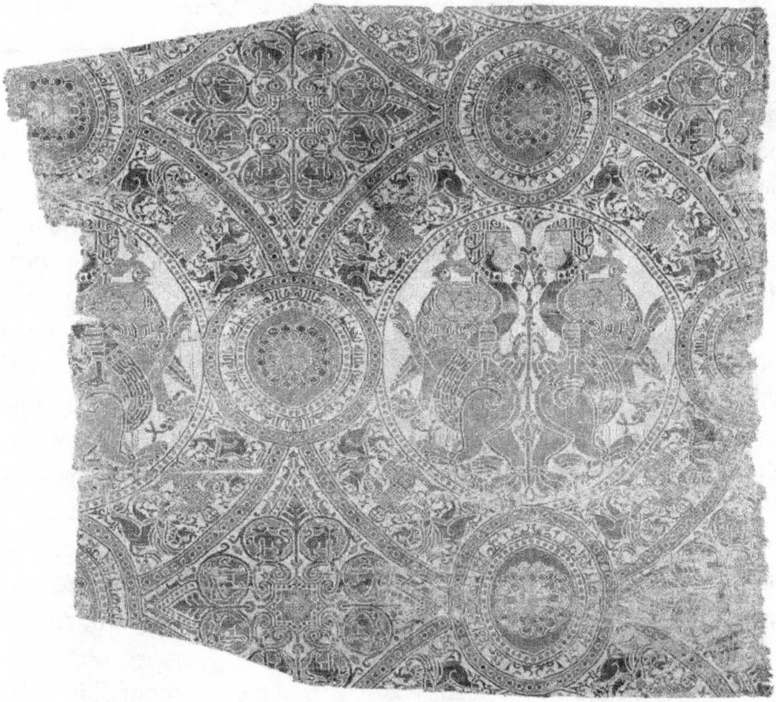

FIGURE 5.2. Fragment from the shroud of San Pedro de Osma, twelfth century. *Photo*: © Museum of Fine Arts, Boston. *Credit*: *Fragment with Wrestling Lions and Harpies*, Spanish (probably Almería), Almoravid, early twelfth century, 50 x 43 cm. Ellen Page Hall Fund, 33.371.

how a textile from Baghdad might have made its way into the tomb of a saint in Soria.[16] But twenty years later, the American textile scholar and Arabist Florence Day proved, through exhaustive analysis of every recorded textile inscription from the eleventh and twelfth centuries, that the unusual spelling of *hādhā* ("this"), with two long *alifs*, was particular to Andalusī contexts.[17] Further research by another American scholar, Dorothy Shepherd, showed that the fabric shared a weave structure with a series of textiles thought to have been produced in the city of Almería in the first half of the twelfth century; she confirmed the connection by finding a dated textile with an inscription dedicated to the Almoravid emir ʿAlī ibn Yūsuf.[18]

16 H. A. Elsberg and R. Guest, "Another Silk Fabric Woven at Baghdad," *Burlington Magazine* 64 (June 1934): 270–72.

17 Day, "Inscription of the Boston 'Baghdad' Silk."

18 Shepherd, "Dated Hispano-Islamic Silk."

Modern scholars long read inscriptions on textiles (and elsewhere) as statements of fact; the name of a ruler or a location woven into a silk provided much desired historical context for its production. But the shroud of Pedro de Osma instead suggests the more complex set of meanings an inscription could evoke, beyond and sometimes in contradiction to the literal meaning of its inscription. Falsifying inscriptions on textiles seems to have been widespread in the period. A manual for market inspectors written by al-Saqaṭī in eleventh- or twelfth-century Malaga urged the market inspector to prevent weavers from changing inscriptions, "a well-known practice of disreputable persons."[19] Whether or not consumers would have seen such textiles as authentically connected to the places or people their inscriptions proclaimed is an open question. The Burgo de Osma silk suggests that for the Arabic-literate market in al-Andalus, silks with figural scenes enclosed in roundels may have been associated with Baghdad, and an inscription labeling it as such might have served like a brand name for this particular form. For the Christians of northern Europe, such textiles were known as Almería silks, though the city was far from the only center of silk production in al-Andalus.

Such silks thus illuminate the transcultural movement of objects and forms, from the Islamic east to North Africa and al-Andalus, and from there to Christian kingdoms of Iberia. Even those Almería textiles that were not labeled as products of Baghdad used motifs—such as fantastical beasts and heroic scenes framed by pearled roundels—that were in vogue in the Abbasid East. The cluster of textiles Shepherd identified seem to indicate that Almería in the twelfth century was a center for the production of counterfeit "Baghdad" silks, along with several other types of textiles that appear in Arabic chronicles with names associated with the Islamic East.[20] Many of these textiles ended up in the tombs of saints, clergymen, and kings in the Christian north.[21] The mechanisms of their production and circulation are obscure, with only hints in chronicles that mention gifts, booty, or trade. But their outsized importance in the

---

19 R. B. Serjeant, "Material for a History of Islamic Textiles up to the Mongol Conquest" [part 5], *Ars Islamica* 15/16 (1951): 36.

20 Writing in the seventeenth century, al-Maqqarī reported that Almería had contained thousands of looms and had produced types of silk fabric including *siqlāṭūn* (scarlet, and perhaps figured with roundels) and *dibāj* as well as imitations of Iraqi and Iranian silks such as *attabī*, *iṣfahānī*, and *jurjānī*.

21 On this question, see María Judith Feliciano, "Muslim Shrouds for Christian Kings?" and "Medieval Textiles in Iberia: Studies for a New Approach."

Mediterranean and beyond, recorded in the new vernacular literatures of medieval Europe and preserved in the most holy and precious contexts of the church, reveal a reality in which ideas about beauty, luxury, power, and holiness traversed the whole known world.

The Almería "Baghdad" silk offers interesting parallels to Ibn Mardanīsh's cultural production. Like Ibn Mardanīsh's coinage, it contained pure gold traded from across the Sahara and an inscription that proclaimed its connection to Abbasid Baghdad. Like his coinage, this silk and similar objects traversed the Iberian Peninsula as gifts and objects of exchange, their ubiquity in Christian Europe evidenced by written references (e.g., to "soies d'Aumarie" or "morabetinos lupinos") across a vast geography. And although it is unlikely that the shroud of Pedro de Osma was produced while Ibn Mardanīsh ruled, the web of connections the textile traced, from the trans-Saharan trade routes to the Mediterranean port of Almería and from the Abbasid capital in the east to the Christian courts and churches of the west, were the same that would define Ibn Mardanīsh's reign.

The silks associated with Almería, like the shroud of San Pedro de Osma, spoke in the visual language of the eastern Islamic world, and were universally coveted in the Christian west. Almería, conquered by a coalition of Christian kings precisely because of its economic importance as a Mediterranean port and center of textile and ceramic production, facilitated the transition of these objects and motifs from Islamic contexts into Christian ones. This does not mean that Almería silks flooded into the courts of Castile, Barcelona, Genoa, and Pisa in 1147 as booty, and were understood as symbols of conquest. On the contrary, new technical analysis of textiles from collections like the treasury of San Isidoro show that a single Iberian church could incorporate textiles produced in Central Asia, Byzantium, the Near East, and Iberia, from the ninth through the thirteenth century.[22] Luxurious silk textiles, many woven with gold, featuring animals in roundels, inscriptions, or human figures, from the east and from the west, were in great demand across the Iberian Peninsula, among Muslims and Christians. As María

---

22 See the remarkable technical analysis of the fourteen textiles held in the treasury of San Isidoro in Leon by Ana Cabrera Lafuente, "Textiles from the Museum of San Isidoro (León): New Evidence for Re-Evaluating their Chronology and Provenance," in *The Medieval Iberian Treasury in the Context of Cultural Interchange*, expanded ed., ed. Therese Martin (Leiden: Brill, 2020). Feliciano's article in the same volume, "Sovereign, Saint and City: Honor and Reuse of Textiles in the Treasury of San Isidoro (León)," analyses how this collection worked to construct ideas about the monarchy, the church, and the city of León over time.

Judith Feliciano writes, imagining that silks from diverse origins had a single meaning across Iberia and across time risks losing sight of the complexity of production, exchange, and consumption that characterized the medieval world:

> Taking for granted that a sumptuous silk in a Northern Iberian, or "Christian," context arrived at its location simply as the product of conquest over Muslim territory or a limited cross-frontier traffic not only closes the door to a rich world of consumption and exchange but also isolates the historically diverse Iberian material world within fictitiously closed borders.[23]

In the mid-twelfth century, when the port and textile workshops of Almería came under Castilian (and perhaps Mardanīshī) control, it helped to facilitate access to goods produced and traded there. The conquest was not the engine that drove desire for such textiles but was instead driven by a confluence of economic and religious opportunism that promised increased access to highly sought-after Mediterranean goods. Perhaps Almería functioned in northern European literature as a synecdoche for the Mediterranean itself, and all of the textiles, woven of silk and gold, that had been circulating through it for centuries.

Almería was famous for its textile manufacturing in Arabic sources as well. Soon after the city's founding in the mid-tenth century, al-Rāzī's geographic description of al-Andalus noted that in Almería "they produce beautiful silk textiles brocaded with gold."[24] This production seems to have increased even further under the Almoravids in the first half of the twelfth century, and sources offer lists of textiles woven in Almería with names derived from places more distant.[25] This reflects what has generally been seen as the Almoravids' "easternizing" mode, adapting techniques and motifs from Central Asia by way of Baghdad and Constantinople.[26] Al-Idrīsī (d. 559/1165) reports in his *Kitāb Rūjar*, written in Palermo for Roger II and completed in 548/1154, that before

---

23 Feliciano, "Medieval Textiles in Iberia," 64–65.

24 Évariste Lévi-Provençal, "La 'Description de l'Espagne' de Rāzī," *al-Andalus* 17, no. 1 (1953): 51–108, here 67.

25 Elsayed Abdel Aziz Salem, "Algunos aspectos del florecimiento económico de Almería islámica durante el período de los Taifas y de los Almorávides," *Revista del Instituto Egipcio de Estudios Islámicos* 20 (1979–80): 7–22, here 21.

26 Cristina Partearroyo Lacaba, "Tejidos Andalusíes," *Artigrama* 22 (2007): 371--419, here 383.

the 542/1147 conquest Almería had eight hundred ṭirāz workshops producing silk cloth and garments:

> There were to be found there (in the time of the Almoravids) all wonderful kinds of crafts, and they counted among others, eight hundred factories (*ṭirāz*) for silk (*ḥarīr*) where they made precious mantles (*ḥulla*), brocades, *siqlāṭūn*, Iṣfahānī, Jurjānī, curtains ornamented with precious stones (*sutūr mukallala*), cloth with patterns of circles, small mats (*khumra*), ʿAttabī, veils (*miʿjar*), and various other kinds of silk cloths. . . . Ships used to come to Almeria from Alexandria and Syria. . . . At the time when we are writing the present work, Almeria has fallen into the power of the Christians. Its comeliness has disappeared, the inhabitants have been enslaved, the houses and public buildings have been destroyed, and there is nothing left.[27]

Iṣfaḥānī was presumably made to look like a textile from Isfahan, a capital of the Saljuqs in present-day Iran, and Jurjānī from Jurjān, south of the Caspian Sea, whereas ʿAttabī was named after a neighborhood in Baghdad. For al-Idrīsī in Sicily, Almería was known as a center for Eastern-style silks, and its conquest by the Christians spelled the end of its fame for textiles. In spite of al-Idrīsī's bitter assessment, Almería seems to have persisted as a major trading port after the conquest. At the moment when al-Idrīsī was writing, it was likely Ibn Mardanīsh was administering Almería for the Castilians, setting up *fanādiq* for Genoese and Pisan merchants, and sending gifts woven by Almerian craftsmen to his allies. Perhaps he was also offering the weavers of Almería new workshops in his own capital in Murcia. In the second half of the twelfth century, new mentions of Murcia as a center of silk production also appear.[28]

The silks associated with Almería were not only coveted in the Christian kingdoms of Iberia but were the defining luxury good in twelfth-century Europe more broadly. They appear across literature and chronicles and survive in noble tombs and reliquary contexts in England, France, and Germany. In literature they are often referred to

---

27 Al-Idrīsī, *Description de l'Afrique et de l'Espagne*, ed. and trans. R. P. A. Dozy and M. J. de Goeje (Leiden: Brill, 1866), 197, translated to English in Serjeant, "Materials for a History of Islamic Textiles" [part 5, 1951], 34.

28 David Jacoby, "The Production and Diffusion of Andalusi Silks and Silk Textiles, Mid-Eighth to Mid-Thirteenth Century," in *The Chasuble of Thomas Becket: A Biography*, ed. Avinoam Shalem (Munich: Hirmer, 2017), 144–45. See further discussion below.

as *siglaton* or *ciclaton*, derived from the Arabic *siqlāṭūn*, which may refer to textiles with roundels containing animals, or as *tirez*, from the Arabic ṭirāz, for inscribed textiles.[29] They are mentioned in works such as the *Cantar de mio Cid* (1140), which mentions *ciclaton* as well as fabric embroidered with gold thread, and the *Roman d'Alexandre* (ca. 1180), which refers to *siglatons d'Espagne* and *pales d'Aumarie* (silks of Almería). Other French romances also refer to silks, *porpre* (dark colored silks), and tirez of Almería. The poem "Parzival" by German poet Wolfram von Eschenbach (ca. 1170–ca. 1220) features Almería silks, and Roger of Hoveden, the English chronicler, mentions them, too.[30] A huge number of textiles associated with twelfth-century Almería ended up as shrouds for saints and relics throughout Europe. It is important to note, however, that like the many other names for textiles derived from places, like the English denim ("de Nîmes") or damask (from Damascus), silks known in literature as those of Almería may have been woven in other places, including, perhaps, in Christian cities.[31]

The textiles associated with Almería share visual characteristics with Sasanian and Byzantine precedents, and though produced in the Islamic west were designed to evoke the east. Images of fantastical creatures like griffins and heroic beasts like lions and eagles, usually enclosed in pearled roundels, were ubiquitous on the silks of Taifa and Almoravid al-Andalus. In fact, such images on textiles had their roots in the pre-Islamic Sasanian world. In a narrative in the *Thousand and One Nights*, a woman is described as being dressed in the clothes of the kings of the Sasanians (*mulūk al-akāsira*), "including a garment adorned (*manqūsh*) with red gold, having pictures of beasts and birds upon it."[32] Similar figurative silks continued being produced in the Byzantine world as well as in Islamic regions. Far before such silks became objects of desire in medieval French romance, they were world-spanning hybrids, echoing

---

29 The best source on the Arabic names of textiles remains Serjeant, "Materials for a History of Islamic Textiles," whose five parts first appeared serially in *Ars Islamica* 9–16 (1942–51). Serjeant argues that *siqlāṭūn* means scarlet silk, while Jacoby says the name derives from Greek, indicating a textile type originally from Byzantium, and argues that it referred to textiles with animals contained in roundels. David Jacoby, "Silk Economics and Cross-Cultural Artistic Interaction: Byzantium, the Muslim World, and the Christian West," *Dumbarton Oaks Papers* 58 (2004): 197–240, here 212.

30 This list is adapted from Jacoby, "Production and Diffusion," 146.

31 Feliciano notes that voracious demand for luxury silks led Mozarabic weavers to set up villages in Castile that produced tiraz, perhaps directly for the royal court. See "Medieval Textiles in Iberia," 55.

32 Cited in Serjeant, "Material for a History of Islamic Textiles" [part 5, 1951], 64.

the robes of long-dead kings centuries after their empires had collapsed, even as the artisans who made them incorporated new materials, techniques and inscriptions.

The silks of Almería, so ubiquitous in the written record of early twelfth-century Europe, continued to be famous even after the Almohad conquest of the city in 552/1157.[33] But such silks also began to be produced in new centers. Contemporary sources write that Murcia and Malaga had become centers of silk production by the late twelfth century, and there are indications that Andalusī silk traded through Genoa later circulated throughout the Mediterranean.[34] Al-Shaqundī (d. 629/1231–32) also mentioned silks of Murcia, and there are records of silks "de Mucia" arriving in London in 1166–67.[35] Regardless of their site of production, silks of this type continued to be called "Almería silks" in the courtly literature of France, England, and Germany well into the thirteenth century.[36]

The trade of luxury goods including these silks likely facilitated Ibn Mardanīsh's vast building projects and the tribute he had to pay his Christian allies. At least some of the money Ibn Mardanīsh was obligated to pay his Christian allies was obtained through the lucrative trade with Genoa and Pisa. The trade conducted with these kingdoms also included substantial quantities of painted ceramics, which were produced in Sharq al-Andalus and were in high demand in the Italian city-states.[37] In addition to its use in households, some Murcian and Valencian lusterware was used as bacini to decorate the exteriors of Genoese and Pisan churches.[38] At least some of these ceramics

33 Salem, "Algunos aspectos del florecimiento económico de Almería islámica," 22.

34 Jacoby, "Production and Diffusion," 144–46.

35 Frederique Lachaud, "Les soieries importées en Angleterre (fin XIIe et XIIIe siecles)," in *Soieries medievales: Techniques et cultures; Pour une ethnologie de l'acte traditionnel efficace* (Paris: Éditions de la Maison des sciences de l'homme, 1999), 182; Jacoby, "Production and Diffusion," 146. Jacoby argues against Lachaud's reading that "de Mucia" means Mozarab and suggests it means Murcia instead (see Jacoby, "Production and Diffusion," 151n100).

36 Sharon Kinoshita, "Almeria Silk and the French Feudal Imaginary: Toward a 'Material' History of the Medieval Mediterranean," in *Medieval Fabrications: Dress, Textiles, Clothwork, and Other Cultural Imaginings*, ed. E. Jane Burns (New York: Palgrave Macmillan, 2004).

37 Painted pottery from Sharq al-Andalus was apparently widely used in domestic settings. Alberto García Porras and Adela Fábregas García cite a will from the second half of the twelfth century that records a modest Genoese family's ownership of "unam scutellam pictam de Almeria." See "La cerámica española en el comercio mediterráneo bajomedieval. Algunas notas documentales," *Miscelánea Medieval Murciana* 27–28 (2004): 10.

38 See, for example, the quatrefoil bowl from San Silvestro Church (Museo Nazionale San Matteo, *bacino* no. 190) and the bowl with bird from Sant' Andrea Church (Museo Nazionale San Matteo, *bacino* no. 232) from Pisa, both attributed to twelfth-century Murcia.

FIGURE 5.3. Lustered ceramics used as bacini, at least some from Murcia, on church of Sant'Andrea, twelfth century, Pisa. *Photo:* Wikimedia Commons; photo uploaded by Sailko, licensed under the Creative Commons Attribution-ShareAlike 3.0 Unported (CC BY-SA 3.0) license (https://creativecommons.org/licenses/by-sa/3.0/).

were ornamented with figural imagery of the kind also found on the walls of Ibn Mardanīsh's palace in Murcia. Genoese records also indicate the city's great desire for "silks of Baghdad" (*panni di bagadello*), imported in vast quantities in the middle of the twelfth century.[39] Presumably the new Genoese and Pisan access to the port of Almería and the textiles produced in its mills facilitated this taste for luxury fabrics. Merchants were aware of the Spanish origin of some of these fabrics, as indicated by the name "bagadelli hispanici" given to textiles exported from Genoa to Ceuta, on the North African coast, in 1201.[40] In these processes of consumption, reproduction, and imitation, place names served as shorthand for luxury and form. They also map layered

39 Jacoby, "Silk Economics," 218.

40 Further complicating the layered meaning of names associated with textiles, Jacoby believes it would have been unlikely for the Genoese to export Spanish silks via Genoa to Ceuta, and argues that this record indicates the Genoese were producing their own Spanish Baghdad silks by the beginning of the thirteenth century. Jacoby, "Silk Economics," 218.

connections: expressions of cultural continuity, patterns of trade, and alliances among kings.

Ideas about Arabness in Christian Europe

Robert of Torigni's chronicle, mentioned above, refers to Ibn Mardanīsh as Rex Lupus and as a Hagarene. These terms shed light on the attitudes of his Christian neighbors and soldiers toward Islam in general and toward him more specifically. These attitudes were quite complex and changed according to political circumstance. But even though Ibn Mardanīsh's reign is typically presented as a time of increasingly intense Christian-Muslim warfare spurred by ideas of crusading and holy war, writings about him in Christian contexts offer a different picture. They reflect constantly shifting relationships of enmity and friendship among kings of different religions. They also show a remarkable awareness among Christians of the different groups of Muslims jockeying for power on the Iberian Peninsula and reveal that ideas about nobility and lineage overlapped in interesting ways.

"Hagarene" was one of the main labels used by medieval Europeans to refer to Muslims; the term was based on Muslims' perceived descent from Hagar and her son, Ishmael. It coexisted with other names, such as the even more common "Saracen," which John of Damascus derived from a Greek pun about Sarah sending Hagar away empty.[41] It therefore situated Muslims within a Christian framework, marking them as heretics descended from biblical figures, the misguided cousins of Jews and Christians. At the same time, as Simon Barton has shown, some medieval Iberian sources use these terms in far more nuanced ways that demonstrate the authors' awareness of multiple groups of competing Muslims with different roots. The *Chronica Adefonsi Imperatoris* differentiates among different Muslim groups on the basis of their geographic or ethnic origins, calling the Almoravids Moabites (a name derived from the Biblical son of Lot, Moab), Almohads Assyrians or Muzmutos (a word derived from the Masmūda tribal group), and Andalusīs Arabs or Hagarenes.[42] Calling Ibn Mardanīsh a Hagarene

41 John Tolan, *Saracens: Islam in the Medieval European Imagination* (New York: Columbia University Press, 2002), 52.

42 Petrus Alfonsi identified the biblical Moabites with Muslims generally in the first half of the twelfth century, but it seems to have come to specifically refer to Almoravids, perhaps, as Hélène Sirantoine has suggested, because of the phonetic similarity between the Latin *Mo(h)abitae* and Arabic *murābiṭ*. Sirantoine, "What's in a Word? Naming 'Muslims' in Medieval

might thus have been a way of emphasizing his difference from the Almohads and consequently of indicating his suitability as an ally for Christian kings confronting the Almohad caliphate.

The perplexing name by which he is consistently known in Latin and Castilian sources, "Rex Lupus" or "Rey Lobo," the Wolf King, has not yet been fully explained. In Latin and Castilian chronicles and treaties, other Muslim rulers are given Latinized versions of their Arabic names or titles, such as Miramolin for *amīr al-mu ʾminīn*. Discussing the Muslim vassals of the kings of Navarre and the count-kings of Barcelona, Lucas of Tuy (d. 1249) referred to Ibn Mardanīsh and his near-contemporaries Ibn Ḥamdīn (d. 547/1152) and Sayf al-Dawla (d. 540/1146) collectively as "the kings of the Saracens" but individually as "Abephandil et Zaphadola et rex Lupus."[43] Why does Ibn Mardanīsh have the title "rex" before his name, and why is he called "wolf"?

There are tantalizing suggestions that the term *wolf* may have implied mixed parentage in Iberian contexts, in both the medieval and early modern periods. In the ninth century, Paul Alvarus's biographies of female Cordoban martyrs born of Muslim fathers and Christian mothers described them as "created out of wolfish union."[44] In the early modern Atlantic world, from at least the seventeenth century onward, children of mixed heritage could be classified as "wolves."[45] In both of these contexts, wolf seems to have been a pejorative name, evoking the danger,

---

Christian Iberia," in *Making the Medieval Relevant: How Medieval Studies Contribute to Improving our Understanding of the Past*, ed. Chris Jones, Conor Kostick, and Klaus Oschema (Berlin: De Gruyter, 2020), 225–38; Meritxell Bru, "Posar un nom. Els Almoràvits com a Moabites a finals del segle XI," *Faventia* 31 (2009):129–49; Simon Barton, "Islam and the West: A View from Twelfth-Century León," in *Cross, Crescent, and Conversion: Studies on Medieval Spain and Christendom in Memory of Richard Fletcher* (Leiden: Brill, 2008), 162.

43 Lucas de Tuy, *El Chronicon Mundi de Lucas de Tuy: Edición crítica y estudio*, ed. O. Valdés García (Salamanca: Ediciones Universidad Salamanca, 1996), 378: "Etenim rex Garsies de Nauarra et Raymundus comes Barchilonensis, qui tunc Aragonense regebat regnum et reges Sarracenorum scilicet, Abephandil et Zaphadola et rex Lupus, uno et aodem tempore eius uassalli fuerunt."

44 Jessica A. Coope, *The Martyrs of Córdoba: Community and Family Conflict in an Age of Mass Conversion* (Lincoln: University of Nebraska Press, 1995), 27.

45 In describing a revolt in Mexico City in 1692, Carlos Sigüenza y Góngora (1645–1700) wrote that it was made up of "a common folk so very common . . . composed of Indians, of Blacks both locally born and of different nations in Africa, *chinos*, mulattos, *moriscos*, mestizos, *zambaigos*, *lobos*, and even Spaniards . . . who are the worst among such a vile mob." Translated and quoted in Ilona Katzew, "Casta Painting: Identity and Social Stratification in Colonial Mexico," in *New World Orders: Casta Painting and Colonial Latin America* (New York: Americas Society Art Gallery, 1996). The eighteenth-century casta paintings produced in New Spain and Spain generally included images of the "lobo," usually classified as a mixture of Black and Indian parentage.

irrationality, and potential for violence of a ferocious wild animal. But the simultaneous use of the term *rex*, king, for Ibn Mardanīsh seems to contradict this assessment, and the surviving uses of "wolf" to indicate mixed parentage are both centuries distant from Ibn Mardanīsh's time. There is also no indication that Ibn Mardanīsh's Christian interlocutors (or any of his contemporaries) saw him as any different ethnically or religiously from other Andalusī rulers.

It is evident that Rex Lupus was not a pejorative name, since it was used alongside words of praise both in Ibn Mardanīsh's time and in subsequent centuries. In the mid-thirteenth century, Pope Alexander IV issued a bull regarding the unification of the churches of Segorbe and Albarracín that referred to the former ruler of Murcia and Valencia as "Wolf King (Rex Lupus) of glorious memory." This king, he wrote, had granted the territory of Albarracín to a noble Christian man, and the city had remained loyal to the church even during Saracen occupation. For the pope in Rome, the distant reign of a Muslim king, now dead, was worth remembering as a model of how even Saracens could rule with justice.[46]

Emilio Molina López has suggested that Ibn Mardanīsh may have had a Castilian nickname—"Lope," or "Lubb" in Arabic—that was latinized into Lupus as a Castilian name would have been.[47] Another fascinating hypothesis was put forward by Al-Ṭāhir Makkī and Mikel de Epalza in the context of discussing the name of the Cid. Makkī argued that the Arabic *al-sīd*, from which the name Cid derives, comes not from *al-sayyid*, or lord, as has been conventionally assumed, but instead from *sīd*, an ancient word used in Arabic poetry to refer to fierce animals,

---

46 Bull of Alexander IV, 1258, in Jaime Villanueva, *Viage literario a las iglesias de España* (Madrid: Imprenta de la Real Academia de la Historia, 1851), 3:235. "Petitio vestra nobis exhibita continebat quod quondam Petrus Roderici, nobilitate sanguinis, et morum honestate praeclarus, a clarae memoriae Lupo Rege quaedam castella, et villa obtinuit, quae a sarracenis fuerant diutias occupata, in quae siquidem idem P. postea sollicitudine operosa christianos habitatores induxit . . . " Villanueva suggests in footnote (b) that Petrus Roderici should be Petrus Ferrandi, or D. Pedro Fernandez de Azagra, who, he states, received Albarracín from Ibn Mardanīsh. On this fascinating figure and the independent *señorío* of Albarracín, granted by Ibn Mardanīsh to the Azagra family of Navarre, see Martín Almagro Basch, *Historia de Albarracín y su sierra*, vol. 3 (Teruel: Instituto de Estudios Terolenses, 1959); José María Lacarra, "El Rey Lobo de Murcia y el señorio de Albarracín," in *Estudios dedicados a Don Ramón Menéndez Pidal III* (Madrid: Consejo Superior de Investigaciones Científicas, 1952).

47 Emilio Molina López, "Ibn Mardanis," *Diccionario Biográfico electrónico de la Real Academia de la Historia* (http://dbe.rah.es/biografias/16905/ibn-mardanis).

especially wolves or lions.[48] De Epalza advanced this argument, noting that the classical Arabic *asad*, for lion, is to this day shortened to *ṣīd* in North African dialects, and that great military leaders in al-Andalus were often called lion or *ṣīd* in praise of their bravery and ferocity.[49] Both scholars point to Ibn Mardanīsh, "el rey lobo," as another example of a military man in Sharq al-Andalus who gained a name associated with a fierce animal.[50] In his case, of course, it was not the Muslim soldiers of a Christian warrior calling their leader by the Arabic name of a beast but rather the Christian soldiers or allies of a Muslim leader giving him a Latin or Castilian nickname after a wild creature. In the cases of the Cid and Rex Lupus alike, it is entirely possible that the names by which they were known shifted in usage and meaning, so that a name that began as a comment about bravery could later be heard or understood as another word entirely. De Epalza further suggested that the Arabic *ṣīd* for lion eventually became *sīdī*, "my lord." Lupus/Lobo/Lubb may have functioned similarly, starting as a compliment and then becoming something closer to a Castilian personal name.

Treaties, Vassalage, and Tribute

The kings of Castile, Leon, Aragon, Navarre, Barcelona, their peers across the Pyrenees, as well as the Wolf King of Murcia and Valencia and the Almohads, formed kaleidoscopic alliances that were constantly realigning into new formations. Noblemen who fell out of favor in one territory traveled to another, finding patronage and status in exchange for their inside knowledge that facilitated their new patrons' battles against their former overlords.[51] Multiple competing kingdoms offered possibilities for soldiers as well as for craftsmen and scholars to find new sources of patronage if they found themselves

48 Al-Ṭāhir Aḥmad Makkī, *Malḥamat al-Sīd: Awwal malḥama andalusiyya kutibat fī al-lugha al-qashtaliyya* (Cairo: Dār al-Maʿārif, 1970), 173–82.

49 M. de Epalza, "El Cid = El León: ¿Epíteto árabe del Campeador?" *Hispanic Review* 45, no. 1 (1977): 67–75.

50 De Epalza, "El Cid = El León," 70; Makkī, *Malḥamat al-Sīd*, 176.

51 For a discussion of some of the fascinating Castilian noblemen who were on the move in the twelfth and thirteenth centuries, between Castile, Leon, the Almohads, and more, see Simon Barton, "From Mercenary to Crusader: The Career of Álvar Pérez de Castro (d. 1239) Re-examined," in *Church, State, Vellum and Stone: Essays on Medieval Spain in Honor of John Williams*, ed. Julie Harris and Therese Martin (Leiden: Brill, 2005); and Barton, "Traitors to the Faith? Christian Mercenaries in al-Andalus and the Maghreb, c. 1100–1300," in *Medieval Spain: Culture, Conflict and Coexistence; Studies in Honour of Angus MacKay*, ed. Roger Collins and Anthony Goodman (New York: Macmillan, 2002).

disgraced. For kings, too, the plethora of potential allies proved a boon in a period of constant low-grade conflict. In the fratricidal kingdoms of the Iberian Peninsula, allies who based their claim to legitimacy on an alternate religious tradition could pose a smaller threat than did the brothers, cousins, or uncles who ruled the kingdoms next door. Such non-coreligionists were less likely to claim rights over neighboring kingdoms. For the Christian kings of Iberia, the fact that alliance with Ibn Mardanīsh brought clear benefits in tribute, protection from the Almohads, and ability to fight ambitious rivals made treaties with him quite desirable.

As Hussein Fancy has shown, however, decisions about alliance and enmity that crossed religious lines were not propelled solely by pragmatism or a practical, pecuniary calculus. In the context of thirteenth-century Aragon, Fancy demonstrates, partnerships could be based on complementary visions of sovereignty: the Aragonese kings received a boost to their imperial claims from the presence of non-Christian knights in their employ, while the North African warriors themselves found an opportunity to wage jihad in fighting other Christians on behalf of the Aragonese.[52] Similarly, for the rulers who alternately aligned with and fought each other, allies of different religions could augment their international stature. At the same time, crusading against Muslims on the Iberian Peninsula also carried enormous prestige, and rulers and soldiers believed it could win them rewards in both this world and the next. Ibn Mardanīsh's treatment in Christian sources demonstrates that he mostly managed to occupy the first of these two zones, as a fellow king to be honored and respected, whose loyalty reflected positively on his Christian allies. But as a Muslim ruler, he was sometimes lumped together with the rest of the "Saracens" and his territories were targeted for conquest.

While Ibn Mardanīsh's cultural production made the case for his legitimacy in religious and ideological terms, his alliances provided him with the economic and military might to maintain his hold on power. As a result, Ibn Mardanīsh was able to create what María Jesús Viguera Molíns calls a third option in the ambit of Andalusī religious relations, preserving an ideological distinction from the Christians while paying them tribute. As she points out, it was this model that would remain the most powerful in Iberia in subsequent centuries, when the Nasrids

52 Hussein Fancy, *The Mercenary Mediterranean: Sovereignty, Religion, and Violence in the Medieval Crown of Aragon* (Chicago: University of Chicago Press, 2017).

would continue paying tribute to Castile while elaborating their own ruling ideology.[53]

Ibn Mardanīsh's alliances with Barcelona and Castile were particularly long-lasting and important to his military success, and his trade agreements with Genoa and Pisa supported his kingdom economically. These alliances were fodder for Ibn Mardanīsh's critics, including the Almohad chronicler Ibn Ṣāḥib al-Ṣalā, who cursed his name and referred to the Christian kings as "his friends" (*aṣḥābihi*).[54] But as a survey of Ibn Mardanīsh's cultural production demonstrates, he was much more than a simple puppet that the Christians deployed against the Almohads. Instead, Ibn Mardanīsh was one of many contemporaneous Muslim rulers who sought to establish an effective form of rule during a moment of massive transition in the Islamic world. He developed a dynamic conception of authority rooted in Almoravid examples that also incorporated the new forms appearing in distant Islamic lands. The adaptability of his articulation of authority shows an Islamic political system in flux and a particularly resourceful ruler who used Islamic models old and new to counter the claims of his rivals and to maintain his independence.

Barcelona provided important military and economic support to Ibn Mardanīsh's territories, and he aided them in turn, paying Ramon Berenguer IV, count-king of Barcelona, some hundred thousand gold dinars a year in *parias*, or tribute. Al-Maqqarī reports that Ibn Mardanīsh asked the count of Barcelona for help to fight the Almohads in 546/1151, and that the count obliged by sending ten thousand soldiers to assist him. This added contingent scared the Almohads so much that they retreated without engaging.[55] Records from Barcelona also report that in March 1152, Ramon Berenguer himself, at the head of a substantial army, came to the aid of the Rey Lobo, because he considered him a vassal, and because he was under threat from the Almohads.[56]

Ibn Mardanīsh's independence from the Almohads was made possible by his alliances with his Christian neighbors. According to Christian documents, Ibn Mardanīsh was a vassal to King Alfonso VII of Castile-Leon, Alfonso VIII's grandfather, from at least 1156. A treaty between

53 Viguera Molíns, *Reinos de taifas*, 197–98.

54 See, for example, Ibn Ṣāḥib al-Ṣalā, *al-Mann bi-l-imāma*, 109. See further discussion of this source and its treatment of Ibn Mardanīsh in chapter 2.

55 Al-Maqqarī, *Nafḥ al-ṭīb*, 4:378. This is a seventeenth-century source and its accuracy is therefore questionable, but it may be based on earlier sources.

56 Francisco Diago, *Historia de los victoriosissimos antigvos Condes de Barcelona* (Barcelona: Sebastian de Cormellas, 1603), 242 v.

Ibn Mardanīsh and Alfonso VII seems to have been signed sometime between 1147 and 1158, in which the rulers agreed to trade Ibn Mardanīsh's fortress of Uclés, some seventy miles east of Toledo, for a fortress of Alfonso's at Alicun, thirty miles northwest of Almería.[57] The fortress of Uclés would continue to operate as currency of legitimacy among the kings of Leon and Castile, as it passed between the family members of Alfonso VII and was donated to their preferred religious groups. Ferdinand II of Leon gave Uclés to the Hospitallers while his nephew Alfonso VIII remained a minor, but when Alfonso VIII reached his majority, he donated it instead to the Order of Santiago, which would turn the fortress into the headquarters of their religious and military activities.[58] It is unclear exactly when this treaty was signed, but the fortress was definitively in Castilian hands by 1157, and Ibn Mardanīsh begins appearing in Castilian sources even earlier. Although no treaties with Castile or Leon survive from the first years of Ibn Mardanīsh's reign, circumstantial evidence suggests that he had a close relationship with Alfonso VII from his earliest period in power. A letter describes a meeting between Alfonso VII, Ibn Mardanīsh (*Rege Valençie Merdenis qui idem Lop*), and Ibn Hamushk (*Rege Murçie Abenfamusco*) in Zorita, in today's Guadalajara, in February 1149.[59]

With the death of Alfonso VII in 1157, the kingdom of Castile faced new challenges. Alfonso VII had divided his kingdom between his two sons, granting Sancho III (r. 1157–58) Castile and Ferdinand II Leon. When Sancho III died, his three-year-old son Alfonso VIII gained power, setting off a fierce contest between the two powerful families of Toledo, the Laras and the Castros, over who would have custody over the young king. It is shortly after Alfonso VIII's succession to the throne that the

57 The precise date on which Ibn Mardanīsh signed a treaty offering Alfonso VII the fortress of Uclés and his vassalage is contested. Julio González argues that the treaty was signed in 1149 but the fortress transferred eight years later in 1157. See González, "Repoblación de las tierras de Cuenca," *Anuario de Estudios Medievales* 12 (1982): 183–204. Bernard Reilly notes, on the basis of the charters of Alfonso VII, that Ibn Mardanīsh begins appearing as a vassal in 1156. Reilly, *The Contest of Christian and Muslim Spain 1031–1157* (Cambridge, MA: Blackwell, 1992), 221.

58 Milagros Rivera Garretas, "El castillo-fortaleza de Uclés: Datos histórico-arqueológico," *Cuenca* 17 (1980): 35–49.

59 Juan Catalina García, *La Alcarria en los dos primeros siglos de su reconquista: discursos leídos ante la Real Academia de la Historia en la recepción publica del sr. Juan Catalina García en 27 de mayo de 1894* (Madrid: El Progreso, 1894), 35n2; Manuel Recuero Astray, *Alfonso VII, 1126–1157* (Burgos: Editorial la Olmeda, 2003), 267.

sources first explicitly mention Ibn Mardanīsh as vassal to this king.[60] A document recording that Alfonso VIII gave the church of Santa María de Valdegunia to the monastery of Retuerta on July 11, 1160, includes the line "Rex Lupus, uasallus regi Ildefonso, conf" ("Wolf King, vassal of King Alfonso, confirms") underneath the name of the king,[61] but above the names of all of his counts, noblemen, archbishops, and bishops—a position that places Ibn Mardanīsh above these highest-ranking members of the Castilian court.[62] The document thus emphasizes both Ibn Mardanīsh's status as a vassal and his importance relative to the other witnesses.

The chronicles suggest that especially in these early years of the young King Alfonso VIII's reign, Ibn Mardanīsh was frequently present at his court. Perhaps Ibn Mardanīsh was an ally of the king's Lara regent, or sought to participate in the debates over his regency. The *Anales Toledanos* records that Ibn Mardanīsh entered Toledo in 1167: "Entró el Rey Lop en Toledo Era MCCV."[63] This moment in 1167 was the crux of the battle between the Laras and the Castros, as Alfonso VIII and his regent, Nuño Pérez de Lara, fought to win back Toledo and push out the Castros and their ally, Alfonso's uncle Ferdinand II of Leon (r. 1157–88), who had been stationing his troops in Toledo and collecting its taxes. Scholars have suggested that Ibn Mardanīsh may have been called to Toledo to help fight the Castros or perhaps to adjudicate the dispute. He may also have traveled to the fractious city to ask for Castile's help for countering Aragonese attacks.[64] Whether his purpose was to help the Laras in their battle with the Castros or to seek their help against the Aragonese, Ibn Mardanīsh's arrival in Toledo at this juncture shows his close involvement in the internal and external politics of Castile.

---

60 For a broad discussion of Ibn Mardanīsh's alliances with Castile, and its importance at a time of political instability, see Ignacio González Cavero, "Una revisión de la figura de Ibn Mardanish: Su alianza con el reino de Castilla y la oposición frente a los almohades," *Miscelánea Medieval Murciana* 31 (2007): 95–110.

61 Julio González, *El reino de Castilla en la época de Alfonso VIII* (Madrid: Consejo Superior de Investigaciones Científicas, 1960), 2:94–96; see also 1:894.

62 Simon Doubleday has shown the importance of such lists of names and their order in determining the hierarchy among nobility in twelfth-century Castile in *The Lara Family: Crown and Nobility in Medieval Spain* (Cambridge, MA: Harvard University Press, 2001), 12–14.

63 *Anales Toledanos*, in Enrique Florez, ed., *España Sagrada* (Madrid: Antonio Marin, 1767), 23:391.

64 See González Cavero, "Una revision de la figura de Ibn Mardanish," 107; Gonzalo Martínez Díez, *Alfonso VIII, Rey de Castilla y Toledo* (Burgos: Editorial la Olmeda, 1995), 104–6.

Other evidence suggests that the conflicts among Muslim rulers and Christian rulers on the Iberian Peninsula facilitated close relationships across religious lines. It was at roughly this moment when the Almohads welcomed Fernando Rodríguez, brother-in-law of Ferdinand II, in Seville, and made a pact with Ferdinand II. Ibn Ṣāḥib al-Ṣalā described the presence of Fernando Rodríguez and his men in Seville for five months in 1168 as a time of mutual admiration between the Castilians and the Almohads, and said the Castilians "nearly converted" to Islam, promising their fidelity to Almohad power.[65] The Almohads also signed a peace treaty with Ferdinand II and promised to fight alongside him against Nuño Pérez de Lara.[66] Thus the battle between the son and grandson of Alfonso VII over Castile became part of the battle between the Almohads and Ibn Mardanīsh over Sharq al-Andalus, and vice versa.

However, relationships among the Christian kings of the Iberian Peninsula could change with new circumstances, and Ibn Mardanīsh's position as favored vassal could be easily threatened. A series of three treaties preserved in the archives of the Crown of Aragon demonstrate the rapid shifts in alliance between Ibn Mardanīsh and different Christian kingdoms that led to changes in fortune for Ibn Mardanīsh. The first treaty preserved in the archives records an alliance between King Alfonso II of Aragon (also Alfons I of Barcelona and Provence; r. 1157–April 25, 1196) and Rex Lupus (represented by Giraldo de Jorba), signed in November 1168.[67] The text reestablishes peace between the two rulers for two years starting May 1, 1169, in exchange for an annual tribute of twenty-five thousand morabetins from Ibn Mardanīsh, of which five thousand would be paid within thirty days.[68] The agreement may have been inspired by the new ten-year peace treaty between Navarre and Castile (signed in 1167), which meant that Sancho VI of Navarre (r. 1150–94) would

65 Ibn Ṣāḥib al-Ṣalā, *al-Mann bi-l-imāma,* 368–70.

66 Ibn Ṣāḥib al-Ṣalā, *al-Mann bi-l-imāma,* 370–71.

67 Archives of the Crown of Aragon (herafter ACA), Chancery, Parchments of Alfonso I, folder 43, no. 62. See Villanueva, *Viage literario,* 17:328–30; Lacarra, "El Rey Lobo," 516. Guillermo de Torroja, the bishop of Barcelona, signed this treaty as a witness. See also Ana Isabel Sánchez Casabón, *Alfonso II Rey de Aragón, Conde de Barcelona y Marqués de Provenza: Documentos* (1162–1196) (Saragossa: Institución Fernando el Católico, CSIC, 1995), 94–96.

68 Morabetins are gold dinars minted in the style of the Almoravids using West African gold. In this case, the term almost certainly refers to Ibn Mardanīsh's dinars, elsewhere called morabetinos lupinos.

have been able to help Ibn Mardanīsh, who had a preexisting alliance with the Castilians, attack the Aragonese, had Aragon not made an alliance with Ibn Mardanīsh. Evidence suggests that Sancho VI had already been an important ally of Ibn Mardanīsh's, traveling to Murcia personally to aid him. A document in the archives of Navarre, dated June 1163, acknowledges a debt of six hundred morabetinos lupinos that a knight named Aznar de Rada and his wife owe a "don Yucef" (perhaps Ibn Mardanīsh's son Yūsuf?), "that we borrowed from you when King Sancho was in Murcia."[69] This visit seems to have taken place in 1161, when a dearth of documents in the Navarre archives suggests the king's long absence.[70] Caught between Barcelona, Navarre, and Castile-Leon, all of which had treaties with Ibn Mardanīsh, Aragon needed a treaty of its own to protect itself from its Christian rivals and the formidable armies of Ibn Mardanīsh.

But the treaty drafted in November 1168 between Alfonso II of Aragon and Ibn Mardanīsh does not seem to have been enforced. Perhaps Ibn Mardanīsh failed to send the first five thousand morabetins he had promised in time. Instead, the next month (on December 19, 1168), Alfonso II of Aragon and Sancho VI of Navarre signed a treaty against Ibn Mardanīsh in Sangüesa.[71] In the treaty, both rulers pledged to endeavor to seize the territories of Rex Lupus and all the other Saracens, both wasteland and inhabited land, and to divide them between themselves.[72] The language of the treaty mirrors another treaty between Ibn Mardanīsh's former allies: that in which Genoa pledged allegiance to Holy Roman Emperor Frederick I and promised to help him against Ibn Mardanīsh and the rulers of the Balearics, and the two rulers vowed to fight the Saracens throughout the kingdom of the Wolf and in the kingdoms of Majorca and Minorca.[73]

---

69 Lacarra, "El Rey Lobo," 516–17: "Que malevamus de uos quando rex Sancius fuit ad Murciam."

70 José de Moret, *Anales de Reino de Navarra* (Pamplona: B. Huarte, 1695), vol. 2, bk. 19, chap. 4, no. 20.

71 ACA, Chancery, Parchments of Alfonso I, folder 43, no. 64. This document was first published by Lacarra in "El Rey Lobo," 523–26. As Lacarra notes on p. 517, the existence of this second document shows that the previous treaty must not have been completed.

72 ACA, Chancery, Parchments of Alfonso I, folder 43, no. 64. "Simili quoque modo sibi ad invicem convenient per bonam fidem, sine engano, quod quidquid ab hac die in antea potuerint capere, vel adquirere in tota terra regis Lupi, vel tota alia terra sarracenorum, per medium divident et habebunt in heremo et populato."

73 Constable, *Housing the Stranger*, 128.

Shifting relations among the Christian kingdoms seem to have intervened once more in the situation before Aragon and Navarre managed to make much progress against Ibn Mardanīsh. In this case, it was Alfonso VIII of Castile who concluded a new treaty to protect his vassal. This third treaty was signed on June 4, 1170, in Sahagún between Alfonso VIII and Alfonso II of Aragon, and it decreed that the Aragonese would cease attacking Ibn Mardanīsh's territory the following year in exchange for an annual tribute of forty thousand morabetins of gold.[74] The treaty addressed Alfonso II as a relative of Alfonso VIII and talked extensively about the love between the two kingdoms. Ibn Mardanīsh's territory was protected by virtue of his close relationship of vassalage with the Castilians. At the same meeting in Sahagún, King Henry II of England helped to broker a lasting peace between Castile and Aragon through a series of marriage alliances: Alfonso VIII would marry Henry's daughter Eleanor and Alfonso II would marry Alfonso VIII's aunt Sancha, securing peace between the two kingdoms of Castile and Aragon. Eleanor was nine at the time and would not marry Alfonso until four years later, in 1174, and the English and the Castilians still disagree about whether Henry promised Gascony to Alfonso as part of her dowry.[75]

The vast quantities of money promised in these treaties were likely responsible for the debasement of Ibn Mardanīsh's coinage over time, as he struggled to meet the financial burdens of his alliances. Though a morabetin or dinar theoretically consisted of four grams of gold, by the late 1160s the standard weight of Ibn Mardanīsh's dinar had fallen closer to two grams.[76] Kassis has also shown that Ibn Mardanīsh minted dinars in two distinct weights throughout his reign, and Kassis speculates that the slightly lighter dinars were used for paying tribute to the Christian kings of Iberia.[77] Nonetheless, the cost of his alliances, as well as of the building projects and military campaigns in which he engaged, are reflected in several criticisms of his authority recorded by Ibn al-Khaṭīb in the fourteenth century, which frequently focus on his heavy taxation of the population.

74 ACA, Chancery, Parchments of Alfonso I, folder 43, no. 85. Sánchez Casabón, *Alfonso II Rey de Aragón, Conde de Barcelona y Marqués de Provenza*, 147–48.

75 John Hosler, *Henry II: A Medieval Soldier at War, 1147–1189* (Leiden: Brill, 2007), 77.

76 Kassis, "Coinage," 225.

77 See the chart in Kassis, "Coinage," 223–25.

In the treaties, Ibn Mardanīsh's portrayal varies according to the political context. In the first treaty, he appears as a king with sovereign claims to his land, whereas in the second he is simply another Saracen to be expelled, along with the Almohads. In the third, he becomes a special figure protected by the Castilian crown. These changes reflect the instability caused by the ongoing territorial conflict among Navarre, Aragon, and Castile. Sharq al-Andalus was a crucial buffer state between the Christian states and the Almohads, and this fact, along with the region's substantial tribute, made it an important ally for each of the kingdoms at various points. Throughout this period, Ibn Mardanīsh was also protected by his close relationship with Castile.

The long twelfth century, between the capture of Toledo in 1085 and that of Seville in 1248, was the height of Christian expansion into al-Andalus. Ibn Mardanīsh's reign began in 1147, just as Pope Eugenius III declared that fighting the Muslims of Iberia constituted a crusade, and the rulers whom Ibn Mardanīsh counted as allies in Castile, Genoa, Pisa, and Aragon formed alliances pledging to divide Muslim-held territories amongst themselves. His success despite these challenges reflects the flexibility of religious and political ideologies in the period. The three treaties examined here demonstrate that Ibn Mardanīsh was sometimes seen as a valued ally against North African enemies, while at other times he was grouped with the latter in an undifferentiated mass of Saracens. His presence could offer a neighboring king the chance to connect himself to imperial ideals of cross-religious alliance, or even vassalage, alongside useful material aid against a common enemy. On the other hand, designating him as an infidel enemy could justify attacking a dangerously ambitious brother or cousin who counted him as an ally. Occupying the physical landscape between the Almohads and the kings of Castile, Navarre, and Aragon, Ibn Mardanīsh also served as a theoretical intermediary between Iberian alliance and holy war, alternately rejected and embraced by those on each side.

A Shared Culture

After Ibn Mardanīsh's death and the disappearance of the protective buffer he had offered his Christian allies against the Almohads, new forms of cultural production appeared in Castile that echoed the gifts and tribute he had once sent. Some of this new production was likely meant to replace the goods that no longer flowed from Sharq al-Andalus to Ibn Mardanīsh's allies. His largest export was doubtless the vast quantities of gold dinars that he paid as tribute to the kingdoms of Castile, Barcelona, and Aragon. These dinars had a profound effect on the coinage of Castile in the years immediately after his death, as will be discussed further below. Written sources and material evidence also suggest the widespread circulation of textiles and ceramics from Sharq al-Andalus throughout the Iberian Peninsula and beyond, many with figural motifs that would have been frowned on by Almohad market inspectors and whose continued production was unlikely after the Almohad conquest. Having access to large quantities of gold coins and figured silks with consistent forms determined consumers' expectations of such items; they became the ideals to be pursued, whether through trade or new production. But ideas about power, friendship, and mutual enmity could also facilitate the transfer of motifs and the development of new forms. For Alfonso VIII of Castile, who had known Ibn Mardanīsh as a loyal vassal and defender from infancy, adopting the techniques, materials, and motifs of his dead ally served as a potent means of asserting his own legitimacy and his continued fight against the Almohads.

Ibn Mardanīsh's coins, given in tribute to the courts of Barcelona, Aragon, and Castile and the cities of Genoa and Pisa, were highly valued and, as noted earlier, remained a currency of record for these kingdoms even after his death. Latin Christian rulers north of Naples did not, with few exceptions, mint gold coins until the mid-thirteenth century, largely because of the difficulty they encountered in finding gold in sufficient quantities. When medieval European rulers did mint gold coins, they often followed the model of Islamic gold coins, as in the case of the eighth-century Mercian king Offa's dinar, which imitated an Abbasid dinar,[78] or King Roger of Sicily's twelfth-century *tari* coins, which were based on Fatimid quarter-dinars.[79] To these rulers, gold coins were Islamic, their value and material inextricably bound with their Arabic inscriptions. As Janet Abu-Lughod has noted, when the Italian city-states of Florence and Genoa began to mint gold coins in the mid-thirteenth century,

78 British Museum CM 1913-12-13-1.
79 British Museum CM 1860.7-3.23.

they did so clearly to supplement rather than replace the Islamic coins already in use.[80]

Many early European gold coins imitating Islamic examples were crude copies, like Roger's *taris* that used pseudo-Arabic inscriptions. Alfonso VII seems to have minted gold dinars in Baeza, a city that was between 542–52/1147–57, like Almería, under the authority of Castile.[81] Unlike earlier European copies of Islamic coins, these are legible and faithful versions of the dinars that Ibn Mardanīsh was minting in Murcia, with the mint name changed to indicate they were produced in Castilian Baeza. The Almohads conquered Baeza along with Almería in 552/1157, but Ibn Mardanīsh took Baeza back and held it as his own territory from 554/1159. Mardanīshī coins then begin to appear with the mint "Baeza," alongside those he minted in Murcia. Jean Gautier-Dalché shows, through close analysis of fiscal records from Toledo, the Castilian capital, that "*mithqāl*s de Baeza" were in widespread, continuous use from 1152 until 1173. A record from Toledo in 1158, when Baeza had been lost and Ibn Mardanīsh had not yet started to issue his own Baezan coins, shows the sale of a house for 40 mithqāls of Baeza, "which were circulating in Toledo."[82]

After Ibn Mardanīsh's death in 1172, the Castilians lost access to the two cities that had been minting the primary currency being used in Toledo. After minting Almoravid-style coins in Baeza, it would have been easy to continue producing copies of earlier Islamic coins in Toledo. But Alfonso VIII, grandson of Alfonso VII and life-long ally of Ibn Mardanīsh, began minting a revolutionary new coin.[83] In 1174, just two

80 Janet Abu-Lughod, *Before European Hegemony: The World System A.D. 1250–1350* (New York: Oxford University Press, 1989), 15.

81 As Tawfiq Ibrahim of the Tonegawa Collection notes on his website, very few coins from this series survive. They appear in Vives as numbers 1992–1995. Ibrahim reads the mint name as *Bayyāsa 'iyar Qashtiliya*, rather than Vives's reading of *Bayyāsa, Jayyān, Ishbiliya*. Ibrahim, "Coins of the al-Andalus Tonegawa collection: Almoravid Taifas," accessed August 24, 2021, http://www.andalustonegawa.50g.com/almoravids_taifas.htm. J. Gautier-Dalché shows that coins called *mithqāl*s "de Baeza" appear in texts from 1152 to 1173, suggesting a longer period of production than the evidence of the surviving coins suggest. Gautier-Dalché, "Le rôle de la Reconquête de Tolède dans l'histoire monetaire de la Castille (1085–1174)," in *Estudios sobre Alfonso VI y la Reconquista de Toledo* (Toledo: Instituto de Estudios Visigótico-Mozárabes, 1988), 11–25.

82 Gautier-Dalché, "Le rôle de la Reconquête de Tolède," 23–24.

83 On the many different types of coins minted in the name of Alfonso VIII over his lifetime, including his gold dinars, see James Todesca, "Selling Castile: Coinage, Propaganda, and Mediterranean Trade in the Age of Alfonso VIII," in *King Alfonso VIII of Castile: Government, Family, and War*, ed. Miguel Gómez, Kyle Lincoln, Damian Smith, Martín Alvira Cabrer, Carlos de Ayala Martínez, and Janna Bianchini (New York: Fordham University Press, 2019), 30–58.

FIGURE 5.4A-B. Alfonsine dinar, Toledo, 1181, obverse and reverse. *Photo:* American Numismatic Society.

years after Ibn Mardanīsh's death, his ally Alfonso VIII began minting gold dinars in Toledo; these dinars continued to be minted in his name until 1217, three years after his death. They are traditionally described as coins of the Almoravid type,[84] and their name in Spanish (morabetinos) reflects this label.[85] As the treaties discussed earlier demonstrate, Ibn Mardanīsh's coins were also called morabetinos. However, a close examination of Alfonso VIII's gold dinars shows that they were not based on Almoravid examples but rather mimicked the specific design and inscriptions of the dinars he had been receiving in tribute from Ibn Mardanīsh for years.[86] Kassis suggests that Alfonso minted these coins because he faced a dearth of reliable gold currency after the

84 See Medina Gómez, *Monedas*, 380.

85 Gautier-Dalché shows that these coins were called *mithqāls alfonsí* in the written records of contemporary Toledo. "Le rôle de la Reconquête de Tolède," 24.

86 Antonio Vives y Escudero noted at the turn of the last century the similarities between Ibn Mardanīsh's coinage and that of Alfonso VIII, but described Ibn Mardanīsh's as copies of an earlier Almoravid model and Alfonso's coins as "una copia de los dinares almoravides tan servil como podía permitirlo la diferencia de religión." See Vives, *La Moneda castellana: discursos leídos ante la Real Academia de la Historia* (Madrid: M. Tello, 1901), 16–17. More recently, Heather Ecker's catalogue *Caliphs and Kings: The Art and Influence of Islamic Spain. Selections from the Hispanic Society, New York* (Washington, DC: Smithsonian Institution, 2004), 134, highlighted the similarity between Alfonso's dinar and an Almoravid dinars. Tom Nickson has also noted the similarity between Ibn Mardanīsh's and Alfonso's dinars but does not discuss why this might be the case, see "'Sovereignty belongs to God': Text, Ornament and Magic in Islamic and Christian Seville," *Art History* 38, no. 5 (2015): 838–61.

death of Ibn Mardanīsh, but the choice to imitate the particulars of Ibn Mardanīsh's coinage reflects more than convenience or fiscal policy.[87] In addition to following the style of Ibn Mardanīsh's coinage, Alfonso included Arabic inscriptions that directly countered the ideological claims of Ibn Mardanīsh's legends with Christian ones, which shows an engagement with the religious and political ideas presented by Ibn Mardanīsh.[88]

In their design, Alfonso's dinars copy the small decoration found on many of Ibn Mardanīsh's dinars under the inscription that starts with *al-Imām*—a series of dots, a star, or a flower. Almoravid dinars do not have this decoration. Alfonso VIII's dinars, like Ibn Mardanīsh's, include it under the inscription about the Imam—a flower above a series of small dots on his earliest dinars of 1174 through 1181,[89] and a series of dots under the large Latin alphabet inscription reading ALF, for the first three letters of his name, on the dinars minted in his name between 1214 and 1217.[90] These later coins, minted under Alfonso's son Enrique I, also include a star underneath the inscription calling Alfonso an emir.

The inscriptions on Alfonso's dinars also clearly respond to those on Ibn Mardanīsh's dinars. The central legend on the reverse of Ibn Mardanīsh's coin from 548 AH reads as follows:

Lā ilāha illā Allāh	There is no god but God
Muḥammad rasūl Allāh	Muḥammad is the Messenger
	of God
Yaʿtaṣimu bi-ḥabl Allāh	The emir Abū ʿAbd Allāh
al-amīr Abū ʿAbd Allāh	Muḥammad ibn Saʿd, whom
Muḥammad ibn Saʿd ayyadahu	God supports,
Allāh	holds fast to the rope of God

The central legend on the obverse of Alfonso's 1181 dinar reads:

Amīr	Commander (emir)
al-qatuliqīn	of the Catholics

---

87 Kassis, "Coinage," 219.

88 As Kassis writes in an article on Qāḍī ʿIyāḍ's coinage, "It is evident that coinage became a medium of exchange of some of the dominant religious-political ideas of the Christian-Muslim confrontation in medieval Spain." Hanna Kassis, "Qāḍī ʿIyāḍ's Rebellion against the Almohads in Sabtah (A. H. 542–543/A. D. 1147–1148): New Numismatic Evidence," *Journal of the American Oriental Society* 103, no. 3 (1983): 505–14.

89 Medina Gómez, *Monedas*, 385, pl. 112.

90 Medina Gómez, *Monedas*, 386, pl. 113.

Alfūns ibn Sanja	Alfonso son of Sancho
ayyadahu Allāh	whom God supports
wa-naṣarahu	and helps[91]

The reverse central legend has a cross at the top, and then the following text:

Al-imām al-bīʿa	The imam of the Christian
al-masīḥiyya bābā	church is the pope
Rūm al-ʿaẓam	of Rome, the most great

Compare this to the obverse central legend of Ibn Mardanīsh's 565 dinar:

Al-imām	The imam
ʿAbd Allāh	ʿAbd Allāh
amīr al-muʾminīn	the Abbasid
al-ʿAbbāsī	Commander of the Faithful

Rome here becomes parallel to Baghdad, and the pope to the Abbasid caliph. Both Alfonso and Ibn Mardanīsh sought legitimacy through a relationship with the spiritual leader (*imām*) of their religion, though like Ibn Mardanīsh on his early and late coins, Alfonso did not specify the name of the leader to whom he referred. Both also presented themselves as being supported by God or invoked God's support (*ayyadahu Allāh*, which can also be translated as "May God support him"). Alfonso added "and grant him victory" (*wa naṣarahu*), suggesting that his many military victories were likewise granted by God.

The recto marginal legend on Alfonso's 1181 coins reads as follows:

Bi-ism-l-Ab wa-l-Ibn wa-l-Rūḥ al-qudus, Allāh al-wāḥid, man āmana wa-ta ʿāmada yakūn salīman	In the name of the Father and the Son and the Holy Ghost, the One God, whoever believes and is baptized will be saved.[92]

Ibn Mardanīsh's 565 recto marginal legend reads:

91 Medina Gómez, *Monedas*, 385. This coin is dated to the year 1219 of the Safar calendar. The Safar calendar, which began in 38 BC, was used in Christian Iberia throughout the Middle Ages. Thus 1219 of Safar corresponds to 1181 of the Common Era.

92 The beginning part of this passage is a *basmala* modified to incorporate the Tripartite Christian God and is followed by Mark 14:16.

Wa-man yabtaghi ghayr al-islām dīnan fa-lan yuqbil minhu wa-huwa fī al-ākhira min al-khāsirīn	Whoever desires a religion other than Islam, it will never be accepted from him, and in the afterlife he will be among the losers.[93]

On Alfonso's dinar an excerpt from the New Testament about the exclusivity of the Christian faith and the importance of being saved through baptism counters Ibn Mardanīsh's use of a Quranic passage, characteristic of Almoravid and later Iberian coinage, which warns that anyone who accepts a religion other than Islam will be condemned in the afterlife. The "translation" of Ibn Mardanīsh's coins into a visually similar version more suitable for a Christian king reflects an engagement with the coins' meaning and their connections across space and time. Alfonso's use of the phrase "The imam of the Christian Church is the pope of Rome, the most great" reveals that he understood that Ibn Mardanīsh was legitimating his authority with reference to a distant imam who was the leader of the Islamic world. Similarly, "In the name of the Father and the Son and the Holy Ghost, the One God" displays an understanding of the doctrinal differences between Islamic and Christian conceptions of God's unity. To Alfonso, Ibn Mardanīsh's coins were not merely illegible chunks of gold with pleasing patterns. Alfonso's dinars show that he understood at least some of the meanings conveyed by the coins, even if he didn't comprehend all of the associations gold coins might have had in an Islamic context. The networks that linked Ibn Mardanīsh's coins to Damascus, Baghdad, and sub-Saharan gold mines may have been invisible to Alfonso. But the power of the gold, which showcased the ruler's wealth and reach, and of the form, which was rooted in centuries of power in the Islamic West, and even of the inscriptions, with their opposition to the Almohads, was clearly legible to Alfonso.

The inscriptions on Alfonso's dinars responded, line by line, to the religious and political claims made by Ibn Mardanīsh on his dinars. Given that Ibn Mardanīsh's coinage in turn responded directly to the ideology of the Almohads, Alfonso's coins implicitly adopted the anti-Almohad propaganda recently abandoned by Ibn Mardanīsh even as they advanced a Christian vision of authority. There is clearly a discrepancy between the two rulers' respective understandings of the

93 Quran 3:85.

relationship of religious and political power—one endorsing a tripartite God mediated through the pope in Rome, the other adhering to a prophetically established rule in God's name and overseen by the caliph in Baghdad—but both opposed Almohad power. Alfonso would have seen his addition of a Christian message and of his own name as augmenting the power and prestige already embodied by Ibn Mardanīsh's dinars. By creating his own version of Ibn Mardanīsh's coinage, filling its lines with a Christian message, and proclaiming himself the emir, Alfonso asserted a new kind of ownership that far surpassed collecting Ibn Mardanīsh's coins. Alfonso's dinars thus demonstrate that the coins of Ibn Mardanīsh that Alfonso possessed had in turn come to possess him, transforming his ideas about coinage and authority.[94] By choosing to imitate Ibn Mardanīsh's dinars, Alfonso sought to claim the mantle of leadership from the anti-Almohad Iberian Muslim rulers. Later Muslim rulers, including the Nasrids, who were also allies to Castile, would not continue this pattern, instead opting to imitate the distinctive form of Almohad coins (squares within circles for dinars, and square dirhams), although their legends were substantially different from Almohad ones. Alfonso's morabetinos remained an important currency of record throughout the Mediterranean long after his death. The crusading records of Count Alphonse of Poitiers (d. 1271) show that he bought four thousand morabetinos alfonsinos to take to the east to finance the crusading activities of his brother Louis IX of France (r. 1226–70).[95]

It was not just Ibn Mardanīsh's coinage that persisted in new forms after his death. The inscription used throughout his palace in Murcia—*al-yumn wa-l-iqbāl*, "good fortune and prosperity," discussed in chapter 3—also continued to reverberate in later Iberian royal culture. At about the same time that Alfonso's son was minting a second set of dinars in his father's name in Toledo, a small church was tacked onto the back of a mosque in Toledo to commemorate Alfonso's victory against the Almohads at the Battle of Las Navas de Tolosa. The diminutive church, called San Cristo de la Luz, is dominated by an image of

---

94 Ian Hodder, *Entangled: An Archaeology of the Relationships between Humans and Things* (Malden, MA: Wiley-Blackwell, 2012), 24: "Things become possessed by us, but we also have become possessed by them, by their colour, beauty, memories, associations, etc. The processes involve paying attention to, becoming associated with, becoming linked in terms of history and memory, finding, keeping, using over time, applying force and the law to control access to things."

95 Todesca, "Selling Castile," 45.

FIGURE 5.5. "Good fortune and prosperity" inscriptions, Church of San Cristo de la Luz, Toledo. *Photo:* Abigail Krasner Balbale.

Christ in Majesty that fills its central wall. In an arch that surrounds the image runs a band with the very same Arabic inscription, *al-yumn wa-l-iqbāl*, that appeared first in Ibn Mardanīsh's palace, and it is painted in the same style and with the same orthographic anomalies as though it were executed in miniature on silk or clay. The inscription is also found in the church of San Roman in Toledo, framing saints, church fathers, and angels. Both churches were decorated around 1220, in the aftermath of the Battle of Las Navas de Tolosa, in celebration of the victory of the Castilians and their allies against the Almohads. San Roman was reconsecrated by the archbishop of Toledo, Rodrigo Jiménez de Rada, after being painted with a remarkable program of religious scenes and this inscription.

FIGURE 5.6. "Good fortune and prosperity" inscriptions, Church of San Roman, Toledo. *Photo:* Abigail Krasner Balbale.

Jiménez de Rada, in addition to holding the archbishopric of Toledo, was a historian and a champion of the series of battles against the Muslims of Iberia that would later be enshrined as the Reconquista. By the mid-thirteenth century, when he sat down to write his history of the Arabs, the *Historia Arabum*, the Almohads had been definitively defeated at the Battle of Las Navas de Tolosa—a battle officially termed a crusade, thanks in part to Jiménez de Rada's intercession with the pope. The *Historia Arabum* describes the wars between the Christians and the North African Berber dynasties that had consumed the previous century.

Within this narrative, Jiménez de Rada pauses to praise Ibn Mardanīsh, who, like his Christian neighbors, had fought the Almohads:

> Now there was . . . a man who was endowed with wisdom and was generous, energetic, and kind, Mahomat Abençahat, who later became known as the Wolf King (Rex Lupus). He won the kingdom of Valencia and the kingdom of Murcia as well as the areas around them, including Lorca and Guadix and many other places. Many Christians also lived there.[96]

For Jiménez de Rada, advocating crusades against the infidel and praising Ibn Mardanīsh were evidently not contradictory. In fact, they seemed to be part of the same ideological program defined by the fight against the Almohads and the assertion of an ecumenical Iberian identity against a "foreign" Muslim power. Perhaps the use of the inscription *al-yumn wa-l-iqbāl* should be seen in a similar light: not as an expression of dominance, as the use of objects or iconography deemed "Islamic" in Christian contexts is often seen, but instead as an expression of cultural and political continuity.

The inscription appears in a wide range of buildings throughout Iberia built between the thirteenth and fifteenth centuries, including Christian churches and palaces, synagogues, and eventually Islamic palaces once more. It appears in fourteenth-century additions to the Castilian palace and convent of Las Huelgas in Burgos, surrounding roundels with regal peacocks. It appears again, in ribbons framing the space occupied by saints such as James and Mary, in the Royal Convent of Santa Clara in Tordesillas, founded by Peter I, king of Castile-Leon (r. 1350–69). And it appears again in bands that surround Hebrew inscriptions from the Torah in the fourteenth-century synagogue of Samuel Halevi, the finance minister of King Peter I.[97]

How did an inscription adapted from portable objects and first used architecturally by Ibn Mardanīsh on the walls of his palace become such an oft-repeated decorative refrain in thirteenth- and fourteenth-century Castilian buildings? Ibn Mardanīsh may have borrowed the inscription from ceramics or silks, perhaps from Fatimid Egypt, for the walls of his

---

96 Jiménez de Rada, *Historia Arabum*, ed. J. Lozano Sánchez (Seville: Secretariado de Publicaciones de la Universidad de Sevilla, 1974), 70–71.

97 See discussion of these uses of the inscription in Jerrilynn Dodds, María Rosa Menocal, and Abigail Krasner Balbale, *The Arts of Intimacy: Christians, Jews, and Muslims in the Making of Castilian Culture* (New Haven, CT: Yale University Press, 2008), 188–89.

FIGURE 5.7. "Good fortune and prosperity" inscriptions, Monastery of Las Huelgas, Burgos. *Photo:* Abigail Krasner Balbale.

palace as part of his claim to legitimate rule. Like the "courtly" images in his palace and the muqarnas on which they appeared, the inscription on the walls of his buildings spoke the languages of Islamic authority and Mediterranean traditions of power. Many of the most desirable luxury objects of the twelfth-century Mediterranean were products of Fatimid Egypt. Ibn Mardanīsh's realm produced similar goods, including silks and lustered ceramics, in increasingly large quantities, and the trade in such products helped produce the great wealth demonstrated by the profusion of his gold coins.

Like his coins, Ibn Mardanīsh's articulation of an Andalusī culture of sovereignty to counteract the austerity of the Almohads served as a model for the Christian kings who allied with him to fight the Berber empire. The use of the inscription throughout the new monuments of Castilian power meant that it became a symbol of Iberian courtly culture as well. Thus, it could be used in palaces, churches, and synagogues as a marker of luxury and good taste. This is confirmed by its use in an Islamic context in the fourteenth century. A famous, nearly six foot tall vase, found in excavations of the Alhambra, is thought to have been

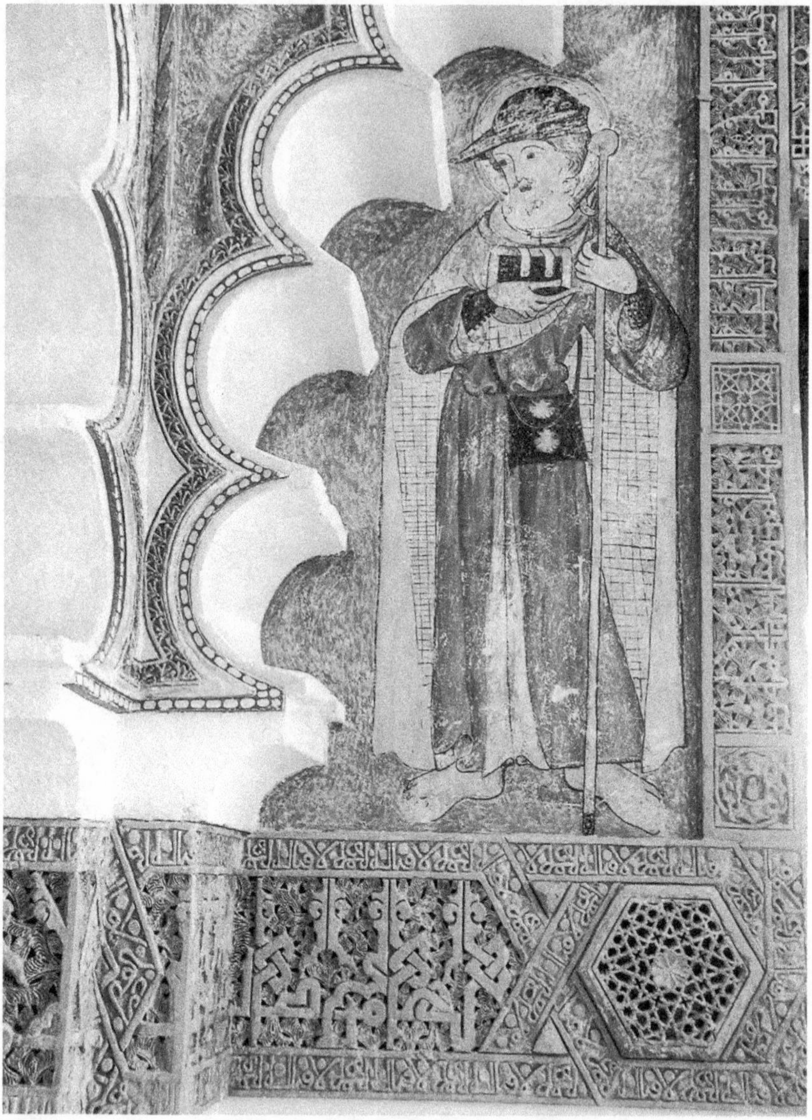

FIGURE 5.8. "Good fortune and prosperity" inscriptions, Royal Convent of Santa Clara, Tordesillas. *Photo:* Abigail Krasner Balbale.

designed to decorate the palace. It, too, is covered with ribbons of the same inscription, which encircle the vase and frame graceful gazelles.[98]

98 Museo de la Alhambra, Granada, inv. no. 290, likely produced during the second reign of Muḥammad V between 763–93/1362–91.

FIGURE 5.9. Alhambra Vase, Museum of the Alhambra, Granada. *Photo:* J. M. Grimaldi/Junta de Andalucía.

The inscription is also found throughout the Alhambra between the longer and more legible poetic inscriptions that cover every surface.

Ibn Mardanīsh's court, as the locus of anti-Almohad resistance in the twelfth century, became a cultural model for the Iberian courts that followed it, both Christian and Muslim. His courtly culture, developed in relation to his contemporaries and predecessors in the Islamic world and in opposition to the Almohads, blossomed even further in the Christian and Muslim courts that fought the Almohads in the twelfth and thirteenth centuries. Two of the most famous textiles of the period—the "Drinking Ladies," now held at the Cooper Hewitt National Design Museum in New York, and the "Pillowcase of Berengaria" at Las Huelgas—reflect a shared fixation on women and drinking. The "Drinking Ladies," a fragment of a larger textile, features a repeated medallion pattern, with two women enclosed by a band of pearls, seated on a platform, raising their glasses to meet each other's in the center.[99] The pillowcase found in the tomb of Queen Berengaria of Leon and Castile (d. 1246), the daughter of Alfonso VIII and Eleanor Plantagenet, and mother of Ferdinand III, shows two figures facing each other within a roundel encircled by illegible *naskhī* Arabic text.[100] One, with dark hair in a braid down her back, holds a stringed instrument. The other, with fair hair, holds a cup toward her companion. Between them, a tree of life divides the roundel, with roots branching beneath their feet and a single trunk that ends in a crownlike shape at the summit. Both figures are raising one knee, as if they have been caught in mid-dance. Four eight-pointed stars punctuate the red silk ground surrounding the central medallion, and two bands enclose the composition with a stylized Kufic inscription that reads *al-baraka al-kāmila*, perfect blessing.

Both of these textiles were made using the distinctive *lampas* brocade form of a group of Andalusī textiles from the twelfth century or later, many associated with Almería. They were woven with an animal substrate wrapped in gold wire to create the shimmering gold surface of the textile.[101] The forms associated with Almería textiles are roundels containing figures of animals or people, with pearled borders and geometric patterns at the interstices. It is likely that craftsmen specializing in the kinds of figured silks for which Almería had become renowned left the city after it came under Almohad control in order to move to realms friendlier to figurative representation, such as Castile, Leon, or Murcia.

The dates of both of these textiles have been contested; suggested dates have ranged from the twelfth to the fifteenth century. They have

---

99 The "Drinking Ladies" fragment is a tapestry-woven textile of about 7 × 13.75 inches, made of silk and gold.

100 The text encircling the roundel is usually described as the testament of faith, *La ilāha illā Allāh*. However, although it has a similar pattern of vertical strokes to the statement of faith, I do not think this text was intended to be legible. Nor do I think that the text's illegibility implies that it was made by craftsmen who could not read Arabic. Scholars have increasingly highlighted the important ways in which text could function beyond linguistic meaning, and a textile such as this one, with a courtly scene at its center, would be unlikely to include explicitly religious text. The use of pseudoscript facilitated the evocation of meaning without the potential problems that using a religious phrase in this context could cause.

101 For a precise description of this textile-weaving technique, see Partearroyo, "Almoravid and Almohad Textiles," 106. As Partearroyo has noted, nearly all of the "Almoravid" textiles that follow this form are thought to have been produced in Almería between the reign of the Almoravid emir ʿAlī ibn Yūsuf (r. 500–37/1106–43) and that of Ferdinand II of Leon (r. 1157–88), in a period spanning Almoravid rule, conquest by a combined force of Iberians, Italians, and French as part of the third crusade, a ten-year period of Castilian control (1147–57), and finally the city's conquest by the Almohads.

FIGURE 5.10. Drinking Ladies fragment, tapestry woven silk with gold wrapped animal substrate, twelfth-thirteenth centuries. *Photo:* Cooper Hewitt National Design Museum. *Credit:* Tapestry Fragment (Spain); previously owned by Francisco Miquel y Badía (Spanish, 1840–1899); silk, metallic (gilded parchment wound around silk core); H x W: 34.9 x 17.8 cm. Gift of John Pierpont Morgan; 1902–1–82.

Figure 5.11. Pillowcase of Berengaria, early thirteenth century. Museo de Telas Medievales, Burgos. *Photo:* Patrimonio Nacional, Monasterio de Santa María La Real de Las Huelgas, 00650512.

been described variously as Almohad or as Castilian. According to several scholars, if they were produced in the Almohad period, they were most likely made in the anti-Almohad Sharq al-Andalus, perhaps in Murcia or Valencia.[102] María Judith Feliciano has argued that the ubiq-

102 For an early assessment of these textiles, see D. G. Shepherd, "The Hispano-Islamic Textiles in the Cooper Union Collection," *Chronicles of the Museum for the Arts of Decoration of*

FIGURE 5.12A-B. Burial robe of Rodrigo Jiménez de Rada. *Photo:* Sheldan Collins / Image © The Metropolitan Museum of Art. *Credit:* Tunic of Don Rodrigo Ximenez de Rada. Almohad or Nasrid period, before 1247. Silk, gold thread, silver thread, and gold-wrapped thread. L. 141 cm. Monasterio de Santa Maria, Santa Maria la Real de Huerta, Spain.

uitous use of such textiles in thirteenth-century Castilian burials demonstrates such a clear preference for Andalusī textiles that they should properly be seen as *Castilian* regalia.[103] She associates the acceptance of these textiles with the richness of the materials and a longstanding taste for other luxury goods that incorporated similar motifs.[104] As she notes, the burial clothes of Rodrigo Jiménez de Rada, which may have been originally gifted to Ferdinand III by his Muslim vassal in Granada and then passed on to the archbishop, were likely worn also in life as part of the archbishop's liturgical costume.[105] Complete with an Arabic inscription reading *al-yumn*, "good fortune"—half of the inscription that appeared in the church of San Roman, consecrated by Jiménez de Rada—the archbishop's robe communicated luxury, power, and Castilian nobility, even as it recalled a long-defunct vassal dynasty in Sharq al-Andalus. To the thirteenth- or fourteenth-century viewers of such robes, or of the churches and palaces adorned with *al-yumn wa-l-iqbāl*, the most legible component of the visual program would have been its Castilianness.

Objects such as Alfonso VIII's gold dinar, modeled on the coins of Ibn Mardanīsh but carrying an Arabic legend asserting Christian superiority, conveyed multiple messages to multiple audiences. Reading the dinar's legend in isolation of its broader context misses the ways in which

---

the Cooper Union 1 (1943): 351–82, as well as Shepherd, "Treasure from a Thirteenth-Century Spanish Tomb." See also Partearroyo, "Almoravid and Almohad Textiles."

103 Feliciano, "Muslim Shrouds for Christian Kings?" 114.

104 Feliciano, "Muslim Shrouds for Christian Kings?" 118.

105 Feliciano, "Muslim Shrouds for Christian Kings?" 120.

it mirrors the earlier form of Ibn Mardanīsh's coinage, yielding the impression that the object speaks at cross-purposes by emulating a Muslim ruler while also asserting the dominance of the pope in Rome rather than the caliph in Baghdad. Taking a broader view reveals that such objects reflect the multiplicity of forms born out of cultural encounter. Alfonso's dinar's visual, material, and written meanings complement rather than contradict each other, portraying the king as all-powerful on a Mediterranean scale, and as the new leader of Ibn Mardanīsh's campaign against the Almohads.

When Ibn Mardanīsh died and his territories were incorporated into the vast Almohad Empire, the kingdoms that had counted him as an ally lost more than a buffer against their enemy. For Castile, especially, and the young king Alfonso VIII, whom Ibn Mardanīsh had served loyally, the loss of this vassal and his territory must have been personally and politically challenging. The vassalage of Ibn Mardanīsh, a fellow king and, even more, a king of another religion, helped legitimate Alfonso's claims to imperial rule. And his tribute, paid in vast quantities of gold coins, in castles, and presumably, in gifts of silk, would have added cosmopolitan glitter to Alfonso's court. His decision to perpetuate many of these forms and motifs in his own court's cultural production betrays just how central they had become to his own political self-fashioning. In subsequent years, the forms born of Ibn Mardanīsh's accumulation of Islamic symbols of authority would accrue new meanings and associations, as they became signs of Castilian royal power.

CHAPTER 6

Resistance and Assimilation after the Almohad Conquest

After Ibn Mardanīsh's death on the last day of Rajab in 567/March 28, 1172, his son Hilāl told the Almohads he would submit to their authority, but it took him a month to go to Seville do so formally. The delegation from Sharq al-Andalus that left Murcia in late Shaʿbān 567/April 1172 included Hilāl, his brothers, and his father's judges and top military officers. They were met a few miles outside Seville by two brothers of the Almohad caliph, members of the Almohad council of ten (*ahl al-jamāʿa*), and a large contingent of soldiers.[1] The Banū Mardanīsh and the Almohads then entered the city together in a triumphant procession and were received by the caliph Abū Yaʿqūb Yūsuf in the "old castle." They arrived just before the Maghrib (sunset) prayer, and according to Ibn Ṣāḥib al-Ṣalā, the new moon (*hilāl*) of Ramaḍān appeared that night.[2] The Almohad judge Abū Mūsā ʿĪsā ibn ʿImrān gave a speech in praise of the caliph, saying, "O our lord,

1 On this group of Almohad leaders, which may or may not have contained ten people, and its relationship to the Prophetic model of the ten people Muḥammad said were guaranteed paradise, see Pascal Buresi and Hicham El Aallaoui, *Governing the Empire: Provincial Administration in the Almohad Caliphate (1224–1269)*, trans. Travis Bruce (Leiden: Brill, 2013), 32–33.

2 Ibn Ṣāḥib al-Ṣalā, *Al-Mann bi-l-imāma*, 472. The first night of Ramaḍān 567 corresponds to April 27, 1172. The symbolic resonance of this moment, with the son of a former rebel with the evocative name "crescent moon" submitting the night of the new crescent moon of the

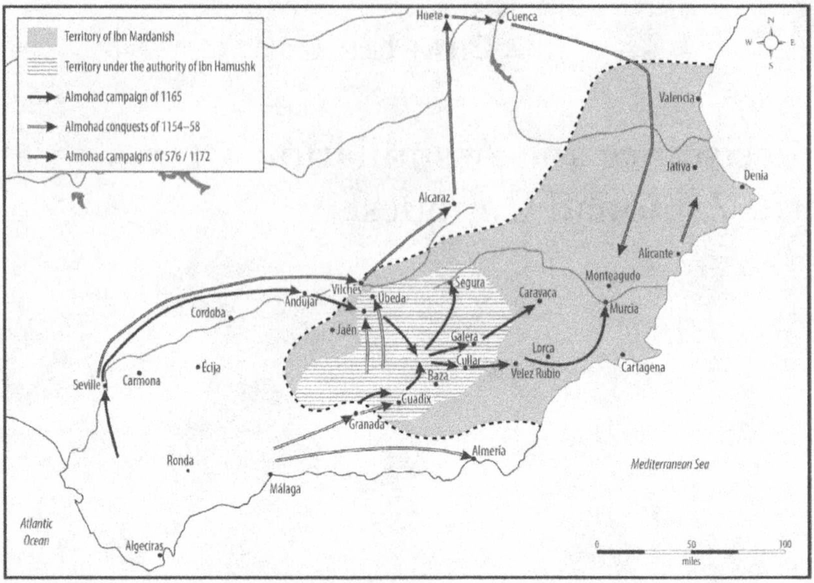

Map 6.1. Almohad conquests in Iberia, 1154–72. Map by Mike Bechthold.

Commander of the Faithful! Tonight, two new moons have risen upon us, that of the month of Ramaḍān and this Hilāl, who has submitted!"[3] The caliph laughed, pleased. He housed Hilāl and his retinue in the former palace of al-Muʿtamid (r. 461–83/1069–90), the Taifa king of Seville, and in houses close by, and Ibn Ṣāḥib al-Ṣalā notes that the caliph gave them "beds and rugs and food and gifts and drinks and all that was necessary, and they understood that they were the most important allies and the closest friends, and the caliphal reign and the power of the imamate welcomed them most cordially."[4]

The following morning, on the first day of Ramaḍān 567, Caliph Abū Yaʿqūb Yūsuf announced the beginning of the construction of the Great Mosque of Seville,[5] a project that would continue for the next three years and eleven months.[6] Ibn Ṣāḥib al-Ṣalā reports that for decades the Almohads in Seville had contented themselves with mosques that were far too

holy month of Ramadan, suggests the Mardanīshī retinue had waited to travel to Seville for a particularly auspicious moment to surrender.

3 Ibn Ṣāḥib al-Ṣalā, *Al-Mann bi-l-imāma,* 472.

4 Ibn Ṣāḥib al-Ṣalā, *Al-Mann bi-l-imāma,* 472–73.

5 Ibn Ṣāḥib al-Ṣalā, *Al-Mann bi-l-imāma,* 478.

6 Ibn Ṣāḥib al-Ṣalā, *Al-Mann bi-l-imāma,* 478.

small, because they had been focused on fighting rebels, and that it was only with Caliph Abū Yaʿqūb, who took control of the peninsula with his victorious armies, that work on this magnificent building could finally be initiated.[7] Thus, the construction of this mosque, and the Almohad turn toward building more generally, was made possible by the conquest and incorporation of Ibn Mardanīsh's territory.

As scholars of the Almohads have noted, the period after the dynasty's conquest of Sharq al-Andalus triggered changes in many aspects of Almohad politics and culture. The Almohads undertook vast building projects using new architectural forms and materials. Scholars began to downplay the doctrine of the mahdī and to promote Mālikī thought more intensively. The Almohad armies, joined now by soldiers and commanders from Ibn Mardanīsh's territory, began a series of significant military campaigns against the Christian kingdoms of the Iberian Peninsula, culminating in the Battle of al-ʿArak/Alarcos in 591/1195. Understanding the mechanisms behind these changes is challenging, not least because later authors tried to minimize the degree to which Almohad doctrine and culture changed over time. But there are hints in Ibn Ṣāḥib al-Ṣalā's work, in biographical dictionaries, and in surviving material culture that these changes originated in the years immediately following Ibn Mardanīsh's death. They suggest that the increasingly Andalusī orientation of the Almohads was due, at least in part, to the incorporation of Ibn Mardanīsh's children, scholars, and military leaders into the Almohad elite and of his buildings and landscapes into Almohad territory.

The Islamic Middle Period overall was a time of political and cultural transformation, as newly Muslim groups began to form dynasties and assert their righteousness. Patricia Crone has described all of the Islamic world as postcolonial, since the Islamic conquests set into motion processes of acculturation that are common in more modern empires as well.[8] The long parallel processes of Arabization and Islamization and the resulting social complexity produced enormous cultural diversity across the Islamic world. In the Maghrib, the conflicts among Ibn Mardanīsh and the Almohads over the legacy of the Arab caliphate were formed in this context. The aftermath of the Almohad incorporation of Sharq al-Andalus also reflected complex dynamics of acculturation.

---

7 Ibn Ṣāḥib al-Ṣalā, *Al-Mann bi-l-imāma,* 476.

8 Patricia Crone, "Post-Colonialism in Tenth-Century Islam," *Der Islam* 83, no. 1 (2006): 2–38.

Recently, scholars of the Middle Ages have argued for the applicability of postcolonial theory to premodern contexts, since it is "inherently about relations of hegemony and resistance in the encounter between different cultures and peoples."[9] Conversion, in particular, had the potential to restructure dynamics of power.[10]

The Almohad conquest of Sharq al-Andalus, involving, as it did, two competing groups of Muslims, has not usually been thought to have required "conversion" or to have led to cultural transformation. And yet, as shown in chapter 2, the Almohads considered the battle against non-Almohad Muslims tantamount to jihad with the ultimate goal of their opponents' conversion and submission. The incorporation of Ibn Mardanīsh's territories into the Almohad realm *was* a conquest, requiring religious and political submission, and like most conquests, the resulting power structures were complex. As the Banū Mardanīsh and their allies became Almohads, the Almohads redefined their own community and the "other"—turning their focus from a great battle between Muslims to one directed at Christians. Alongside this military change in direction came other, more subtle shifts. Two of Ibn Mardanīsh's daughters married the Almohad caliph and his son, the future caliph Abu Yūsuf Yaʿqūb, and raised their children in al-Andalus; Ibn Mardanīsh's family members administered provinces for the Almohads; and the scholars, craftsmen, and objects that had once spoken for his kingdom had to find new homes.

This chapter explores the interactions of the competing rulers of the twelfth-century Islamic West in a time of flux. As the rulers formed alliances, sought to assert their superiority, waged wars, and sponsored cultural production, the people, lands, goods, and ideas they traded expressed their stances of affiliation with or resistance to one another. Sometimes resistance was conveyed explicitly in armed conflict or in dynastic chronicles that denigrated the enemy, while affiliation manifested itself in treaties or marriages. Other times, evidence of enmity or alliance can be gleaned from the choice of specific architectural forms, from the

9 Ato Quayson, "Translations and Transnationals," in *Postcolonial Approaches to the European Middle Ages: Translating Cultures,* ed. Ananya Jahanara Kabir and Deanne Williams (Cambridge: Cambridge University Press, 2005).

10 As Janina Safran has observed about al-Andalus, "Engagement with the other and the process of differentiation were not unidirectional and not comfortable. In this context, as in others, power relations were ambivalent and ambiguous." Janina Safran, *Defining Boundaries in al-Andalus: Muslims, Christians, and Jews in Islamic Iberia* (Ithaca, NY: Cornell University Press, 2013), 21.

presence of a particular figure in a ruler's court, or from the catalogue of a scholar's teachers. I read both historical chronicles and these other kinds of sources against and alongside each other to understand the dynamics of the newly Almohad territories of Sharq al-Andalus and to trace how the people who had fought the Almohad caliphate for so long were incorporated into their former enemy's regime. Rather than take these sources at their word, I seek to probe their contradictions, the gaps glossed over, and the fissures that reveal the complexities of their contexts. Such an examination reveals that even after Ibn Mardanīsh's dynasty failed, its people, landscapes, ideas, and objects continued to challenge the Almohad caliphate.

Analyzing the relationships of hegemony and resistance among Muslims, instead of assuming that cultural difference and conflict fall along a binary Christian-Muslim line, reveals fragmented and constantly shifting groups within what might otherwise be seen as a unified category. The incorporation of Hilāl and the elite of the Mardanīshī polity into the Almohad caliphate seems, on the surface, to have been complete. But assimilation can mask more complex processes of acculturation, as the conquered quietly transform their conquerors.

The Almohad Incorporation of Sharq al-Andalus

From its first sentence to its last paragraph, Ibn Ṣāḥib al-Ṣalā's history demonstrates the immense importance of Ibn Mardanīsh and his family in the construction and consolidation of Almohad power.[11] His work opens with a critical narrative about how Ibn Mardanīsh and his Christian "companions" set out to fight the Almohads, and it ends with the assimilation of Ibn Mardanīsh's children into Almohad power structures. As discussed in chapter 2, the history presents Ibn Mardanīsh as impious, dangerously close to and reliant on Christians. The trope of Ibn Mardanīsh's "Christian companions" appears throughout Ibn Ṣāḥib al-Ṣalā's work, as Linda Gale Jones has shown, and through it the author attempts to paint the quotidian battles among the rulers of the twelfth-century western Mediterranean as a cosmic showdown

11 Pierre Guichard has noted how Ibn Ṣāḥib al-Ṣalā's emphasis on Ibn Mardanīsh's regime, and particularly its incorporation into the Almohad Empire, offers the Mardanīshī state a certain legitimacy. *Les musulmans de Valence,* 1: 126.

between Islam and Christianity, good and evil.[12] He also insinuates that Ibn Mardanīsh's mind had been damaged by excessive wine drinking and that any rebellion against the Almohads could be explained only by mental instability or religious laxity. The volume's narrative arc is one of rebellion followed by submission and redemption; accordingly, it closes on the Almohads and Ibn Mardanīsh's children turning to fight the Christians of the north together. The final chapters of the volume also describe the massive building projects that Abū Ya'qūb Yūsuf undertook after the consolidation of his control over al-Andalus.

In spite of its clear pro-Almohad bias, Ibn Ṣāḥib al-Ṣalā's chronicle is the best source of information about Ibn Mardanīsh's time in power and about how he was seen by the Almohads. All later sources, including the thirteenth-century works by Ibn 'Idhārī and 'Abd al-Wāḥid al-Marrākushī, rely heavily on Ibn Ṣāḥib al-Ṣalā's narration of events. As the distance between the authors of historical chronicles and the period chronicled grows, their narratives become imbued with layers of contemporary meaning and, as will be shown in chapter 7, are sometimes transformed and distorted. In addition to being the chronicler closest in time to Ibn Mardanīsh, Ibn Ṣāḥib al-Ṣalā was an important member of the Almohad elite and an eyewitness to many of the events he describes. He thus offers a unique perspective on contemporary Almohad attitudes toward the Banū Mardanīsh before and after their capitulation.

According to Ibn Ṣāḥib al-Ṣalā, Hilāl and his retinue were treated with great honor after meeting the caliph on the first night of Ramaḍān. The following morning, the caliph received homage from the leaders and soldiers of Sharq al-Andalus. On that day, Ibn Mardanīsh's soldiers and commanders pledged their obedience to the caliph and asked him to be allowed to undertake an expedition against Huete, a Castilian city on the eastern edge of the kingdom, close to Sharq al-Andalus.[13] They explained that the city would be easy to conquer because it was newly built with poorly defended walls, and that it would be easy to maintain the Almohad army's provisions. The caliph was pleased with their request and promised they could set off as soon as Ramaḍān was over. Ibn Ṣāḥib al-Ṣalā notes that Hilāl and his companions made themselves at home in al-Mu'tamid's former palace and received such abundant gifts that they forgot the customs of their independent reign and "admired the

12 Linda Gale Jones, "'The Christian Companion': A Rhetorical Trope in the Narration of Intra Muslim Conflict," *Anuario de Estudios Medievales* 38 (2008): 793–829.

13 Ibn Ṣāḥib al-Ṣalā, *al-Mann bi-l-imāma*, 473.

generosity and good government that they saw in this illustrious regime, and they were made happy with an enormous happiness, and a great liveliness showed in their faces and their carriage."[14]

Later in the chronicle, Ibn Ṣāḥib al-Ṣalā writes about the expedition to Huete, which took place in Shawwāl 576/June 1172. The caliph Abū Yaʿqūb and his armies set out with the intention of undertaking jihad. They embarked on a remarkable campaign of Ibn Mardanīsh-focused conquest, beginning with a siege of the castle of Balj (modern Vilches), which Ibn Mardanīsh had "given to the Christians" after Ibn Hamushk began to consider switching his allegiance to the Almohads.[15] Accompanied by Ibn Hamushk, Abū Yaʿqūb and his troops encircled the castle, which submitted within a day, and Abū Yaʿqūb granted the castle to Ibn Hamushk.[16] Next the Almohad armies turned to the castle of al-Karaz (Alcaraz) "in order to cleanse it of infidelity as well," because Ibn Mardanīsh had given it, too, to the Christians.[17] This castle also ended up being abandoned by its defenders within a day and given to Ibn Hamushk. The Almohad armies then began to raid Christian territory on the route to Huete. The caliph's brother and an advance force arrived outside Huete on the thirteenth of Dhū al-Qaʿda 576/July 7, 1172, with the caliph and his armies joining them four days later. The following week, the Almohad *sayyid* Abū Ḥafṣ, who had been appointed governor of Sharq al-Andalus, arrived together with Abū al-Ḥajjāj Yūsuf ibn Mardanīsh, Ibn Mardanīsh's brother, who would eventually succeed Abū Ḥafṣ as governor of Valencia. They and their armies joined the Almohad armies already besieging Huete, terrifying the Christians within.[18] The siege lasted ten days. The city's residents nearly ran out of water while awaiting the arrival of Alfonso VIII, but a storm refilled their water reservoirs and allowed them to continue holding out. Writing a century after Ibn Ṣāḥib al-Ṣalā, al-Marrākushī would described these events as a miracle, writing that the inhabitants of Huete were dying of thirst, and requested permission from Alfonso VIII to submit, but he refused.[19] Al-Marrākushī wrote that the Almohad soldiers besieging the

14 Ibn Ṣāḥib al-Ṣalā, *al-Mann bi-l-imāma*, 473–74.

15 Ibn Ṣāḥib al-Ṣalā, *al-Mann bi-l-imāma*, 489.

16 Ibn Ṣāḥib al-Ṣalā, *al-Mann bi-l-imāma*, 490.

17 Ibn Ṣāḥib al-Ṣalā, *al-Mann bi-l-imāma*, 490.

18 Ibn Ṣāḥib al-Ṣalā, *al-Mann bi-l-imāma*, 499.

19 Al-Marrākushī, *al-Muʿjib fī talkhīs*, 180–81. As Huici Miranda notes in his translation, this is a significant departure from the story told by Ibn Ṣāḥib al-Ṣalā, who was an eyewitness to these events. Ambrosio Huici Miranda, *Crónicas árabes de la reconquista*, vol. 4, trans. of ʿAbd

city overheard a great sound of yelling and crying within the city one night, and realized it was the city's priests and monks praying and the rest of the people responding "amen." Suddenly, a torrential downpour arrived, filling the city's cisterns and wells with water, and allowing the city to continue to resist the siege.[20]

Eventually, with no victory in sight and the threat of Alfonso VIII's imminent arrival, the Almohads gave up. Ibn Ṣāḥib al-Ṣalā frames the Almohads' failure to capture the city as a consequence of the impurity of their intentions in jihad, and he records a Friday sermon in Arabic and Berber (*al-lisān al-gharbī*) that chastised the soldiers for being insincere and desiring the prohibited.[21] Nevertheless, the Almohad armies conducted successful raids in the region of Cuenca, in areas that had likewise reverted to the Christians through Ibn Mardanīsh's donations of Muslim land to Christians as part of pacts and tribute payments.[22] By turning against the very Christians who had benefited from Ibn Mardanīsh's agreements and tribute, his children and soldiers proved themselves loyal Almohads.

After nearly two months of raiding, the caliph decided to cease campaigning and give his armies a break; he and the rest of the Almohad elite went to visit their new territory in Sharq al-Andalus. The soldiers who had joined the campaign from Ibn Mardanīsh's former territories returned home, well paid for their service to the Almohads. Upon the Almohads' arrival in the province of Valencia, Abū al-Ḥajjāj Yūsuf ibn Mardanīsh delivered vast quantities of food to the caliph and his entourage, and Ibn Ṣāḥib al-Ṣalā, who was present, proclaimed the great beauty of the region.[23] Moving slowly through Sharq al-Andalus, the caliph and his armies stayed in the palaces at Monteagudo. There, according to Ibn Ṣāḥib al-Ṣalā, they were met by all of the people of Murcia, who welcomed them with drums and banners and proclaimed, "Praise be to God, who has united us with you in the best state and in the most agreeable situation and has removed injustice and impiety!"[24] The caliph and his retinue then moved into the palace in Murcia, and Hilāl ibn Mardanīsh was tasked with ensuring the perfect comfort of the Almohad guests in

al-Wāḥid al-Marrākushī, *Kitāb al-Muʿjib fī talkhīṣ akhbār al-mugrib* (Tetouan: Editora Marroquí, 1955), 203–4. This raises fascinating questions about what other sources (perhaps Christian?) al-Marrākushī might have relied on to craft his narrative.

20 Al-Marrākushī, *al-Muʿjib fī talkhīs*, 181.

21 Ibn Ṣāḥib al-Ṣalā, *Al-Mann bi-l-imāma,* 500–501.

22 Ibn Ṣāḥib al-Ṣalā, *Al-Mann bi-l-imāma,* 504.

23 Ibn Ṣāḥib al-Ṣalā, *Al-Mann bi-l-imāma,* 512.

24 Ibn Ṣāḥib al-Ṣalā, *Al-Mann bi-l-imāma,* 513–14.

Murcia. "They found," writes Ibn Ṣāḥib al-Ṣalā, "houses prepared, full of clothes, and provisioned, and nubile girls and beautiful young slaves had been brought from those that his father had in great number for such an occasion."[25] That night, the new moon marking the start of Muḥarram appeared (corresponding to August 23, 1172).

Over the course of Muḥarram, most of the Almohads and their soldiers requested to return to their homes, but the family of Ibn Mardanīsh and the Almohad caliphal family and nobles stayed in Murcia together, conducting "noble sessions" (*majālis*) and discussing the future of their collaboration.[26] The caliph granted Abū al-Ḥajjāj the governorship of Valencia, a level of position that had previously been open only to *sayyids*, or descendants of ʿAbd al-Muʾmin, because the caliph "recognized the sincerity of his obedience."[27] After Muḥarram, both families returned to Seville, where Ibn Mardanīsh's sons and their families were given the Taifa palace of al-Muʿtamid and the adjoining houses as their residence. They continued to fight alongside the Almohads in raids against the Christian north, and Ibn Ṣāḥib al-Ṣalā particularly commends Ghānim ibn Muḥammad ibn Mardanīsh for his bravery in battle and his loyalty to the Almohads.[28]

In the last pages of the surviving volume of Ibn Ṣāḥib al-Ṣalā's chronicle, he describes how the Almohads turned toward Toledo and Portugal, winning concessions from the Christian kings of those regions. Raiding the region of Toledo, he writes, the Almohad armies captured so much booty and so many captives that they made the Castilians "drink from a bitter cup," and that Nuño Pérez de Lara (Ar. *Nūnoh*), Lord of Toledo (*ṣāḥib Ṭulayṭula*), protector of the young Alfonso, sent an embassy begging for peace.[29] In describing Alfonso VIII's regent as humiliated and desperate, Ibn Ṣāḥib al-Ṣalā imposes cosmic justice on Ibn Mardanīsh's closest Christian ally. Fifteen years earlier, the Almohad armies had fought against Nuño alongside Alfonso VIII's uncle Ferdinand II; now, in raiding his territory directly, with Ibn Mardanīsh's children and soldiers at their side, they had transformed a proxy conflict into a direct one.

---

25 Ibn Ṣāḥib al-Ṣalā, *Al-Mann bi-l-imāma,* 514.
26 Ibn Ṣāḥib al-Ṣalā, *Al-Mann bi-l-imāma,* 514–15.
27 Ibn Ṣāḥib al-Ṣalā, *Al-Mann bi-l-imāma,* 515.
28 Ibn Ṣāḥib al-Ṣalā, *Al-Mann bi-l-imāma,* 516.
29 Ibn Ṣāḥib al-Ṣalā, *Al-Mann bi-l-imāma,* 526.

Although Ibn Ṣāḥib al-Ṣalā's continuation of his chronicle has been lost, other Almohad sources emphasize the important roles Ibn Mardanīsh's children continued to play in the following generation. Al-Marrākushī, writing in the early thirteenth century, recounted several stories about the caliph Abū Ya'qūb Yūsuf's generosity to Hilāl, including an enigmatic, fablelike story about a dream Hilāl had.[30] The story, which al-Marrākushī says he heard from one of Hilāl's sons, is written in Hilāl's voice. In the dream the caliph presented Hilāl with a key. When he awoke, Hilāl went to the palace and came into the presence of the caliph, who presented him with a key identical to the one he had seen in the dream. Fearful, Hilāl asked him what it was, and the caliph told him had been sent from Murcia, and that it opened a chest the governor there had discovered in his father's treasury, but that the caliph had not opened it, since it belonged to Hilāl. He urged Hilāl to take the key and to open the chest, but Hilāl begged him to send for the chest so he could open it in the caliph's presence. The caliph refused, ordering him to open the chest himself and keep its contents himself. When Hilāl did so, he discovered jewels and treasures that had belonged to his father, worth more than forty-thousand dinars.

In this narrative, Abū Ya'qūb is presented as not only generous to the children of his dead former rival, but as encouraging them to continue their family's legacy. By sending the very jewels and treasures of Ibn Mardanīsh to Hilāl, he allows the continued inheritance of royal symbols and wealth among the Banū Mardanīsh. The foretelling of this event in a dream, a common trope in Arabic historiography, frames it as providential, part of the Almohad caliph's God-given rule. In other narratives in al-Marrākushī, Hilāl demonstrates devotion to the caliph and the Almohad regime, for example, by preserving a tablet (*lawḥ*) the caliph gives him to learn with and requesting that he be buried with it next to his skin.[31] The caliph responds by giving Hilāl and his sons horses, robes of honor, and money. In these first years after the submission of Ibn Mardanīsh, his children and the Almohad elite stitch their families together through performances of mutual respect and generosity. The culmination of this integration took place on the fifth of Rabī' al-Awwal 570/fourth of October 1174, when one of Ibn Mardanīsh's daughters married Abū Ya'qūb, and another daughter, named Ṣafīya, married his son, the future caliph Abū Yūsuf Ya'qub, in an elaborate

30 Al-Marrākushī, *al-Mu'jib fī talkhīs*, 182–83.
31 Al-Marrākushī, *al-Mu'jib fī talkhīs*, 183.

public ceremony.[32] Ibn al-Khaṭīb reported that Abū Yaʿqūb married Ibn Mardanīsh's daughter "to mix his [Ibn Mardanīsh's] people with his own and thus made them inherit sovereignty over the eastern lands for a not insignificant time."[33] He concluded his discussion of the wedding by stating that Abū Yaʿqūb fell in love with this daughter, and she triumphed over him so completely that people began to describe being madly in love using the saying "like the caliph and the blue-eyed Mardanīshī girl."[34]

Almohad Architecture, Post–1172

Nearly every element of Almohad culture was transformed in the years after the incorporation of Ibn Mardanīsh's family and territory into the Almohad realm in 567/1172. Although these transformations can probably not be attributed to any direct efforts on the part of the Banū Mardanīsh and their allies to change the Almohad dynasty, it is clear that the complete conquest of al-Andalus allowed the Almohads to direct their attention to their Christian enemy. Ibn Ṣāḥib al-Ṣalā's narrative of the construction of the Great Mosque of Seville makes it clear that it was precisely because of the submission of the Banū Mardanīsh that the caliph Abū Yaʿqūb Yūsuf commissioned the greatest mosque ever seen in al-Andalus ("There is not in al-Andalus a mosque that equals it in width and length and number of naves").[35] It seems likely that this new construction also relied on the talent of craftsmen from the Almohads' newly acquired territories. The chief architect of the Great Mosque of Seville was one Aḥmad ibn Bāsuh, whom Ibn Ṣāḥib al-Ṣalā described as working alongside architects from all of al-Andalus, as well as others from Marrakech, Fez, and the Strait. Ibn Ṣāḥib al-Ṣalā writes that carpenters and workmen from all of these locations assembled in Seville to obey the command of the caliph who had been distinguished by God for his piety, and worked to similarly distinguish Seville.[36] He also notes that the building incorporated marble from the coasts of the Strait, which

---

32 Ibn ʿIdhārī, *Bayān al-mughrib, qism al-Muwaḥḥidīn,* 135; Ibn al-Khaṭīb, *Aʿmāl al-aʿlām,* ed. Sayyid Kasrawī Ḥasan, 2:241; Al-Maqqarī, *Nafḥ al-ṭīb,* 1:445. See also discussion of these wedding ceremonies in Marín, *Mujeres en al-Andalus,* 443–44, 549–50.

33 Ibn al-Khaṭīb, *Aʿmāl al-aʿlām,* ed. Sayyid Kasrawī Ḥasan, 2:241.

34 Ibn al-Khaṭīb, *Aʿmāl al-aʿlām,* ed. Sayyid Kasrawī Ḥasan, 2:241.

35 Ibn Ṣāḥib al-Ṣalā, *Al-Mann bi-l-imāma,* 476.

36 Ibn Ṣāḥib al-Ṣalā, *Al-Mann bi-l-imāma,* 474–75.

no previous ruler in al-Andalus had been able to procure.[37] By bringing together people and materials from across the empire in this manner, the Great Mosque of Seville was an expression of the imperial ambitions of the Almohad caliphate.

The mosque was nearly completely destroyed in subsequent centuries, so direct analysis of the building is impossible. But Ibn Ṣāhib al-Ṣalā's descriptions of the mosque and its minaret give a sense of the scale and luxury of the building's ornamentation and convey what the architecture might have looked like.[38] He mentions a dome (*qubba*) that crowned the mihrab, with muqarnas plasterwork (*ṣan'at al-jibs*), and a *maqṣūra*, or enclosed area in front of the mihrab, that was reserved for the caliph.[39] There was also a new *sabāṭ*, or passageway connected to the palace, for the caliph to use to get to the mosque in privacy. The Almohads had already constructed a sabāṭ in a palace/mosque complex in Marrakech, and as Amira Bennison has noted, this feature, used in both of their two capitals, echoed similar structures in Umayyad Cordoba.[40] The Almohads also had already constructed muqarnas vaults in their mosques in Tīnmallal and Marrakech, and there are records of a maqṣūra in both the first and the second versions of the Kutubiyya mosque in Marrakech.

Other elements of the mosque's architecture seem to point to disjuncture from earlier Almohad buildings. The minaret, which survives as the bell tower of the cathedral of Seville, now known as La Giralda, and the copper-alloy plated doors of the entrance to the courtyard are the best-preserved elements of the structure.[41] As Jessica Streit has shown, both exhibit considerable differences from earlier Almohad architecture in North Africa.[42] The minaret, constructed beginning between 1184 and 1198, displays a remarkably complex ornamental program on its four walls, in seven distinct levels. Most of the ornament consists of *sebka*,

37 Ibn Ṣāḥib al-Ṣalā, *Al-Mann bi-l-imāma,* 476.

38 Ibn Ṣāḥib al-Ṣalā, *Al-Mann bi-l-imāma,* 477–78.

39 On the muqarnas, see Ibn Ṣāḥib al-Ṣalā, *Al-Mann bi-l-imāma,* 477, esp. n7, where the editors note that he means muqarnas. On the *maqṣūra*, see ibid., 478.

40 Amira Bennison, "Power and the City in the Islamic West from the Umayyads to the Almohads," in *Cities in the Pre-Modern Islamic World*, eds. Amira Bennison and Alison Gascoigne (London: RoutledgeCurzon, 2007), 66.

41 On these bronze doors, their inscriptions, and their connections to other Iberian and North African objects, see Tom Nickson, "'Sovereignty Belongs to God.'"

42 Jessica Streit, "Well-Ordered Growth: Meanings and Aesthetics of the Almohad Mosque of Seville," in *"His Pen and Ink Are a Powerful Mirror": Andalusi, Judaeo-Arabic, and Other Near Eastern Studies in Honor of Ross Brann*, ed. Adam Bursi, S. J. Pearce, and Hamza Zafer (Leiden: Brill, 2020).

FIGURE 6.1. La Giralda, the Almohad minaret of the former Great Mosque of Seville, constructed 1184–98. *Photo:* Abigail Krasner Balbale.

panels of interlacing rhomboids, rising from thin marble columns and contained within rectangular frames. These sebka panels frame arched seven levels of windows, which open onto the interior ramp within the minaret. The windows are mostly doubled arches, alternating between two horseshoes or two multilobed arches, and surmounted by larger lambrequin arches. Like most Almohad architecture, the minaret is constructed of mud brick, but here the brick has been shaped into forms that allow delicate tracery. The sebka panels represent two layers of ornament, one surface, and one web offset underneath, providing the illusion of greater depth and recalling the "three-dimensional" stucco carving of both Ibn Mardanīsh and the Almoravids.

Streit argues that the increased subtlety and complexity of Seville's minaret, which may have been constructed at the same moment as the far simpler Kutubiyya minaret at their mosque in Marrakech, reflects cultural and intellectual strands of their Andalusī milieu. Specifically, she connects the increasing naturalism of Almohad architectural ornamentation to the philosophy being developed by Ibn Rushd and Ibn Ṭufayl, two Andalusī scholars employed by the Almohad court in the late twelfth century, and to their arguments that the proof of God could be found in His rationally ordered natural world.[43] Dominique Urvoy has seen a similar approach to well-ordered and logical rationalism in the work of Ibn Ṭufayl, in an Almohad culinary compendium, and throughout Almohad cultural production.[44]

Further evidence of considerably more elaborate ornamentation on the interior of the mosque has also come to light. Archaeological excavations in 1997–98 uncovered fragments of carved stucco that have been attributed to what was once the mihrab wall of the mosque.[45] These fragments were deeply carved, and appear to have constituted a large sebka frame, through which vegetal ornamentation wove.[46] As Streit observes, the combination of a trellislike sebka screen and vegetal ornamentation creates a far more mimetic representation than is typical in Almohad art, evoking the plants that would have been growing in the architectural frame of the mosque courtyard.[47] The verisimilitude of the scrolling vegetal elements would have been amplified by the polychrome painting of the stucco, in rich reds and greens—a use of color highly unusual in Almohad mosque architecture. The interior of the mosque,

---

43 Streit, "Well-Ordered Growth," 319–22.

44 Dominique Urvoy, "The *Rationality* of Everyday Life: An Andalusian Tradition? (Apropos of Ḥayy's First Experiences)," in *The World of Ibn Tufayl: Interdisciplinary Perspectives on Ḥayy ibn Yaqẓān*, ed. Lawrence I. Conrad (Leiden: Brill, 1996), 38–52.

45 Miguel Ángel Tabales Rodríguez and Álvaro Jiménez Sancho, "Intervención arqueológica en el Pabellón de oficinas de la Catedral de Sevilla (1997–1998)," *Anuario arqueológico de Andalucía* 3 (2001): 432; Rosario Huarte Cambria, "Fragmentos de yeserías relacionados con la aljama Almohade de Sevilla," *Laboratorio de Arte* 14 (2001): 181–96.

46 Huarte Cambria, "Fragmentos de yeserías," 183; Streit, "Well-Ordered Growth," 314–15.

47 Streit, "Well-Ordered Growth," 314–15.

described by Ibn Ṣāḥib al-Ṣalā as beginning construction immediately after the arrival of the Banū Mardanīsh in Seville, therefore reflects a considerable departure from earlier forms of Almohad architecture and toward forms—deeply carved stucco and polychromy—familiar from Taifa, Almoravid, and Mardanīshī examples. Perhaps the submission of the Banū Mardanīsh, and the end of the threat of their opposition, made the symbols of their kingdom fair game for incorporation into Almohad aesthetics.

Archaeological investigations of the Almohad remnants of the Alcazar of Seville, adjacent to the new mosque, also provide evidence of a new stage of construction starting in 1172.[48] The northern portico of the Palacio del Yeso, reconstructed in 1172, remains visible today. The façade is organized in a symmetrical tripartite structure, divided by two massive brick piers.[49] The central zone contains a wide polylobed arch, pointed at the top, with forms like stalactites descending on either side of the apex. Two brick piers support the central arch. On each side, in a symmetrical arrangement, two small columns support three polylobed arches that intertwine at the top to support an open network of sebka lattice. Behind this open façade rests another, with two horseshoe arches and two windows that provide an entrance to the palace itself. The doubled façade, with a narrow arcade in between, and the polylobed arches resemble Taifa architecture, especially the northern façade of the Aljafería in Saragossa. But the use of a larger central arch has been associated with Abbasid architecture, with its emphasis on a strong central axis.[50]

As Arnold has noted, the immediate precedents for the Almohads' use of such a central focus in their architecture can be found in in the Almoravid palace in Marrakech and, especially, in Ibn Mardanīsh's palace in Monteagudo.[51] Speculating about why the Almohads might have

---

48 Rafael Manzano Martos, "Casas y palacios en la Sevilla Almohade: Sus antecedents Hispánicos," in *Casas y palacios de al-Andalus*, ed. Navarro Palazón; Miguel Ángel Tabales Rodríguez, *El Alcázar de Sevilla: Primeros estudios sobre estratigrafía y evolución constructiva* (Seville: Junta de Andalucía, 2002), 40–56.

49 On the Palacio del Yeso, see Arnold, *Islamic Palace Architecture*, 199–204.

50 Arnold, *Islamic Palace Architecture*, 215–18.

51 Arnold, *Islamic Palace Architecture*, 216–17. "Only in Monteagudo did the architect go one step further, by adding a niche to the back of the broad hall and thus giving the hall essentially a T-shaped ground plan. No other example of this kind has been found in the West from the twelfth century. In the thirteenth century this second feature of Abbasid architecture would come to new prominence, in the shape of the mirador" (ibid., 218). Antonio Almagro also noted the clear relationship between the architecture at Monteagudo and the Almohad palace at the Alcazar. Antonio Almagro Gorbe and Rafael Manzano Martos, "Palacios

FIGURE 6.2. Patio del Yeso, Alcazar of Seville, reconstructed in 1172. *Photo:* Wikimedia Commons; photo uploaded by Jose Luis Filpo Cabana, licensed under the Creative Commons Attribution 3.0 Unported (CC BY-SA 3.0) license (https://creativecommons.org/licenses/by/3.0/).

adopted this element of Abbasid architecture in spite of their ideological opposition to the Abbasids, Arnold suggests that they used this Abbasid form to express their own concept of power.[52] But given the date of the Palacio del Yeso's construction and its reliance on a central arch and axis, perhaps the associations this form carried for the Almohads should be sought in Sharq al-Andalus rather than in the Abbasid East.

Other elements of the Almohads' architecture and garden design seem already to have responded to developments in Sharq al-Andalus. Huici Miranda showed that ʿAbd al-Muʾmin's love of gardens, and his construction of the Buḥayra estate outside Marrakech, was facilitated by the submission of Aḥmad ibn Milḥān, formerly of Guadix in Sharq al-Andalus, who had fled Ibn Mardanīsh's territory for Marrakech in 546/1151 and subsequently designed the garden and waterways there.[53]

---

medievales hispanos: discurso del académico electo Excmo. Sr. D. Antonio Almagro Gorbea leído en el acto de su recepción pública el día 27 de enero de 2008 y contestación del Excmo. Sr. D. Rafael Manzano Martos" (Granada: Real Academia de Bellas Artes de San Fernando, 2008), 47–48.

52 Arnold, *Islamic Palace Architecture*, 216.

53 Ambrosio Huici Miranda, *Crónicas árabes de la reconquista*, Vol. 4, 164, note 1.

FIGURE 6.3. Reconstruction of an axial view across the interior courtyard of the Castillejo of Monteagudo, by Antonio Almagro Gorbea. Inventory no. AA-301_i05, "Arquitectura de Al-Andalus," Academia Colecciones, Real Academia de Bellas Artes de San Fernando, Madrid.

Ibn Mardanīsh's country estate at Monteagudo was conquered by the Almohads in 560/1165, and much of it was destroyed.[54] In 567/1171, Abū Yaʿqūb ordered his architect Aḥmad ibn Bāsuh to renovate the Almohad country estate outside of Seville known as al-Buḥayra. The renovation included elaborate hydraulic works, which brought water via an aqueduct to a large square reservoir (140 × 140 feet). In the middle of the southern side of the reservoir was a small square pavilion, and along the eastern side there are remnants of a larger, rectangular pavilion that seems to stretch the whole length of the reservoir.[55] New excavations in Monteagudo in 2018–19 have uncovered an aqueduct that supplies a central reservoir, as well as a similar series of pavilions and palaces overlooking the waterways and cultivated landscapes.[56] Did the Almohad caliph seek to compete with the luxurious rural estate (*munya*) of his rival in Sharq al-Andalus? Ibn Mardanīsh's architecture, with the use of cross-axial gardens, miradors over cultivated landscape, and dispersed palaces and pavilions through productive landscapes, was only the latest in a long tradition of palatine complexes outside cities. The Almohads may have sought to claim this tradition from the Umayyads of Cordoba

54 Ibn Ṣāḥib al-Ṣalā, *al-Mann bi-l-imāma*.
55 Arnold, *Islamic Palace Architecture*, 211–12.
56 Excavations led by Julio Navarro Palazón, as yet unpublished.

or the more distant Fatimids or Abbasids, but the closest and most recent example they had of this kind of space was in Ibn Mardanīsh's Sharq al-Andalus.

Almohad calligraphic style seems to have shifted in this period as well. María Antonia Martínez Núñez argues that the introduction of monumental cursive inscriptions is an Almohad innovation, but she notes several Saljuq examples and "scarce" Almoravid and Mardanīshī examples that predate or coincide with the inscriptions of the Almohads.[57] She dates the shift in the Almohad use of cursive to the mid-twelfth century, which saw monetary reform under ʿAbd al-Mu'min along with the building of the mihrab of the Kutubiyya (553/1158) and the mihrab of the mosque of the Qasba in Marrakech (584/1188).[58] And she suggests that Ibn Mardanīsh's inscriptions, which slightly predate those of the Almohads and share several characteristics with them, "may find their explanation in the need to compete with the same modes of propaganda as their opponents, at least in epigraphic materials."[59] This explanation could hold in the other direction as well. In fact, the respective datings proposed by archaeologists for the structures suggest that it was the Almohads responding to Mardanīshī examples rather than the reverse. In a brief article published in 1987, María Jesús Rubiera Mata argued that the earliest peninsular cursive inscriptions dated precisely from the moment and region of Ibn Mardanīsh's authority, and that it was from Murcia, Játiva, and pro-Mardanīshī Granada that this new form of script percolated into broader usage.[60]

At the mosque in Seville, one monumental portal survives, and includes the original Almohad door. Made of a thin surface of copper alloy placed on a wooden substructure, this massive door was stamped with calligraphic cartouches in Kufic, reading *al-mulk li-llāh, al-baqā li-llah*—"Sovereignty is God's, Permanence is God's."[61] Traces of gold suggest the

57 María Antonia Martínez Núñez, "Escritura árabe ornamental y epigrafía andalusí," *Arqueología y territorio medieval* 4 (1997): 127–62; Martínez Núñez, "Ideologia y epigrafia Almohades," in *Los Almohades*, ed. Cressier, Fierro, and Molina, 1:8.

58 Martínez Núñez, "Ideología y epigrafía Almohades," 9.

59 Martínez Núñez, "Ideología y epigrafía Almohades," 35n131: "Tal vez encuentren su explicación en la necesidad de competir con los mismos medios de propaganda que sus oponentes, al menos en materia epigráfica." See also Martínez Núñez, "Escritura árabe ornamental," 140–41.

60 María Jesús Rubiera Mata, "Las inscripciones árabes de Játiva: una hipótesis y una propuesta sobre la denominación de un estilo," in *Homenaje al profesor Darío Cabanelas Rodríguez, O.F.M., con motivo de su LXX aniversario* (Granada: Universidad de Granada, Departamento de Estudios Semíticos, 1987).

61 Martínez Núñez, "Ideología y epigrafía Almohades," 13–14.

whole door might once have been gilded.[62] The door's massive bronze handles or knockers, however, are inscribed in cursive, making them some of the earliest surviving cursive inscriptions found on the Iberian Peninsula.[63] The inscriptions weave around the curves of the substantial handle, surrounded by scrolling vines, and include five Quranic verses. On one handle are written two ayas from Sūrat al-Nūr (24:36–37), "In temples God has allowed to be raised up, and His Name to be commemorated therein, therein glorifying Him, in the mornings and the evenings, / are men whom neither commerce nor trafficking diverts from the remembrance of God and to perform the prayer," and, on the other, three ayas from Sūrat al-Ḥijr (15:46–48), "Enter you them, in peace and security! / We shall strip away all rancour that is in their breasts; as brothers they shall be upon couches set face to face; / no fatigue there shall smite them, neither shall they ever be driven forth from there."[64] These inscriptions transform the monumental portal of the Almohads' new mosque to a passage into a heavenly realm, a place devoted to prayer and glorifying God, in which brothers may sit face to face without malice. In the construction of this great mosque in Seville, the Andalusī capital of the Almohads, where the caliph lived alongside his Mardanīshī brethren, the Almohads began to knit together their dynasty with the territories, aesthetics, and ideas of their erstwhile rivals.

These parallels between the modes of articulating sovereignty used by Ibn Mardanīsh's regime and those used by the Almohads increased in the years following the incorporation of his dynasty into theirs. However, by pointing them out, I do not mean to argue that the art and architecture of the Almohads was in some way derivative of al-Andalus. As already discussed, Ibn Mardanīsh's material culture was consciously formulated to emulate and evoke North African, Andalusī, and eastern models. The direction in which these goods, motifs, and modes moved in is not always clear, and neither is the timeline of their arrival in different cities and dynasties. What is clear is that Ibn Mardanīsh and the Almohads both sought to demonstrate their superior might and

62 Abd al-Aziz Salem, "La Puerta del Perdón en la gran mezquita de la alcazaba almohade de Sevilla," *Al-Andalus* 43 (1978), 203.

63 Salem, writing in 1978, called them the earliest cursive inscriptions in Spain. "La Puerta del Perdón," 204. The inscriptions in Ibn Mardanīsh's structures predate them, however.

64 The second part of the final aya from Sūrat al-Nūr is missing on the handle, and both Quranic inscriptions are preceded by the basmala and prayers for Muḥammad. Salem was the first to transcribe these inscriptions and push back against the argument that they were of Christian construction. See "La Puerta del Perdón," 204–6.

FIGURE 6.4. Bronze handle of the Puerta del Perdón, formerly the Great Mosque of Seville, constructed 1172–74. *Photo:* Abigail Krasner Balbale.

wealth through cultural production, and that the modes they used to articulate their political and religious ideals in material form could overlap. In the period after the Almohad incorporation of Sharq al-Andalus, as Ibn Mardanīsh's family and administration were integrated into the Almohad state, his craftsmen were put to work on Almohad projects,

Almohad caliphs inhabited his palaces, and his daughters bore the caliphs' children, these cultural formations became even more layered.

On the complexities of cultural interaction in modern America, James Clifford wrote: "Stories of cultural contact and change have been structured by a pervasive dichotomy: absorption by the other *or* resistance to the other. . . . Yet what if identity is conceived not as a boundary to be maintained but as a nexus of relations and transactions actively engaging a subject?"[65] Following Clifford in thinking of cultural contact as a series of exchanges breaks down the linear trajectory along which the history and art of al-Andalus and North Africa are often organized. Instead, it allows a consideration of the relationships and exchanges that structured individual and dynastic identities. Objects and spaces exerted their own powerful draw in these relationships. Clifford notes that considering cultural interaction in terms of complex processes of absorption and resistance yields new ways of thinking about identity, in which it is being constantly reformulated in transactions and interactions. As the Almohads encountered spaces and objects created as part of Ibn Mardanīsh's quest for power, rich in symbolic language and made of the most luxurious materials, they absorbed and resisted them, expanded and destroyed them. Their public displays of honor for Ibn Mardanīsh's family and for the elites who had made up his dynasty demonstrate that theirs was not a conquest of unmitigated violence and destruction, but rather a complex negotiation. As the Almohad realm and Mardanīshī Sharq al-Andalus became one political territory, the people, places, and objects that mingled in the new, combined empire reformulated their identities in relation to one another.

Scholars from Sharq al-Andalus and the Almohads

The leaders of Ibn Mardanīsh's religious establishment, including the imams, judges, and khaṭībs appointed by his government, formed part of the delegation that went with Hilāl to submit to the Almohads in 567/1172. Ibn al-Faras, Ibn Ḥubaysh, and Ibn Ḥamīd, the three khaṭībs who alternated in giving the Friday sermon in Murcia's great mosque in the period just before the fall of the dynasty, were likely among this

65 James Clifford, *The Predicament of Culture: Twentieth-Century Literature, Ethnography and Art* (Cambridge, MA: Harvard University Press, 1998), 344.

group.[66] Ibn al-Abbār notes that Ibn al-Faras died in Seville while taking part in this mission, in the middle of the night on the nineteenth of Shawwāl 567 (June 14, 1172)—roughly six weeks after the delegation's arrival at the beginning of Ramaḍān and just before the combined forces of Ibn Mardanīsh's men and Almohad soldiers would set out on jihad toward Huete.

Although the other two men's biographies do not mention their participation in this delegation, they both became important Almohad religious figures. Ibn Ḥamīd (d. 586/1190), a Friday preacher under Ibn Mardanīsh, became the judge of Valencia under the Almohads. His biography in Ibn al-Abbār's work mentions his great knowledge of hadith, grammar, and Quranic readings and notes that he became judge in the year 581/1185, when he was already in his seventies. It also discusses the large number of students he taught.[67] One of his students was the author Ibn ʿAmīra al-Ḍabbī, whose biographical dictionary offers a series of stories about Ibn Ḥamīd that al-Ḍabbī collected personally from the scholar and his friends and acquaintances.[68] Al-Ḍabbī writes that Ibn Ḥamīd had been his first teacher and that his lessons had taken place when he, al-Ḍabbī, had been less than ten years old, which would have been during Ibn Mardanīsh's rule, around 560/1165.[69] Al-Ḍabbī talks about the scholars from whom Ibn Ḥamīd transmitted hadith and focuses on the scholar's incredible work ethic.

According to a story that al-Ḍabbī narrates from one of the author's friends, Ibn Ḥamīd once said, "I would like it if the Commander of the Faithful were to charge me with writing a commentary of the book of Sībawayh. I would do it in such a way that my explanations would break the pages of the two masters (*ustādhayn*), and no one would need a

66 Ibn al-Abbār mentions two groups of three khaṭībs as alternating in giving the sermon in Friday prayers. The biographies of Ibn Ḥubaysh and Ibn Saʿāda both mention each other and Abū ʿAlī Ibn ʿArīb as the other members of the group of three. But in the biography of Ibn al-Faras, Ibn al-Abbār writes that it was he, Ibn Ḥamīd, and Ibn Ḥubaysh who alternated in the position. It seems likely that all five of these scholars served as khaṭībs at slightly different times, with Ibn Ḥubaysh as the constant. See discussion of these figures in Carmona, "El saber y el poder," 115n167, and in Aguilar, "Identidad y vida intelectual," 19, 22–23. Aguilar notes (19) that covering the distance between Murcia and Valencia would have taken roughly five to six days, and that moving scholars across such distances would have served to ensure the cohesion of the territories under Ibn Mardanīsh and maximized the benefits conferred by the prestige of these scholars.

67 Ibn al-Abbār, *Takmila*, ed. Codera, 255–56, no. 823; Carmona, "El saber y el poder," 114–17.

68 Al-Ḍabbī, *Bughyat al-multamis*, 63–64, no. 79.

69 See al-Ḍabbī's biography of him and Carmona's note in "El saber y el poder," 116n169.

teacher with it." The friend inquired why he did not go ahead and do it, and Ibn Ḥamīd replied, "I cannot because of all of my work, which does not allow me to grab even a moment. But if I received the order of the Commander, it would put me under obligation and provide a dispensation that would authorize me to set aside the time for my work and separate myself [to do it]."[70] The book written by Sībawayh (d. 161/777), a Persian Muslim from Shiraz, was still, four centuries after its author's death, unsurpassed as the most important book of Arabic grammar, and writing commentaries on it was a frequent pastime of scholars working in rulers' courts. The grammarian al-Zajjāj (d. ca. 316/928), for example, wrote a commentary on Sībawayh's book and also served as tutor to the children of the Abbasid caliph al-Muʿtaḍid. Ibn al-Ḥamīd's eagerness to write his own commentary on this great book reflects the continuing importance of mastery of Arabic grammar in the far-flung courts of the Middle Period and Andalusī scholars' deep awareness of the textual canon of the eastern Islamic world. It also points to the importance of official sponsorship or dispensation from rulers in the commissioning of new scholarship. Ibn al-Ḥamīd never wrote his commentary on Sībawayh, presumably since the caliph never asked him to, and his duties as judge consumed his time.

Ibn Ḥubaysh, by contrast, did receive commissions from the Almohad caliph to write for him. The caliph Abū Yaʿqūb Yūsuf appointed Ibn Ḥubaysh judge of Murcia in 575/1179–80 and, on the day of his appointment, also commissioned him to write a book on the Islamic conquests under the first three of the *Rāshidūn* or "rightly guided" caliphs after the death of the Prophet Muḥammad, Abū Bakr, ʿUmar, and ʿUthmān.[71] The fourth of these caliphs, ʿAlī, was omitted from this book, probably because he was venerated as imām by Shiʿī groups, including the rival Fatimid caliphate. Ibn Ḥubaysh's book, *Kitāb al-Ghazawāt* ("The book of the conquests") emphasized the caliphs' roles as warriors who had expanded the lands of Islam through pious violence. Like narratives of the mahdī Ibn Tūmart's life, which echoed the rise of Islam and especially events connected to the Prophet Muḥammad, this work

70 Al-Ḍabbī, *Bughya,* 64; Carmona, "El saber y el poder," 117.

71 Ibn Ḥubaysh claims his appointment and the commissioning of the book took place on the same day in the preface to his book, *Kitāb al-Ghazawāt* (Cairo: Maṭbaʿat Ḥassān, 1983), 1:1. See also Ibn al-Abbār, *Takmila*, ed. Codera, 2:573–75, no. 1617; Carmona, "El poder y el saber," 109–13; *EI*², s.v. "Ibn Ḥubaysh" (D. M. Dunlop); D. M. Dunlop, "The Spanish Historian Ibn Ḥubaish," *Journal of the Royal Asiatic Society of Great Britain and Ireland*, n.s., 73 (1941): 359–62.

of history served to highlight the parallels between the early Rāshidūn caliphs and the first four Almohad caliphs. Years later, Abū Yaʿqūb Yūsuf's successors would expand on the idea of the first four Almohad caliphs as a new group of "Rāshidūn." The fifth and eighth Almohad caliphs, Yūsuf al-Mustanṣir (r. 610–20/1213–23) and Yaḥyā al-Muʿtaṣim (r. 624–33/1227–35), both minted coins on which they referred to themselves *ibn al-khulafāʾ al-rāshidīn*, "the son of the Rāshidūn caliphs," thus transferring the designation "rightly guided" from the first four caliphs to succeed the Prophet to the first four caliphs to succeed the Almohad mahdī.[72]

As Javier Albarrán has shown, Ibn Ḥubaysh's book was an integral part of Abū Yaʿqūb Yūsuf's broader program of promoting holy war against the Christian kingdoms of the Iberian Peninsula and legitimating these battles by linking them to the battles of the early Islamic period.[73] His campaign against the Christian kingdoms, which entered a new stage in the aftermath of the incorporation of Ibn Mardanīsh's territories and armies, was accompanied by a series of intellectual projects aimed at underscoring the vital importance of holy war. In addition to commissioning Ibn Ḥubaysh's work, Abū Yaʿqūb Yūsuf also asked the philosopher Ibn Ṭufayl (d. 581/1181–82) to write a poem encouraging jihad.[74] The caliph seems to have been invested in presenting Ibn Tūmart as equally focused on battle against Christians, even though the Almohads had been primarily occupied in fighting fellow Muslims until long after the mahdī's death.[75] To this end, Abū Yaʿqūb Yūsuf added a chapter on jihad to Ibn Tūmart's *Kitāb*, completing it, according to the colophon, in Shaʿbān of 579/1183—a few years after commissioning Ibn Ḥubaysh's work.[76] The new chapter consists almost entirely of canonical hadith relating to jihad. Similarly, the body of Ibn Ḥubaysh's work is based on earlier Eastern histories of the early Islamic conquests, and their

---

72 Martínez Núñez, "Ideología y epigrafía almohades," 23; A. Prieto y Vives, "La reforma numismática de los almohades," in *Miscelánea de estudios y textos árabes* (Madrid: Centro de Estudios Históricos, 1915), 27–28.

73 Albarrán, "*Jihād* of the Caliphs," 123–33.

74 E. García Gómez, "Una qaṣīda política inédita de Ibn Ṭufayl," *Revista del Instituto Egipcio de Estudios Islámicos* 1 (1953): 21–28; Albarrán, "*Jihād* of the Caliphs," 128.

75 Albarrán, "De la conversión y expulsión al mercenariado: La ideología en torno a los cristianos en las crónicas almohades," in *La Península Ibérica en tiempos de las Navas de Tolosa*, ed. M. A. Carmona and C. Estepa (Madrid: Sociedad Española de Estudios Medievales), 79–91.

76 A manuscript of Ibn Tūmart's *Kitāb* survives in the Bibliothèque nationale de France, Arab. 1451; it was published by Luciani as *Le Livre d'Ibn Toumert*. See Huici Miranda, *Historia política*, 95–100, 247; Albarrán, "*Jihād* of the Caliphs," 127.

presentation in the book is no different from what it would have been in a work written under any other dynasty. The difference, as Albarrán has shown, lies in the work's introduction, which frames the Almohad caliphs as parallel to the Rāshidūn caliphs, continuing the divine project of the mahdī just as the Rāshidūn carried on the mission of the Prophet Muḥammad.[77] By incorporating Ibn Ḥubaysh into the Almohad political and religious system, Abū Ya'qūb Yūsuf could exploit his traditional Sunnī, Mālikī training to weave together narratives of holy war in the early Islamic period and his own campaigns against Christian powers and to turn himself, his father, and his son into reincarnations of 'Umar, Abū Bakr, and 'Uthmān.

Just as Abū Ya'qūb sought to emphasize the anti-Christian jihad of the early Almohads in an effort to legitimate his own role as caliph/mujāhid, so, too, did Almohad attitudes toward Mālikī thought seem to shift in the decade after the conquest of Sharq al-Andalus. Maribel Fierro has argued that the "reformed Mālikism" of the Almohads was rooted in their conquest of al-Andalus and their assimilation of its largely Mālikī population.[78] The positions of authority given to scholars such as Ibn al-Ḥamīd and Ibn Ḥubaysh, both trained by the top Mālikī scholars of al-Andalus, served to legitimate Almohad rulers in the eyes of their Andalusī subjects. It also allowed Abū Ya'qūb and his successors to augment their religious credibility by linking themselves and their campaigns of holy war to illustrious figures and battles of the past. Whereas Ibn Tūmart had been content to reject earlier caliphates altogether, Abū Ya'qub harnessed the scholarly power of Andalusī intellectuals to reclaim the mantle of the early caliphate for himself and his family.

Veneration and Destruction: The Ibn Ghaṭṭūs Quran

A series of magnificent Qurans made by the famous Valencian calligrapher Ibn Ghaṭṭūs (active 556–78/1161–82) during Ibn Mardanīsh's time in power may offer some clues to the complex processes by which Ibn Mardanīsh's dynasty was simultaneously incorporated into and effaced by the Almohad regime.[79] Ibn al-Abbār reports that Ibn Ghaṭṭūs was said

77 Albarrán, "*Jihād* of the Caliphs," 130–32.

78 Fierro, "La religion," 446–48.

79 For more on these Qurans and their relation to other Almohad Qurans, see Élisabeth Dandel, "Ibn Gaṭṭūs: Une famille de copistes-enlumineurs à Valence (Espagne)," *Histoire de l'Art* 24 (December 1993): 13–24; Marianne Barrucand, "Les Enluminures de l'époque Almohade: Frontispices et *'Unwān*-s," in *Los Almohades*, ed. Cressier, Fierro, and Molina; Martin

to have produced one thousand Qurans and that their fame and quality were such that kings had fought to possess them and continued to do so in his own time.[80] Several of these Qurans survive in collections around the world. Élisabeth Dandel studied several of them and argued that the Banū Ghaṭṭūs were a Quran-making family with at least two members active in the trade and that they worked in Valencia from at least 556/1161 to 578/1182. This period spans the arrival of the Almohads in Valencia in 567/1172, and several of the Qurans the Banū Ghaṭṭūs produced are classified in scholarship as Almohad Qurans. But the forms, calligraphy, and design of these Qurans remained consistent across the change in dynasty.

Most of the Qurans include colophons with information about the calligrapher, known as Ibn Ghaṭṭūs, and sometimes the names of the patrons. One, now in Cairo, produced in Valencia in 557/1162, was commissioned by "the most high first minister (*al-wazīr al-awwal al-ajall*), Abū Muḥammad ibn ʿAbd Allāh ibn ʿAbd al-Raḥmān ibn ʿAbd Allāh al-Madhḥijī, known as al-Lawshī," and it was copied by "ʿAbd Allāh ibn Muḥammad ibn ʿAlī," who, Dandel argues, was the original Ibn Ghaṭṭūs, the father.[81] On this "prime minister" of Ibn Mardanīsh, no other clear information survives. The biographical dictionary *Kitāb Ṣilat al-Ṣila* mentions a figure with a similar name, who belonged to the important scholarly family of the Banū Saʿāda. This figure died in the Granadan city of Lawsha 573/1177, placing him within geographic and chronological proximity to Ibn Mardanīsh's regime, and is described as "among the most honorable and distinguished of shaykhs" (*min jillat al-ashyākh wa-fuḍalāʾihim*).[82] This figure does not correspond to either of the two men Pierre Guichard has identified as *wazīr*s under Ibn Mardanīsh.[83] Nevertheless, this Quran's inscription suggests that Ibn Ghaṭṭūs and

---

Lings, "Andalusian Qurans," *British Museum Quarterly* 24 (1961): 94–96; *Maroc medieval: Un empire de l'Afrique à l'Espagne* (Paris: Musée du Louvre, 2014), nos. 208, 209; Umberto Bongianino, "The Origin and Development of Maghribī Round Scripts: Arabic Palaeography in the Islamic West (4th/10th–6th/12th Centuries)" (PhD diss., Oxford University, 2017), 149–58; Nourane Ben Azzouna, "Les corans de l'Occident musulman médiéval: État des recherches et nouvelles perspectives," *Perspective* 2 (2017): 103–30.

80 Ibn al-Abbār, *al-Takmila li-kitāb al-ṣila* (Beirut: Dār al-Fikr, 1995), 2:105–6.

81 Dandel, "Ibn Gaṭṭūs;" Dodds, ed., *Al-Andalus,* 306.

82 A scholar named Saʿd al-Khayr ibn ʿUbayd Allāh ibn ʿAbd al-Raḥmān al-Madhḥijī, who died in 573/1177 in Lawsha (mod. Loja, in the province of Granada), may be the same figure, although there is no mention of Ibn Mardanīsh in his biography. Abū Jaʿfar Aḥmad ibn Ibrāhīm Ibn al-Zubayr, *Ṣilat al-ṣila*, ed. ʿA. S. al-Harrās and S. Aʿrāb (Rabat: Wizārat al-Awqāf wa-l-Shuʿūn al-Islāmiyya, 1993–95), 4: 216–17, number 432.

83 Pierre Guichard, *Les musulmans de Valence et la Reconquête* (*XIe-XIIIe siècle*) (Damascus: Institut français de Damas, 1991), 1:121.

FIGURE 6.5A-C. The first two pages of the Ibn Ghaṭṭūs Quran, with the colophon blacked out, and the first verse of the Quran with the ink bleeding through from the reverse. *Photo:* Bibliothèque Nationale de Tunisie, no. 13728.

his son were producing Qurans for important political leaders in Ibn Mardanīsh's regime.

Perhaps the most significant Quran attributed to Ibn Ghaṭṭūs, discovered in 2018 in the collection of Tunisia's national library, may have been made for Ibn Mardanīsh himself.[84] It is the smallest in size, at

84 Bibliothèque nationale de Tunisie, no. 13728. This Quran, discovered in the collection of the BNT in March 2018, has not yet been published, but on the basis of its style it has been attributed Ibn Ghaṭṭūs. For details on the analysis of the Quran, its materials and script, and the scholars of the BNT's attribution of it to Ibn Ghaṭṭūs, see the following newspaper article: "Muṣḥaf Ibn Ghaṭṭūs . . . al-ʿuthūr ʿalā naskha thālitha," *Al-ʿArabī al-Jadīd,* 17 March 2018, https://www.alaraby.co.uk/مصحف-ابن-غطوس-العثور-على-نسخة-ثالثة accessed 3/26/2019.

barely four inches square, and its twenty lines per page require a minuscule script. Written in thin brown Maghribī calligraphy on fine parchment—characteristic of the Banū Ghaṭṭūs—the Quran is adorned with elaborately illuminated *'unwāns*, verse markers and indications for prostration, many executed in gold leaf. The patron or intended recipient was either extremely wealthy or extremely important. But the part of the manuscript that would tell the reader for whom and by whom this masterpiece was made has been carefully and completely destroyed. The two pages where one would expect the colophon to appear have been entirely blacked out, save for the ornamented square frames.

The text of the Quran itself remains intact, but the traces of the patron's name and his role in commissioning this pious object have disappeared. Whoever obliterated the colophon did it with such a generous quantity of ink that it bled through to the reverse of the page, which contains the final verse of the Quran, framing the verse with a ghostly dark shadow. This purposeful damage seems to support the hypothesis that the Quran either was commissioned by Ibn Mardanīsh or mentioned his name in the colophon. It is hard to imagine another figure associated with Valencia between 556/1161 and 578/1182 whose legacy would be equally contested and whom unknown successors would wish to erase with such vehemence. The obscuring of the name of the copyist alongside that of the patron would have made the object less valuable to the kings whom Ibn al-Abbār described as fighting over these Qurans. The blacking out of the colophon must have been a deliberate act meant to make the Quran acceptable to a recipient who did not want to be reminded of a recalcitrant rebel.[85]

As Jean-Pierre van Staëvel has noted, the Almohads' "nearly surgical" destruction of just the names of the Almoravid sovereign from the Qubbat al-Barudiyyīn in Marrakech, the minbar of the Kutubiyya Mosque, and the foundation inscription of the Almoravid mosque at Tlemcen suggest that their standard response to the monuments and objects of their predecessors was to carefully efface their names.[86] Far from the

85 My plans to analyze this Quran using UV light and other methods that might reveal what lies under the obliterated area were thwarted by global travel restrictions enacted during the coronavirus pandemic of 2020. I hope we are someday able to decipher more of this object's history.

86 Jean-Pierre van Staëvel, "L'art almohade fut-il révolutionnaire?" *Perspective: Actualité en histoire de l'art* 2 (2017): 81–102, here 92–93.

kind of wholesale destruction of monuments and objects described in a few Almohad sources and repeated by many modern scholars, van Staëvel argues that the Almohads preserved the vast majority of the landscape they inherited, adding their own monumental spaces alongside their predecessors' buildings. The diminutive Quran in Tunis may have entered an Almohad library, even as the Banū Ghaṭṭūs family that produced it pivoted to making Qurans for new masters. But the name of the sovereign who commissioned it, like that of ʿAlī ibn Yūsuf at Qubbat al-Barudiyyīn, was meticulously destroyed.

The Quran in question survived in the Aḥmadiyya library of the Zaytūna mosque in Tunis into the twentieth century before being transferred to the National Library of Tunisia, and it was evidently preserved as a treasure even though its dedication to a ruler who challenged Almohad authority had been entirely effaced. The mechanisms of this careful and complete obliteration of Ibn Mardanīsh's memory and the transfer of the censored object to North Africa are invisible, but the fact that they occurred speaks to the complexity of memory and assimilation in the aftermath of conflict. This Quran's blackened colophon, like the whitewashed muqarnas ceiling of Dār al-Ṣughrā, speak to the forms of erasure or conversion that could facilitate survival.

Mardanīshī Almohads and the Transformations of the Caliphate

Even as the figural cycle in Ibn Mardanīsh's palace was covered, his name on his Quran obliterated, and his territory absorbed, his dynasty and its memory lived on in other ways. His territory and his objects were incorporated into the Almohad realm, transforming the visual and material culture of the Almohads in the process. His daughters, one whose name is unknown and another named Ṣafiyya, married the caliph Abū Yaʿqūb Yūsuf and future caliph Abū Yūsuf Yaʿqūb, respectively. Ṣafiyya bore Abū Yūsuf a child, who later ruled as the Almohad caliph Abū al-ʿUlā al-Maʾmūn from 624/1227 to 629/1232.[87] As caliph, al-Maʾmūn renounced the Almohad doctrine of the infallible mahdī, removed all mention of the mahdī from coins, and sent a letter to the Almohad elite

87 Al-Marrākushī, *al-Muʿjib fī talkhīs*, 202; Ibn Abī Zarʿ, *Rawḍ al-Qirṭās*, 2:483.

stating that there was no mahdī other than Jesus, son of Mary.[88] The letter claimed that his father, Abū Yūsuf Ya'qūb, husband to Ṣafiyya, had also opposed the Almohad doctrine of the mahdī.[89] Al-Ma'mūn is reported to have studied the *Muwaṭṭā'* of Mālik and the hadith collections of al-Bukhārī and Abū Dāwūd and to have affiliated himself with the Mālikī madhhab.[90] This shift away from Almohad doctrine and toward a Sunnī Mālikī understanding of law is also visible in the standards of appointment (*taqādīm*) issued under his authority.[91] In addition, to fight his nephew Yahyā, who was contesting his authority, al-Ma'mūn formed an alliance with Ferdinand III of Castile that allowed him to reconquer Marrakech from his opponents. According to the chronicles of Ibn 'Idhārī, Ibn Abī Zar', and Ibn Khaldūn, he promised the king that he would build a church for his Christian mercenaries in the center of Marrakech, a city that had been theoretically off limits to Christians since the arrival of the Almohads, and that they would be permitted to ring their church bells.[92]

Al-Ma'mūn's rejection of Almohad ruling ideology and traditions has been seen as a reason for the subsequent failure of the caliphate, and it was a proximate cause of the splitting off of the Hafsid dynasty of Ifrīqiya, which remained loyal to the idea of the mahdī.[93] Should it also be seen as the ultimate victory of the Banū Mardanīsh and its Sunnī ideology over the caliphate proclaimed by the Almohads? Al-Ma'mūn

---

88 *Rasā'il Muwaḥḥidiyya, majmū'a jadīda*, 1:384–86. On the rejection of Almohad doctrine, see also Roger Le Tourneau, "Sur la disparition de la doctrine almohade," *Studia Islamica* 32 (1970): 193–201, esp. 194–97.

89 *Rasā'il Muwaḥḥidiyya, majmū'a jadīda*, 1:385.

90 Ambrosio Huici Miranda, *Historia política del imperio almohade*, vol. 2 (Tetouan: Editora Marroquí, 1957), 465–66, n. 3.

91 On the legal attitudes of al-Ma'mūn, see Buresi and El Aallaoui, *Governing the Empire*, 74–76, 204–5.

92 Ibn Abī Zar', *Rawḍ al-Qirṭās*, 329; Ibn 'Idhārī, *al-Bayān al-Mughrib*, 284; Ibn Khaldūn, *Kitāb al-'Ibar*, 6:530–31. On debates over the ringing of church bells in Islamic contexts in the medieval Mediterranean, see Olivia Remie Constable, "Regulating Religious Noise: The Council of Vienne, the Mosque Call and Muslim Pilgrimage in the Late Medieval Mediterranean World," *Medieval Encounters* 16 (2010): 64–95. The same concession allowing Western Christians housed in fondacos in Tunis to ring their church bells was granted by a thirteenth-century Ḥafṣid would-be ruler to Western Christians in a treaty made with Alfonso III of Aragon in 686/1287. See Olivia Remie Constable, "Ringing Bells in Ḥafṣid Tunis: Religious Concessions to Christian *Fondacos* in the Later Thirteenth Century," in *Histories of the Middle East: Studies in Middle Eastern Society, Economy and Law in Honor of A.L. Udovitch*, ed. Margariti Eleni Roxani, Adam Sabra, and Petra M. Sijpesteijn (Leiden: Brill, 2011), 53–72.

93 Le Tourneau argues as much in his "Sur la disparition de la doctrine almohade."

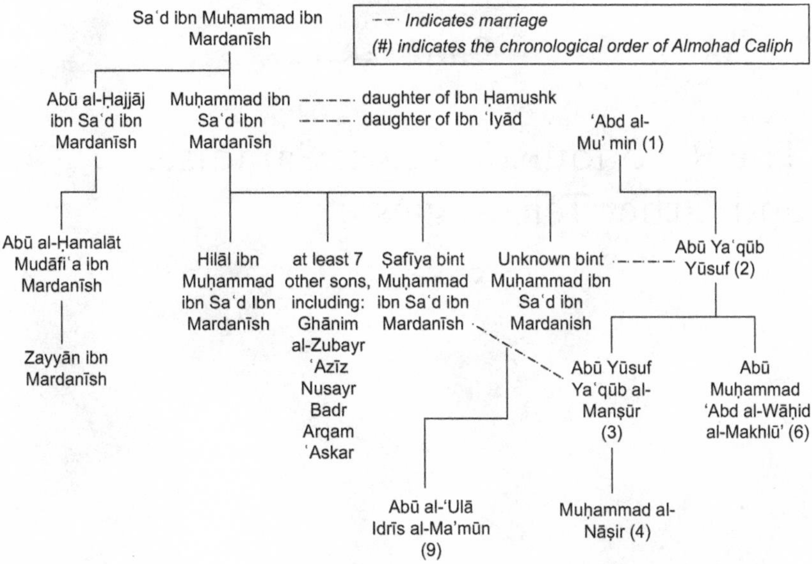

FIGURE 6.6. Genealogy of the Almohad Ruling Family with the Banū Mardanīsh.

was succeeded by his son al-Rashīd, who reinstated the doctrine of the mahdī, so ideology (unsurprisingly) does not map neatly onto genealogy. But the continued contestation over the idea of the mahdī, the sources of law, and attitudes toward Christian neighbors that had characterized the reign of Ibn Mardanīsh shows that these debates did not disappear with his death. Instead, the incorporation of the people and the territories of Sharq al-Andalus into the Almohad Empire meant that the challenges it once posed for the Almohads became internal.

Chapter 7

The Reconquista, a Lost Paradise, and Other Teleologies

ʿAbd al-Wāḥid al-Marrākushī's early thirteenth-century history, describing the rise of the Almohads' greatest Andalusī rival, Muḥammad ibn Saʿd Ibn Mardanīsh, notes that Ibn Mardanīsh's predecessor had declared that he "had abundant bravery and was very capable" and predicted that "maybe God will benefit the Muslims through him."[1] But in a twentieth-century edition of al-Marrākushī's text, the editors insert a cautionary footnote after the first mention of Ibn Mardanīsh:

> A hereditary disposition had inclined him [Ibn Mardanīsh] toward Spain [*al-Asbāniyya*], because he resembled the Christian kings in his clothes and his weapons, and most of his army was Spanish mercenaries, and therefore [he was] suspicious in his religion; and he was linked with the kings of the Christians, giving them presents and kindnesses, and perhaps asking them for help against the Muslims in his wars![2]

---

1 This statement is also quoted in chapter 2; al-Marrākushī, *al-Muʿjib*, ed. al-ʿAryān, 3:279 (*Fa innahu ẓāhir al-najda kathīr al-ghanāʾ wa-laʿalla Allāh an yanfaʿa bihi al-muslimīn*). This passage appears in the 1949 edition discussed here on p. 210.

2 Al-Marrākushī, *al-Muʿjib*, 1949, 209.

The idea that Ibn Mardanīsh's blood inclined him toward the Christians is evidently not an Almohad-era one: as discussed in the first two chapters of this book, Almohad sources criticized Ibn Mardanīsh for his "Christian companions" and his impious behavior, but they did not suggest that his ancestry was Christian. For the Almohads, challenging a rival's lineage and implying it made him less Muslim would have been a dangerous game to play, since the Almohads, as well as many of their Andalusī rivals, did not have clear Arab genealogies.[3] Like many who sought authority in the Islamic Middle Period, the Almohads worked hard to present themselves as noble and to connect themselves to Arab tribal ancestors. Ultimately, their contest was over different ideas of righteous authority, and for the Almohads Ibn Mardanīsh was an infidel simply because of his refusal to accept their sovereignty. The discrepancy between the treatment of Ibn Mardanīsh in al-Marrākushī's original text and the note inserted by the twentieth-century editors reflects the influence of modern ideas of race and religion. But it is also the result of seven centuries of historiographic debate over figures such as Ibn Mardanīsh, and about the history of al-Andalus more broadly.

When Ibn Mardanīsh died in Rajab 567/March 1172 and the Almohads conquered his territory, the so-called second Taifa period came to a close. The Almohads enjoyed forty more years of power in Iberia and North Africa, turning with increasing dedication toward battles against the Christian kings of Iberia with whom Ibn Mardanīsh had once been allied. It was this conflict—later endorsed by Pope Innocent III as a crusade—that would eventually force the Almohads out of al-Andalus.

Ibn Mardanīsh's dynasty failed, and his memory—honored by his allies, variously respected and reviled by his rivals—was subsequently filtered by generations of later historians who sought to use his story to impart lessons or warnings. These later chronicles, written across the course of the next five centuries, adapted and transformed the narratives about Ibn Mardanīsh that appeared in contemporary Almohad sources, many of which are themselves now lost. The resulting image of Ibn Mardanīsh and his kingdom has emphasized his impiety, his closeness to his Christian allies and soldiers, and his sinfulness in resisting the Almohads. The historical treatment of Ibn Mardanīsh's battles against the Almohads reveals the gradual crystallization of a teleological

3 As discussed earlier, the Almohad caliphs did claim an Arab genealogy, descending from the Quraysh, though through the maternal line rather than the more traditionally required agnatic descent. See Fierro, "Las genealogías de ʿAbd al-Muʾmin."

vision of Christian-Muslim warfare on the Iberian Peninsula. This later reinterpretation made him into a character doomed to fail; indeed, it turned him into a parable for al-Andalus itself: flexible, tolerant, luxury-loving, irreligious, and unwilling to place the preservation of al-Andalus ahead of his own self-interest. Tracing the genealogy of this vision of Ibn Mardanīsh offers insight not only into the evolution of Ibn Mardanīsh's portrayal over time but also the development of an understanding of al-Andalus as exceptional, as the preeminent locus of jihad and of nostalgic yearning.

The period from the fourteenth to the seventeenth century marks an important shift in how Ibn Mardanīsh's lineage and religion were presented. Regardless of the origins of the name Mardanīsh (discussed in chapter 3), it is highly likely that Ibn Mardanīsh, like many Iberian Muslims, was at least partially of Christian descent and may have also had Berber and Arab blood. Berbers had a substantial and long-standing presence in Iberia, and the Muslim population was decisively shaped by intermarriage and conversion.[4] Since the eighth century and the time of the first Umayyad ruler of Iberia—ʿAbd al-Raḥmān I, the son of a Berber princess and a Qurayshī father—ethnicity had been a layered and complex matter. Ruggles has shown that many of the royal mothers of the Umayyad rulers of al-Andalus were of Christian descent.[5] If Ibn Mardanīsh was the great-great-grandson of a convert from Christianity to Islam, he was one of many Iberian Muslims who had Christian roots. But as a ruler who made alliances with Christians against fellow Muslims, Ibn Mardanīsh was described by later Arabic sources as close to the Christians in everything from his appearance to his actions. Their suggestion that his religious allegiance might lie outside the umma, like his diplomatic alliances did, has tainted the historiography of the period ever since. Interestingly, the sources that emphasize his disloyalty to Islam and his Christian roots tend to call him Ibn Mardanīsh, while more neutral depictions usually use the name he used himself, Muḥammad ibn Saʿd. This usage also corresponds to a temporal division: most sources that are definitely contemporary to Ibn Mardanīsh

4 Ramzi Rouighi argues that the entire concept of "Berberness" was invented in the context of al-Andalus to describe inhabitants of the Iberian Peninsula who were of North African origin, and that it was applied to people in Northwest Africa only later. See Rouighi, *Inventing the Berbers*.

5 Ruggles, "Mothers of a Hybrid Dynasty."

call him Muḥammad ibn Saʿd, whereas later sources tend to opt for the name Ibn Mardanīsh.

This shift to conceiving of Ibn Mardanīsh's genealogy as the key to his religious identity and political affiliations occurred at a time when lineage began to play a similar role in the Iberian Peninsula more generally. As David Nirenberg has argued, the shift seems to have taken place over the course of the fourteenth to sixteenth centuries. Focusing particularly on the Jewish and Christian communities, he observes that "although in both communities lineage was clearly important at the level of the family, the dynasty, and the individual line, in neither, before the fifteenth century, did it emerge as a central form of cultural memory or communal identification establishing a group identity."[6] The move to define group identity as being rooted in lineage accompanied the massacres and mass conversions of Jews in the late fourteenth and early fifteenth centuries and the associated anxiety about the integrity of religious communities. A focus on genealogy offered a possible solution both for Jews seeking to maintain communal cohesion amid forced conversion and displacement and for Christians striving to ensure the sincerity of believers: who was really a Jew or really a Christian could be determined by simply tracing an individual's forebears. For both groups, relying on lineage held the promise of certainty, since no matter what people may have done or claimed, they were what their blood was. As Nirenberg writes:

> Confronted by these displacements, problems of intermediacy, and crises of classification, Jews, Christians and conversos turned more or less simultaneously to lineage as one means of reestablishing the integrity of religious categories of identity. In doing so, each group drew largely upon its own traditions, but each was also aware of, and responding to, the changes taking place in the others' genealogical imaginations.[7]

The problem with this approach was that according to the Pauline epistles, like according to the Quran, conversion was supposed to erase difference, yielding Christians (or Muslims) indistinguishable from each other except in their good deeds.[8] Nonetheless, in this period,

---

6 Nirenberg, *Neighboring Faiths,* 147.

7 Nirenberg, *Neighboring Faiths,* 152.

8 Galatians 3:28: "There is neither Jew nor Greek, there is neither slave nor free, there is no male and female, for you are all one in Christ Jesus." Quran 49:13: "O mankind, We have

Christian heritage constituted a prerequisite for nobility, good behavior, and sincere faith in the eyes of many Christians. This perception gained strength over the following centuries, culminating in ideas about purity of blood. As Henry Kamen has noted, this concept of "limpieza de sangre" was deployed at various moments of conflict between different groups to justify the dominance of those of "pure blood" over those deemed contaminated.[9] Although it never carried the force of law and was deployed only at strategic moments in particular contexts in fifteenth- and sixteenth-century Castile, the "genealogical imagination" it relied on seems to have had wide-ranging influence in Castile and beyond.

Beginning in the thirteenth century, but accelerating over the course of the next three hundred years, Christians across Europe began to use lineage to justify the exclusion of not only Jews but also those who had converted from Judaism to Christianity. Extending the theory of the dangerousness of Jewish blood further, they imagined that contact with Jews could bring God's wrath on even the most noble and righteous.[10] In the late thirteenth century, Sancho IV of Castile (r. 1284–95) wrote a narrative of his great-grandfather Alfonso VIII's time in power that blamed Alfonso's failure to defeat the Almohads at Alarcos in 1195 on his affair with a Jewess in Toledo. According to Sancho, God had been so angered by his sin that he caused the defeat, but after Alfonso repented and built the monastery of Las Huelgas in Burgos as penance, God finally granted him victory at Las Navas de Tolosa in 1212.[11]

Similar concepts of purity and contamination seem to have operated in Islamic contexts in Iberia as well. In the early fourteenth century, as the Nasrids of Granada faced internal and external challenges, ideas

created you male and female, and appointed you races and tribes, that you may know one another. Surely the noblest among you in the sight of God is the most god-fearing of you. God is All-knowing, All-aware."

9 Henry Kamen, "Limpieza and the Ghost of Américo Castro: Racism as a Tool of Literary Analysis," *Hispanic Review* 64, no. 1 (1996): 19–29. Kamen pushes back against the claim that *limpieza* was an all-consuming framework in Spain in the early modern period. As he notes, those in power, including Ferdinand and Isabella, were vehemently opposed to the idea, and conversos achieved important political and religious roles even at the height of its popularity.

10 For an anthropological approach to the demarcation of boundaries through ideas of purity and contamination, see Mary Douglas, *Purity and Danger: An Analysis of the Concepts of Pollution and Taboo* (London: Routledge, 1966).

11 David Nirenberg, *Neighboring Faiths*, 56. Nirenberg cites Sancho IV's *Castigos* (completed in 1292–93), published as *Castigos e documentos para bien vivir*, ed. Agapito Rey (Bloomington: Indiana University Press, 1952), 133.

about the contamination of lineages and its effects begin to appear in the literature. The fourth sultan Naṣr (r. 708–13/1309–14), who would be the last ruler from the direct descendants of the dynasty's founder, Ibn al-Aḥmar, came to power as the Marinids of North Africa, the Castilians, and the Aragonese were all fighting to win Nasrid territory. He managed to make peace on all fronts, in part by concluding a pact with Ferdinand IV of Castile in which he promised to pay tribute and pledged his vassalage to Ferdinand. Ibn al-Khaṭīb, the fourteenth-century Granadan polymath, wrote about Naṣr's fall from power in ways that highlighted his Christianness. His teacher, the court poet Ibn Jayyāb, seems to have opposed Naṣr and instead supported his successor, Ismā'īl I (r. 713–25/1314–25).[12] According to Ibn al-Khaṭīb, Naṣr had been educated by his Christian mother, who had inclined him toward the Christians, and in addition to being a vassal to Ferdinand IV of Castile and paying him tribute, Naṣr also dressed in the Christian style. Ibn al-Khaṭīb indicated that Naṣr's own court (*khāṣṣa*) and the population of Granada were opposed to him and his vizier, who also dressed like a Christian, and that they begged his brother-in-law Abū Saʿīd Faraj to depose him.[13]

In Ibn al-Khaṭīb's description of Naṣr, a foreign policy seen as too generous to the Christians becomes conflated with Christian blood. It is Naṣr's purportedly Christian mother who has made him look favorably on the Christians and to sponsor science and neglect jihad. The course correction that Ibn al-Khaṭīb supported, in the form of a rebellion by Abū Saʿīd Faraj and the eventual replacement of Naṣr with Abū Saʿīd's son Ismāʿīl, was a genealogical one, and it created a new line, *al-dawla al-Ismāʿīliyya al*-Naṣriyya, that ruled for the rest of the Nasrid period.[14] Whether or not Naṣr had a Christian mother and whether or not he wore Christian-style clothes, what is important is that saying he did served to delegitimate him. By the fourteenth century, suggesting that those whom one opposed had been contaminated by contact with religious outsiders or that they might, because of their lineage, be loyal to the enemy had become a potent mode of political opposition.

These changes in later medieval and early modern thinking about lineage led to the transformation of the historiographic treatment of

---

12 On Ibn al-Jayyāb, see M. J. Rubiera Mata, *Ibn al-Ŷayyāb: El otro poeta de la Alhambra* (Granada: Patronato de la Alhambra, 1994), 133–35.

13 Ibn al-Khaṭīb, *al-Iḥāṭa*, ed. ʿInān, 1:394.

14 Antonio Fernández-Puertas, "The Three Great Sultans of al-Dawla al-Ismāʿīliyya al-Naṣriyya who built the fourteenth-century Alhambra: Ismāʿīl I, Yūsuf I, Muḥammad V (713–793/1314–1391)," *Journal of the Royal Asiatic Society*, 3rd ser., 7, no. 1 (1997): 1–25.

Ibn Mardanīsh. In what follows, I will focus particularly on the changes wrought by Ibn al-Khaṭīb and his later admirer, the seventeenth-century Tlemceni chronicler al-Maqqarī. Paralleling Spanish histories of the seventeenth century, which portrayed the "restoration" of Christian Spain as a singular, providential process, al-Maqqarī presented the fall of al-Andalus as a judgment from God and reimagined the twelfth century as a time of implacable Christian-Muslim warfare.[15] The resulting narrative had no place for a figure of Ibn Mardanīsh's complexity, so he was transformed to fit into an overarching narrative of holy war. These narratives of holy war, decline, and a lost paradise, born in the early modern period, would exert considerable influence on descriptions of Ibn Mardanīsh and al-Andalus in the modern period, too.

Blood and Loyalty in Changing Visions of al-Andalus

Ibn Mardanīsh justified his wars as jihad, and the Almohads also saw their fight against him in those terms. But in both cases, jihad constituted a battle over righteous Islamic authority, not a Christian-Muslim showdown. Over time, as more and more of the Iberian Peninsula was won by Christians, and especially after the fall of Granada, Arabic historians recast these intra-Muslim battles to fit into a vision of Christian-Muslim holy war. Such visions thus distort modern understandings of earlier periods and of figures such as Ibn Mardanīsh.

Following the historiographic treatment of one battle across chronicles from the twelfth to the seventeenth century is illustrative of the ways in which the narratives could shift. The Battle of Faḥṣ al-Jallāb in 560/1165 and the Battle of al-Jallāb in 567/1172 were two of the biggest confrontations between Ibn Mardanīsh and his Almohad rivals. Because of the similar names by which these battles were known, and the fact that they were both substantial Almohad victories, later chroniclers often referred to both interchangeably. In early descriptions of these battles, including those written by Almohad loyalists, Ibn Mardanīsh and his "Christian companions" oppose the Almohads and their Berber and Arab tribal troops and are defeated. By the seventeenth century, however, two Muslim armies fighting each other seemed incongruous, and

15 On the idea of the "restoration" (and, later, "reconquest") of Christian Spain in Spanish historiography, see Martín Ríos Saloma, *La reconquista: Una construcción historiográfica (siglos XVI–XIX)* (Madrid: Marcial Pons Ediciones de Historia, 2011).

al-Maqqarī's narrative of a crucial part of the story turns Ibn Mardanīsh's enemies into Christians.

In the late twelfth century, writing in Almohad territory, Ibn Ṣāḥib al-Ṣalā described the Battle of Faḥs al-Jallāb, in 560/1165, thus:

> On the Friday, the seventh of Dhū al-Ḥijja in the year 560, the Almohads arrived at daybreak at the plain of Murcia, where the plain of Murcia begins, at a place known as Ḥāma bi-l-Quwād and Faḥs al-Jallāb, ten miles from Murcia. The army of Ibn Mardanīsh stopped and prepared for the defense, while the Almohads deployed their numerous troops and raised their victorious flags, formed their lines, and revisited their classes and categories in all the tribes of the Almohad groups, constant and faithful—of Harga and the people of Tīnmallal, of Hintāta and Qadmīwa and Janfīsa and the other tribes, according to their categories, and of the Arabs, the Hilālīs, the Riḥāḥīs, the Hāshimīs, the Zughbīs, and all the slaves inscribed for this most high matter, who were prepared for the meeting and had committed themselves to resist and stay firm in obedience to God the Most High and to defeat their enemies and, with this, enter into Paradise forever. Ibn Mardanīsh and his army fell upon them with his Christian companions in three attacks: the first against the Arabs and the second two against the Almohads. God helped the believers in these attacks and sustained them, comforting their hearts with His decision. A cloud of darkness grew among them, and the sun of daylight left and darkness approached, followed by total obscurity. Horseman fell on horseman and injuries from penetrating lances and the time-tested cutting swords used by the Arabs grew, until God granted victory to the Muslims and turned the swords against the infidels, which was, with the help of God the Most High, their perdition. God erased their traces with the sword. They killed them with a rapid slaughter, and most of them fell down prostrate.[16]

Ibn Ṣāḥib al-Ṣalā's detailed description of the Almohad armies, arrayed in ranks of Berber tribes and Arab tribes, determined to defeat their enemies and win paradise, against Ibn Mardanīsh and his generic "Christian companions," sets up the conflict as a religious one. On one side

16 Ibn Ṣāḥib al-Ṣalā, *al-Mann bi-l-imāma*, 273–75.

are the "Muslims," in all their tribal variety, on the other, undifferentiated "infidels," erased by God's sword.

Early the next century, in 621/1224, the chronicler al-Marrākushī, born and raised in Almohad territories but retelling the story of the battles between the Almohads and Ibn Mardanīsh for his Abbasid audience, also focused on the religious makeup of Ibn Mardanīsh's army and the crushing defeat he and his Christian "companions" suffered.[17] Al-Marrākushī's description of the later Battle of al-Jallāb, four miles from Murcia, which took place in 567/1172, emphasizes the destruction of Ibn Mardanīsh's mostly Christian army just as Ibn Ṣāḥib al-Ṣalā had in his discussion of the early Battle of Faḥṣ al-Jallāb: "Ibn Mardanīsh advanced with his soldiers, the majority of whom were Christian, and he and the Almohads met in a place known as al-Jallāb, four miles from Murcia, and the companions of Ibn Mardanīsh suffered a terrible defeat, leaving many of the Christians dead."[18]

The following century, Ibn al-Khaṭīb, in his biographical dictionary, *al-Iḥāṭa fī Akhbār Gharnāṭa*, described a series of events that occurred during the Battle of al-Jallāb. The description forms part of the biography of Ḥātim ibn Saʿīd, a companion of Ibn Mardanīsh's who fought alongside him.

> He [Ḥātim] was present one day with the emir Muḥammad ibn Saʿd, on the day of the battle of Jallāb, and the emir was extraordinarily patient. He continued attacking again and again, without interruption. He did this within view of Ḥātim, and he turned his head to him and said, "O Commander Abū Karam, what do you see?" Ḥātim replied to him, "If only the sultan could see you today, he surely would increase your salary!"[19] Ibn Mardanīsh laughed,

---

17 On the trope of the "Christian companion" in Ibn Ṣāḥib al-Ṣalā's work and in those that relied on it, see Jones, "'Christian Companion.'"

18 Although al-Marrākushī calls this battle the Battle of al-Jallāb, it is evidently the 560/1165 Battle of Faḥṣ al-Jallāb, four miles from Murcia, rather than the 1172 Battle of al-Jallāb to which he refers. Al-Marrākushī, *al-Muʿjib* (1949 edition), 179.

19 It is unclear who the "sultan" mentioned in this narrative could be. Ibn Mardanīsh was not paid a salary by any higher authority, and he did not claim this title as an independent ruler; nor did his successors. The Almohad ruler, meanwhile, was called caliph. Indeed, the title sultan was exceedingly rare in the Islamic West, though by the twelfth century it was in widespread use in much of the Islamic East. Al-Maqqarī uses the title throughout his works to refer to rulers, although according to the *EI*^{2}, the term *sulṭān* was not adopted by rulers in North Africa until the eighteenth century. See *EI*^{2}, s.v. "Sulṭān" (J. H. Kramers and C. E. Bosworth). Another possibility is that Ibn al-Khaṭīb or later copyists misread *sulṭān* when the text said *salīṭīn*, a title used by Arabic authors such as Ibn Abī Zarʿ to refer to the Castilian king Alfonso VII. See Ibn Abī Zarʿ, *al-Anīs al-muṭrib bi-rawḍ al-qirṭās fī akhbār*

and Ḥātim knew that what he meant was that it was not a matter of risk but rather of endurance and planning.[20]

After describing Ibn Mardanīsh's extraordinary bravery on the battle, Ibn al-Khaṭīb recounts an exchange between Ḥātim, Ibn Mardanīsh, and one of the latter's viziers in which the two subordinates teased each other, Ḥātim by pointing out how poorly his rival lived up to his namesake among the companions of the Prophet Muḥammad.[21] According to Ibn al-Khaṭīb, Ibn Mardanīsh was moved (*ṭariba*) by a reference to a pious early companion of the Prophet Muḥammad. Whereas the previous narrative highlighted Ibn Mardanīsh's possession of the traditional Islamic virtues of manliness and bravery in battle accompanied by modesty, the story of this exchange depicts him as so pious that a passing reference to a companion of the Prophet affects him emotionally. Unlike the two earlier Almohad descriptions of the battle, this narrative must have had its roots in an earlier, pro-Mardanīshī biography that reflected admiration for Ibn Mardanīsh (here called Muḥammad ibn Saʿd), and described him as righteous, brave, and pious.

By contrast, in Ibn al-Khaṭīb's later historical work, *Aʿmāl al-aʿlām*, which he wrote while in exile from the Nasrid court in Marinid North Africa between 774/1372 and 776/1374 shortly before being executed for heresy by the Nasrid ruler Muḥammad V, the details about Ibn Mardanīsh's bravery and piety are nowhere to be found in narratives of his battles. In Ibn al-Khaṭīb's description of the Battle of Faḥṣ al-Jallāb, a typically terse account focuses on Ibn Mardanīsh's defeat by the Almohads: "Then the power of Ibn Mardanīsh began to decline: the Almohads defeated him in Faḥṣ al-Yandūn on Friday, the seventh of Dhū al-Ḥijja in the year 560."[22]

This process of turning a complex and often positive view of Ibn Mardanīsh into a flatter and more polemical presentation can also be observed in other parallel discussions in Ibn al-Khaṭīb's two works. In in his earlier work, the *Iḥāṭa*, Ibn al-Khaṭīb treats Ibn Mardanīsh from

---

mulūk al-Maghrib wa-tārīkh madīnat Fās, ed. ʿAbd al-Wahhāb Bin Manṣūr (Rabat: al-Maṭbaʿa al-Malikiyya, 1999), 252.

20 Ibn al-Khaṭīb, *al-Iḥāṭa*, ed. Ṭawīl, 1:272–73, in the biography of Ḥātim ibn Saʿīd, the addressee of this speech.

21 Ibn al-Khaṭīb, *al-Iḥāṭa*, ed. Ṭawīl, 1:272–73. Ḥātim refers to the tradition according to which ʿAbd al-Raḥmān ibn ʿAwf, a companion of the Prophet Muḥammad, would be among the companions guaranteed a place in heaven. See *Sunan Abī Dāwūd*, hadith number 4648, 5: 183.

22 Ibn al-Khaṭīb, *Kitāb aʿmāl al-aʿlām*, ed. E. Lévi-Provençal (Beirut: Dār al-Makshūf, 1956), 262.

several different angles, reflecting the wide range of available sources the scholar collected to write his biographical dictionaries. He discusses Ibn Mardanīsh's name and his acquisition of power, lays out his circumstances, describes his heroism and bravery as well as his disgraceful behavior, recounts some of the events that he participated in, including his conquest of Granada, and finally records his death.[23] Each section relies on reports by earlier historians, sometimes named and other times referred to vaguely as "chroniclers."[24] The section on Ibn Mardanīsh's disgraceful behavior is by far the longest, close to six times the length of any other section. Ibn al-Khaṭīb claims that the majority of its information comes from a no longer extant book by Ibn Ṣāḥib al-Ṣalā (*Thawrat al-Murīdīn*), which matches the tenor of surviving works by this author. According to Ibn al-Khaṭīb, it is from Ibn Ṣāḥib al-Ṣalā that we learn of Ibn Mardanīsh's powerful body, his chivalry, and his bravery, but also of his drinking habits. Ibn al-Khaṭīb reports, from Ibn Ṣāḥib al-Ṣalā, that Ibn Mardanīsh designated Mondays and Thursdays as days for drinking with his boon companions, who included his military commanders. He would slaughter a cow and distribute its meat to his soldiers, and he would entertain them with the songs of singing slave girls (*qiyān*) until "he gained control over the hearts of the army." Among the many anecdotes included in this section is an unattributed story of Ibn Mardanīsh's sleeping with a group of serving girls under a single blanket, followed by a discussion of his great love of wind instruments and dancing. Ibn al-Khaṭīb also reports that Ibn Mardanīsh used to get drunk and beat one of his serving boys but would subsequently repent and give the boy generous gifts. He mentions Ibn Mardanīsh's peace treaties with Barcelona and Castile and the tribute he paid these kingdoms, and he notes disapprovingly that Ibn Mardanīsh provided houses and wine taverns in Murcia for the Christians in his armies. The bulk of the long section on Ibn Mardanīsh's objectionable behavior consists of a single story, "reported by several trustworthy chroniclers," about a resident of Murcia who fled to Jaén (Jayyān) and told of his experience of forced labor and imprisonment because he had been unable to pay the excessive and un-Islamic taxes demanded by Ibn Mardanīsh.

---

23 Interestingly, in this section Ibn al-Khaṭīb calls the ruler Muḥammad ibn Saʿd and does not comment on the potential origins of the name Mardanīsh, but in later, more negative discussions he calls him Ibn Mardanīsh.

24 Ibn al-Khaṭīb, *al-Iḥāṭa*, ed. Ṭawīl, 2:70–74.

In the *A'māl al-a'lām*, Ibn al-Khaṭīb repeated many of the elements of his earlier treatment of Ibn Mardanīsh but consolidated the complex descriptions of his earlier work into a simpler and more polemical narrative.[25] In an illustrative passage, Ibn al-Khaṭīb first provides a description of Ibn Mardanīsh's great physical strength and gallantry but then focuses on the ruler's love of wine, describing his drinking games with fellow warriors with prizes that included silver drinking vessels and carpets. In this portrayal, Ibn Mardanīsh was not only a great drinker but also a great lover, who could bed two hundred serving girls under a single blanket. Further, Ibn al-Khaṭīb reports,

> He had a propensity for wearing Christian clothes [*ziyy al-rūm*] and tight clothes, riding ambling workhorses, and using saddles with thick saddlebows. He sought help from them [the Christians] in his planning, and he arranged for helpers and soldiers from them, and he built buildings for them in Murcia that included taverns and churches. He was in need of money, so he violated his subjects with every kind of injustice [*bi-kull wajḥ min wujūḥ al-jūr*], and he made too many agreements [*istakthara min al-qabālāt*],[26] and he prescribed astonishing [levels of] customs taxes [*mukūs*].[27]

In an echo of his critique of the Nasrid sultan Naṣr, Ibn al-Khaṭīb described Ibn Mardanīsh as wearing tight, Christian clothes. This portion of Ibn al-Khaṭīb's text reflects fourteenth-century understandings of Christian clothing, since Christians did not wear tight clothes in the twelfth century. The change in Christian clothing from loose-fitting to tight corresponded to the introduction of plate armor, which

25 Ibn al-Khaṭīb, *A'māl al-a'lām*, ed. Lévi-Provençal, 259–62.

26 Lévi-Provençal's edition of *A'māl al-a'lām* has this word as *qabālāt*, meaning contracts or agreements, whereas Sayyid Kasrāwī Ḥasan's edition writes *qiyālāt*, a word of less common usage that could mean rescinding or annulling agreements.

27 Ibn al-Khaṭīb, *A'māl al-a'lām*, ed. Lévi-Provençal, 261. *Mukūs*, sg. *maks*, are pre-Islamic customs taxes, adopted by Muslim rulers even though a hadith decried them as oppressive (*Inna ṣāḥib al-maks fī al-nār*, "The tax-collector will go to hell"); see *EI*[2] s.v. "Maks" (W. Björkman). Taxation was frequently the basis of criticism of those in power and sometimes led to revolution. It is interesting to note that the Almohads gained power in North Africa by pledging to abolish Almoravid customs taxes and to condemn to death anyone who levied them. See al-Idrīsī, *Description de l'Afrique et de l'Espagne*, 69–70. Ibn al-Khaṭīb also notes that Ibn Mardanīsh taxed his population heavily in order to finance his wars and tells the story, mentioned earlier, of a desperate man forced into slave labor because he was unable to pay the extra-Islamic taxes Ibn Mardanīsh demanded. See Ibn al-Khaṭīb, *al-Iḥāṭa*, ed. Ṭawīl, 2:72–73. Although we have no other indication of Ibn Mardanīsh's tax practices, the substantial tributes he owed Barcelona and Castile as part of his peace treaties may well have required the imposition of new taxes on his population.

required tighter clothes underneath.[28] If Ibn Mardanīsh had been wearing Christian-style clothes in the twelfth century, they would not have been tight. By dwelling on Ibn Mardanīsh's dissolute behavior, Ibn al-Khaṭīb followed Almohad sources in suggesting a moral equivalency between the ruler and his Christian allies. This critique, familiar from Ibn Ṣāḥib al-Ṣalā, that Ibn Mardanīsh's brain was wine-addled, and that he built taverns and churches for Christians, that he was more loyal to his Christian allies than to his Muslim subjects, constituted a potent delegitimizing tactic. Ibn al-Khaṭīb's new emphasis on his tendency to look, fight, and dress like a Christian represents an evolution in thinking about religious identity from the twelfth- and thirteenth-century sources, which still relied on the trope of the "Christian companion" to undermine the legitimacy of the Almohads' rivals.

By the mid-fourteenth century, what it meant to call someone an infidel had acquired new valences, implying a genealogical cause for perceived disloyalty. By the time Ibn al-Khaṭīb was writing the *Aʿmāl al-aʿlām*, when al-Andalus had been reduced to a small territory that was increasingly dependent on the goodwill of its royal Christian protectors, the ubiquitous alliances across religious lines that had defined much of the high Middle Ages had come to be seen in a different light. Ibn al-Khaṭīb's criticism of the Nasrid sultan Naṣr, in which he insinuated that the sultan's true loyalties lay with the Christians by referring to his allegedly Christian genealogy, reflected a world view in which behavior could reveal "true" identity, formed by blood.[29] Ibn al-Khaṭīb may have read genealogical implications into Ibn Ṣāḥib al-Ṣalā's work; later modern scholars certainly did. The assumed connection between genealogy, sartorial tendencies, and political and religious allegiances is on full display in the *Aʿmāl al-aʿlām*. Ibn al-Khaṭīb's description of Ibn Mardanīsh as an impious and unjust ruler who preferred Christians over Muslims should perhaps be seen as a criticism of the scholar's erstwhile Nasrid patrons.

In the *Iḥāṭa*, Ibn al-Khaṭīb included multiple narratives about Ibn Mardanīsh that revealed both his bravery and his lively court life. In the later *Aʿmāl al-aʿlām*, his more succinct treatment of Ibn Mardanīsh focused on the latter aspect, and it is this condensation of the more widely ranging medieval sources that is most frequently reproduced by later scholars. It is this flattened and largely negative vision of Ibn Mardanīsh

---

28 See F. Piponnier and P. Mane, *Dress in the Middle Ages,* trans. Caroline Beamish (New Haven, CT: Yale University Press, 2000).

29 Ibn al-Khaṭīb, *al-Iḥāṭa,* ed. ʿInān, 1:394; Rubiera Mata, *Ibn al-Ŷayyāb,* 134.

that Ibn al-Khaṭīb's most admiring reader and greatest champion, Aḥmad al-Maqqarī, would inherit and adopt—with an important exception, discussed below. Born in Ottoman Tlemcen in the late sixteenth century to a family that claimed Granada as its ancestral home, Aḥmad al-Maqqarī (d. 1041/1632) was a jurist and hadith transmitter who also studied the history and literature of al-Andalus in the course of a series of visits to Marrakech and Fez. He served as the imam of al-Qarawiyyīn in Fez from 1022/1613 to 1027/1617, but after falling out of favor with the Saʿdian sultan Mawlāy Zaydān, he left to perform the pilgrimage and spent the rest of his life in the Islamic East. He settled in Cairo and married there but continued to travel regularly to Mecca, Medina, and Damascus.

It was during a visit to Damascus in 1039/1627 that al-Maqqarī began to conceive of a massive work on the history of al-Andalus and on Ibn al-Khaṭīb as its preeminent literary scholar (*adīb*).[30] Al-Maqqarī began to compose *Nafḥ al-ṭīb* as soon as he returned to Cairo. In the book's introduction, al-Maqqarī describes his initial reluctance to start writing, even after his friends in Damascus had encouraged him, because he felt underequipped to undertake such an ambitious project without all of the books on al-Andalus he had left behind in Fez. He begins the book with his own autobiography, describing the twists of fate that have led him to exile. He emphasizes the same theme again in the last part of the book, a biography of Ibn al-Khaṭīb, who was exiled from al-Andalus in the fourteenth century and was then condemned to death for heresy in Marinid Fez in 776/1374.

Al-Maqqarī's work, like that of Ibn al-Khaṭīb, incorporated many earlier narratives that record both Ibn Mardanīsh's bravery and his degeneracy. Al-Maqqarī took several elements of his coverage of Ibn Mardanīsh, including his narrative of Ibn Mardanīsh's siege of Almería, nearly verbatim from other extant sources, but adds later ideas about lineage and loyalty adapted from Ibn al-Khaṭīb.[31] In al-Maqqarī's telling, the Almohads

30 Ralph Elger, "Adab and Historical Memory: The Andalusian Poet/Politician Ibn al-Khaṭīb as Presented by Aḥmad al-Maqqarī (986/1577–1041/1632)," *Die Welt des Islams* 42, no. 3 (2002): 293. Elger focuses particularly on the fascination of seventeenth-century Damascene literary scholars with the theme of fate and the ability of literature to offer immortality. This theme, already associated with the lost world of al-Andalus, made studies of the people and literature of the region even more intriguing and, Elger argues, held particular appeal for al-Maqqarī, who was exiled from his own homeland as Ibn al-Khaṭīb had once been from al-Andalus.

31 Al-Maqqarī, *Nafḥ al-Ṭīb*, 4:463. The story of the siege of Almería is told in much the same way in Ibn Abī Zarʿ, *al-Anīs al-Muṭrib*, 252.

were besieging the Christian fortress of Almería when Ibn Mardanīsh raised an army that pinned the Almohads against the Christians in the fortress. Then, al-Maqqarī says, Ibn Mardanīsh suddenly realized the shame inherent in attacking his coreligionists who were fighting the Christians and decamped with his army.[32] Al-Maqqarī goes on to describe Ibn Mardanīsh as a man of Christian origin who profited from the chaotic end of Almoravid rule by seizing control of eastern al-Andalus. In explicitly pointing out Ibn Mardanīsh's Christian roots, al-Maqqarī seems to explain his questionable moral character, and his willingness to make a period of political chaos work to his advantage. Nevertheless, in occasional moments, like the narrative of the siege of Almería, al-Maqqarī's Ibn Mardanīsh recognizes that he *should* be loyal to his fellow Muslims, and recognizes the wickedness of his actions.

But this attitude—that hereditary religion should determine loyalty—clearly challenged al-Maqqarī when he tried to incorporate narratives from earlier sources in which Ibn Mardanīsh was praised in battles against fellow Muslims. This is visible most immediately in al-Maqqarī's retelling of the narrative of al-Jallāb from Ibn al-Khaṭīb's *Iḥāṭa*. Ibn al-Khaṭīb's original story highlights Ibn Mardanīsh's bravery and describes him as moved by the mention of a companion of the Prophet. But al-Maqqarī makes an important change to the narrative.

> One day he [Ibn Mardanīsh] was fighting a convoy of Christians, throwing them down and killing them in such a way that he himself was astonished, and he said to an old man from among his military commanders, who was knowledgeable in the ways of war and famous for them: "What do you see?" And the old man replied, "If only the sultan could see you, he would surely increase what he gives you from the treasury [*bayt māl*] and your salary, for who could be head of the army and achieve such courage? But he would object to your perishing, for it would lead to the perishing of the army." Ibn Mardanīsh responded, "Be that as it may, I will not die twice, and if I die, perhaps it will allow those who come after me to live."[33]

Whereas Ibn al-Khaṭīb wrote about Ibn Mardanīsh's battleground bravery against unspecified enemies (in actuality, the Almohads), al-Maqqarī

32 al-Maqqarī, *Nafḥ al-Ṭīb*, 4:463.
33 al-Maqqarī, *Nafḥ al-ṭīb*, 3:210.

states explicitly that these enemies were Christians. To al-Maqqarī in the seventeenth century (or, perhaps, to an earlier intermediary whose version of the events al-Maqqarī repeated), it was inconceivable that Ibn al-Khaṭīb might have transmitted a narrative praising the bravery of a Muslim ruler fighting fellow Muslims; accordingly, he changed the ruler's enemies into Christians. Subsequent scholars who have depended on al-Maqqarī's version of Ibn al-Khaṭīb's work have largely remained blind to the transformation that made the Battle of al-Jallāb yet another conflict between Christian and Muslim foes, rather than the intra-Muslim fight it was.

Al-Maqqarī's reworking of Ibn al-Khaṭīb's narrative parallels the rise of a vision of totalizing Christian-Muslim warfare in Spanish historiography. This vision, as Martín Ríos has shown, gained strength in the seventeenth century, as historians sought to clarify and formalize the narrative of the "restoration" of Christianity on the Iberian Peninsula.[34] This development raises the fascinating question of how historiographic topoi traveled between historians writing in Castilian on the Iberian Peninsula and those working in Arabic in North Africa. Scholars have noted that Ibn al-Khaṭīb seems to have adapted narratives from the thirteenth-century Castilian chronicle *Estoria de España,* sponsored by King Alfonso X, in his own work.[35] Similarly, al-Maqqarī's outline of the history of enmity between Muslims and Christians on the Iberian Peninsula follows the same narrative structure as do those sixteenth- and seventeenth-century Christian works that cast the Christian conquest of al-Andalus as a singular and continuous ideological mission.[36]

Al-Maqqarī, like the authors of these earlier Christian works, begins his narrative of the history of the loss of al-Andalus with Pelayo. This figure, a Visigothic nobleman who is said to have founded the kingdom of Asturias in 718, is credited in the histories of what would be imagined as the "Reconquista" as being the first champion of the Christians against Islamic hegemony on the Iberian Peninsula. Like Christian chronicles that turned the figure of Pelayo into a hero who resisted the Islamic presence on the Iberian Peninsula from the moment of al-Andalus's genesis, al-Maqqarī described how Pelayo and his tiny band of followers

34 Ríos, *Reconquista.*

35 Justin Stearns, "Two Passages in Ibn al-Khaṭīb's Account of the Kings of Christian Iberia," *Al-Qanṭara* 25 (2004): 157–82; M. M. Antuña, "Una versión árabe compendiada de la 'Estoria de España' de Alfonso el Sabio," *Al-Andalus* 1, no. 1 (1933): 105–28.

36 Al-Maqqarī, *Nafḥ al-Ṭīb,* 4:350–85.

fled Muslim armies to a cave, where they survived a siege by subsisting, miraculously, on honey gathered from holes. Eventually emerging from their refuge in the cave, they were able to defeat the Muslim army. He then recounts the Battle of Las Navas de Tolosa, the fall of the Almohads, and the emergence of Ibn al-Aḥmar, founder of the Nasrid dynasty. At the beginning, he frames the entire narrative in providential terms, claiming that God had chosen to give the Peninsula to the unbelievers after having previously granted it to the Muslims, and ending with a prayer:

> And the enemies came to the peninsula from behind it and from between its hands; may God the Most High bring back to it the word of Islam and make rise in it the *sharīʿa* of the master of mankind, upon him be the most favored prayers and peace, and remove the hand of the disbelievers from it and from what is around it. Amen.[37]

This remarkable idea of a territory granted to Muslims by God and then taken by unbelievers, with the possibility of territorial redemption through prayer, mirrors the Christian historiography described by Ríos, which explains the Muslim conquest as "a just punishment for the sins committed by the Goths" and views the ensuing long war with the Muslims as "an eight-hundred-year-long penance that allowed the Christians to remove the stains of the sin."[38] Fierro has shown that many earlier Arabic chronicles about al-Andalus employ similar providential frameworks that depict victory as a sign of God's favor.[39] But al-Maqqarī's narrative parallels the Christian historical writing of his time even more closely: he states, in words nearly identical to those of his contemporary Diego Saavedra Fajardo (d. 1648), that Pelayo was the ancestor of all Iberian kings until his own day.[40] By incorporating a foundational myth of the Spanish nation into his own historical narrative, al-Maqqarī presents al-Andalus as a territory with which God

37 Al-Maqqarī, *Nafḥ al-Ṭīb*, 4:351.

38 Ríos, *Reconquista*, 44: "Un justo castigo por los pecados cometidos por los godos y que la lucha mantenida contra los musulmanes fuera tenida por una larga penitencia de ochocientos años que permitió a los cristianos borrar las manchas del pecado."

39 Maribel Fierro, "Christian Success and Muslim Fear in Andalusī Writings during the Almoravid and Almohad Periods," in *Dhimmis and Others: Jews and Christians and the World of Classical Islam*, ed. U. Rubin and D. Wasserstein (Winona Lake, IN: Eisenbrauns, 1997) 165.

40 Al-Maqqarī, *Nafḥ al-Ṭīb*, 4:351. On Saavedra and his conception of the continuity of the Spanish monarchy from Pelayo to Felipe IV, see Ríos, *Reconquista*, 102–7.

had once graced the Muslims but which, in spite of his prayer to the contrary, had been lost to a triumphant and divinely favored Christian kingdom.

This providential vision of decline created the framework within which the totality of the history of al-Andalus was understood. The works of these two exiled scholars, Ibn al-Khaṭīb in fourteenth-century Fez and al-Maqqarī in seventeenth-century Cairo, demonstrate the beginning and the apotheosis of the myth of al-Andalus. For both of these figures, scholarship offered a chance at restoration—of their reputation as well as of a glorious culture they saw as in decline or lost. María Jesús Rubiera Mata and Mikel de Epalza have noted that "the myth of al-Andalus . . . was probably born among the exiled Muslims of al-Andalus" and that it "was particularly collected and amplified by al-Maqqarī."[41] This myth, which Rubiera Mata and de Epalza define as a fixation on al-Andalus's cultural splendor and nostalgia for a lost paradise, informed the ways in which many Arab and European authors presented al-Andalus in the centuries after al-Maqqarī.

The teleology defined by the inevitable decline and fall of al-Andalus conditioned historians' perception of earlier periods. The narrative arc of Ibn al-Khaṭīb's *Aʿmāl al-aʿlām* and al-Maqqarī's *Nafḥ al-ṭīb* emphasizes a period of glory that is followed by a time of decline, and it thus mirrors their own professional rise and subsequent fall into exile. In order to fit the history of al-Andalus into this framework, al-Maqqarī celebrated littérateurs, *mujāhid*s, and other individuals whose lives he saw as exemplifying Andalusī virtues and maligned others he saw as responsible for the region's decline. Like all works of history, *Nafḥ al-ṭīb* reflects its author's preoccupations and is filled with literary topoi. Nevertheless, later scholars have seen and used it as a compendium of earlier sources about al-Andalus that offers an unbiased archive for the benefit of modern scholarship.

In his introduction to the 1855–61 edition of *Nafḥ al-ṭīb*, Gustave Dugat wrote that it constituted "a kind of historical and literary library of the Arabs of Spain."[42] Since the early nineteenth century, a series of European Arabists have mined this source for information about al-Andalus and for literary treasures, yielding works such as John Shakespear's

41 María Jesús Rubiera Mata and Mikel de Epalza, "Al-Andalus: Between Myth and History," *History and Anthropology* 18, no. 3 (2007): 270.

42 "Une sorte de bibliothèque historique et littéraire des Arabes d'Espagne." Al-Maqqarī, *Analectes sur l'histoire et la littérature des Arabes d'Espagne* (Leiden: Brill, 1855–61), bk. 5, vi.

History of the Mahometan Empire in Spain (1816) and Pascual de Gayangos's abridged translation, *The History of the Mohammedan Dynasties in Spain* (1840).[43] Évariste Lévi-Provençal, in the first edition of the *Encyclopaedia of Islam*, called *Nafḥ al-ṭīb* an "immense compilation of historical and literary information, poems, letters and quotations very often taken from works now lost" and argued that this feature made it the most valuable source on the history of al-Andalus.[44] Like other scholars of al-Andalus in the twentieth century, Lévi-Provençal used al-Maqqarī as an archive of historical information from which he constructed his own historical narratives.

As my close examination of al-Maqqarī's treatment of Ibn Mardanīsh demonstrates, however, *Nafḥ al-ṭīb* is no dispassionate archive. Instead, it reflects a mythification of al-Andalus that accompanied the exile of its intellectuals, many of whom settled in Fez and, like Ibn al-Khaṭīb, began to rewrite its history in a nostalgic mode. Al-Maqqarī lived at the moment when the last descendants of the Muslims of al-Andalus were forced to depart the territory, many of them settling in North Africa and agitating for the restoration of al-Andalus.[45] The same sultan who employed al-Maqqarī in Fez encouraged these exiled Moriscos to support him and to join his army by claiming that he would be the ruler who would reconquer al-Andalus from the Christians and resurrect its glory.[46] Later, in exile in Cairo without his library and without access to many of the surviving sources, al-Maqqarī further mythified al-Andalus, eliding conflict among Muslims and emphasizing the tragic decline of al-Andalus at the hands of the Christians.

In mythifying the history of al-Andalus to create a compelling narrative, al-Marrākushī was simply practicing the tools of his trade. Nicola Clarke has observed that when it came to writing in and about al-Andalus:

> History-writing was for a purpose, and that purpose was creating and disseminating an understanding of the world through an image of its past. It was written in an overtly factual style, in anecdotal forms such as the *khabar* and with devices such as *isnād*s

---

43 See Dugat's introduction for discussion of these translations and their approach to al-Maqqarī's work in al-Maqqarī, *Analectes sur l'histoire*, bk. 5, vii.

44 *EI1*, s.v. "al-Makkarī" (É. Lévi-Provençal).

45 See Mercedes García-Arenal, "The Moriscos in Morocco," in *The Expulsion of the Moriscos of Spain*, ed. Mercedes García-Arenal and Gerard Wiegers (Leiden: Brill, 2014).

46 García-Arenal, "Moriscos in Morocco," 311–12.

> that were meant to protect and advertise the accounts' adherence to the truth, but this history was placed in a literary framework, that of narrative, for ease of retelling and by the very rules of the game.[47]

As she notes, *akhbār*, the discrete building blocks of narrative, presented with chains of transmission, were used flexibly. They could be used independently of each other, moved to new contexts, or used with new names in the service of emplotment, leading to systematic distortion.[48] Echoes of the same story across chronicles written centuries apart could serve different ends or feature different protagonists tailored to the contexts of the authors or compilers and the moralizing goals of their narratives.[49]

In such use, Ibn Mardanīsh became not just a man whose relationships with Christians were sometimes too close for comfort—as Ibn al-Khaṭīb had depicted him in his later work—but a proximate cause of the fall of al-Andalus. This new role is clear in al-Maqqarī's discussion of the Battle of Las Navas de Tolosa (which he calls by its Arabic name, al-ʿUqāb). The battle took place forty years after Ibn Mardanīsh's death, but al-Maqqarī nevertheless attributes to him a share of the blame for the outcome.

> God purified the Muslims at a site known as al-ʿUqāb, and a number were martyred, and the reason was the weakness of the Maghrib and al-Andalus—that of the Maghrib lying in the emptiness of its villages and quarters, and that of al-Andalus in the demands for enmity against it, when after al-Nāṣir ibn al-Manṣūr the *sayyid*s agitated violently in the regions of al-Andalus, everyone in his own service, and their sovereignty in Marrakech weakened. They began to raise armies against each other in tyranny, and the castles of the Muslims began to submit, and the men of distinction and the rest of the Arabs from the Umayyad dynasty dispersed and fled all together; and they sprang upon them all at once and dislodged them and seized power. The main ones among

47 Nicola Clarke, *The Muslim Conquest of Iberia: Medieval Arabic Narratives* (London: Routledge, 2012), 103.

48 Clarke, *Muslim Conquest of Iberia*, 104.

49 See Maribel Fierro, "La Falsificación de la Historia: Al-Yasaʿ b. Ḥazm y su Kitāb al-Mughrib," Al-Qanṭara 16 (1995): 1–37, esp. 35–37.

> them were Muḥammad ibn Hūd al-Judhāmī, the rebel in al-Andalus, and Ibn Mardanīsh and other rebels.[50]

It is possible that al-Maqqarī in this passage refers not to Muḥammad ibn Saʿd Ibn Mardanīsh but to his great-grandnephew, Zayyān ibn Mardanīsh (d. 1270), who would rule Valencia after the Battle at Las Navas, as Almohad power disintegrated. But the narrative of Andalusī decline that al-Maqqarī outlines here, focusing on the weakness of al-Andalus and the Maghrib caused by the rebellion of men such as Ibn Mardanīsh, conflates individuals and centuries into an overall story of rebellion, tyranny, and decay. The only thread tying Ibn Mardanīsh to Las Navas was that he also fought the Almohads and, as both Almohad chroniclers and al-Maqqarī point out, did so with Christians among his soldiers. But Ibn Mardanīsh and his Christian "companions" were not the immediate cause of the weakness of the Almohads at the time of Las Navas, nor for the broader loss of al-Andalus.

As Robert Hoyland has demonstrated, historians writing in Arabic often used causal frameworks to make sense of their material.[51] In addition to offering greater drama and creating orderly narratives, teleological framing allowed authors and compilers to present history as a morality lesson that reinforced the ultimate justice of God. People lost power because they had failed to show gratitude to God.[52] It is not surprising, therefore, that al-Maqqarī's portrayal of the final centuries of Andalusī history might take a moralizing tone and emphasize the reasons the Muslims lost power. Highlighting the dangers of collaboration with Christians, as Ibn al-Khaṭīb did in his later critique of Ibn Mardanīsh, served as both an explanation for the decline of al-Andalus and a cautionary tale for contemporary Muslim rulers. Ibn Mardanīsh's contradictory treatment in sources such as Ibn al-Khaṭīb's two works reflects his polarizing role as an opponent of the Almohads. But in the shift from complex attitudes toward a fixation on "Christianness" and Christian roots we can also see growing anxieties among Muslim writers in Iberia and North Africa about close relationships with their increasingly powerful Christian neighbors.

---

50 Al-Maqqarī, *Nafḥ al-ṭīb*, 1:446.

51 Robert Hoyland, "History, Fiction and Authorship in the First Centuries of Islam," in *Writing and Representation in Medieval Islam*, ed. Julia Bray (London: Routledge, 1996), esp. 22 ff.

52 Hoyland, "History, Fiction and Authorship," 28.

Modern Transformations

In late medieval and early modern chronicles, and continuing well into modern scholarship, earlier writers' long and diverse treatments of Ibn Mardanīsh were condensed into shorter and more anecdotal ones, producing a one-dimensional image of an impious Muslim with Christian ancestry and loyalties. As a result, Ibn Mardanīsh has come to be seen either as an ideologically toothless Andalusī Muslim who lacked the religious fervor necessary to defend the besieged al-Andalus against the Christians or as a protosecular Spanish nationalist hero who resisted the intolerance of the foreign Almohad invaders because his loyalty to his fellow Iberians surpassed his loyalty to his fellow Muslims. Both of these visions are aimed at explaining why an Andalusī ruler might ally with Christians against Muslims at a time when the Christians of the Iberian Peninsula were imagined to be uniting in the Reconquista to expel the Muslim interlopers after centuries of conflict. The two major schools of nineteenth-century Spanish historiography also made use of these conflicting images of Ibn Mardanīsh: one reified the idealized vision of the Reconquista, positing a fundamental break between Spain and al-Andalus, while the other claimed to find the roots of Spanish identity in al-Andalus.[53] Ibn Mardanīsh's complex history allowed him to be inserted into either of these narratives as evidence—either as a rare Muslim fighting alongside his Christian neighbors in the Reconquista or as an exemplary "Spanish Muslim," loyal to his nation over his religion.

The first modern historians of al-Andalus, committed to a positivist vision of history, brought together narratives from multiple Arabic sources to reveal a historical truth. But in their reliance on Arabic chronicles with diverse perspectives on Ibn Mardanīsh, historians such as José Antonio Conde, Reinhart P. Dozy, and Francisco Codera incorporated multiple conflicting attitudes toward Ibn Mardanīsh in their works, calling him by different names in different sections and reflecting a range of ideological perspectives. For example, Conde, the earliest historian of al-Andalus in Spain to rely primarily on Arabic sources, used various names for Ibn Mardanīsh, including Mohamed Aben Sad, Aben Sad, Aben Sad ben Mardanis, Muhamad Aben Sad ben Mardanis, Abu

53 Alejandro García-Sanjuan, "Rejecting al-Andalus, Exalting the Reconquista: Historical Memory in Contemporary Spain," *Journal of Medieval Iberian Studies* 10, no. 1 (2018): 127–45. On the Almohads in Spanish historiography in particular, see Isabel O'Connor, "The Fall of the Almohad Empire in the Eyes of Modern Spanish Historians," *Islam and Christian-Muslim Relations* 14, no. 2 (2003): 145–62.

Abdala ben Sad, Muhamad Ben Sadi Aben Mardanis, Aben Sadi, Abdala ben Sad, and Muhamad ben Sad el Gazamī Aben Mardenis.[54] It is not clear whether he was aware that these names referred to one and the same figure. But the divisions among and ideologies of his sources were largely invisible to him, since he conceived of the whole project as being fundamentally about the "Arab" side of the history of Spain, as opposed to the "Christian" side. His introduction framed the work as predicated on a Rankean ambition to access the whole "truth" of Spanish history, rather than only the winning, Christian side: "A healthy and fair criticism asks that we not content ourselves with the testimonies of a sole side, and that we compare the accounts of both with impartiality and discretion, and with only the desire to discover the truth."[55] Because history was always written by the victors, Conde suggested that the Arabic sources could offer the perspective of the dynasty that had been swept away, which he refers to as "nuestros árabes," our Arabs.[56] But because he was not sensitive to the distortions caused by victorious and vanquished groups within the Islamic context, he did not recognize the divergent modes in which Ibn Mardanīsh was treated in the Arabic sources. The result of Conde's approach, much like that of Ibn al-Khaṭīb's early work, is a fragmented picture of Ibn Mardanīsh that depicts him alternately as a brave hero of the Andalusī factions against the Almohads and as a perfidious, bad Muslim who was too close to his Christian allies.

The Dutch Orientalist Dozy critiqued Conde's understanding of his sources ("Conde worked on Arabic documents without knowing much more of this language than the characters with which it is written, replacing with an extremely fertile imagination the absence of knowledge of the most basic facts") and produced a series of substantial translations of medieval Arabic sources.[57] His deep knowledge of these sources and his careful citations, which often include the original Arabic, enabled

54 A nonexhaustive list of references for the names used in Conde's *Historia de la dominación de los Árabes en España* (first published 1840; citations here are from the Madrid: Marín y Compañía, editors, 1874 edition): Aben Sad: 225, 229, 239, 241, 242, 243; Muhamad ben Sad ben Mardanis: 223; Abu Abdala ben Sad: 224; Muhamad Aben Sad ben Mardanis: 225; Muhamad ben Sad el Gazamī Aben Mardenis: 229; Abu Abdala Muhamad ben Sad: 229, 241, 243; Muhamad ben Sad: 238, 239; Muhamad ben Sadi: 238; Muhamad ben Sad Aben Mardenis: 241; Aben Sad ben Mardanis: 243.

55 Conde, *Dominacion de los Árabes,* 3: "Pero una sana y justa critica pide que no nos contentemos con los testimonios de un solo partido, y que comparemos las relaciones de ambos con imparcialidad y discrecion, y con solo el ánimo de hallar la verdad."

56 Conde, *Dominacion de los Árabes,* 4.

57 Dozy, *Recherches,* xii.

a deeper analysis of the differences among the sources and opened the way for new generations of scholars to study al-Andalus. But as the passage with which I opened this book indicates, Dozy was a man of his times, operating in a largely national framework and thus fixated on determining what "nation" Ibn Mardanīsh belonged to. Reading Ibn al-Khaṭīb's fourteenth-century narratives at face value, Dozy described Ibn Mardanīsh drinking, bedding his slave girls, and distributing silver to his soldiers. He concluded that Ibn Mardanīsh's generosity made his warriors idolize him, but cautioned: "At the same time—and this is what would make his life difficult—his prurience was insatiable, and if the pope Alexander IV had had knowledge of what is said in this regard, he would perhaps have thought twice before calling him *wolf king of glorious memory*."[58] For Dozy, then, Ibn Mardanīsh was defined above all by his debauchery, and his lofty reputation was possibly only because those who admired him did not know the full story. Dozy contrasted him with the "religious" Almohads and pointed to his alliances with Christians as evidence of his doctrinal and political flexibility. For Dozy, as for many other liberal historians of the late nineteenth century, describing figures like Ibn Mardanīsh or the Cid as irreligious and flexible constituted part of their broader critique of religion, making these figures into harbingers of "the modern."[59] In a world divided according to religion and ethnicity, Ibn Mardanīsh thus fell on the Christian, Spanish side—even if Christians would not fully approve of his licentiousness either.

This view of Ibn Mardanīsh persisted into the twentieth century. In 1959, Martín Almagro Basch echoed the conclusions of Dozy, Codera, and Gaspar Remiro by writing that Ibn Mardanīsh, of Christian origin, "was wise, strong and brave, valiant and loved by his soldiers. But he was spoiled by lasciviousness, which contributed to his ruin."[60]

58 Dozy, *Recherches*, 367–68: "Mais en même temps—et c'est ce qui fait tache dans sa vie—sa lubricité était insatiable, et si le pape Alexandre IV avait eu connasissance de ce que l'on racontait à ce propos, il y aurait peut-être regardé à deux fois avant de l'appeler *clara memoria Lupus rex*."

59 See discussion of this trend in Hussein Fancy, "What was Convivencia?" (unpublished article, many thanks to the author for sharing it); more generally on the Spanish historiography of the Islamic period in the nineteenth and twentieth century, see John Tolan, "Using the Middle Ages to Construct Spanish Identity: 19th- and 20th-century Spanish Historiography of Reconquest," in *Historiographical Approaches to Medieval Colonization of East Central Europe*, ed. Jan M. Piskorski (Boulder, CO: East European Monographs, 2002); James Monroe, *Islam and Arabs in Spanish Scholarship (Sixteenth Century to the Present)* (Leiden: E. J. Brill, 1970), 84–127.

60 Almagro Basch, *Historia de Albarracín*, 3:15–16: "Era sagaz, fuerte y bravo, valeroso y querido de sus soldados. Pero estaba estragado por la lujuria, que contribuyó a su ruina." See also Gaspar Remiro, *Historia de Murcia musulmana*, 181–91.

Claudio Sánchez-Albornoz described Ibn Mardanīsh as following a path of "heroic resistance of the African invader for his Spanish fatherland; for him, a fatherland common to Muslims and Christians."[61] He lamented that this "son of Martínez" had been mistreated by Almohad chroniclers and had eventually succumbed to the superior power of the "African conquerors." But, he wrote, what the valiant Murcian had been unable to accomplish through force of arms had been subsequently accomplished by his daughters by means of their beauty, through their marriage to two Almohad caliphs: "Once again Spanish women conquered the conquerors."[62]

Isidro de las Cagigas, an Arabist and diplomat who served as Franco's consul in the Spanish protectorate in Tetouan, saw the Almohads and their religious intolerance as a rupture in the "Spanish tradition of convivencia."[63] For him, men like Ibn Mardanīsh represented what was best in that tradition, as chiefs of a "nationalist" or "peninsular" party that fought for independence from African Berbers.[64] Like Dozy and Codera, Cagigas emphasized Ibn Mardanīsh's names and background and noted "other indirect evidence" of his "Spanish origin," including his Christian-style clothing and weapons, his use of the Spanish language, and his close alliances with Christian kings. Cagigas concluded: "For being Spanish in everything, he was Spanish even in his vices; Latin and Arabic chroniclers praise him for his unbridled lust."[65] Cagigas even speculated that Ibn Mardanīsh's inherited Spanishness passed down through his daughters into certain Almohads: the Almohad caliph al-Ma'mūn Abū al-'Ulā ibn Ya'qūb was "Spanish," not only because he was born in Malaga but also because he had "Spanish blood," since his mother was Ṣafiyya, the daughter of Ibn Mardanīsh.[66] He had not been raised with the sacred rite of visiting Ibn Tūmart's tomb but rather was well versed in Andalusī traditions of religious science, and he therefore rejected the Almohad doctrine. Cagigas also suggested that it was this

61 Claudio Sánchez-Albornoz, *La España musulmana* (Madrid: Espasa-Calpe, 1982), 286: "Su camino que era de la heroica resistencia al invasor africano de su patria española; para él, patria común de musulmanes y cristianos."

62 Sánchez-Albornoz, *La España musulmana*, 286: "Y otra vez las mujeres españolas conquistaron a los conquistadores."

63 Isidro de las Cagigas, "Problemas de minoría y el caso de nuestro medievo," *Hispania* 40 (1950): 534: "rompio' la verdadera tradición española de convivencia."

64 Isidro de las Cagigas, *Los mudéjares* (Madrid: Instituto de Estudios Africanos, 1948), 263–64.

65 Cagigas, *Los mudéjares*, 265.

66 Cagigas, *Los mudéjares*, 345.

biological and regional inheritance that made it possible for al-Maʾmūn to accept twelve thousand horsemen from Ferdinand III to augment his army, under onerous conditions.[67] In writing about both Ibn Mardanīsh and his Almohad grandson's rejection of Almohad power and doctrine, Cagigas framed the conflict in ethnic and religious terms, one side being Spanish, flexible, and lusty, the other African, rigid, and religious.

These visions of Ibn Mardanīsh's decadence and closeness to Christians are ultimately rooted in Almohad descriptions of their rival's irreligiosity, but they have been filtered through modern ideas about lineage, religion, and ethnicity. If, as Ibn al-Khaṭīb claimed, the source of the narratives about Ibn Mardanīsh bedding two hundred slave girls under a single blanket or designating two days for drinking with his soldiers was a lost book by Ibn Ṣāḥib al-Ṣalā, how should the scholar understand these stories? Ibn Ṣāḥib al-Ṣalā, in the service of the Almohad caliphs, was eager to reinforce an image of Ibn Mardanīsh as debauched, lascivious, and drunk in order to highlight his lack of piety and righteousness in contrast to the Almohads, who conscientiously enjoined the good and forbade the wrong. As discussed in chapter 2, fixating on Ibn Mardanīsh's Christian soldiers and friends also reinforced his classification as an infidel who had to be conquered. But imagining, as modern scholars have done, that this made Ibn Mardanīsh "Spanish," or a Christian, reflects a misreading of the Almohad sources and a projection of modern-day attitudes toward Islam, ethnicity, and nationalism.

Whereas Almohad writers contemporary to Ibn Mardanīsh depicted him as an infidel for his refusal to accept Almohad rule, later authors, whose conception of membership in the umma was less narrow, interpreted these sources to mean that Ibn Mardanīsh was actually a Christian (or at least a "Hispanified," and therefore more secular, Muslim). Doing so allowed these later scholars, writing after the fall of Almohad Iberia to the Christian kingdoms, to recast the conflict between the Almohads and their rivals such as Ibn Mardanīsh as part of a broader holy war between Christians and Muslims. The result has been a vision of Ibn Mardanīsh as a traitor to Islam, and of the twelfth century as the apogee of Christian-Muslim enmity and violence in Iberia.

Some twentieth-century scholars have recognized the ways in which Almohad propaganda has distorted the image of Ibn Mardanīsh. Guichard, writing about the costs of Ibn Mardanīsh's military campaigns and

67 Cagigas, *Los mudéjares*, 345–46.

alliances and suggesting they could only have been possible thanks to illegal taxes like those mentioned by Ibn al-Khaṭīb, noted that these taxes may have been "what made Ibn Mardanīsh the impious and bloodthirsty tyrant described by later sources, doubtless influenced by Almohad propaganda."[68] To identify an explanation other than weakness or Andalusī "idiosyncrasy" for the fall of al-Andalus, Guichard turned to analysis of the social and political structures of al-Andalus.[69] At the same time, however, Guichard suggested, like al-Maqqarī did, that it was Ibn Mardanīsh and the discordant Taifa kings of the thirteenth century who caused the defeat of the Almohads and facilitated the expansion of the Christian kingdoms. According to Guichard, the decline of al-Andalus was due to Ibn Mardanīsh's and his contemporaries' lack of an ideology of jihad.[70] Following Urvoy, Guichard argued that in the Islamic West of the later twelfth century, jihad was only a "political instrument of the state," not an "ardent obligation."[71] For Ibn Mardanīsh, engaging in open war against fellow Muslims with the participation of Christian mercenaries, rather than what Guichard envisions as proper jihad, created "a situation increasingly unacceptable in the eyes of Muslim subjects and Andalusī public opinion."[72] Yet a study of the uses of jihad in the Early and Middle Islamic Periods reveals that it was almost always a political instrument of the state, labile and flexible, to be deployed against rivals and enemies.[73] Jihad was central to the political legitimation of a vast range of dynasties in the Middle Period because it facilitated claims to legitimacy even as it also served to eliminate rivals. Even the juridical boundaries of what constituted jihad were relatively unstable until the late Middle Period.[74]

---

68 Pierre Guichard, *Al-Andalus frente a la conquista cristiana*, trans. Josep Torro (Valencia: Biblioteca Nueva, 2001), 136: "Cabe preguntarse si no fue esta situación, difícilmente sostenible, la que hizo de Ibn Mardanīš el tirano impío y sanguinario que describen las fuentes posteriores, influenciadas sin duda por la propaganda almohade."

69 Guichard, *Al-Andalus frente a la conquista*, 133.

70 Guichard, *Al-Andalus frente a la conquista*, 135–37.

71 Guichard, *Al-Andalus frente a la conquista*, 137; Dominique Urvoy, "Sur l'evolution de la notion de ǧihād dans l'Espagne musulmane," *Mélanges de la Casa de Velázquez* 9 (1973): 335–71.

72 Guichard, *Al-Andalus frente a la conquista*, 135.

73 For an excellent study of the meanings and uses of jihad in Andalusī contexts, see Javier Albarrán, *Ejércitos benditos: Yihad y memoria en al-Andalus (siglos X-XIII)* (Granada: Universidad de Granada, 2020).

74 Roy P. Mottahedeh and Ridwan al-Sayyid, "The Idea of *Jihād* in Islam before the Crusades," in *The Crusades from the Perspective of Byzantium and the Muslim World*, ed. A. E. Laiou and R. P. Mottahedeh (Washington, DC: Dumbarton Oaks, 2001), 29.

Guichard and Urvoy did not contrast Ibn Mardanīsh's "jihad ideology" directly with that of the Almohads, since they argued that the Almohads were also insufficiently focused on fighting the Christians until after their conquest of Sharq al-Andalus. But in much of the twentieth-century discourse about this region, the idea of Ibn Mardanīsh as flexible, decadent, and friendly toward Christians is juxtaposed with an image of the Almohads as rigid fundamentalists. Like Sánchez-Albornoz's description of Ibn Mardanīsh as "Murcian" and "Spanish" and that of his Almohad rivals as "African invaders," this juxtaposition presented Andalusīs as fundamentally different from and *better than* Muslims from elsewhere.[75] Ramón Menéndez Pidal, Sánchez-Albornoz's teacher, also saw al-Andalus as different, because it was *Spanish*. For Menéndez Pidal, the children of a "Galician, Catalan or Basque slave" were Spanish regardless of the Arab or African ancestry of their fathers.[76] In the nineteenth and twentieth centuries, such arguments served to reinforce Spain's and France's colonial ambitions by supporting the civilizational superiority of Europeans over Africans and Arabs. They also, as Eric Calderwood has shown, articulated a bond between Spain and North Africa, rooted in the culture of al-Andalus, that could be used to justify both Spain's rule over Morocco and Moroccan nationalism.[77]

Whereas Spanish scholars seeking to naturalize their country's Islamic past harnessed Ibn Mardanīsh as an exemplar of the gulf separating Andalusīs from their North African rivals, Arab reformers adopted him as a model of a Muslim operating within European modernity. Shakīb Arslān, the Lebanese Druze prince and writer, traveled to Spain and Morocco to explore the history of al-Andalus and to conduct

---

75 Similarly, discussions of drinking and other activities seen as contravening the strictures of Islam are often presented in discussions of al-Andalus as evidence of the region's flexibility and superiority. Manuela Marín highlights both how similar drinking cultures seemed to be in the Islamic east and west and how Spanish scholars like Claudio Sánchez-Albornoz pointed to it as evidence of the Spanishness of Andalusī Muslims. Marín, "En los márgenes de la ley: El consumo de alcohol en al-Ándalus," in *Identidades marginales*, Estudios onomástico-biográficos de al Andalus 13, ed. Cristina de la Puente (Madrid: Consejo Superior de Investigaciones Científicas, 2003), 271–328.

76 Rámon Menéndez Pidal, *La España del Cid* (Madrid: Editorial Plutarco, 1929), 669, cited in O'Connor, "Fall of the Almohad Empire," 148. This claim parallels Menéndez Pidal's broader argument regarding how Spaniards had reshaped ("reformado") their Islam (77). For a critical view of this racially oriented perspective on Spanish history, see Thomas Glick and Oriol Pi-Sunyer, "Acculturation as an Explanatory Concept in Spanish History," *Comparative Studies in Society and History* 11, no. 2 (1969): 136–54.

77 Calderwood, *Colonial al-Andalus: Spain and the Making of Modern Moroccan Culture* (Cambridge, MA: Harvard University Press, 2018).

research for his book on the subject, *al-Ḥulal al-sundusiyya fī al-akhbār wa-l-āthār al-Andalusiyya* ("The brocaded garments about the news and monuments of al-Andalus," published in three volumes between 1936 and 1939). While in Tetouan, Arslān attended a tea party at the home of the Spanish consul Cagigas and stayed with the leaders of the Moroccan nationalist movement.[78] Describing al-Andalus as a "lost paradise" (*al-firdaws al-mafqūd*), Arslān posited it as a symbol of the greatness of Islamic civilization and as part of the common heritage of the Muslim world, which had been lost but which could serve as a model for future reform. As Calderwood observes, Arslān saw al-Andalus as "past tense and potential future tense, but not present tense."[79]

Arslān used the metaphor of al-Andalus as a bridge between European modernity and the potential of Islamic civilization, offering a path forward. In his book, he mentions Ibn Mardanīsh dozens of times, describing his treatment in earlier Arabic sources and focusing on his lineage, his bravery, power, and close relationships with Christian neighbors.[80] Ibn Mardanīsh was "probably of Christian Spanish origin," he writes, though the Banū Mardanīsh had always presented themselves as Arabs in order to claim the community group feeling (*ʿasabiyya*) that would support their rule.[81] Arslān does not move significantly beyond the depictions of Ibn Mardanīsh found in the work of Ibn al-Khaṭīb or in the history of Lévi-Provençal, both of which he cites extensively. But his use of Ibn Mardanīsh as a king who operated in Europe and brought together Christians and Muslims seems to highlight a utopian vision of the ruler, a model for the future of Christian-Muslim relations.

All of these visions of Ibn Mardanīsh seek to fit him into frameworks in which the West and the Islamic world are separate, and race is determined biologically and affects culture and politics. Ibn Mardanīsh is a "Western" Muslim, and therefore, definitionally more flexible than those "Eastern" or "African" ones. Islam itself, defined according to the Western academic framework of religion that made normative the structures of Christianity, is imagined as legalistically defined, as austere and violent. Ibn Mardanīsh, measured against these ideals of what a Muslim

78 Calderwood, *Colonial al-Andalus*, 257.

79 Calderwood, *Colonial al-Andalus*, 266.

80 See, for example, Shakīb Arslān, *al-Ḥulal al-sundusiyya fī al-akhbār wa-l-āthār al-Andalusiyya* (Beirut: Dār al-Kutub al-ʿIlmiyya, 1997), 2:162–64; 3:189, 406–7, 497, 511.

81 Arslān, *al-Ḥulal al-sundusiyya*, 3:189: *min aṣl isbānyūlī masīḥī*. On *ʿasabiyya*, see 3:511.

ruler "should" be, falls short. Much like Shahab Ahmed's observation about historians' descriptions of the Saljuqs, fellow non-Arab claimants to power in the twelfth century, Ibn Mardanīsh is presented as having a "sincerity-deficit," or even an "Islam-deficit."[82] His turn toward figurative imagery in his palaces, narratives about his drinking, his bedding of slave girls, even his taxation policies, are gathered as evidence of his cosmopolitanism, as opposed to his identity as a Muslim. Ahmed's forceful critique of this kind of binary framework when it comes to the study of Islam argues that privileging the legalistic, the Arab, and the earliest period of Islam has made the vast majority of Islamic history and culture incomprehensible. Rather than demonstrating the "Westernness" of al-Andalus, or the power of blood to determine ideology, what Ibn Mardanīsh's reign shows is precisely the inextricability of the strands that are imagined as opposed. It shows how cultural forms including images of musicians and drinkers could form part of theological debates, the ease with which people and things traversed the vast lands of Islam and beyond, and how the earliest articulations of European courtly culture were born out of Christian kings' encounters with their Muslim neighbors.

82 Ahmed, *What is Islam?* 220–21.

Postscript

Medieval Stories, Modern Anxieties

In the fall of 2019, the city of Murcia hosted an unprecedented three exhibitions focused on Ibn Mardanīsh. The first, "Castillejo de Monteagudo: Poder y producción en la almunia del Rey Lobo" ("The Castillejo of Monteagudo: Power and Production in the *Munya* of the Wolf King"), appeared at the Palacio de San Esteban and focused on the palaces and gardens at Monteagudo, outside the city, and the broader use of productive palatial estates in the Islamic West. The second, "Rey Lobo: El Legado de Ibn Mardanīš, 1147–1172" ("Wolf King: The Legacy of Ibn Mardanīsh"), was housed at the Museo Arqueológico de Murcia and brought together hundreds of artifacts from around Spain that never before had been exhibited together, from the fragments of Dār al-Ṣughrā's painted muqarnas ceiling to coins, textiles, and potsherds. The third, opening just after the first closed, was "Recorrer la memoria: Ibn Mardanis" ("Revisiting Memory: Ibn Mardanīsh"), in the Museo de la Ciudad de Murcia, and consisted of contemporary art and objects inspired by Ibn Mardanīsh. All three exhibits were promoted together by the municipality and its museums, though they were organized and curated by different groups of scholars.[1] The confluence of the three exhibitions, alongside two new

1 "Castillejo de Monteagudo: Poder y producción en la almunia del Rey Lobo" was curated by Julio Navarro Palazón, Pedro Jiménez Castillo, Juan A. García Granados, and

archaeological excavations in the neighborhood of San Esteban in Murcia and in Monteagudo, demonstrates a new surge of interest in Ibn Mardanīsh's reign and suggests his continued salience in the construction of national and regional memory.[2]

The final exhibit, on the memory of Ibn Mardanīsh, offers insight into the ways in which this twelfth-century ruler's memory operates in a twenty-first century autonomous region in Spain. The exhibit included artwork featuring imagined medieval scenes and photographs of historical sites by local artists, informational posters made by schoolchildren, and both handmade and mass-produced objects inspired by Ibn Mardanīsh. The latter included soccer jerseys for the local team known as the Lobos, or wolves, as well as costumes, standards, and medals used by the Cabila, or tribe, of Ibn Mardanīsh in the annual festival of Moors and Christians. The festival, introduced in 1983, is organized around a parade made up of twelve "tribes," each named for an important Muslim or Christian connected to Murcia. In the exhibit, the first shield for the "Wolf King" tribe, made in 1983, was displayed alongside later iterations. All contained images of a fearsome wolf howling toward a crescent moon.

The exhibition also displayed original art produced for a comic book focused on the history of Ibn Mardanīsh that was published in the early twenty-first century and that sought to educate local youth about a

Maurizio Toscano and was exhibited at San Esteban Espacio Abierto from April 24 to September 30, 2019. See the guide to the exhibition published under the same title in 2019. "Rey Lobo: El legado de Ibn Mardanīš, 1147–1172" was curated by Jorge A. Eiroa Rodríguez and Mariángeles Gómez Ródenas at the Museo Arqueológico de Murcia and was exhibited from June to September 2019. The catalogue was edited by Eiroa and Gómez under the same title as the exhibit and incorporated essays on Ibn Mardanīsh and Sharq al-Andalus by seven other Spanish scholars. "Recorrer la memoria: Ibn Mardanis" was presented at the Museo de la Ciudad, Murcia and curated by its director, Consuelo Oñate Marín, with the assistance of Clara María Alarcón Ruiz and Carmen Clemente Martínez. The exhibit was on display from October 2019 to March 2020, and the museum published a small catalogue with text by Antonio Luis Martínez Rodríguez under the same title.

2 All of the curators of these exhibits, and other recent scholars on Ibn Mardanīsh in general, have emphasized that one should not see a contradiction between the ruler's Christian allies, enmity against the Almohads, and loyalty to a distant caliph. Eiroa and Gómez emphasize the commonalities between Ibn Mardanīsh and other Taifa or Mediterranean figures: "El emirato de Ibn Mardanīš," 23. Such scholarly work in the twenty-first century is usually very careful to distinguish a historical perspective on Ibn Mardanīsh from the more ideological appreciations as a regional or national hero one finds in the popular sphere. But the popular reception of such scholarship and exhibits is another story. The "Rey Lobo" exhibit at the Museo Arqueológico de Murcia had so many visitors it shattered the museum's previous records, and the many events, teams, and objects adorned with his name in the region of Murcia reflects his current outsized role in the popular imagination.

glorious moment in their region's past. The cover of the comic book, *El Rey Lobo: El valeroso rey de Murcia que fundó un gran reino y batalló incansable contra el imperio Almohade* ("The Wolf King: the brave king of Murcia who founded a great kingdom and fought tirelessly against the Almohad Empire"), published by the Ayuntamiento de Murcia in 2006, depicts Ibn Mardanīsh in blue on horseback, bareheaded, wearing the chain mail of a medieval European knight, with the Castillo de Monteagudo rising above his shoulders.[3] Teeming around his horse is a sea of presumably Almohad soldiers with dark brown skin wearing white robes and turbans. The Wolf King raises a heavy, European-style sword above his head, ready to bring it down on one of these white-robed men, who is attacking with a spear. Another white-robed man turns to attack the viewer in the foreground of the image, wielding a spear threateningly and making a ferocious face. Another threatens the hero with a sinister curved sword. Who the hero is and who the enemy is, in this cover image and the images throughout the twelve-page book, is in no doubt at all. One has all the markers of a medieval hero—horse, sword, armor, bravely fighting even though vastly outnumbered. The people he fights are marked as foreign, terrifying, and a threat, not only to him but to the viewer as well.

The vision of Ibn Mardanīsh in this third exhibit, as fundamentally Murcian, a local hero whose name adorns soccer teams, road races, street signs, is supported by the ways he ties into both a multicultural vision of Spanish past, in which Muslims could play an important role in the construction of the nation, and an antiforeigner agenda, in which Muslims from North Africa constitute the true risk to Spanish identity. Both of these constructions of Ibn Mardanīsh imagine him as fundamentally different from Muslims elsewhere; genealogically, religiously, ethnically. Yet, as the exhibit down the street at the Museo Arqueológico shows through the objects collected from his reign, Ibn Mardanīsh's material culture connected him more closely to the Islamic east than that of any previous ruler in al-Andalus. As I have argued here, material culture can encode ideology and reveal connections across space and time. What tracing Ibn Mardanīsh's material culture shows, in the incorporation of distant inspiration through processes of dynamic transformation, is the

3 The comic book was the first of the Ayuntamiento de Murcia's historical comic book series, *Historietas de la Historia. El Rey Lobo* was written by the archaeologist Pedro Jiménez Castillo and illustrated by Manuel Martínez Meseguer, and published in 2006. It was also the first of the trilogy entitled "La Murcia Islámica."

FIGURE P.1. Cover of the comic book, *El Rey Lobo*, written by Pedro Jiménez Castillo, design and drawings by Manuel Martínez Meseguer. Published by Ayuntamiento de Murcia, 2006.

interpenetration of ideas and forms, people and materials, across the Mediterranean. Ibn Mardanīsh, the Almohads, and the kings of Castile, Sicily, Aragon, and beyond all fought—and allied—to distinguish themselves as righteous and powerful, and their battles and treaties served as conduits for the movement of people, ideas, and goods.

The loss of al-Andalus, and the emergence of teleological narratives of Christian success or Muslim failure, began to create the still-potent vision of al-Andalus as a place apart, distinct from other regions of what are now called the Middle East *and* Europe. This was further exacerbated by the imposition of Enlightenment binaries, in what Bruno Latour called a process of purification, that separated the world into a series of dualisms, predicated most importantly on "modern" and nonmodern.[4] This scaffolding of modern/medieval, Western/non-Western, secular/religious is pernicious and distorting everywhere, but its failures are particularly visible in the discourse surrounding al-Andalus, which

4 Bruno Latour, *We Have Never Been Modern*, trans. Catherine Porter (Cambridge, MA: Harvard University Press, 1993).

is alternately forced into one side or the other of these dichotomies. If, following Latour, we allow for more than two modes of description, the myriad connections that link Ibn Mardanīsh; his rivals, allies, and successors; the objects they traded and gifted; men they employed; women they married; and buildings they constructed map a world of dynamic links, of flows, of transformations and continuities.[5]

But the power of the dichotomy, and of civilizational frameworks, has become so ingrained in popular culture that even as the story of Ibn Mardanīsh loses some of its nationalist luster, it is expanded to fit into a broader clash of civilizations. In the twenty-first century, as heightened anxieties about terrorism and refugees define much discussion in the West about Islam, Ibn Mardanīsh and the Almohads have been thrust into even more anachronistic roles. Having previously played the characters of a Spanish nationalist and rigid African invaders, they now appear as a fighter for freedom, secularism, and modernity and "the al-Qaeda of the Middle Ages," respectively.[6] Ibn Mardanīsh and the Almohads have been assessed following the same pattern Mahmood Mamdani detected in the op-ed pages of the New York Times after 9/11, in which "good Muslims are modern, secular and Westernized, but bad Muslims are doctrinal, antimodern and virulent."[7] Thus, the Almohads are imagined as terrorists fixated on killing Christians, and Ibn Mardanīsh is celebrated as a "good" (i.e., secular or assimilated) Muslim. These portrayals, omnipresent in popular histories, local commemorations, and news reports, offer another vision of "Spanish" Islam in a new era of violence.

In the aftermath of the Madrid bombings in March 2004, President José María Aznar was defeated at the polls and became a lecturer at Georgetown. In a lecture he gave there, he argued that Spain's battle against Islamic terrorism had begun already in the eighth century, "when a Spain recently invaded by the Moors refused to become just

---

5 As Latour argues, moving beyond these dualisms requires us to "manage *at last* to count beyond two," since "the raw and the cooked, nature and culture, words and things, the sacred and the profane, the real and the constructed, the abstract and the concrete, the savage and the civilized, and even the dualism of the modern and the premodern, do not seem to get our investigator very far." Latour, *An Inquiry into Modes of Existence: An Anthropology of the Moderns,* trans. Catherine Porter (Cambridge, MA: Harvard University Press, 2013), 146.

6 This label appears in passing in Hugh Thomas, *Rivers of Gold: The Rise of the Spanish Empire from Columbus to Magellan* (New York: Random House, 2003). For a critique, see Simon Doubleday, "Introduction: 'Criminal non-intervention'; Hispanism, Medievalism and the Pursuit of Neutrality," in *In the Light of Medieval Spain: Islam, the West, and the Relevance of the Past,* ed. S. Doubleday and D. Coleman (New York: Springer, 2008), 14.

7 Mamdani, *Good Muslim, Bad Muslim,* 24.

another piece in the Islamic world and began a long battle to recover its identity."[8] The idea that the Reconquista constituted the "first" war on terror and that it was Spaniards' fighting invading "Moors" that had given birth to the nation derived from Aznar's readings of Ménendez Pidal and Sánchez-Albornoz.[9] In more recent years, calls for a "nueva Reconquista," rejecting Muslim immigrants and politically correct attitudes toward Islam in favor of a militant return to an imagined medieval Christian national identity, have found unexpected support at the polls, as the ultra-right Vox party has swept into power across Spain.[10] In 2019, Vox won the largest share of the votes in the region of Murcia, making it the only region dominated by this party. Vox's leadership describes the Middle Ages as a period of glory, when Spain saved Europe by fighting Islam, and promises to reassert a unified Christian identity against encroaching forces of secularism and Islam that it sees as threatening Europe anew.[11]

In this context, Ibn Mardanīsh seems to be having a new moment in the limelight. For those who see Islam as dangerous and the Reconquista as heroic history, Ibn Mardanīsh's alliance with Christians against Muslim "invaders" offers a narrative that can assimilate some of Andalusī history into a Christian Spanish framework. In 2012, the writer Sebastián Roa published a novel called *La Loba de al-Ándalus* ("The she-wolf of al-Andalus") that focused on Ibn Mardanish's wife and includes much of the narrative of his loyalty to Christians and enmity to the Almohads found in historical sources.[12] In the book, Ibn Mardanīsh is described as descended from Christians, brave and loyal to his Christian allies, who is devoted to fighting the fearsome military machine of the Almohads, powered by fanaticism, who have abandoned their African mountains to attack the lovers of the Cross. The Christians are too caught up in their own rivalries to stop the Almohads—only Ibn

8 Quoted in Alejandro García-Sanjuan, "Rejecting al-Andalus," 133.

9 García-Sanjuan, "Rejecting al-Andalus," 134.

10 On Vox and its use of the Middle Ages, see, for example, Guillermo Altares, "Why the Middle Ages Have Become Incredibly Relevant: Far-Right Parties like Vox in Spain Use Doubtful Historical Facts to Justify Their Vision of a Modern-Day Islamic Invasion," *El Pais*, August 1, 2019, https://elpais.com/elpais/2019/08/01/inenglish/1564673082_675360.html.

11 Ivan Espinosa de los Monteros, Vox's vice-secretary of international relations, said: "Europe is what it is, thanks to Spain. Thanks to our contribution, ever since the Middle Ages, of stopping the spread of Islam. History matters and we shouldn't be afraid of that." See Francis Ghilès, "Vox Reinvents History to Claim 'Reconquista' of Spain," *The Arab Weekly*, November 17, 2019, https://thearabweekly.com/vox-reinvents-history-claim-reconquista-spain.

12 Sebastián Roa, *La loba de al-Ándalus* (Madrid: Ediciones B, 2012).

Mardanīsh, in this vision, can save Spain from a terrible fate. A vision of invading hordes from Africa carried particular meaning in the moment when this book was published, of course—in 2011, the year before the book was published, record numbers of Tunisians and other North Africans fleeing the instability caused by the Arab Spring began to arrive in Southern Europe. In the years that followed the publication of this book, the number of migrants continued to increase. The author Roa lives in Valencia, within the former territories of Ibn Mardanīsh, where he works as a police inspector when he is not writing novels. This region, alongside Cataluña to its north and Andalucía to the south, have the largest populations of foreign residents in Spain. Murcia, too, has substantial numbers of immigrants, many of whom work in the region's agricultural areas, and some 42 percent of whom are of African origin.[13] This rise in immigration has contributed to a backlash that has brought a wave of ultraright parties campaigning on anti-immigration agendas to power.

Ibn Mardanīsh has become steadily more visible in popular culture in exactly the same years that Islamophobic and anti-immigrant discourse has increased. In 2018, Roa published an article about Ibn Mardanīsh in the right-wing newspaper *ABC* that extended his reading of Ibn Mardanīsh's significance more explicitly to the present day. In the article, he called Ibn Mardanīsh "the scourge of the jihadis" and positioned his cultural production and alliances within a framework of Christian-Muslim enmity.[14] The article opens with a discussion of the image of the *mizmār* player in Dār al-Ṣughrā, writing:

> Although anthropomorphic representation—opposed by the Muslim tradition—was not strange for the Andalusis, this [image] stands out in its temporal context. Half of the Iberian Peninsula found itself invaded by the most fanatical Muslim caliphate of all of those that North Africa has disgorged: the Almohad empire. And the Andalusi king who dared to defy them for a quarter of a

---

13 *La inmigración en España: Efectos y oportunidades,* Consejo Económico y Social España, Informe 02|2019. http://www.ces.es/documents/10180/5209150/Inf0219.pdf. See especially the map on p. 74 and table on p. 75.

14 Sebastián Roa, "El Rey Lobo, el azote de los yihadistas del siglo XII," *ABC*, August 20, 2018, https://www.abc.es/cultura/abci-lobo-azote-yihadistas-siglo-201808190211_noticia.html.

century was Muhammad ibn Saʿd ibn Mardanish, better known as the Wolf King.[15]

Later, Roa notes Ibn Mardanīsh's Christian blood and asserts that he "hated radical Islam." He refers to the Almohads as the "Daesh" of their period because of their *takfīr* (calling fellow Muslims unbelievers), their emphasis on *tawḥīd*, and their treatment of Jews and Christians, and he says that Ibn Mardanīsh was known for speaking Romance, dressing like a Christian, permitting the construction of churches in his realm, and enjoying wine and other "non-Moorish" pleasures.[16] The article concludes with the claim that Ibn Mardanīsh's death and the conquest of his territories by the Almohads led to an "Iberian agony" "from which our ancestors were only able to deliver us in the summer of 1212"—at the Battle of Las Navas de Tolosa.[17] Ibn Mardanīsh is here made part of the national narrative rooted in the Reconquista, fighting the "African invaders" and "radical Islam"—a Spanish Muslim hero who can be used to integrate the Islamic past into a proud national identity.

The narrative elements (the *akhbār*) present in this 2018 article have their roots in medieval sources. We can trace the topoi of Ibn Mardanīsh's decadence, his drinking and womanizing, and his concessions to Christians to Ibn al-Khaṭīb and to earlier Almohad chronicles. But in the article these elements are interpreted through an entirely modern framework in which national boundaries and bloodlines determine ideology and religious practice is defined by the letter of the law. Ibn Mardanīsh is a regional and national hero precisely because he does not follow the "Moorish" restrictions on pleasures, because he is "Spanish" in his love of drink and women, and because his daughters "conquer" the enemy through seduction, like Spanish women have allegedly done throughout history. This vision of Ibn Mardanīsh risks not only misunderstanding the attitudes and intentions of the twelfth-, fourteenth-, and seventeenth-century authors from whose writings it is ultimately drawn but also

15 Roa, "El Rey Lobo": "Aunque la representación antropomórfica—contraria a la tradición musulmana—no es extraña a los andalusíes, ésta destaca en su contexto temporal. Media península ibérica se encontraba invadida por el califato musulmán más fanático de cuantos ha vomitado el norte de África: el imperio almohade. Y el Rey andalusí que se atrevió a desafiarlo durante un cuarto de siglo fue Muhammad ibn Saʿd ibn Mardánish, mejor conocido como Rey Lobo."

16 Roa, "El Rey Lobo": "También se dice que hablaba en romance, vestía al modo cristiano, permitía la construcción de iglesias en sus dominios y se daba al vino y a otros placeres poco morunos."

17 Roa, "El Rey Lobo."

reifying pernicious attitudes about religion and identity that carry significant ideological weight today. If Ibn Mardanīsh is a "good" Muslim for his fight against other Muslims and for his sinfulness, is a Muslim who does *not* drink and have promiscuous sex a jihadi threat? Such patently absurd ideas have been recently gaining ground in Europe and the United States, as politicians such as President Emmanuel Macron of France advocate a "society of vigilance" against an Islamist "hydra" whose signs, his interior minister suggested, can be seen in prayer, fasting in Ramaḍān, and refusing to drink alcohol.[18]

In Roa's 2018 article, and in the other popular depictions of Ibn Mardanīsh, the framework for understanding the history of the Iberian Peninsula is one of implacable Christian-Muslim enmity, a polarized vision in which Christians and Muslims were not simply at war on the battlefield but rooted in fundamentally different systems. This vision—a historiographic construct, as Alejandro Garcia Sanjuan has shown so compellingly—is also predicated on a series of polarized dualities that posit as incommensurable Europe/non-Europe, modern/nonmodern, legitimate violence/illegitimate violence, and so forth.[19] In this framework, the Christian knights and kings of the northern Iberian Peninsula are presented as the progenitors of modern Spain and Portugal, and the Almohads as terrifying, irrational invaders, as the "Daesh" of the Middle Ages. In such a framework, Ibn Mardanīsh can be inserted on the "Christian" side—he is flexible, a brave defender, a European, a Spaniard.

Following Ibn Mardanīsh's treatment in sources from the thirteenth century to the present offers instructive insight into the ways in which historical narratives can be deployed in debates over contemporary concerns. It also shows how the idea of al-Andalus as a cautionary tale, an imagined paradise, and a locus of premodern protosecularism and tolerance developed and how these divergent visions continue to distort

---

18 "France Needs 'Society of Vigilance' against Islamist 'Hydra': Macron," Reuters, October 8, 2019, https://www.reuters.com/article/us-france-security-victims-macron/france-needs-society-of-vigilance-against-islamist-hydra-macron-idUSKBN1WN168; "Castaner Bristles after Social Media Backlash over Muslims and Beards List," RFI, October 10, 2019, http://en.rfi.fr/france/20191010-france-s-interior-christophe-minister-condemns-social-media-backlash.

19 On the continuing relevance of this National-Catholic discourse of invasion and "reconquest," see especially García Sanjuan, "La persistencia del discurso nationalcatólico sobre el Medievo peninsular en la historiografía española actual," *Historiografías* 12 (2016): 132–53. As García Sanjuan notes, contemporary historiography on the Spanish past is often rooted in a kind of Islamophobia that is more subtle than that expounded by the far-right politicians but which nevertheless cannot imagine space for Muslims within Europe, even in the past.

our understanding of the past. For Ibn al-Khaṭīb, writing in exile, Ibn Mardanīsh posed a warning to his former patrons that they, like their twelfth-century predecessor, could lose power and be remembered as helpers to the Christians and traitors to their own people. Later scholars such as al-Maqqarī, writing after al-Andalus had fallen, could not conceive of a Muslim who fought his fellow Muslims and, knowing where the story was heading, remade him into a secret Christian or his enemies into Christian infidels. Transforming Ibn Mardanīsh in this way seemed to explain the collapse of the wealthy and powerful dynasties of al-Andalus. Ironically, by emphasizing Ibn Mardanīsh's connections to Christians, Arabic historians facilitated his later reification as a Spanish nationalist hero who fought the Almohads out of loyalty to his Iberian identity, or as a warrior for the "secular" west against forces of intolerance. Today, his fierce resistance to the Almohads has made him one of the "good" Andalusī Muslims who can be celebrated by historians and regional governments alike.

No doubt Ibn Mardanīsh would be puzzled by his later depiction in sources across the centuries and by twenty-first-century Murcians purporting to dress up like him and his retinue. The genealogies examined here work at cross-purposes: Ibn Mardanīsh's own cultural production sought to connect his dynasty to the Islamic East, whereas later writers have created a new lineage for him that emphasizes his difference from Eastern actors. The Arab genealogy Ibn Mardanīsh claimed and the language, iconography, and materials he deployed to articulate his connections to the power centers of the Islamic East reflected and helped constitute networks linking people and objects across space and time. They show a Mediterranean crisscrossed by connections, a world in which an upstart on the western edge of the Mediterranean could conjure the potent phrases and imagery of his imperial forebears and the distant caliph to support his bid for power.

But beginning with Ibn al-Khaṭīb and accelerating in the centuries after the conquest of Granada, we see the development of a teleological notion of the decline of the Islamic West that seeks to sever these connections and turn al-Andalus into a region unlike its southern or eastern peers. This notion has given rise to a new genealogy for Ibn Mardanīsh, one that focuses on his difference from other Muslim actors, either locating the cause of Andalusī decline in his insufficient piety or celebrating him as an emblem of the emergence of a secular, protonationalist Iberian identity. Ibn Mardanīsh has come to stand in for what was wrong about Andalusī Islam *and* for what was right about the Spain that would eventually emerge. In each of the periods studied in this book, historical arguments about Ibn Mardanīsh were really arguments about the present; he serves as a tool for arguing over anachronistic ideas of secularism, religiosity, Europe, and the Middle East. Like the idea of al-Andalus itself, Ibn Mardanīsh's biography has become fodder for contemporary debates over the relationships of Christianity and Islam, art and piety, East and West.

Bibliography

Primary Sources

ʿAbd al-Ḥamīd. *ʿAbd al-Ḥamīd al-kātib wa mā tabaqqā min rasāʾilihi*. Edited by Iḥsān ʿAbbās. Amman: Dār al-Shurūq, 1988.

ʿAbd al-Muʾmin. *Majmūʿat rasāʾil muwaḥḥidiyya min inshāʾ kuttāb al-dawla al-muʾminiyya*. Edited by Évariste Lévi-Provençal. Rabat: Maṭbūʿāt Maʿhad al-ʿUlūm al-ʿUlyā al-Maghribiyya, 1931.

ʿAllām, Mahdī. *Dirāsāt adabiyya*. Al-Qāhirah: Maktabat al-Shabāb, 1984.

ʿAzzāwī, Aḥmad, ed. *Rasāʾil muwaḥḥidiyya: Majmūʿa jadīda*. 2 vols. al-Qunayṭira: Jāmiʿat Ibn Ṭufayl, Kulliyyat al-Ādāb wa-l-ʿUlūm al-Insāniyya, 1995.

Abū Dāwūd. *Sunan Abu Dawud*. 5 vols. Edited by Imām Hāfiz Abū Dāwūd, Sulaiman bin Ash'ath, and Hāfiz Abu Tāhir Zubair ʿAlī Zaʿī. Translated by Yaser Qadhi. Vol. 1. Riyadh: Maktaba Dar-us-Salam, 2008.

Amari, Michele, ed. *I diploma arabi del R. Archivio Fiorentini*. Florence: F. le Monnier, 1863.

Anonymous. *al-Hulal al-mawšiyya: Crónica árabe de las dinastias almorávide, almohade y benimerín*. Translated by Ambrosio Huici Miranda. Tetouan: Editora Marroquí, 1951.

—. *al-Ḥulal al-mawshiyya fī dhikr al-akhbār al-marrākshiyya*. Edited by Abd al-Qādir Zamāma and Suhayl Zukkār. Casablanca: Dār al-Rushshād al-Ḥadītha, 1979.

Arberry, A. J., trans. *The Koran Interpreted*. New York: Macmillan, 1955.

Barton, Simon, and Richard Fletcher, ed. and trans. "Chronica Adefonsi Imperatoris." In *The World of the Cid*, 148–263. Manchester: Manchester University Press, 2000.

al-Ḍabbī, Aḥmad b. Yaḥyā b. ʿAmīra. *Bughyat al-multamis fī tārīkh rijāl ahl al-Andalus*. Edited by al-Hawarī. Beirut: Dār al-Kutub al-ʿIlmiyya, 2005.

Deverdun, Gaston. *Les inscriptions arabes de Marrakech*. Rabat: Imprimerie de l'Agdal, 1956.

al-Dhahabī, Muḥammad b. Aḥmad. *Siyar aʿlām al-nubalāʾ*. Edited by Shu'ayb al-Arnāʾūṭ. Beirut: Mu'assasat al-Risāla, 1985.

Diago, Francisco. *Historia de los victoriosissimos antigvos Condes de Barcelona*. Barcelona: Sebastian de Cormellas, 1603.

Dozy, Reinhart Pieter Anne, ed. *Notices sur quelques manuscrits arabes*. Leiden: Brill, 1847.

Flórez, Enrique, ed. "Anales Toledanos." In *España Sagrada*, Vol. 23. Madrid: Antonio Marin, 1767.

al-Ghazālī. *Faḍā'iḥ al-bāṭiniyya wa-faḍā'il al-mustaẓhiriyya*. Edited by ʿAbd al-Raḥmān Badawī. 4 vols. Cairo: al-Dār al-Qawmiyya, 1964.

—. *Freedom and Fulfillment: An Annotated Translation of al-Ghazālī's al-Munqidh Min al-Ḍalāl and Other Relevant Works of al-Ghazālī*. Translated by Richard Joseph McCarthy. Boston: Twayne Publishers, 1980.

—. *Iḥyā ʿulūm al-dīn = The Book of Knowledge*. Translated by Nabih Amin Faris. Delhi: Islamic Book Service, 1962.

al-Ḥakīm, ʿAlī ibn Yūsuf. "al-Dawḥa al-mushtabika fī ḍawābit dār al-sikka." Edited by Hussein Mónes. *Revisto del Instituto de Estudios Islámicos en Madrid* 6, no. 1–2 (1958): 63–204.

Ibn al-Abbār. *al-Takmila li-kitāb al-ṣila*. Edited by Ibrāhīm al-Abyārī. Beirut: Dār al-Kitāb al-Lubnānī, 1989.

—. *Kitāb al-takmila li-kitāb al-ṣila: Complementum libri assilah (dictionarium Biographicum)*. Edited by Francisco Codera y Zaidín. Madrid: Romero, 1886.

Ibn Abī Zarʿ. *al-Anīs al-muṭrib bi-rawḍ al-qirṭās fī akhbār mulūk al-Maghrib wa-tārīkh madīnat Fās*. Edited by ʿAbd al-Wahhāb Bin Manṣūr. Rabat: al-Maṭbaʿa al-Malikiyya, 1999.

—. *Rawḍ al-qirṭās*. Translated by Ambrosio Huici Miranda. Valencia: Anubar, 1964.

Ibn Ḥamdīs. *Dīwān*. Edited by I. ʿAbbās. Beirut: Dār Bayrūt, 1960.

Ibn Ḥubaysh. *Kitāb al-ghazawāt*. Edited by Aḥmad Ghunaym. Cairo: Maṭbaʿat Ḥassān, 1983.

Ibn ʿIdhārī al-Marrākushī. *al-Bayān al-mughrib fī akhbār al-Andalus wa-l-Maghrib*. Edited by G. S. Colin and Évariste Lévi-Provençal. Beirut: Dār al-Kutub al-ʿIlmiyya, 2009.

—. *al-Bayān al-mughrib fī akhbār al-Andalus wa-l-Maghrib: Qism al-Muwaḥḥidīn*. Edited by M. I. al-Kattānī, M. Ibn Tāwīt, M. Znaybar and ʿA. Q. Zamāma. Beirut: Dār al-Gharb al-Islāmī, 1985.

Ibn Khaldūn, ʿAbd al-Raḥmān ibn Muḥammad. *Kitāb al-ʿIbār = Histoire des Berbères et des dynasties Musulmanes de l'Afrique septentrionale*. Edited by Paul Casanova. Translated by William MacGuckin de Slane. Paris: Geuthner, 1982.

—. *The Muqaddimah: An Introduction to History—Abridged Edition*. Translated by Franz Rosenthal. New York: Pantheon, 1958.

Ibn Khallikān. *Wafayāt al-aʿyān*. Edited by Ihsān ʿAbbās. Beirut: Dār al-Thaqāfa, 1971.

Ibn al-Khaṭīb. *al-Iḥāṭa fī akhbār gharnāṭa*. Edited by Yūsuf ʿAlī Ṭawīl. Beirut: Dār al-Kutub al-ʿIlmiyya, 2003.

—. *Aʿmāl al-aʿlām*. Edited by Évariste Lévi-Provençal. Beirut: Dār al-Makshūf, 1956.

—. *Aʿmāl al-aʿlām*. Edited by Sayyid Kasrawī Ḥasan. Beirut: Dār al-Kutub al-ʿIlmiyya, 2003.

Ibn Māja. *Sunan Ibn Mâjah*. Edited by Imām Muhammad Bin Yazeed, Ibn Majah Al-Qazwinī, and Hāfiz Abu Tāhir Zubair 'Ali Za'i. Translated by Nasiruddin al-Khattab. Vol. 5.5 vols. Riyadh: Maktaba Dar-us-Salam, 2007.

Ibn al-Qalānisī, Abū Yaʿlā Ḥamza ibn Asad. *Tārīkh Abī Yaʿlā Ḥamza Ibn al-Qalānisī: al-Maʿrūf bi-dhayl tārīkh Dimashq*. Edited by Hilāl ibn al-Muḥassin Ṣābī and H. F. Amedroz. Beirut: Maṭbaʿat al-Ābāʾ al-Yasūʿiyyīn, 1908.

Ibn al-Qaṭṭān. *Nuẓum al-jumān li-tartīb mā salafa min akhbār al-zamān*. Edited by Maḥmūd Makkī. Beirut: Dār al-Gharb al-Islāmī, 1990.

Ibn Qasī. *Kitāb khal' al-na'layn wa-iqtibās al-nūr min mawḍi' al-qadamayn*. Edited by Muḥammad al-Amrānī. Safi, Morocco: IMBH, 1997.

Ibn Ṣāḥib al-Ṣalā. *Tārīkh al-mann bi-l-imāma 'alā al-mustaḍ'afīn bi-an ja'alahum Allāh a'imma wa-ja'alahum al-wārithīn*. Edited by 'Abd al-Hādī Tāzī. Beirut: Dār al-Andalus, 1964.

Ibn Tūmart. *Le livre d'Ibn Toumert* (*Kitāb al-a'azz mā yuṭlab*). Edited by J. D. Luciani. Algiers: P. Fontana, 1903.

Ibn al-Zubayr, Abū Ja'far Aḥmad ibn Ibrāhīm. *Ṣilat al-ṣila*. Edited by 'A. S. al-Harrās and S. A'rāb. Rabat: Wizārat al-Awqāf wa-l-Shu'ūn al-Islāmiyya, 1993.

al-Idrīsī. *Description de l'Afrique et de l'Espagne*. Edited and translated by Reinhart Pieter Anne Dozy and Michael Jan de Goeje. Leiden: Brill, 1866.

Imperiale di Sant'Angelo, Cesare, ed. *Codice diplomatico della repubblica di Genova*. Vol. 1. Rome: Tipografia del Senato, 1936.

Jiménez de Rada. *Historia Arabum*. Edited by J. Lozano Sánchez. Seville: Secretariado de Publicaciones de la Universidad de Sevilla, 1974.

Lévi-Provençal, Évariste, ed. *Documents inédits d'histoire almohade*. Paris: P. Geuthner, 1928.

—, ed. *Inscriptions arabes d'Espagne*. Leiden: Brill, 1931.

Lucas de Tuy. *El Chronicon Mundi de Lucas de Tuy: Edición crítica y estudio*. Edited by O. Valdés García. Salamanca: Ediciones Universidad de Salamanca, 1996.

al-Maqqarī, Aḥmad ibn Muḥammad. *Analectes sur l'histoire et la littérature des Arabes d'Espagne*. Edited by Ludolf Krehl. Vol. 5. Leiden: Brill, 1855.

—. *Nafḥ al-ṭīb min ghuṣn al-Andalus al-raṭīb*. Edited by Iḥsān Abbās. Beirut: Dār Ṣādir, 1968.

al-Marrākushī, 'Abd al-Wāḥid. *al-Mu'jib fī talkhīṣ akhbār al-Andalus*. Edited by Khalīl 'Umrān al-Manṣūr. Beirut: Dār al-Kutub al-'Ilmiyya, 2003.

—. *Crónicas árabes de la reconquista = Kitāb al-Mu'jib fī* talkhīṣ *akhbār al-mugrib*. Translated by Ambrosio Huici Miranda. Tetouan: Editora Marroquí, 1955.

—. *Kitāb al-mu'jib fī al-talkhīṣ*. Edited by Muḥammad Sa'īd al-'Aryān. Cairo: Lajna Iḥyā al-Turāth al-Islāmī, 1962.

al-Marrākushī, Muḥammad ibn 'Abd al-Mālik. *Kitāb al-dhayl wa-l-takmila*. Edited by Muḥammad Bencherifa. 2 vols. Beirut: Dār al-Thaqāfa, 1971.

al-Māwardī. *Kitāb al-aḥkām al-sulṭāniyya*. Edited by Aḥmad Mubārak al-Baghdādī. Kuwait: Maktabat Dār al-Qutayba, 1989.

—. *The Ordinances of Government = Al-Aḥkām al-Sulṭāniyya w'al-Wilāyāt al-Dīniyya*. Translated by Wafaa Hassan Wahba. Reading: Garnet, 2006.

de Moret, José. *Anales de Reino de Navarra*. Pamplona: B. Huarte, 1695.

Ralph of Diceto. *Radulfi de Diceto Decani Lundoniensis Opera Historica: The Historical Works of Master Ralph de Diceto, Dean of London, Edited from the Original Manuscripts*. Edited by William Stubbs. London: H.M. Stationery Office, 1876.

Rey, Agapito, ed. *Castigos é documentos del Rey don Sancho IV*. Bloomington: Indiana University Press, 1952.

Robert of Torigni. *Chronique de Robert de Torigni, abbé du Mont-Saint-Michel.* Edited by Léopold Delisle. Rouen: Le Brument, 1872.

Roger of Hoveden. *The Annals.* Translated by Henry T. Riley. 2 vols. London: H. G. Bohn, 1853.

Secondary Sources

Abd al-Aziz Salem, Elsayed. "Algunos aspectos del florecimiento económico de Almería islámica durante el período de los Taifas y de los Almorávides." *Revista del Instituto Egipcio de Estudios Islámicos* 20, no. 80 (1979): 7–22.

—. "La Puerta del Perdón en la gran mezquita de la alcazaba almohade de Sevilla." *al-Andalus* 43 (1978): 201–8.

Abu-Lughod, Janet. *Before European Hegemony: The World System A.D. 1250–1350.* New York: Oxford University Press, 1989.

Aguilar, Victoria. "Fatima, Amat al-Rahman y otras mujeres en el mundo del saber de Murcia en el siglo XII." In *Mujeres de letras pioneras: En el arte, el ensayismo y la educación*, edited by María Gloria Ríos Guardiola, María Belén Hernández González, and Encarna Esteban Bernabé, 27–45. Murcia: Comunidad Autónoma de la Región de Murcia, 2016.

—. "Identidad y vida intelectual en la Murcia de Ibn Mardaniš." In *Política, sociedad e identidades en el occidente islámico (siglos XI-XIV)*, edited by M. A. Manzano and Rachid El Hour, 13–41. Salamanca: Ediciones Universidad de Salamanca, 2016.

—. "Tres generaciones y varios siglos de historia: Los Banū Burṭuluh de Murcia." In *Homenaje a José María Fórneas,* Estudios onomástico-biográficos de al-Andalus 7, edited by Manuela Marín and Helena de Felipe, 19–40. Madrid: Consejo Superior de Investigaciones Científicas, 1995.

Ahmed, Shahab. *What Is Islam? The Importance of Being Islamic.* Princeton, NJ: Princeton University Press, 2016.

Albarrán, Javier. "De la conversión y expulsión al mercenariado: La ideología en torno a los cristianos en las crónicas almohades." In *La Península Ibérica en tiempos de las Navas de Tolosa*, edited by Carlos Estepa Díez and María Antonia Carmona Ruiz, 79–91. Madrid: Sociedad Española de Estudios Medievales, 2014.

—. *Ejércitos benditos: Yihad y memoria en al-Andalus (siglos X–XIII)*. Granada: Universidad de Granada, 2020.

—. "The *Jihād* of the Caliphs and the First Battles of Islam." *Al-ʿUṣūr al-Wusṭā* 26 (2018): 113–50.

Ali, Nadia. "The Road from Decadence: Agendas and Personal Histories in the Study of Early Islamic Art." In *Empires of Faith in Late Antiquity: Histories of Art and Religion from India to Ireland*, edited by Jaś Elsner, 189–222. Cambridge: Cambridge University Press, 2020.

—. "The Royal Veil: Early Islamic Figural Art and the Bilderverbot Reconsidered." *Religion* 47, no. 3 (2017): 425–44.

Ali-de-Unzaga, Miriam. "Qur'anic Inscriptions on the 'Pennon of Las Navas de Tolosa' and Three Marinid Banners." In *Word of God, Art of Man: The Qur'an and Its Creative Expressions*, edited by Fahmida Suleman, 239–70. Oxford: Oxford University Press, 2007.

Almagro Basch, Martín. *Historia de Albarracín y su sierra.* Vol. 3. Teruel: Instituto de Estudios Terolenses, 1959.

Almagro Gorbe, Antonio, and Rafael Manzano Martos. "Palacios medievales hispanos: discurso del académico electo Excmo. Sr. D. Antonio Almagro Gorbea leído en el acto de su recepción pública el día 27 de enero de 2008 y contestación del Excmo. Sr. D. Rafael Manzano Martos." Granada: Real Academia de Bellas Artes de San Fernando, 2008.

Altares, Guillermo. "Why the Middle Ages Have Become Incredibly Relevant: Far-Right Parties like Vox in Spain Use Doubtful Historical Facts to Justify Their Vision of a Modern-Day Islamic Invasion." *El Pais*, August 1, 2019. https://elpais.com/elpais/2019/08/01/inenglish/1564673082_675360.html.

Anderson, Glaire D. "Villa (*Munya*) Architecture in Umayyad Córdoba: Preliminary Considerations." In *Revisiting Al-Andalus: Perspectives on the Material Culture of Islamic Iberia and Beyond*, edited by Glaire D. Anderson and Mariam Rosser-Owen, 53–81. Leiden: Brill, 2007.

Antuña, M. M. "Una versión árabe compendiada de la 'Estoria de España' de Alfonso el Sabio." *Al-Andalus* 1, no. 1 (1933): 105–28.

Appadurai, Arjun. "Introduction: Commodities and the Politics of Value." In *The Social Life of Things: Commodities in Cultural Perspective*, edited by Arjun Appadurai, 3–63. Cambridge: Cambridge University Press, 1986.

Arnold, Felix. *Der islamische Palast auf der Alcazaba von Almería.* Wiesbaden: Reichert, 2008.

——. *Islamic Palace Architecture in the Western Mediterranean: A History*. Oxford: Oxford University Press, 2017.

Arslān, Shakīb. *al-Ḥulal al-sundusiyya fī al-akhbār wa-l-āthār al-Andalusiyya*. Beirut: Dār al-Kutub al-ʿIlmiyya, 1997.

Asad, Talal. *Formations of the Secular: Christianity, Islam, Modernity*. Stanford, CA: Stanford University Press, 2003.

Aʿrāb, Saʾīd. "Mawqif al-Muwaḥḥidīn min kutub al-furūʿ wa-ḥaml al-nās ʿalā al-madhhab al-ḥazmī." *Daʿwat al-Haqq* 249 (1985): 26–30.

Bacharach, Jere L. "Laqab for a Future Caliph: The Case of the Abbasid al-Mahdī." *Journal of the American Oriental Society* 113, no. 2 (1993): 271–74.

——. "Signs of Sovereignty: The Shahada, Qur'anic Verses, and the Coinage of ʿAbd al-Malik." *Muqarnas* 27 (2010): 1–30.

Baer, Eva. "The 'Pila' of Játiva: A Document of Secular Urban Art in Western Islam." *Kunst Des Orients* 7 no. 71 (1970): 142–66.

Balbale, Abigail. "Affiliation and Ideology at the End of the Almohad Caliphate." *Al-Masāq* 30, no. 3 (2018): 266–83.

——. "Bridging Seas of Sand and Water: The Berber Dynasties of the Islamic Far West." In *A Companion to Islamic Art and Architecture*, edited by Finbarr Barry Flood and Gülru Necipoğlu, 1:356–77. Hoboken, NJ: Wiley-Blackwell, 2017.

Barceló, Carmen. "Estructura textual de los epitafios andalusíes (siglos IX–XIII)." In *Homenaje a Manuel Ocaña Jiménez*, 123–37. Cordoba: Junta de Andalucía, 1990.

Barrucand, Marianne. "Les enluminures de l'époque Almohade: Frontispices et *ʿUnwān*-s." In *Los Almohades: Problemas y perspectivas*, edited by Patrice

Cressier, Maribel Fierro, and Luis Molina, 1:71–121. Madrid: Consejo Superior de Investigaciones Científicas, 2005.

Barton, Simon. *The Aristocracy in Twelfth-Century León and Castile*. Cambridge: Cambridge University Press, 1997.

—. *Conquerors, Brides and Concubines: Interfaith Relations and Social Power in Medieval Iberia*. Philadelphia: University of Pennsylvania Press, 2015.

—. "Islam and the West: A View from Twelfth-Century León." In *Cross, Crescent and Conversion: Studies on Medieval Spain and Christendom in Memory of Richard Fletcher*, 153–74. Leiden: Brill, 2008.

—. "From Mercenary to Crusader: The Career of Álvar Pérez de Castro (d. 1239) Re-Examined." In *Church, State, Vellum and Stone: Essays on Medieval Spain in Honor of John Williams*, edited by Julie Harris and Therese Martin, 111–29. Leiden: Brill, 2005.

—. "Traitors to the Faith? Christian Mercenaries in al-Andalus and the Maghreb, c. 1100–1300." In *Medieval Spain: Culture, Conflict and Coexistence; Studies in Honour of Angus MacKay*, edited by Roger Collins and Anthony Goodman, 23–45. Basingstoke & New York: Palgrave Macmillan, 2002.

Bates, Michael. "Names and Titles on Islamic Coins: An Index." Unpublished, 2019. https://www.academia.edu/26072179/Names_and_Titles_on_Islamic_Coins.

Baxandall, Michael. "The Period Eye." In *Painting and Experience in Fifteenth Century Italy: A Primer in the Social History of Pictorial Style*, by Michael Baxandall, 29–108. Oxford: Oxford University Press, 1988.

Bellver, José. "'Al-Ghazālī of al-Andalus': Ibn Barrajān, Mahdism, and the Emergence of Learned Sufism on the Iberian Peninsula." *Journal of the American Oriental Society* 133, no. 4 (2013): 659–81.

Ben Azzouna, Nourane. "Les corans de l'occident musulman médiéval: État des recherches et nouvelles perspectives." *Perspective* 2 (2017): 103–30.

Bennison, Amira. *The Almoravid and Almohad Empires*. Edinburgh: Edinburgh University Press, 2016.

—. "Power and the City in the Islamic West from the Umayyads to the Almohads." In *Cities in the Pre-Modern Islamic World*, edited by Amira Bennison and Alison Gascoigne, 65–95. London: Routledge Curzon, 2007.

Bennison, Amira, and Maria Angeles Gallego. "Religious Minorities under the Almohads: An Introduction." *Journal of Medieval Iberian Studies* 2, no. 2 (2010): 143–54.

Berkey, Jonathan. *The Formation of Islam*. Cambridge: Cambridge University Press, 2003.

Bisson, T. N. *Fiscal Accounts of Catalonia under the Early Count-Kings (1151–1213)*. Berkeley: University of California Press, 1984.

Blair, Sheila. *The Monumental Inscriptions from Early Islamic Iran and Transoxiana*. Leiden: Brill, 2014.

Blankinship, Khalid Yahya. *The End of the Jihād State: The Reign of Hishām Ibn ʿAbd Al-Malik and the Collapse of the Umayyads*. Albany: State University of New York Press, 1994.

Blessing, Patricia, ed. "Draping, Wrapping, Hanging: Transposing Textile Materiality in the Middle Ages." *Textile Museum Journal* (special issue) 45 (2018): 3–21.

Bloom, Jonathan M. "Almoravid Geometrical Designs in the Pavement of the Cappella Palatina in Palermo." In *The Iconography of Islamic Art: Studies in Honour of Robert Hillenbrand*, edited by Bernard O'Kane, 61–80. Edinburgh: Edinburgh University Press, 2005.

—. "The Minbar from the Kutubiyya Mosque." In *The Minbar from the Kutubiyya Mosque*, edited by Jonathan M. Bloom, Ahmed Toufiq, Stefano Carboni, Jack Soultanian, Antoine M. Wilmering, Mark D. Minor, Andrew Zawacki, and El Mostafa Hbibi, 3–30. New York: Metropolitan Museum of Art, 1998.

Bongianino, Umberto. "The Origin and Development of Maghribī Round Scripts: Arabic Palaeography in the Islamic West (4th/10th–6th/12th Centuries)." PhD diss., Oxford University, 2017.

Bonine, Michael. "Sacred Direction and City Structure: A Preliminary Analysis of the Islamic Cities of Morocco." *Muqarnas* 7 (1990): 50–72.

Bonner, Michael. *Jihad in Islamic History: Doctrines and Practice*. Princeton, NJ: Princeton University Press, 2008.

Bosch Vilá, Jacinto. "¿Mocárabes en el arte de la taifa de Almería?" *Cuadernos de Historia del Islam (Universidad de Granada)* 8 (1977): 139–60.

Brett, Michael. "Le Mahdi dans le Maghreb médiéval." *Revue des mondes musulmans et de la Mediterranée* 91–94 (2000): 93–106.

—. *The Rise of the Fatimids: The World of the Mediterranean and the Middle East in the Fourth Century of the Hijra, Tenth Century CE*. Leiden: Brill, 2001.

Brett, Michael, and Elizabeth Fentress. *The Berbers*. Oxford: Blackwell, 1996.

Brockelmann, Carl. *Geschichte der arabischen Litteratur*. 2nd ed. Leiden: Brill, 1937.

Brown, Jonathan A. C. *Hadith: Muhammad's Legacy in the Medieval and Modern World*. Oxford: Oneworld, 2009.

Bru, Meritxell. "Posar un nom. Els Almoràvits com a Moabites a finals del segle XI." *Faventia* 31 (2009): 129–49.

Brubaker, Leslie. "The Elephant and the Ark: Cultural and Material Interchange across the Mediterranean in the Eighth and Ninth Centuries." *Dumbarton Oaks Papers* 58 (2004): 175–95.

Bulliet, Richard W. *Conversion to Islam in the Medieval Period: An Essay in Quantitative History*. Cambridge, MA: Harvard University Press, 1979.

Buresi, Pascal. "Les documents arabes et latins échangés entre Pise et l'Empire almohade en 596-598/1200-1202." In *Documents et histoire, Islam VIIe–XVIe siècles*, edited by A. Regourd, 13–96. Geneva: Droz, 2013.

Buresi, Pascal, and Hicham El Aallaoui. *Governing the Empire: Provincial Administration in the Almohad Caliphate (1224–1269)*. Translated by Travis Bruce. Leiden: Brill, 2013.

Cabrera Lafuente, Ana. "Textiles from the Museum of San Isidoro (León): New Evidence for Re-Evaluating Their Chronology and Provenance." In *The Medieval Iberian Treasury in the Context of Cultural Interchange*, edited by Therese Martin, expanded ed., 81–117. Leiden: Brill, 2020.

de las Cagigas, Isidro. *Los mudéjares*. Madrid: Instituto de Estudios Africanos, 1948.

—. "Problemas de minoría y el caso de nuestro medievo." *Hispania* 40 (1950): 506–38.

Calderwood, Eric. *Colonial Al-Andalus: Spain and the Making of Modern Moroccan Culture*. Cambridge, MA: Harvard University Press, 2018.

Calvo Capilla, Susana. "El arte de los reinos taifas: tradición y ruptura." *Anales de Historia del Arte* 69, no. 2 (2011): 69–92.

Carillo Calderero, Alicia. "Architectural Exchanges between North Africa and al-Andalus: The Introduction of Muqarnas." *Journal of North African Studies* 19 (2014): 68-82.

—. "La decoración de mocárabes de la *Dār al-Ṣughrā* en Murcia: orientalismo en el arte de Ibn Mardanīš." In *Rey Lobo: El legado de Ibn Mardanīš, 1147–1172,* edited by Jorge A. Eiroa and Mariángeles Gómez Ródenas, 68–81. Murcia: Comunidad Autónoma de la Región de Murcia, 2019.

—. "Decoración tridimensional en Al-Ándalus: Introducción y uso de mocárabes." *Boletín del Museo el Instituto Camón Aznar* 104 (2009): 47–74.

—. "Origen geográfico de los muqarnas: Estado de la cuestión." *Al-Mulk: Anuario de estudios arabistas* 5 (2005): 33–48.

Carmona, Alfonso. "Represión y abuso de poder en el régimen de Ibn Mardanīš." In *De muerte violenta: política, religión y violencia en Al-Andalus*, Estudios onomástico-biográficos de al Andalus 14, edited by Maribel Fierro, 321–48. Madrid: Consejo Superior de Investigaciones Científicas, 2004.

—. "El saber y el poder: Cuarenta biografías de ulemas levantinos de época de Ibn Mardaniš." In *Biografías almohades*, Estudios onomástico-biográficos de al-Andalus 10, edited by María Luisa Ávila and Maribel Fierro, 2:57–129. Madrid: Consejo Superior de Investigaciones Científicas, 2000.

Cary, George. *The Medieval Alexander.* Edited by D. J. A. Ross. Cambridge: Cambridge University Press, 1956.

Casado Lobato, Concepción. "¿Un intento de secesión asturiana en el siglo XII?" *Asturiensia medievalia* (*Universidad de Oviedo, Departmento de Historia Medieval*) 3 (1979): 163–72.

Casamar Pérez, Manuel. "The Almoravids and Almohads: An Introduction." In *Al-Andalus: The Arts of Islamic Spain*, edited by Jerrilyn D. Dodds, 74–83. New York: Abrams, 1992.

Casewit, Yousef. *The Mystics of Al-Andalus: Ibn Barrajān and Islamic Thought in the Twelfth Century.* Cambridge: Cambridge University Press, 2017.

"Castaner Bristles after Social Media Backlash over Muslims and Beards List." *RFI*, October 10, 2019. http://en.rfi.fr/france/20191010-france-s-interior-christophe-minister-condemns-social-media-backlash.

Catalina García, Juan. *La Alcarria en los dos primeros siglos de su reconquista : discursos leídos ante la Real Academia de la Historia en la recepción publica del sr. Juan Catalina García en 27 de mayo de 1894.* Madrid: El Progreso, 1894.

Chakravorty Spivak, Gayatri. "Can the Subaltern Speak?" In *Marxism and the Interpretation of Culture,* edited by Cary Nelson and Lawrence Grossberg, 271–313. Basingstoke: Macmillan, 1988.

Clarke, Nicola. *The Muslim Conquest of Iberia: Medieval Arabic Narratives.* London: Routledge, 2012.

Clément, François. *Pouvoir et légitimité en Espagne musulmane à l'époque des taifas (Ve-XIe siècle): L'imam fictif.* Paris: Harmattan, 1977.

Clifford, James. *The Predicament of Culture: Twentieth-Century Literature, Ethnography and Art.* Cambridge, MA: Harvard University Press, 1998.

Codera y Zaidín, Francisco. *Decadencia y desaparición de los almoravides de España.* Edited by María Jesús Viguera Molíns. Pamplona: Urgoiti Editores, 2004.

Conde, José Antonio. *Historia de la dominación de los Árabes en España*. Madrid: Marín y Compañía, Editores, 1874.

Constable, Olivia Remie. *Housing the Stranger in the Mediterranean World: Lodging, Trade, and Travel in Late Antiquity and the Middle Ages*. New York: Cambridge University Press, 2003.

—. "Regulating Religious Noise: The Council of Vienne, the Mosque Call and Muslim Pilgrimage in the Late Medieval Mediterranean World." *Medieval Encounters* 16 (2010): 64–95.

—. "Ringing Bells in Ḥafṣid Tunis: Religious Concessions to Christian Fondacos in the Later Thirteenth Century." In *Histories of the Middle East: Studies in Middle Eastern Society, Economy and Law in Honor of A.L. Udovitch*, edited by Roxani Eleni Margariti, Adam Sabra, and Petra M. Sijpesteijn, 53–72. Leiden: Brill, 2011.

—. *Trade and Traders in Muslim Spain: The Commercial Realignment of the Iberian Peninsula, 900–1500*. Cambridge: Cambridge University Press, 1994.

Contadini, Anna. "Fatimid Ivories within a Mediterranean Culture." Edited by K. von Folsach and J. Meyer. *The Ivories of Muslim Spain: The Journal of the David Collection* 2 (2005): 226–47.

—. "The Pisa Griffin and the Mari-Cha Lion: History, Art and Technology." In *The Pisa Griffin and the Mari-Cha Lion. Metalwork, Art and Technology in the Medieval Islamicate Mediterranean*, edited by Anna Contadini, 197–256. Pisa: Pacini Editore, 2018.

Cook, Michael. *Commanding Right and Forbidding Wrong in Islamic Thought*. Cambridge: Cambridge University Press, 2000.

Coope, Jessica A. *The Martyrs of Córdoba: Community and Family Conflict in an Age of Mass Conversion*. Lincoln: University of Nebraska Press, 1995.

Cornell, Vincent J. "Understanding Is the Mother of Ability: Responsibility and Action in the Doctrine of Ibn Tūmart." *Studia Islamica* 66 (1987): 71–103.

Cressier, Patrice. "Les portes monumentales urbaines almohades: symbols et fonctions." In *Los Almohades: Problemas y perspectivas*, edited by Patrice Cressier, Maribel Fierro, and Luis Molina, 1:149–87. Madrid: Consejo Superior de Investigaciones Científicas, 2005.

Crone, Patricia. *God's Rule: Government and Islam*. New York: Columbia University Press, 2004.

—. *Medieval Islamic Political Thought*. Edinburgh: Edinburgh University Press, 2004.

—. "Post-Colonialism in Tenth-Century Islam." *Der Islam* 83, no. 1 (2006): 2–38.

Crone, Patricia, and Martin Hinds. *God's Caliph: Religious Authority in the First Centuries of Islam*. Cambridge: Cambridge University Press, 1986.

Curtin, Philip. *Cross-Cultural Trade in World History*. Cambridge: Cambridge University Press, 1984.

Dahmani, Fatma. "Remarques sur quelques fragments de peinture murale trouvés a Murcie." *Tudmir: Revista del Museo Santa Clara, Murcia* 1 (2009): 163–75.

Dandel, Élisabeth. "Ibn Gaṭṭūs: Une Famille de Copistes-Enlumineurs à Valence (Espagne)." *Histoire de l'art* 24 (1993): 13–24.

Day, Florence. "The Inscription of the Boston 'Baghdad' Silk: A Note on Method in Epigraphy." *Ars Orientalis* 1 (1954): 191–94.

De Smet, Daniel. "The Prophet Muḥammad and His Heir ʿAlī: Their Historical, Metahistorical and Cosmological Roles in Ismāʿīlī Shīʿism." In *The Presence of the Prophet in Early Modern and Contemporary Islam*, edited by Denis Gril, Stefan Reichmuth, and Dilek Sarmis, 299–326. Leiden: Brill, 2022.

Dodds, Jerrilyn D. "Jativa Basin." In *Al-Andalus: The Arts of Islamic Spain*, edited by Jerrilyn D. Dodds, 261–63. New York: Abrams, 1992.

Dodds, Jerrilyn D., María Rosa Menocal, and Abigail Balbale. *The Arts of Intimacy: Christians, Jews and Muslims in the Making of Castilian Culture*. New Haven, CT: Yale University Press, 2008.

Domémech-Belda, Carolina. "Moneda y poder en tiempos de Ibn Mardanīš." In *Rey Lobo: El legado de Ibn Mardanīš, 1147–1172,* edited by Jorge A. Eiroa and Mariángeles Gómez Ródenas, 116–133. Murcia: Comunidad Autónoma de la Región de Murcia, 2019.

Donner, Fred. "The Sources of Islamic Conceptions of War." In *Just War and Jihad: Historical and Theoretical Perspectives on War and Peace in Western and Islamic Traditions*, edited by James Turner Johnson, 31–69. New York: Greenwood Press, 1991.

Doubleday, Simon. "Introduction: 'Criminal Non-Intervention'; Hispanism, Medievalism and the Pursuit of Neutrality." In *In the Light of Medieval Spain: Islam, the West and the Relevance of the Past*, edited by Simon Doubleday and David Coleman, 1–31. New York: Springer, 2008.

—. *The Lara Family: Crown and Nobility in Medieval Spain*. Cambridge, MA: Harvard University Press, 2001.

Douglas, Mary. *Purity and Danger: An Analysis of the Concepts of Pollution and Taboo*. London: Routledge, 1966.

Dozy, Reinhart Pieter Anne. *Recherches sur l'histoire et la littérature de l'Espagne pendant le moyen âge*. Leiden, 1881.

Dunlop, D. M."The Spanish Historian Ibn Ḥubaish." *Journal of the Royal Asiatic Society of Great Britain and Ireland* 73 (1941): 359–62.

Ebstein, Michael. "Was Ibn Qasī a Ṣūfī?" *Studia Islamica* 110 (2015): 196–232.

Ecker, Heather. *Caliphs and Kings: The Art and Influence of Islamic Spain. Selections from the Hispanic Society, New York*. Washington, DC: Smithsonian Institution, 2004.

Écochard, Michel. *Filiation de monuments grecs, byzantins et islamiques: Une question de géométrie*. Paris: P. Geuthner, 1977.

Eggen, Nora. "A Book Burner or Not? History and Myth: Revisiting al-Qāḍī ʿIyāḍ and the Controversies over al-Ghazālī in the Islamic West." *Journal of Arabic and Islamic Studies* 18 (2018): 87–109.

Eiroa, Jorge A., and Mariángeles Gómez Ródenas, "El emirato de Ibn Mardanīš: Un breve síntesis interpretiva." In *Rey Lobo: El legado de Ibn Mardanīš, 1147–1172,* edited by Jorge A. Eiroa and Mariángeles Gómez Ródenas, 16–41. Murcia: Comunidad Autónoma de la Región de Murcia, 2019.

—. eds. *Rey Lobo: El legado de Ibn Mardanīš, 1147–1172*. Murcia: Comunidad Autónoma de la Región de Murcia, 2019.

Elger, Ralph. "Adab and Historical Memory: The Andalusian Poet/Politician Ibn al-Khaṭīb as Presented by Aḥmad al-Maqqarī (986/1577–1041/1632)." *Die Welt Des Islams* 42, no. 3 (2002): 289–306.

El Hour, Rachid. "The Andalusian Qāḍī in the Almoravid Period: Political and Judicial Authority." *Studia Islamica* 90 (2000): 67–83.

——. "Le *ṣāḥib al-aḥkām* à l'époque almoravide." *Al-Andalus Magreb* (Universidad de Cadiz) 8–9 (2001): 49–64.

Elsberg, H. A., and R. Guest. "Another Silk Fabric Woven at Baghdad." *Burlington Magazine* 64 (June 1934): 270–72.

de Epalza, Mikel. "El Cid = El León: ¿Epíteto árabe del Campeador?" *Hispanic Review* 45, no. 1 (1977): 67–75.

Ettinghausen, Richard. "Painting in the Fatimid Period: A Reconstruction." *Ars Islamica* 9 (1942): 112–24.

Fancy, Hussein. *The Mercenary Mediterranean: Sovereignty, Religion, and Violence in the Medieval Crown of Aragon*. Chicago: University of Chicago Press, 2017.

——. "What Was Convivencia?" Unpublished, n.d.

Feliciano, María Judith. "El corpus epigráfico de los tejidos medievales en Iberia: Nuevas aportaciones." In *Arte y producción textil en el Mediterráneo medieval*, edited by Laura Rodríguez Peinado and Francisco de Asís García García, 289–317. Madrid: Polifemo, 2019.

——. "Medieval Textiles in Iberia: Studies for a New Approach." In *Envisioning Islamic Art and Architecture: Essays in Honor of Renata Holod*, edited by David J. Roxburgh, 46–65. Leiden: Brill, 2014.

——. "Muslim Shrouds for Christian Kings? A Reassessment of Andalusi Textiles in Thirteenth Century Castilian Life and Ritual." In *Under the Influence: Questioning the Comparative in Medieval Castile*, edited by Cynthia Robinson and Leyla Rouhi, 101–32. Leiden: Brill, 2005.

——. "Sovereign, Saint and City: Honor and Reuse of Textiles in the Treasury of San Isidoro (León)." In *The Medieval Iberian Treasury in the Context of Cultural Interchange*, edited by Therese Martin, expanded ed., 118–44. Leiden: Brill, 2020.

de Felipe, Helena. "Berber Leadership and Genealogical Legitimacy: The Almoravid Case." In *Genealogy and Knowledge in Muslim Societies: Understanding the Past*, edited by Sarah Bowen Savant and Helena de Felipe, 55–70. Edinburgh: Edinburgh University Press, 2014.

——. "Leyendas árabes sobre el origen de los beréberes." *Al-Qanṭara* 11 (1990): 379–96.

Fernández-Puertas, Antonio. "The Three Great Sultans of Al-Dawla al-Ismāʿīliyya al-Naṣriyya Who Built the Fourteenth-Century Alhambra: Ismāʿīl I, Yūsuf I, Muḥammad V (713–793/1314–1391)." *Journal of the Royal Asiatic Society* 3rd ser., 7, no. 1 (1997): 1–25.

Ferrandis Torres, José. "Tesorillo de dīnāres almorávides hallado en la Alcazaba de Almería." *al-Andalus* 11 (1945): 389–94.

Fierro, Maribel. "Christian Success and Muslim Fear in Andalusī Writings during the Almoravid and Almohad Periods." In *Dhimmis and Others: Jews and Christians and the World of Classical Islam*, edited by Uri Rubin and David Wasserstein, 155–78. Israel Oriental Studies, XVII. Winona Lake, IN: Eisenbrauns, 1997.

——. "Conversion, Ancestry and Universal Religion: The Case of the Almohads in the Islamic West (Sixth/Twelfth-Seventh/Thirteenth Centuries)." *Journal of Medieval Iberian Studies* 2, no. 2 (2010): 155–73.

—. "La falsificación de la historia: Al-Yasaʿ b. Ḥazm y su *Kitāb al-Mughrib*." *Al-Qanṭara* 16 (1995): 1–37.

—. "Las genealogías de ʿAbd al-Muʾmin, primer califa almohade." *Al-Qanṭara* 24 (2003): 77–107.

—. "Heraclius in Al-Andalus." In *The Study of Al-Andalus: The Scholarship and Legacy of James T. Monroe*, edited by Michelle Hamilton and David Wacks, 180–210. Cambridge, MA: Harvard University Press, 2018.

—. "The Legal Policies of the Almohad Caliphs and Ibn Rushd's *Bidāyat al-Mujtahid*." *Journal of Islamic Studies* 10, no. 3 (1999): 226–48.

—. "Le mahdi Ibn Tûmart et al-Andalus: L'élaboration de la légitimité Almohade." *Revue des mondes musulmans et de la Mediterranée* 91–94 (2000): 107–24.

—. "El Mahdī Ibn Tūmart: Más allá de la biografía 'oficial.'" In *Política, sociedad e identidades en el Occidente islámico (siglos XI-XIV)*, edited by Miguel Angel Manzano Rodriguez and Rachid El Hour Amro, 73–98. Salamanca: Ediciones Universidad de Salamanca, 2016.

—. "*Mawālī* and *Muwalladūn* in al-Andalus." In *Patronate and Patronage in Early and Classical Islam*, edited by Monique Bernards and John Nawas, 195–245. Leiden: Brill, 2005.

—. "A Muslim Land without Jews or Christians: Almohad Attitudes Regarding the 'Protected People.'" In *Christlicher Norden—Muslimischer Süden: Ansprüche Und Wirklichkeiten von Christen, Juden Und Muslimen Auf Der Iberischen Halbinsel Im Hoch- Und Spätmittelalter*, edited by Matthias Tischler and Alexander Fidora, 231–48. Frankfurt am Main: Aschendorff, 2011.

—. "The *Qāḍī* as Ruler." In *Saber religioso y poder político en el Islam*, edited by Manuela Marín and Mercedes García-Arenal, 71–116. Madrid: Agencia Española de Cooperación Internacional, 1994.

—. "La religión." In *El retroceso territorial de al-Andalus: Almorávides y Almohades siglos XI al XIII*, edited by María Jesús Viguera Molíns, 437–550. Madrid: Espasa Calpe, S.A., 1997.

—. "Revolución y tradición: Algunos aspectos del mundo del saber en al-Andalus durante las épocas Almorávide y Almohade." In *Biografías almohades*, Estudios onomástico-biográficos de al-Andalus 10, edited by María Luisa Ávila and Maribel Fierro, 2:131–65. Madrid: Consejo Superior de Investigaciones Científicas, 2000.

—. "Sobre monedas de época Almohade: El dinar del cadí ʿIyāḍ que nunca existió. Cuándo se acuñaron las primeras monedas almohades y la cuestión de la licitud de acuñar moneda." *Al-Qanṭara* 27, no. 2 (2006): 457–76.

—. "Spiritual Alienation and Political Activism: The Ġurabāʾ in al-Andalus during the Sixth/Twelfth Century." *Arabica* 47, no. 2 (2000): 230–60.

—. "Terror y cambio dinástico en el Occidente islámico medieval." In *Por política, terror social. Reunió Científica XIV Curs d'Estiu Comtat d'Urgell celebrat a Balaguer els dies 30 de Juny i li 2 Juliol de 2010 sota la direcció de Flocel Sabaté i Maite Pedrol*, 93–114. Lleida: Pagés editors, 2013.

—. "Violence against Women in Andalusi Historical Sources (Third/Ninth-Seventh/Thirteenth Centuries)." In *Violence in Islamic Thought from the*

Quran to the Mongols, edited by Robert Gleave and István Kristó-Nagy, 155–74. Edinburgh: Edinburgh University Press, 2015.

—. "Why Ibn Ḥazm Became a Ẓāhirī: Charisma, Law and the Court." *Hamsa* 4 (March 2018): 1–21.

Firestone, Reuven. *Jihad: The Origin of Holy War in Islam*. Oxford: Oxford University Press, 1999.

Fletcher, Madeleine. "The Almohad Tawḥīd: Theology Which Relies on Logic." *Numen* 38, no. 1 (1991): 110–27.

—. "Ibn Tūmart's Teachers: The Relationship with al-Ghazālī." *Al-Qanṭara* 18, no. 2 (1997): 305–30.

Flood, Finbarr Barry. *Objects of Translation: Material Culture and Medieval "Hindu-Muslim" Encounter*. Princeton, NJ: Princeton University Press, 2009.

Foucault, Michel. "Nietzsche, Genealogy, History." In *Language, Counter-Memory, Practice: Selected Essays and Interviews*, edited by Donald F. Bouchard, translated by Donald F. Bouchard and Sherry Simon, 139–64. Ithaca, NY: Cornell University Press, 1977.

Fowden, Garth. *Quṣayr ʿAmra: Art and the Umayyad Elite in Late Antique Syria*. Berkeley: University of California Press, 2004.

"France Needs 'Society of Vigilance' against Islamist 'Hydra': Macron." *Reuters*, October 8, 2019. https://www.reuters.com/article/us-france-security-victims-macron/france-needs-society-of-vigilance-against-islamist-hydra-macron-idUSKBN1WN168.

Fricaud, Emile. "Les *Ṭalaba* dans la société Almohade (Le temps d'Averroès)." *Al-Qanṭara* 18 (1997): 331–88.

Gabrieli, Francesco. "Omayyades d'Espagne et Abbasides." *Studia Islamica* 31 (1970): 93–100.

García Anton, José. "Castillos musulmanes que dominaban la vía Cartagena-Murcia." In *Historia de Cartagena*, edited by Julio Mas García, 5:397–412. Murcia: Mediterráneo, 1986.

García-Arenal, Mercedes, ed. "Mahdisme et millénarisme en Islam." *Revue des mondes musulmans et de la Mediterranée* (special issue) 91–4 (2000).

—. *Messianism and Puritanical Reform: Mahdīs of the Muslim West*. Leiden: Brill, 2005.

—. "The Moriscos in Morocco: From Granadan Emigration to the *Hornacheros* of Salé." In *The Expulsion of the Moriscos of Spain*, edited by Mercedes García-Arenal and Gerard Wiegers, 286–328. Leiden: Brill, 2014.

—." La práctica del precepto de *ʿal-amr bi-l-maʿrūf wa-l-nahy ʿan al-munkar'* en la hagiografia magrebí." *Al-Qanṭara* 13, no. 1 (1992): 143–65.

García Avilés, Alejandro. "Arte y poder en Murcia en la época de Ibn Mardanish (1147–1172)." In *El Mediterráneo y el Arte Español: actas del XI Congreso del CEHA. Valencia, septiembre 1996*, edited by Joaquín Bérchez, Mercedes Gómez-Ferrer Lozano, and Amadeo Serra Desfillis, 31–37. Valencia: Comité Español de Historia del Arte, 1998.

García Gómez, Emilio. "Observaciones sobre la 'Qaṣīda Maqṣūra' de Abū-l-Ḥasan Ḥāzim al-Qarṭāyannī." *al-Andalus* 1 (1933): 81–103.

—. "Una qasida política inédita de Ibn Ṭufayl." R*evista del Instituto Egipcio de Estudios Islámicos* 1 (1953): 21–28.

García Porras, Alberto, and Adela Fábregas García. "La cerámica española en el comercio mediterráneo bajomedieval. Algunas notas documentales." *Miscelánea Medieval Murciana* 27–28 (2004): 7–34.

García Sanjuan, Alejandro. "La persistencia del discurso nationalcatólico sobre el Medievo peninsular en la historiografía española actual." *Historiografías* 12 (2016): 132–63.

—. "Rejecting Al-Andalus, Exalting the Reconquista: Historical Memory in Contemporary Spain." *Journal of Medieval Iberian Studies* 10, no. 1 (2018): 127–45.

Garofalo, Vicenza. "A Methodology for Studying Muqarnas: The Extant Examples in Palermo." *Muqarnas* 27 (2010): 357–406.

Garrido, Pilar. "Aproximación a las fuentes árabes sobre Abū ʿAbd Allāh Muḥammad b. Saʿd b. Muḥammad b. Aḥmad al-Yudāmī al-Tuyībī, ibn Mardanīš (518/1124-5–567/1172)." In *Rey Lobo: El legado de Ibn Mardanīš, 1147–1172,* edited by Jorge A. Eiroa and Mariángeles Gómez Ródenas, 42–49. Murcia: Comunidad Autónoma de la Región de Murcia, 2019.

Gaspar Remiro, Mariano. *Historia de Murcia musulmana*. Saragossa: Tip. de Andrés Uriarte, 1905.

Gautier-Dalché, J. "Le rôle de la Reconquête de Tolède dans l'histoire monetaire de la Castille (1085–1174)." In *Estudios sobre Alfonso VI y la Reconquista de Toledo*, 11–25. Toledo: Instituto de Estudios Visigótico-Mozárabes, 1988.

Ghilès, Francis. "Vox Reinvents History to Claim 'Reconquista' of Spain." *Arab Weekly*, November 17, 2019. https://thearabweekly.com/vox-reinvents-history-claim-reconquista-spain.

Gibb, H. A. R. "Al-Māwardī's Theory of the Khilāfah." *Islamic Culture* 11, no. 3 (1937): 291–302.

—. "The Social Significance of the Shuʿūbiyya." In *Studies on the Civilization of Islam*, edited by Stanford J. Shaw and William R. Polk, 62–73. London: Routledge, 1962.

Glick, Thomas. *Islamic and Christian Spain in the Early Middle Ages*. Princeton, NJ: Princeton University Press, 1979.

Glick, Thomas, and Oriol Pi-Sunyer. "Acculturation as an Explanatory Concept in Spanish History." *Comparative Studies in Society and History* 11, no. 2 (1969): 136–54.

Goitein, S. D. *A Mediterranean Society*. 5 vols. Berkeley: University of California Press, 1967–88.

Goldziher, Ignaz. "Introduction." In *Le Livre d'Ibn Toumert* (*Kitāb al-aʿazz mā yuṭlab*), by Ibn Tūmart, 5–12. edited by J. D. Luciani. Algiers: P. Fontana, 1903.

Golombek, Lisa. "The Draped Universe of Islam." In *Content and Context of Visual Arts in the Islamic World: Papers from a Colloquium in Memory of Richard Ettinghausen*, edited by Priscilla Soucek and Carol Bier, 25–50. University Park: Pennsylvania State University Press, 1988.

Gombrich, E. H. *Norm and Form: Studies in the Art of the Renaissance*. London: Phaidon Press, 1966.

González Cavero, Ignacio. "Una revisión de la figura de Ibn Mardanish: Su alianza con el reino de Castilla y la oposición frente a los almohades." *Miscelánea Medieval Murciana* 31 (2007): 95–110.

González, Julio. *El reino de Castilla en la época de Alfonso VIII*. Madrid: Consejo Superior de Investigaciones Científicas, 1960.

—. "Repoblación de las tierras de Cuenca." *Anuario de Estudios Medievales* 12 (1982): 183–204.

Grabar, André. *Christian Iconography: A Study of Its Origins*. Princeton, NJ: Princeton University Press, 1968.

Grabar, Oleg. "Imperial and Urban Art in Islam: The Subject-Matter of Fatimid Art." In *Early Islamic Art, 650–1100*. Vol. 1. *Constructing the Study of Islamic Art*, 215–41. Hampshire: Ashgate, 2005.

—. "The Shared Culture of Objects." In *Byzantine Court Culture from 829 to 1204*, 115–30. Washington, DC: Dumbarton Oaks, 2004.

Graves, Margaret. *Arts of Allusion: Objects, Arts and Ornament in Medieval Islam*. Oxford: Oxford University Press, 2018.

Griffel, Frank. "Ibn Tūmart's Rational Proof for God's Existence and Unity, and His Connection to the Niẓāmiyya *Madrasa* in Baghdad." In *Los Almohades: Problemas y Perspectivas*, edited by Patrice Cressier, Maribel Fierro, and Luis Molina, 2:753–813. Madrid: Consejo Superior de Investigaciones Científicas, 2005.

Grube, Ernst J. "A Coloured Drawing of the Fatimid Period in the Keir Collection." *Rivista Degli Studi Orientali* 59, 1/4 (1985): 147–74.

Grube, Ernst J., and Jeremy Johns, eds. *The Painted Ceilings of the Cappella Palatina*. Genoa: Bruschettini Foundation for Islamic and Asian Art, 2005.

Guichard, Pierre. *Al-Andalus frente a la conquista cristiana*. Translated by Josep Torro. Valencia: Biblioteca Nueva, 2001.

—. *Les musulmans de Valence et la Reconquête (XIe-XIIIe siècle)*. 2 vols. Damascus: Institut français de Damas, 1991.

Halevi, Leor. *Muhammad's Grave: Death Rites and the Making of Islamic Society*. New York: Columbia University Press, 2007.

Halm, Heinz. *The Empire of the Mahdi: The Rise of the Fatimids*. Leiden: Brill, 1996.

Harrison, Alwyn. "Behind the Curve: Bulliet and Conversion to Islam in al-Andalus Revisited." *Al-Masāq* 24, no. 1 (35–51): 2012.

Hautecoeur, Louis. "De la trompe aux 'Mukarnas.'" *Gazette des Beaux-Arts* 6 (1931): 26–51.

Ḥāyik, Sīmūn. *Ibn Mardanīsh aw al-Muwaḥḥidūn*. Jūnīya, Lebanon: al-Maṭbaʿa al-Būlīya, 1993.

Hazard, Harry. *The Numismatic History of Late Medieval North Africa*. New York: American Numismatic Society, 1952.

Heck, Paul. "'Jihad' Revisited." *Journal of Religious Ethics* 32 (2004): 95–128.

Heidenreich, Anja, and Carmen Barceló. "El inicio de la loza dorada autóctona en la península ibérica: Una aproximación desde sus epígrafas." In *Las artes en al-Andalus y Egipto: Contextos y intercambios*, edited by Susana Calvo Capilla, 85–110. Madrid: La Ergástula, 2017.

Hernández Jiménez, Félix. "Travesía de la Sierra de Guadarrama en el acceso a la raya musulmana del Duero." *al-Andalus* 38, no. 1 (1973): 69–186.

Hillenbrand, Robert. "*La Dolce Vita* in Early Islamic Syria: The Evidence of the Later Umayyad Palaces." *Art History* 5 (1982): 1–35.

Hodder, Ian. *Entangled: An Archaeology of the Relationships between Humans and Things*. Malden, MA: Wiley-Blackwell, 2012.

Hoffman, Eva. "Between East and West: The Wall Paintings of Samarra and the Construction of Abbasid Princely Culture." *Muqarnas* 25 (2008): 107–32.

—. "A Fatimid Book Cover: Framing and Re-Framing Cultural Identity in the Medieval Mediterranean World." In *L'Egypte Fatimide: Son Art et Son Histoire*, edited by Marianne Barrucand, 403–19. Paris: Presses de l'université de Paris-Sorbonne, 1999.

—. "Pathways of Portability: Islamic and Christian Interchange from the Tenth to the Twelfth Century." *Art History* 24 (2001): 17–50.

Hopkins, J. F. P. *Medieval Muslim Government in Barbary until the Sixth Century of the Hijra*. London: Luzac, 1958.

Hosler, John. *Henry II: A Medieval Soldier at War, 1147–1189*. Leiden: Brill, 2007.

Hoyland, Robert. "History, Fiction and Authorship in the First Centuries of Islam." In *Writing and Representation in Medieval Islam*, edited by Julia Bray, 16–46. London: Routledge, 1996.

Huarte Cambria, Rosario. "Fragmentos de yeserías relacionados con la aljama Almohade de Sevilla." *Laboratorio de Arte* 14 (2001): 181–96.

Huici Miranda, Ambrosio. *Historia musulmana de Valencia*. Valencia: Ayuntamiento de Valencia, 1970.

—. *Historia política del imperio almohade*. 2 vols. Tetouan: Editora Marroquí, 1957.

—. "Prefacio." In *Al-Mann bil-Imāma: Estudio preliminar, traducción e índices*, by Ibn Ṣāḥib al-Ṣalā, 5–8. Translated by Ambrosio Huici Miranda. Valencia: Anubar, 1969.

Hunwick, John. "Gao and the Almoravids: A Hypothesis." In *West African Cultural Dynamics: Archaeological and Historical Perspectives*, 413–30. The Hague: De Gruyter Mouton, 1980.

Ibrāhīm, Tawfīq. "A Dinar of ʿAli ibn ʿUbaid Struck in Murcia." In *XII Congreso Internacional de Numismática*, 1593–97. Madrid: Ministerio de Cultura, 2005.

"La inmigración en España: Efectos y oportunidades." Consejo Económico y Social España, Informe 02, 2019. http://www.ces.es/documents/10180/5209150/Inf0219.pdf.

ʿĪsā, Fawzī Saʿd. *al-Shiʿr al-Andalusī fī ʿaṣr al-Muwaḥḥidīn*. Alexandria: al-Hayʾa al-Miṣriyya al-ʿĀmma li-l-Kitāb, 1979.

Jābir, Jābir Khalīfa. *Banū Mardanīsh wa-dawrahum al-siyāsī wa-l-ʿaskarī fī al-Andalus*. Damascus: Dār Amal al-Jadīda, 2017.

Jacoby, David. "The Production and Diffusion of Andalusi Silks and Silk Textiles, Mid-Eighth to Mid-Thirteenth Century." In *The Chasuble of Thomas Becket: A Biography*, edited by Avinoam Shalem, 142–51. Munich: Hirmer/The Bruschettini Foundation, 2017.

—. "Silk Economics and Cross-Cultural Artistic Interaction: Byzantium, the Muslim World, and the Christian West." *Dumbarton Oaks Papers* 58 (2004): 197–240.

Jiménez Castillo, Pedro (w), and Manuel Martínez Meseguer (p). *El Rey Lobo: El valeroso rey de Murcia que fundó un gran reino y batalló incansable contra el imperio Almohade*. Historietas de la Historia. Murcia: Ayuntamiento de Murcia, 2006.

Johns, Jeremy. "Arabic Inscriptions in the Cappella Palatina: Performativity, Audience, Legibility and Illegibility." In *Viewing Inscriptions in the Late Antique and Medieval Mediterranean*, edited by Antony Eastmond, 124–47. Cambridge: Cambridge University Press, 2015.

—. "Muslim Artists and Christian Models in the Painted Ceilings of the Cappella Palatina." In *Romanesque and the Mediterranean: Patterns of Exchange across the Latin, Greek and Islamic Worlds c. 1000–c. 1250*, edited by Rosa Maria Bacile and John McNeill, 59–89. Leeds: British Archaeological Association, 2015.

Jones, Linda G. "'The Christian Companion': A Rhetorical Trope in the Narration of Intra Muslim Conflict." *Anuario de Estudios Medievales* 38 (December 2008): 793–829.

—. "The Preaching of the Almohads: Loyalty and Resistance across the Strait of Gibraltar." *Medieval Encounters* 19 (2013): 71–101.

Kamen, Henry. "Limpieza and the Ghost of Américo Castro: Racism as a Tool of Literary Analysis." *Hispanic Review* 64, no. 1 (1996): 19–29.

Kapitaikin, Lev. "David's Dancers in Palermo: Islamic Dance Imagery and Its Christian Recontextualization in the Ceilings of the Cappella Palatina." *Early Music* 47, no. 1 (2019): 3–23.

Kassis, Hanna. "The Coinage of Muḥammad Ibn Saʿd (Ibn Mardanīsh) of Mursiya: An Attempt at Iberian Islamic Autonomy." In *Problems of Medieval Coinage in the Iberian Area*, edited by Mário Gomes Marques, 209–29. Santarém, Portugal: Instituto Politécnico, 1988.

—. "Muslim Revival in Spain in the Fifth/Eleventh Century: Causes and Ramifications." *Der Islam* 67 (1990): 78–110.

—. "Qadi Iyad's Rebellion against the Almohads in Sabta (A.H. 542–543/A.D. 1147–1148): New Numismatic Evidence." *Journal of the American Oriental Society* 103 (1983): 505–14.

Katzew, Ilona. "Casta Painting: Identity and Social Stratification in Colonial Mexico." In *New World Orders: Casta Painting and Colonial Latin America*, edited by Ilona Katzew, 8–29. New York: Americas Society Art Gallery, 1996.

King, David. "The Enigmatic Orientation of the Great Mosque of Cordoba." *Suhayl* 16–17 (2018): 33–111.

—. "The Sacred Direction in Islam: A Study of the Interaction of Religion and Science in the Middle Ages." *Interdisciplinary Science Reviews* 10, no. 4 (1985): 315–28.

Kinoshita, Sharon. "Almeria Silk and the French Feudal Imaginary: Toward a 'Material' History of the Medieval Mediterranean." In *Medieval Fabrications: Dress, Textiles, Clothwork, and Other Cultural Imaginings*, edited by E. Jane Burns, 165–76. New York: Palgrave Macmillan, 2004.

Kleinberg, S. Jay, ed. *Retrieving Women's History: Changing Perceptions of the Role of Women in Politics and Society*. Oxford: Berg Publishers, 1988.

Knipp, David. "Almoravid Sources for the Wooden Ceiling in the Nave of the Cappella Palatina in Palermo." In *Die Cappella Palatina in Palermo:*

Geschichte, Kunst, Funktionen, edited by Thomas Dittelbach, 571–78. Künzelsau: Swiridoff Verlag, 2011.

Kopytoff, Igor. "The Cultural Biography of Things: Commoditization as Process." In *The Social Life of Things: Commodities in Cultural Perspective*, edited by Arjun Appadurai, 64–91. Cambridge: Cambridge University Press, 1986.

Kühnel, Ernst. *Die Islamischen Elfenbeinskulpturm, VIII–XIII Jahrhundert*. Berlin: Deutscher Verlag für Kunstwissenschaft, 1971.

Kurtz, Lester. "The Politics of Heresy." *American Journal of Sociology* 88, no. 6 (1983): 1085–1115.

Lacarra, José María. "El Rey Lobo de Murcia y el señorio de Albarracín." In *Estudios dedicados a Don Ramón Menéndez Pidal III*, 3:515–26. Madrid: Consejo Superior de Investigaciones Científicas, 1952.

Lachaud, Frederique. "Les soieries importées en Angleterre (fin XIIe et XIIIe siecles)." In *Soieries medievales: Techniques et cultures; Pour une ethnologie de l'acte traditionnel efficace*, 179–92. Paris: Éditions de la Maison des sciences de l'homme, 1999.

Lafuente Vidal, José. "El tesoro de monedas árabes de Elche." *Boletín de la Real Academia de la Historia* 96 (1930): 846–56.

Lagardère, Vincent. *Les Almoravides, le djihād andalou*. Paris: L'Harmattan, 1999.

—. "Le ǧihād almohade: Théorie et practique." In *Los Almohades: Problemas y perspectivas*, edited by Patrice Cressier, Maribel Fierro, and Luis Molina, 2:617–31. Madrid: Consejo Superior de Investigaciones Científicas, 2005.

Landau-Tasseron, Ella. "Unearthing a Pre-Islamic Arabian Prophet." *Jerusalem Studies in Arabic and Islam* 21 (1997): 42–61.

Larsson, Göran. *Ibn García's Shuʿūbiyya Letter: Ethnic and Theological Tensions in Medieval al-Andalus*. Leiden: Brill, 2003.

Latour, Bruno. *An Inquiry into Modes of Existence: An Anthropology of the Moderns*. Translated by Catherine Porter. Cambridge, MA: Harvard University Press, 2013.

—. *We Have Never Been Modern*. Translated by Catherine Porter. Cambridge, MA: Harvard University Press, 1993.

Le Tourneau, Roger. "Sur la disparition de la doctrine almohade." *Studia Islamica* 32 (1970): 193–201.

Lévi-Provençal, Évariste. "La 'Description de l'Espagne' de Rāzī." *al-Andalus* 17, no. 1 (1953): 51–108.

—. "Le titre souverain des almoravides et sa légitimation par le califat 'abbaside." *Arabica* 2 (1955): 265–88.

Lings, Martin. "Andalusian Qurans." *British Museum Quarterly* 24 (1961): 94–96.

Lintz, Yannick, Bahija Simou, Claire Déléry, Bulle Tuil Leonetti, and Adil Boulghallat. *Le Maroc Médiéval. Un empire de l'Afrique à l'Espagne*. Paris: Musée du Louvre, 2014.

Makariou, Sophie, ed. *L'Orient de Saladin: L'Art des Ayyoubides*. Paris: Institut du monde arabe, 2001.

Makdisi, George. "The Sunni Revival." In *Islamic Civilisation, 950–1150*, edited by D. S. Richards, 155–68. Oxford: Cassirer, 1973.

Makkī, Al-Ṭāhir Aḥmad. *Malḥamat al-Sīd: Awwal malḥama andalusiyya kutibat fī al-lugha al-qashtaliyya*. Cairo: Dār al-Maʿārif, 1970.

Mamdani, Mahmood. *Good Muslim, Bad Muslim: America, The Cold War and the Roots of Terror*. New York: Penguin Random House, 2005.

Manzano Martínez, José A. "Arquitectura defensiva: Delimitación de entornos y documentación histórica de 20 torres y castillos." *Memorias de Arqueología* 10 (1995): 662–71.

—. "Fortificaciones islámicas en la huerta de Murcia: Sector septentrional; Memoria de las actuaciones realizadas." *Memorias de Arqueología* 7 (1992, rev. 1998): 389–441.

Manzano Martínez, José A., and Francisca Bernal Pascual. "Un palacio fortificado musulmán en la huerta de Murcia: El Castillo de Larache; Estado actual de la investigación." *Verdolay* 4 (1993): 153–66.

Manzano Martos, Rafael. "Casas y palacios en la Sevilla Almohade: Sus antecedents Hispánicos." In *Casas y palacios de al-Andalus*, edited by Julio Navarro Palazón, 315–52. Granada: El Legado Andalusí, 1995.

Marçais, Georges. *L'Architecture musulmane d'Occident. Tunisie, Algérie, Maroc, Espagne et Sicile*. Paris: Arts et Métiers grafiques, 1954.

Marcos Cobaleda, María. "En torno al arte y la arquitectura almorávides: Contribuciones y nuevas perspectivas." In *al-Murābiṭūn (los almorávides): Un Imperio islámico occidental. Estudios en memoria del Profesor Henri Terrasse*, edited by María Marcos Cobaleda, 314–44. Granada: Junta de Andalucía, 2018.

Marín, Manuela. "En los márgenes de la ley: El consumo de alcohol en al-Ándalus." In *Identidades marginales*, Estudios onomástico-biográficos de al Andalus 13, edited by Cristina de la Puente, 271–328. Madrid: Consejo Superior de Investigaciones Científicas, 2003.

—. *Mujeres en al-Ándalus,* Estudios Onomástico-Biográficos de al-Andalus 11. Madrid: Consejo Superior de Investigaciones Científicas, 2000.

—. "Šūrā et ahl al-šūrā dans al-Andalus." *Studia Islamica* 62 (1985): 25–51.

Marshak, Boris I. "An Early Seljuq Silver Bottle from Siberia." *Muqarnas* 21 (Essays in Honor of J. M. Rogers) (2004): 255–65.

Martínez Enamorado, Virgilio. "Poder y epigrafía Mardanīšíes: Confirmando (otra vez) a Ibn Jaldūn." In *Rey Lobo: El legado de Ibn Mardanīš, 1147–1172,* edited by Jorge A. Eiroa and Mariángeles Gómez Ródenas, 104–15. Murcia: Comunidad Autónoma de la Región de Murcia, 2019.

Martínez Díez, Gonzalo. *Alfonso VIII, Rey de Castilla y Toledo*. Burgos: Editorial la Olmeda, 1995.

Martínez Núñez, Maria Antonia. "Escritura árabe ornamental y epigrafía andalusí." *Arqueología y territorio medieval* 4 (1997): 127–62.

—. "Ideología y epigrafía almohades." In *Los Almohades: Problemas y perspectivas*, edited by Patrice Cressier, Maribel Fierro, and Luis Molina, 1:13–52. Madrid: Consejo Superior de Investigaciones Científicas, 2005.

Martínez Núñez, Maria Antonia, Isabel Rogríguez Casanova, and Alberto Canto García. *Epigrafía árabe: Catálogo del gabinete de antigüedades*. Madrid: Real Academia de la Historia, 2008.

Martínez Rodríguez, Antonio Luis. *Recorrer la memoria: Ibn Mardanis*. Murcia: Ayuntamiento de Murcia, 2019.

Massaiu, Maurizio. "The Use of *Muqarnas* in Ḥammādid Architecture: Some Preliminary Observations." In *Mapping Knowledge: Cross-Pollination in*

Late Antiquity and the Middle Ages, edited by Charles Burnett and Pedro Mantas-España, 209–30. Cordoba: CNERU/Oriens, 2014.

Mateu y Llopis, Felipe. "Morabetinos lupinos y alfonsinos desde Ramón Berenguer IV de Barcelona a Jaime I de Aragón (1131–1276): Datos documentales sobre su curso en Navarra, Aragón, Barcelona, Lérida y Valencia con referencias a otras especies monetarias de igual valor." In *II Jarique de Numismatica Hispano-Árabe*, 93–116. Lleida: Quaderns de l'Institut d'Estudis Ilerdencs, 1990.

Mathews, Karen. "Plunder of War or Objects of Trade? The Reuse and Reception of Andalusi Objects in Medieval Pisa." *Journal of Medieval Iberian Studies* 4, no. 2 (2012): 233–58.

Medina Gómez, Antonio. *Monedas hispano-musulmanas.* Toledo: Instituto Provincial de Investigaciones y Estudios Toledanos, 1992.

Melikian-Chirvani, Assadullah Souren. *Islamic Metalwork from the Iranian World, 8th–18th Centuries.* London: H.M. Stationery Office, 1982.

Menéndez Pidal, Rámon. *La España del Cid.* Madrid: Editorial Plutarco, 1929.

Messier, Ronald. *The Almoravids and the Meanings of Jihad.* Santa Barbara, CA: Praeger, 2010.

Mitha, Farouk. *Al-Ghazālī and the Ismailis: A Debate on Reason and Authority in Medieval Islam.* London: I. B. Tauris & Institute of Ismaili Studies, 2001.

Molina López, Emilio. "Apuntes en torno al perfil biográfico de un dirigente local andalusí, Muḥammad b. Sa'd b. Mardanīš (siglo XII)." In *Regnum Murciae: Génesis y configuración del Reino de Murcia*, edited by A. Robles Fernández and I. Pozo Martínez, 87–101. Murcia: Comunidad Autónoma de la Región de Murcia, 2008.

——. "El gobierno de Zayyān b. Mardanīsh en Murcia (1239–1241)." *Miscelánea Medieval Murciana* 7 (1981): 159–88.

——. "Ibn Mardanis." In *Diccionario Biográfico electrónico de la Real Academia de la Historia*, n.d. http://dbe.rah.es/biografias/16905/ibn-mardanis.

Monroe, James. *Islam and Arabs in Spanish Scholarship (Sixteenth Century to the Present).* Leiden: Brill, 1970.

Monzón Moya, Fabiola, and Concepción Martín Morales. "El antiguo convento de Santa Fe de Toledo. Recuperación de algunas dependencias de época musulmana." *Revista del Instituto de Patrimonio Histórico Español y Bienes Culturales* 6 (2005): 53–76.

Mottahedeh, Roy. "The Shu'ūbiyyah Controversy and the Social History of Early Islamic Iran." *International Journal of Middle East Studies* 7, no. 2 (1976): 161–82.

Mottahedeh, Roy, and Ridwan al-Sayyid. "The Idea of Jihād in Islam before the Crusades." In *The Crusades from the Perspective of Byzantium and the Muslim World*, edited by Angeliki E. Laiou and Roy Mottahedeh, 23–30. Washington, DC: Dumbarton Oaks, 2001.

Mulder, Stephennie. *The Shrines of the 'Alids in Medieval Syria: Sunnis, Shi'is and the Architecture of Coexistence.* Edinburgh: Edinburgh University Press, 2014.

Müller, Christian. "Administrative Tradition and Civil Jurisdiction of the Cordoban *Ṣāḥib al-Aḥkām*." *Al-Qanṭara* 21, no. 1 (2000): 57–84.

"Muṣḥaf Ibn Ghaṭṭūs . . . al-ʿuthūr ʿalā naskha thālitha," *Al-ʿArabī al-Jadīd*, 17 March 2018, https://alaraby.co.uk/مصحف-ابن-غطوس-العثور-على-نسخة-ثالثة (accessed 3/26/2019).

Nagel, Tilman. "La destrucción de la ciencia de la *šarīʿa* por Muḥammad ibn Tūmart." *Al-Qanṭara* 18, no. 2 (1997): 295–304.

—. "Le mahdisme de Ibn Tūmart et Ibn Qasī: Une analyse phénoménologique." *Revue des mondes musulmans et de la Mediterranée* 91–94 (2000): 125–36.

Navarro Palazón, Julio. "La Dār aṣ-Ṣugrà de Murcia: Un palacio andalusí del siglo XII." In *Colloque international d'archéologie islamique, IFAO, le Caire, 3–7 février 1993*, edited by Roland-Pierre Gayraud, 97–139. Cairo: Institut Français d'Archéologie Orientale, 1998.

—. "Nuevas aportaciones al estudio de la loza dorada andalusí: el ataifor de Zavellá." In *Les illes orientals d'al-Andalus (V Jornades d'Estudis Històrics Locals), 28–30 noviembre 1985*, edited by Guillem Rosselló-Bordoy, 225–238. Palma de Mallorca: Institut d'estudis Baleàrics, 1987.

Navarro Palazón, Julio, and Pedro Jiménez Castillo. "La arquitectura de Ibn Mardanīš: Revisión y nuevas aportaciones." In *La Aljafería y el arte del Islam occidental en el siglo XI*, edited by Gonzalo Borrás Gualís and Bernabé Cabañero Subiza, 291–350. Saragossa: Institución "Fernando el Católico," Consejo Superior de Investigaciones Científicas, 2012.

—. "La arquitectura mardanisí." In *La arquitectura del Islam occidental*, edited by Rafael López Guzmán, 117–36. Barcelona: Lunwerg Editores/Legado Andalusí, 1995.

—. "Casas y palacios de al-Andalus: Siglos XII–XIII." In *Casas y palacios de al-Andalus*, edited by Julio Navarro Palazón, 17–32. Granada: El Legado Andalusí, 1995.

—. "El Castillejo de Monteagudo: Qasr ibn Saʿd." In *Casas y palacios de al-Andalus*, edited by Julio Navarro Palazón, 63–104. Granada: El Legado Andalusí, 1995.

—. "Evolution of the Andalusi Urban Landscape: From the Dispersed to the Saturated Medina." In *Revisiting Al-Andalus: Perspectives on the Material Culture of Islamic Iberia and Beyond*, edited by Glaire D. Anderson and Mariam Rosser-Owen, 115–42. Leiden: Brill, 2007.

—. "La producción cerámica medieval de Murcia." In *Spanish Medieval Ceramics in Spain and the British Isles*, edited by C. M. Gerrard, A. Gutiérrez, and A. Vince, 185–214. Oxford: Tempus Reparatum, 1995.

—. "La yesería en época almohade." In *Los Almohades: Problemas y perspectivas*, edited by Patrice Cressier, Maribel Fierro, and Luis Molina, 1:249–303. Madrid: Consejo Superior de Investigaciones Científicas, 2005.

Navarro Palazón, Julio, Pedro Jiménez Castillo, Juan A. García Granados, and Maurizio Toscano. *Castillejo de Monteagudo. Poder y producción en la almunia del rey Lobo. Guía de la exposición*. Murcia: Región de Murcia, Ayuntamiento de Murcia, Consejo Superior de Investigaciones Científicas and FECYT, 2019.

Necipoğlu, Gülru. *The Topkapı Scroll: Geometry and Ornament in Islamic Architecture; Topkapı Palace Museum Library MS H. 1956*. Santa Monica, CA: Getty Center for the History of Art and the Humanities, 1995.

Nickson, Tom. "'Sovereignty Belongs to God': Text, Ornament and Magic in Islamic and Christian Seville." *Art History* 38, no. 5 (2015): 838–61.

Nirenberg, David. *Neighboring Faiths: Christianity, Islam and Judaism in the Middle Ages and Today*. Chicago: University of Chicago Press, 2014.

O'Connor, Isabel. "The Fall of the Almohad Empire in the Eyes of Modern Spanish Historians." *Islam and Christian-Muslim Relations* 14, no. 2 (2003): 145–62.

Partearroyo, Cristina. "Almoravid and Almohad Textiles." In *Al-Andalus: The Arts of Islamic Spain*, edited by Jerrilyn D. Dodds, 105–13. New York: Abrams, 1992.

—. "Tejidos Andalusíes." *Artigrama* 22 (2007): 371–419.

Pavón Maldonado, Basilio. "La decoración monumental: Maderas y mocárabes." In *Arquitectura y decoración en el Islam Occidental: España y Palermo*, 123–49. Self-published online, 2011. http://www.basiliopavonmaldonado.es/Documentos/EspanapalermoI.pdf.

—. "El maylis del taifa al-Mu'tasim de la alcazaba de Almería: Muqarnas = muqarbas = mucarnas = almocárabes = mocárabes en el arte hispanomusulmán." *Revista del Instituto Egipcio de Estudios Árabes en Madrid* 32 (2000): 221–59.

Peláez Martín, Alejandro. *El califa ausente: cuestiones de autoridad en al-Andalus durante el siglo XI*. Madrid: La Ergástula, 2018.

Peña Martín, Salvador. "El término de origen coránico Amr Allāh ('Disposición de Dios') y el linguocentrismo trascendente islámico, en torno al siglo XII." *Anaquel de Estudios Árabes* 22 (2011): 197–224.

Piponnier, Françoise, and Perrine Mane. *Dress in the Middle Ages*. Translated by Caroline Beamish. New Haven, CT: Yale University Press, 2000.

Pozo Martínez, Indalecio, Alfonso Robles Fernández, and Elvira Navarro Santa-Cruz. "Arquitectura y artes decorativas del siglo XII: el alcázar menor de Santa Clara, Murcia (Dār aṣ-Sugra)." In *Las artes y las ciencias en el Occidente musulmán: sabios mursíes en las cortes mediterráneas*, edited by A. Robles Fernández, 203–33. Murcia, Ayuntamiento de Murcia, 2007.

Prieto y Vives, Antonio. "La reforma numismática de los almohades: ensayo sobre la numismática de los estados musulmanes hispano-africanos de los siglos XII al XV." In *Miscelánea de estudios y textos árabes*, edited by R. Besthorn, Ángel González Palencia, and Antonio Prieto y Vives, 11–114. Madrid: Centro de estudios históricos, 1915.

Puente, Cristina de la. "Obras transmitidas en al-Ándalus por Abū 'Alī al-Ṣadafī." *Al-Qanṭara* 20 (1999): 195–200.

Qaddūrī, 'Abd al-Majīd. *Mahdisme: Crise et changement dans l'histoire du Maroc*. Rabat: Université Mohammad V Faculté des lettres et des sciences humaines, 1994.

al-Qāḍī, Wadād. "The Religious Foundation of Late Umayyad Ideology." In *Saber religioso y poder político en el Islam*, edited by Manuela Marín and Mercedes García-Arenal, 231–73. Madrid: Agencia Española de Cooperación Internacional, 1994.

Quayson, Ato. "Translations and Transnationals." In *Postcolonial Approaches to the European Middle Ages: Translating Cultures*, edited by Ananya Jahanara

Kabir and Deanne Williams, 253–68. Cambridge: Cambridge University Press, 2005.

Rabasco García, Victor. "El arte textile y su impacto en la cultura visual de los Reinos de Taifas." In *Arte y producción textil en el Mediterráneo medieval*, edited by Laura Rodríguez Peinado and Francisco de Asís García García, 479–99. Madrid: Polifemo, 2019.

Recuero Astray, Manuel. *Alfonso VII, 1126–1157*. Burgos: Editorial la Olmeda, 2003.

Reilly, Bernard. *The Contest of Christian and Muslim Spain 1031–1157*. Oxford: Blackwell, 1992.

Reynolds, Dwight. *The Musical Heritage of Al-Andalus*. New York: Routledge, 2021.

Rice, D. S. "The Fermo Chasuble of St. Thomas a Becket Revealed as the Earliest Fully Dated and Localised Major Islamic Embroidery Known." *Illustrated London News*, October 3, 1959.

Richardson, Kristina. "Singing Slave Girls (Qiyan) of the ʿAbbasid Court in the Ninth and Tenth Centuries." In *Children in Slavery through the Ages*, edited by Gwyn Campbell, Suzanne Miers, and Joseph C. Miller, 105–18. Athens: Ohio University Press, 2009.

Ríos Saloma, Martín. *La reconquista: Una construcción historiográfica (siglos XVI–XIX)*. Madrid: Marcial Pons Ediciones de Historia, 2011.

Rivera Garretas, Milagros. "El castillo-fortaleza de Uclés: Datos histórico-arqueológico." *Cuenca* 17 (1980): 35–49.

Roa, Sebastián. *La loba de al-Ándalus*. Madrid: Ediciones B, 2012.

——. "El Rey Lobo, el azote de los yihadistas del siglo XII." *ABC*, August 20, 2018. https://www.abc.es/cultura/abci-lobo-azote-yihadistas-siglo-201808190211_noticia.html.

Robinson, Cynthia. "The Arts of the Taifa Kingdoms." In *Al-Andalus: The Arts of Islamic Spain*, edited by Jerrilyn D. Dodds, 49–62. New York: Abrams, 1992.

——. "Love in the Time of Fitna: 'Courtliness' and the 'Pamplona' Casket." In *Revisiting Al-Andalus: Perspectives on the Material Culture of Islamic Iberia and Beyond*, edited by Glaire D. Anderson and Mariam Rosser-Owen, 99–113. Leiden: Brill, 2007.

——. *Medieval Mediterranean Courtly Culture in Al-Andalus:* Ḥadīth Bayāḍ Wa-Riyāḍ. London: Routledge, 2006.

——. *In Praise of Song: The Making of Court Culture in al-Andalus and Provence, 1005–1134 AD*. Leiden: Brill, 2002.

Robles Fernández, Alfonso. "Estudio arqueológico de los palacios andalusíes de Murcia (ss. X–XV): Tratamiento ornamental e influencia en el entorno." PhD diss., Universidad de Murcia, 2016.

——. "Los programas ornamentales de los palacios reformados y fundados por el emir Ibn Mardanīš." In *Rey Lobo: El legado de Ibn Mardanīš, 1147–1172*, edited by Jorge A. Eiroa and Mariángeles Gómez Ródenas, 50–67. Murcia: Comunidad Autónoma de la Región de Murcia, 2019.

Rodríguez Lorente, Juan José. *Numismática de la Murcia musulmana*. Madrid: Distributed by Carols Castán, 1984.

Rosenthal, E. I. J. *Political Thought in Medieval Islam*. London: Cambridge University Press, 1962.

Rosser-Owen, Mariam. "Andalusi Spolia in Medieval Morocco: Architectural Politics, Political Architecture." *Medieval Encounters* 20 (2014): 152–98.

—. "Poems in Stone: The Iconography of ʿĀmirid Poetry, and Its 'Petrification' on ʿĀmirid Marbles." In *Revisiting Al-Andalus: Perspectives on the Material Culture of Islamic Iberia and Beyond*, edited by Glaire D. Anderson and Mariam Rosser-Owen, 83–98. Leiden: Brill, 2007.

Rouighi, Ramzi. *Inventing the Berbers: History and Ideology in the Maghrib*. Philadelphia: University of Pennsylvania Press, 2019.

Rubiera Mata, María Jesús. *Ibn al-Ŷayyāb: El otro poeta de la Alhambra*. Granada: Patronato de la Alhambra, 1994.

—. "Las inscripciones árabes de Játiva: una hipótesis y una propuesta sobre la denominación de un estilo." In *Homenaje al profesor Darío Cabanelas Rodríguez, O.F.M., con motivo de su LXX aniversario*, 2:293–295. Granada: Universidad de Granada, Departamento de Estudios Semíticos, 1987.

—. "El Rey Lobo de Murcia, Ibn Mardanîs (1147–1172), promotor de la construcción de alcázares viales." In *Imágenes y promotores en el arte medieval: Miscelánea en homenaje a Joaquín Yarza Luaces*, edited by María Luisa Melero Moneo, 191–94. Bellaterra: Universidad Autónoma de Barcelona, 2001.

Rubiera Mata, María Jesús, and Mikel de Epalza. "Al-Andalus: Between Myth and History." *History and Anthropology* 18, no. 3 (2007): 269–73.

Ruggles, D. Fairchild. *Gardens, Landscape, and Vision in the Palaces of Islamic Spain*. University Park: Pennsylvania State University Press, 2000.

—. "The Mirador in Abbasid and Hispano-Umayyad Garden Typology." *Muqarnas* 7 (1990): 73–82.

—. "Mothers of a Hybrid Dynasty: Race, Genealogy, and Acculturation in al-Andalus." *Journal of Medieval & Early Modern Studies* 34, no. 1 (winter 2004): 65–94.

Sachedina, Abdulaziz Abdulhussein. *Islamic Messianism*. Albany: State University of New York Press, 1981.

Safran, Janina. "The Command of the Faithful in Al-Andalus: A Study in the Articulation of Caliphal Legitimacy." *International Journal of Middle East Studies* 30, no. 2 (1998): 183–98.

—. *Defining Boundaries in Al-Andalus: Muslims, Christians, and Jews in Islamic Iberia*. Ithaca, NY: Cornell University Press, 2013.

—. *The Second Umayyad Caliphate: The Articulation of Caliphal Legitimacy in al-Andalus*. Cambridge: Harvard University Press, 2000.

Sánchez-Albornoz, Claudio. *La España musulmana*. Madrid: Espasa-Calpe, 1982.

Sánchez Casabón, Ana Isabel. *Alfonso II Rey de Aragón, Conde de Barcelona y Marqués de Provenza: Documentos (1162–1196)*. Saragossa: Institución Fernando el Católico, Consejo Superior de Investigaciones Científicas, 1995.

Sánchez Pravia, José Antonio, and Luis Alberto García Blánquez. "Fulgor en el alcázar musulmán de Murcia: El conjunto religioso-funerario de San Juan de Dios." In *Las artes y las ciencias en el Occidente musulmán*, edited by Maribel Parra Lledó and Alfonso Robles Fernández, 235–52. Murcia: Museo de la Ciencia y el Agua, 2007.

Savant, Sarah Bowen, and Helena de Felipe. "Introduction." In *Genealogy and Knowledge in Muslim Societies: Understanding the Past*, edited by Sarah Bowen Savant and Helena de Felipe, 1–8. Edinburgh: Edinburgh University Press, 2014.

Serjeant, R. B. "Material for a History of Islamic Textiles up to the Mongol Conquest, Parts 1–5." *Ars Islamica* 9–16 (1942–51).

Serrano Ruano, Delfina. "Porque llamaron los Almohades a los Almoravides antropomorfistas?" In *Los Almohades: Problemas y perspectivas*, edited by Patrice Cressier, Maribel Fierro, and Luis Molina, 2:815–52. Madrid: Consejo Superior de Investigaciones Científicas, 2005.

—. "Why Did the Scholars of Al-Andalus Distrust al-Ghazali? Ibn Rushd al-Jadd's Fatwā on Awliyā' Allāh." *Der Islam* 83 (2006): 137–56.

Sezgin, Fuat. *Coins and Coinage of Al-Andalus*. Frankfurt am Main: Institute for the History of Arabic-Islamic Science at the Johann Wolfgang Goethe University, 2003.

Shalem, Avinoam. "Architecture for the Body: Some Reflections on the Mobility of Textiles and the Fate of the So-Called Chasuble of Saint Thomas Becket in the Cathedral of Fermo in Italy." In *Dalmatia and the Mediterranean: Portable Archeology and the Poetics of Influence*, edited by Alina Payne, 246–67. Leiden: Brill, 2014.

—, ed. *The Chasuble of Thomas Becket: A Biography*. Munich: Hirmer/The Bruschettini Foundation, 2017.

Shaw, Wendy M. K. *What Is "Islamic" Art? Between Religion and Perception*. Cambridge: Cambridge University Press, 2019.

Shepherd, Dorothy G. "A Dated Hispano-Islamic Silk." *Ars Orientalis* 2 (1957): 373–82.

—. "The Hispano-Islamic Textiles in the Cooper Union Collection." *Chronicles of the Museum for the Arts of Decoration of the Cooper Union* 1 (1943): 351–82.

—. "A Treasure from a Thirteenth-Century Spanish Tomb." *Bulletin of the Cleveland Museum of Art* 65, no. 4 (1978): 111–34.

Siddiqi, Amir H. *Caliphate and Kingship in Medieval Persia*. Lahore: Shaikh Muhammad Ashraf, 1942.

Simon-Cahn, Annabelle. "The Fermo Chasuble of St. Thomas Becket and Hispano-Mauresque Cosmological Silks: Some Speculations on the Adaptive Reuse of Textiles." *Muqarnas* 10 (1993): 1–5.

Sirantoine, Hélène. "What's in a Word? Naming 'Muslims' in Medieval Christian Iberia." In *Making the Medieval Relevant: How Medieval Studies Contribute to Improving Our Understanding of the Past*, edited by Chris Jones, Conor Kostick, and Klaus Oschema, 225–38. Berlin/Boston: De Gruyter, 2020.

Sokoly, Jochen. "Between Life and Death: The Funerary Context of Tiraz Textiles." In *Islamische Textilkunst des Mittelalters. Aktuelle Probleme*, edited by Muhammad Abbas Muhammad Salim, 71–78. Riggisberger Berichte 5. Bern: Abegg Stiftung, 1997.

—. "Textiles and Identity." In *A Companion to Islamic Art and Architecture*, edited by Finbarr Barry Flood and Gülru Necipoğlu, 1:275–99. Hoboken: Wiley-Blackwell, 2017.

van Staëvel, Jean-Pierre. "L'art almohade fut-il révolutionnaire?" *Perspective* 2 (2017): 81–102.

Stearns, Justin. "Two Passages in Ibn Al-Khaṭīb's Account of the Kings of Christian Iberia." *Al-Qanṭara* 25 (2004): 157–82.

Stockstill, Abbey. "A Tale of Two Mosques: Marrakesh's Masjid al-Jami' al-Kutubiyya." *Muqarnas* 35, no. 1 (2018): 65–82.

Stoneman, Richard, Kyle Erickson, and Ian Netton, eds. *Alexander Romance in Persia and the East.* Groningen: Barkhuis, 2012.

Stones, Alison. "A Note on the Beard-Pulling Motif: A Meeting between East and West, or a Northern Import?" In *Early Medieval Art and Archaeology in the Northern World: Studies in Honour of James Graham-Campbell*, edited by Andrew Reed and Leslie Webster, 877-92. Leiden: Brill, 2013.

Streit, Jessica R. "Well-Ordered Growth: Meanings and Aesthetics of the Almohad Mosque of Seville." In *"His Pen and Ink Are a Powerful Mirror": Andalusi, Judaeo-Arabic, and Other Near Eastern Studies in Honor of Ross Brann*, edited by Adam Bursi, S.J. Pearce, and Hamza Zafer, 298–325. Leiden: Brill, 2020.

Tabales Rodríguez, Miguel Ángel. *El Alcázar de Sevilla: Primeros estudios sobre estratigrafía y evolución constructiva.* Seville: Junta de Andalucía, 2002.

Tabales Rodríguez, Miguel Ángel, and Álvaro Jiménez Sancho. "Intervención arqueológica en el Pabellón de oficinas de la Catedral de Sevilla (1997–1998)." *Anuario arqueológico de Andalucía* 3 (2001): 429–43.

Tabbaa, Yasser. "Andalusian Roots and Abbasid Homage in the Qubbat Al-Barudiyyin in Marrakech." *Muqarnas* 25 (2008): 133–46.

—. "The Muqarnas Dome: Its Origin and Meaning." *Muqarnas* 3 (1985): 61–74.

—. *The Transformation of Islamic Art during the Sunni Revival.* Seattle: University of Washington Press, 2001.

Talib, Adam. "Topoi and Topography in the Histories of Al-Ḥīra." In *Historian and Identity in the Late Antique Near East*, edited by Philip Wood, 123–47. Oxford: Oxford University Press, 2012.

Taragan, Hana. "Constructing a Visual Rhetoric: Images of Craftsmen and Builders in the Umayyad Palace at Qusayr 'Amra." *Al-Masāq* 20 (2008): 141–60.

Telles Antunes, Miguel, and Adel Sidarus. "Mais um quirate cunhado em Beja em nome de Ibn Qasi e Abu Talib al-Zuhri." *Arqueología Medieval* 1 (1992): 221–23.

Terrasse, Henri. *L'Art Hispano-Mauresque des origines au XIIIe siècle.* Paris: Van Ouest, 1932.

Thomas, Hugh. *Rivers of Gold: The Rise of the Spanish Empire from Columbus to Magellan.* New York: Random House, 2003.

Todesca, James. "Selling Castile: Coinage, Propaganda, and Mediterranean Trade in the Age of Alfonso VIII." In *King Alfonso VIII of Castile: Government, Family and War*, edited by Miguel Gómez, Kyle Lincoln, Damian Smith, and Martín Alvira Cabrer, 30–58. New York: Fordham University Press, 2019.

Tolan, John. *Saracens: Islam in the Medieval European Imagination.* New York: Columbia University Press, 2002.

—. "Using the Middle Ages to Construct Spanish Identity: 19th- and 20th-Century Spanish Historiography of Reconquest." In *Historiographical Approaches to Medieval Colonization of East Central Europe*, edited by Jan M. Piskorski, 329–48. Boulder, CO: East European Monographs, 2002.

Torres Balbás, Leopoldo. *Ars Hispaniae: historia universal del arte hispánico*. Vol. 4. Arte Almohade, Arte nazarí, Arte mudéjar. Madrid: Plus-Ultra, 1949.

—. "Crónica arqueológica de la España musulmana." *al-Andalus* 2/2 (1934): 337–91.

—. "Paseos arqueológicos por la España musulmana. Murcia." *Boletín de la Junta del Patronato del Museo Provincial de Bellas Artes de Murcia* 11–12 (1933).

Tronzo, William. *The Cultures of His Kingdom: Roger II and the Cappella Palatina in Palermo*. Princeton, NJ: Princeton University Press, 1997.

Trouillot, Michel-Rolph. *Silencing the Past: Power and the Production of History*. Boston: Beacon Press, 1995.

"Una investigación detecta 7 'hoteles' de época islámica en Dénia, más que en ninguna otra ciudad del país." *La Marina Plaza*. February 10, 2020. https://lamarinaplaza.com/2020/02/10/una-investigacion-detecta-7-hoteles-de-la-era-islamica-en-denia-mas-que-en-ninguna-otra-ciudad-del-pais/.

Urvoy, Dominique. *El mundo de los ulemas andaluces del siglo V/XI al VII/XIII: Estudio Sociológico*. Translated by Francisco Panel. Madrid: Ediciones Pegaso, 1983.

—. "La pensée d'Ibn Tūmart." *Bulletin d'études orientales* 27 (1974): 19–44.

—. *Pensers d'al-Andalus: La vie intellectuelle à Cordoue et Seville au temps des Empires Berberes (fin Xie siècle–début XIIIe siècle)*. Toulouse: Centre National de la Recherche Scientifique, 1990.

—. "The Rationality of Everyday Life: An Andalusian Tradition? (Apropos of Ḥayy's First Experiences)." In *The World of Ibn Tufayl: Interdisciplinary Perspectives on Ḥayy Ibn Yaqẓān*, edited by Lawrence I. Conrad, 38–52. Leiden: Brill, 1996.

—. "Sur l'evolution de la notion de *ğihād* dans l'Espagne musulmane." *Mélanges de la Casa de Velázquez* ix (1973): 335–71.

Vega Martín, Miguel, Salvador Peña Martín, and Manuel C. Feria García. *El mensaje de las monedas Almohades: Numismática, traducción y pensamiento islámico*. Cuenca: Ediciones de la Universidad de Castilla La Mancha, 2002.

Viguera Molíns, María Jesús. "Las cartas de al-Gazālī y al-Ṭurṭūšī al soberano almorávid Yūsuf b. Tāšufīn." *al-Andalus* 42, no. 2 (1977): 341–74.

—. "Las reacciones de los Andalusíes." In *Los Almohades: Problemas y perspectivas*, edited by Patrice Cressier, Maribel Fierro, and Luis Molina, 2:705–35. Madrid: Consejo Superior de Investigaciones Científicas, 2005.

—. *Los reinos de taifas y las invasions magrebíes*. Madrid: Mapfre, 1992.

—. "Sobre el nombre de Ibn Mardanīš." *Al-Qanṭara* 17 (1996): 231–38.

Villanueva, Jaime. *Viage literario a las iglesias de España*. Madrid: Imprenta de la Real Academía de la Historia, 1851.

Vives y Escudero, Antonio. *La moneda castellana: discursos leídos ante la Real Academia de la Historia*. Madrid: M. Tello, 1901.

—. *Monedas de las dinastías Arábigo Españolas*. Madrid: Juan R. Cayón, 1893.

Wallach Scott, Joan. *Gender and the Politics of History*. 30th anniversary ed. New York: Columbia University Press, 2018.

—. "The Problem of Invisibility." In *Retrieving Women's History: Changing Perceptions of the Role of Women in Politics and Society*, edited by S. Jay Kleinberg, 5–29. Oxford: Berg Publishers, 1988.

Wasserstein, David. *The Caliphate in the West: An Islamic Political Institution on the Iberian Peninsula*. Oxford: Clarendon Press, 1993.

—. "A Jonah Theme in the Biography of Ibn Tūmart." In *Culture and Memory in Medieval Islam: Essays in Honour of Wilferd Madelung*, edited by F. Daftary and J. Meri, 232–49. London: I. B. Tauris, 2003.

White, Graeme J. *Restoration and Reform, 1153–1165: Recovery from Civil War in England*. Cambridge: Cambridge University Press, 2000.

Yücesoy, Hayrettin. *Messianic Beliefs and Imperial Politics in Medieval Islam: The ʿAbbāsid Caliphate in the Early Ninth Century*. Columbia: University of South Carolina Press, 2009.

Yus Cecilia, Silvia, and Mariángeles Gómez Ródenas. "El repertorio cerámico del siglo XII en la Medina *Mursiya*." In *Rey Lobo: El legado de Ibn Mardanīš, 1147–1172*, edited by Jorge A. Eiroa and Mariángeles Gómez Ródenas, 82–93. Murcia: Comunidad Autónoma de la Región de Murcia, 2019.

Index